ADVANCES IN PSYCHOBIOLOGY

Volume Two

ADVANCES IN PSYCHOBIOLOGY

GRANT NEWTON AND AUSTIN H. RIESEN, EDITORS

Advances in Psychobiology, Volume One, edited by Grant Newton and Austin H. Riesen

Advances in Psychobiology, Volume Two, edited by Grant Newton and Austin H. Riesen

ADVANCES IN PSYCHOBIOLOGY

VOLUME TWO

EDITED BY

GRANT NEWTON

Santa Susana, California

AUSTIN H. RIESEN

University of California, Riverside

A WILEY-INTERSCIENCE PUBLICATION

John Wiley & Sons
New York · London · Sydney · Toronto

SERIES PREFACE

As a new and burgeoning area of research, comparative psychobiology has gained a true identity during the past two decades. The interdependence of behavioral and somatic processes makes imperative the active cooperation of scientists in all disciplines that have as their subject matter some aspect or grouping of the many factors and facets of change occurring throughout the life cycle of organisms. Such collaboration has long been apparent in the field of psychology which recognizes the fundamental contributions of biochemistry, biophysics, genetics, medicine, physiology, zoology, and their myriad subdisciplines. Thus, whereas the massive proliferation of data demands increasing specialization, paradoxically it has become necessary to penetrate those artificial boundaries that currently define the territorial limitations of various specialists.

The thorough study of behavior urgently requires a continuing resynthesis of the findings of specialists who work in the life sciences, too often unaware of advances in the closely related studies of other workers. Many new journals have begun publication of interdisciplinary empirical findings that have opened up a vast potential for understanding behavioral development. If this potential is to flourish and fulfill its promise, there must be a deliberate and spirited "meeting of minds."

Between the broadest theoretical perspectives of biological principles and the empirical research of the laboratory, as published in the experimental journals, a great need has arisen for a medium that will juxtapose the data and the issues of their interpretation, and build upon their relevancy to each other.

Advances in Psychobiology is offered as a major thrust in the direction of meeting this need. It is international as well as interdisciplinary in scope. It will publish, in English, the contributions of notable researchers on the current world scene of biobehavioral investigation, while reducing as much as possible the problems of communication across technical language barriers. The overall series will attempt to be comprehensive, though individual volumes will of necessity be colored by the authorship of the year at hand.

GRANT NEWTON
AUSTIN H. RIESEN

August 1971

PREFACE

This volume pursues the goals of interdisciplinary investigation into behavioral biology, and again, as in Volume One, most of its chapters concern themselves at least in part with developmental psychobiology. Current research interest and areas of major recent advances are emphasized. Effects on brain development of such basic growth-supporting factors as the following are reviewed and evaluated: nutritional supports, hormonal influences, sensory inputs and deprivations, experiential (learning) effects, and drug usage. Two chapters deal with the nature of memory storage.

The effects of endocrine activity on the nervous system and the control of later neuroendocrine functions by the brain are the subject of Chapter 1. The development of sexual behavior and its manifestations at maturity are experimentally open to study in animals. Most of Roger Gorski's review presents data and discusses neuroendocrine mechanisms and issues as these are revealed in animal research. Implications for human sexuality and reference to clinical investigations are briefly examined.

Fine structure of the nervous system is both essential to its functioning and responsive to environmental inputs. In Chapter 2, on plastic changes in the visual system, Fifková presents the results of ultramicroscopic studies of synaptic alterations. These studies exemplify a currently intense interest in relationships between neural function and structure.

Protein nutrition in neural and behavioral development is of major significance but the effort to implicate learning deficiencies proves to be extremely difficult. Zimmermann, Geist, and Wise, in Chapter 3, examine the background of research on protein malnutrition and behavioral consequences. Based on results of their own primate research in this area they propose that early environmental deprivation and protein malnutrition during infancy produce similar behavioral malfunctions. Exploratory behavior, problem solving, and social behaviors are impaired.

The physiology of memory storage is currently under intense investigation by electrophysiological and neurochemical methods. In Chapter 4, Gold, Zornetzer, and McGaugh evaluate an extensive literature on the production of retrograde amnesia by electrical brain stimulation and the implications of these studies for an understanding of the nature and locus of memory storage processes. Such questions as the significance of the effect of subseizure stimulation of the amygdala or hippocampus on memory and whether disruption of memory implies the exact reciprocal of engram storage are critically examined.

The biochemistry of learning and memory is a new area of research of only the past two decades. John Gaito has been an active participant. In Chapter 5, he reviews progress and current problems after tracing the origins of this scientific quest to Ward Halstead and Ralph Gerard and thus to the University of Chicago *circa* 1950. Molecular theories are currently controversial.

Chapters 6, 7, and 8 are all concerned with brain function in perception, but each approaches this problem from a different vantage point. Implications for human perception, including perceptual development, are indicated by the chapter titles. Direct applicability to the human condition calls them to the attention of parents and educators as well as specialists in the neurosciences.

Austin H. Riesen

Riverside, California
December 1973

CONTENTS

CHAPTER SEVEN

CHAPTER EIGHT

ADVANCES IN PSYCHOBIOLOGY

Volume Two

Chapter 1

THE NEUROENDOCRINE REGULATION OF SEXUAL BEHAVIOR*

ROGER A. GORSKI

University of California, Los Angeles

The science of neuroendocrinology encompasses the study of several processes: (*a*) releasing-factor physiology and chemistry; (*b*) neural control of endocrine activity, for which process the feedback action of peripheral hormones on regulatory systems is critical; and (*c*) the action of hormones upon the brain that alter its activity and the behavior of the individual. This chapter will discuss the neuroendocrine regulation of sexual behavior as a relatively independent construct, although the question of the interaction between the regulation of gonadotropin (GTH) secretion and sexual behavior will also be considered. The former task is itself very difficult, because the regulation of sexual behavior is highly complex. We must consider the following questions: How is sexual behavior measured? Which hormones are required? Where and how may they act? And, as we shall document below, it is essential to consider the male and female independently. Finally, sexual behavior varies greatly with different species of animals, so to simplify our task the laboratory rat will be considered as the model system, although not to the exclusion of other species.

The Measurement of Sexual Behavior

The scientific evaluation and quantification of sexual behavior in animals is difficult and subject to severe criticism. In the situation, admittedly artificial, in which a sexually receptive female is introduced into

* Reproduced from an original article appearing in Spanish in *Neuroendocrinologia*, O. Schiaffini, A. O. Bosch, M. Motta, and L. Martini (Eds.) Toray S. A., Barcelona, Spain, 1973.

1

the home cage of a male rat, the following important behavioral events occur more or less in sequence. The male investigates the female, particularly her anal–genital region. The receptive female displays several behaviors that have been termed *solicitory*. She rapidly shakes her head so that her ears appear to vibrate. She abruptly darts about and stops equally as abruptly. The male will frequently pursue the female as he continues his investigation of her genital region. At intervals the male will mount the female, palpate her flanks with his forelegs, and show pelvic thrusting as he attempts insertion of the penis into the vagina (intromission). In order for the male to achieve intromission the sexually receptive female will exhibit a characteristic behavioral response called *lordosis*. During lordosis the female arches her back so that both her head and perineum are elevated, and she deviates her tail to one side.

After a brief mount the male dismounts in a characteristic way depending on whether or not he has achieved intromission. During the interval before the next mount the male may lick his genitalia and resume his investigation of the genital region of the female. After a series of intromissions the male will ejaculate, an event that can be recognized behaviorally by the type of dismount and immediate postejaculatory behavior. Normally the male exhibits a period of sexual refractoriness before resuming sexual behavior that culminates in subsequent ejaculations.

Quantification of Female Behavior

Although most experimenters (and this chapter) concentrate on the lordosis response (actually only one component of female sexual behavior), there are different methods of analysis of this response, having varying validity. These methods range from a timed test, considered to be positive for female sexual behavior as long as one lordosis response is exhibited, to a complex rating system that takes into account the degree of lordosis. In many laboratories, including the author's, behavioral data are reduced to a lordosis quotient (LQ, number of lordosis responses divided by the number of mounts, times 100), which is based on at least 10 mounts. In this manner one can distinguish between animals that occasionally lordose (low LQ, low sexual receptivity) and those that lordose upon almost every mount (high LQ, high receptivity). A behavioral test that considers the display of a single lordosis as the sole indication of female behavior provides less information than the LQ, and may be misleading. Because the lordosis response itself may vary from a weak arching of the back to a very pronounced response, several authors have recently devised an elegant scoring system, which takes into account the degree of lordosis as well as its duration, and the presence or absence of soliciting behavior (Gerall & Kenney, 1970; Hardy, 1972; Hendricks, 1972). As elegant an estimate of sexual receptivity as this may appear, one must still consider that each mount by a given male may not be of equal intensity. It is possible, therefore, that as the analysis of the lordosis response becomes more complex, it begins to measure male behavior as well.

Attempts have been made to eliminate the male, and to substitute perineal manipulation by the experimenter (Powers & Zucker, 1969). The mounting stimulus may be more complex, however, inasmuch as the author has observed animals that clearly lordose to the male but not to manipulation, and vice versa. Both the quantification of lordosis and its artificial induction have been highly developed by Komisaruk (1971). In these studies vaginal and cervical probing have been applied with a glass rod, and the response quantified in detail from photographs taken of the female against a background grid. By this procedure lordosis has been reduced to a numerical estimate of upward deviation of the animal's nose and rump. Application of this method of analysis has clearly shown that the reflex pattern of lordosis can be elicited in the absence of ovarian hormones, although estrogen markedly facilitates it (Komisaruk, 1971). In the following discussion we shall concentrate on those experiments that express female sexual behavior in terms of the response elicited by the mounting male.

Quantification of Male Behavior

In the case of the male rat there are several parameters that can be quantified precisely: the number of mounts, intromissions, or ejaculations per test, or per unit time; the time intervals between these events; the number of intromissions that precede each ejaculation; the duration of the postejaculatory refractory period; and the latency between introduction of the female into the testing cage and the first mount, intromission, and ejaculation. The three specific behavioral events, mount, intromission, and ejaculation, are rigidly defined and readily distinguished after some experience. A proper mount is registered when the male mounts the female from the rear in the correct orientation, palpates the sides of the female with his forepaws, and exhibits pelvic thrusting. The pelvic thrusts appear to be related to attaining the proper orientation so that the penis can be inserted into the vagina. The dismount from a mount without intromission is not remarkable, the male backs away from the female. An intromission is registered when the mounting male exhibits a deeper pelvic thrust, dismounts more abruptly, thrusting himself backward away from the female. During ejaculation the male raises his forepaws from the female and may stand on his hindlegs, and dismounts by falling backwards. After ejaculation the male grooms his genitalia and rests for a period before beginning a new series of mounts and intromissions, which culminate in another ejaculation.

Nonhormonal Factors That Affect Sexual Behavior

There are many factors that alter the behavioral response of an animal to a given hormone regime. In the case of the male rat, for example, prior copulatory experience appears to improve sexual performance as judged by mount, intromission and ejaculation latencies, and intromission frequency (Dewsbury, 1969). The sexually naive male is a markedly poor performer in comparison to experienced stud males. In the male cat, previous mating activity prolongs the display of sexual behavior following castration (Rosenblatt, 1965). In addition, early experience not sexual in nature can also alter subsequent sexual performance (see Rosenblatt, 1965; Lehrman, 1971).

In the case of the female rat even the effect of experience within an individual behavior test can be detected. In rats rendered relatively nonresponsive behaviorally to progesterone and/or estrogen by neonatal androgenization, a significant facilitation of the LQ was observed as a result of repeated mounting and, presumably, intromission although the latter was not quantified (Clemens, Shryne, & Gorski, 1970). In contrast, Hardy & DeBold (1972) demonstrated, in a cleverly designed experiment in which intromission was prevented by a "vaginal mask," that repeated intromission actually decreased the probability of a subsequent lordosis. In the same experiment, these authors noted that in ovariectomized rats treated only with estradiol benzoate (EB) and thus showing low levels of lordosis-responding, there was a general increase in LQ with repeated behavioral testing. Therefore, it appears that prior copulatory experience immediately increases the probability of lordosis in animals not fully receptive, whereas in females that are responding at high levels, continued sexual activity reduces receptivity. It is likely that the latter phenomenon is related to painful stimuli rather than to a general central mechanism of lordosis suppression. These two experiments emphasize the fact that one must critically analyze the experimental design when attempting to compare the results of one experiment with another, whether within one laboratory, or between different laboratories. The lordosis response appears to be a dynamic phenomenon subject to change even within the short period of an individual behavioral test.

The environmental conditions under which a behavioral test is conducted are also of potential significance. It is so well known that the male rat will not perform sexually when introduced into a novel environment that most investigators provide the male with a period of time to adapt to the behavioral testing arena before introducing a receptive or test animal; often the latter is introduced into the home cage of the male. Inasmuch as behavior of the receptive female rat does not appear to be adversely affected by her introduction into a novel environment, the behavioral test is commonly initiated immediately upon presentation of the female to the male. However, it has been shown that reactivity to a novel environment can suppress lordosis behavior in females that are not highly receptive (Clemens, Hiroi, & Gorski, 1969). Thus, although the rat injected with a low dose of testosterone propionate (TP; 10 μg) postnatally achieves only a low LQ when ovariectomized, primed with EB and progesterone, and introduced into a testing arena containing a waiting male, the LQ attained by these same animals is significantly increased when they are allowed a 2 hr period to adapt to the testing arena before a well-trained stud male is introduced to start the test (Fig. 1). A similar facilitation of lordosis behavior by adaptation to the testing arena is seen in normal ovariectomized rats in which low levels of sexual receptivity are produced by priming with EB and low doses of progesterone (Clemens et al., 1969).

The time period required for adaptation is unknown, either for the female or for the male. A survey of the literature reveals that the period of adaptation for the male has ranged from a few minutes to more than an hour, or to a condition of *permanent adaptation,* that is, testing behavior in the male's home cage. Although it would appear that the novel stimuli of a new environment inhibit sexual behavior, one cannot generalize to all nonsexual stimuli. Larsson (1963) demonstrated that old male rats (20–24 months of age) that did not perform as vigorously as males only 5–6 months of age became as sexually active as the young animals when handled by the experimenter every 2 min during the test. Painful stimulation applied to the skin of the back evokes copulatory behavior, and periodic stimuli actually pace masculine behavior (Barfield & Sachs, 1968). Similarly, electric shock applied to the tail of sexually naive male rats facilitates mating behavior (Caggiula & Eibergen, 1969). It has been suggested that these stimuli increase the arousal state of the male, but it is likely that introducing the male to a novel environment, which inhibits behavior, is also an arousing stimulus although obviously of different quality. In addition, a given stimulus may have a different effect on the initiation of behavior than on its maintenance.

In the author's laboratory, lordosis tests are often carried out to 50

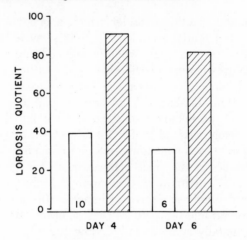

Fig. 1.   Facilitation of lordosis behavior (based on a 10 mount test) induced by a 2 hr adaptation (shaded columns) to the mating arena. The open columns indicate the behavioral response of these same animals when they were introduced into the mating arena just before the start of another test. The rats had received an injection of 10 μg TP on day 4 or 6 of age. All behavioral tests were performed after estrogen–progesterone priming of the adult ovariectomized animal. Numbers of animals are indicated by numbers at base of columns. Data from Clemens et al. (1969).

mounts, and it it not uncommon to find the interest of the male wane toward relatively nonreceptive females. The mere act of lifting the female from the testing arena, and reintroducing her immediately, stimulates renewed mating activity on the part of the male. Does this occur because the male now responds to the female as a new, potentially receptive partner, perhaps because he has learned from his period of service as stud male, or do the stimuli related to manipulating the female increase the state of arousal of the male? Unfortunately, the relationship between environmental factors and male sexual behavior is too complex to be explained at the present time. Although the elucidation of these complex interrelationships might appear to be an esoteric problem, it is important to note that differences between experimental groups, or between apparently similar but conflicting experiments in different laboratories, might in fact be due to these environmental factors rather than to possible differences in the neural or hormonal basis of behavior. Careful attention to the details of experimental design and execution is particularly essential for valid interpretation of the literature in this field.

Sexual Behavior of Other Animals

This chapter cannot serve as an anthology of sexual behavior, yet it should be emphasized that there is great variation among species, which markedly affects the methods for the experimental analysis of this behavior. A few examples of the variety in female behavior will suffice to illustrate this fact. The female hamster displays lordosis to the mounting stimulus, but the female normally holds this posture for long periods of time. The male may mount, dismount, even ejaculate many times while the female holds the lordosis posture. In a 10 min test, for example, the female may be in lordosis for more than 500 sec. Clearly, in such an animal the LQ as defined for the rat cannot be calculated. In the ewe, sexual behavior consists of the female standing motionless to accept the mounting ram, rather than her moving away to avoid his advances. In the case of the rhesus monkey, the female must actually bear the entire weight of the generally larger male during copulation.

In very general terms, female sexual behavior represents the acquiescence of the receptive female to the mounting male. The male frequently appears to be the more aggressive partner. The manner of the acquiescence of the female and the approach of the male may vary markedly among species. Because of this fact, the experimental evaluation of sexual behavior is highly species specific. Although a comparative description of sexual behavior would be informative, in order to arrive at a general concept of the neuroendocrine regulation of sexual behavior, it is important to consider the hormone specificity and the identity of the neural substrate for sexual behavior in our model species, the rat.

The Hormonal Control of Sexual Behavior

Although it is well established that reproductive behavior is dependent on gonadal hormones (Young, 1961), specific understanding of the process is very limited. The site and mechanism of gonadal steroid action will be discussed in later sections in this chapter. At this point we will consider the identity of the hormones involved in sexual behavior, and the probable changes in gonadal activity that facilitate such behavior at appropriate phases of the reproductive cycle.

In the castrated male rat, treatment with TP can restore male sexual behavior, and it is interesting to note that treatment with excess androgen restores behavior only to precastration levels (Larsson, 1966). Current concepts suggest that fluctuations in testicular activity in the male rat are minimal, and that the male is generally primed to display sexual behavior at any time. However, there is significant uncertainty about the precise identity of the steroid(s) ultimately responsible for male sexual behavior.

In the female, the inhibitory effect of ovariectomy on sexual behavior is quite dramatic, and complete receptive behavior can be restored by exogeneous hormone administration. In the ovariectomized rat sexual receptivity can be facilitated by treatment with estrogen alone, although progesterone appears to enhance this behavior further. This enhancement is so marked that progesterone is thought to have an important role in the regulation of sexual behavior in the intact female. Finally, progesterone may have a biphasic action on sexual receptivity, an initial facilitatory phase followed by a period of suppression. Let us now consider these statements in detail.

The injection of approximately 1 μg EB daily for about 1 week is sufficient to facilitate normal levels of sexual receptivity in ovariectomized females as measured by the LQ (Davidson, Smith, Rodgers, & Bloch, 1968b). Even after 12 days of treatment this level of EB had restored uterine weight only to control levels; thus, by this criterion, this treatment appears to be in the physiological range. In contrast, the minimum daily dose of EB required to induce vaginal cornification in this same study was only 0.2 μg for 4 days. Note that the peripheral tissues, particularly the vaginal epithelium, appear to be more sensitive to estrogen replacement that the lordosis system. Although it could be argued that in experiments of this type, exogenous estrogen interacts with progesterone of adrenal origin to facilitate lordosis behavior, Davidson, Rodgers, Smith, & Bloch (1968a) repeated the above study in ovariectomized and adrenalectomized rats, yet found that daily injection of EB alone facilitated lordosis behavior.

On the other hand, there is no doubt that progesterone can markedly potentiate the facilitation of lordosis behavior by exogenous estrogen (see Edwards, Whalen, & Nadler, 1968). In most laboratories in which lordosis behavior is studied, ovariectomized rats are given a single injection of EB, or several daily injections that alone do not markedly facilitate lordosis. Progesterone is injected 4–8 hr before the behavioral test. Data from the authors' laboratory have repeatedly confirmed the fact that the low levels of lordosis-responding induced by a single injection of 5 μg EB/kg (Arai & Gorski, 1968), or three daily injections of 2 μg EB (Clemens et al., 1969) are markedly and significantly increased by the subcutaneous administration of progesterone (Fig. 2).

Because it is clear that either estrogen alone or estrogen and proges-

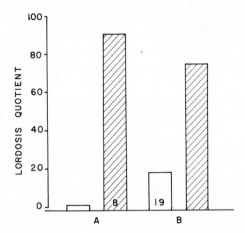

Fig. 2. Facilitation of lordosis behavior induced by the subcutaneous injection of 0.5 mg progesterone (shaded columns) either 48 hr after the injection of 5 μg EB/kg (A), or on the day after three consecutive daily injections of 2 μg EB (B). Behavioral tests were performed at comparable intervals following EB injection whether progesterone was administered or not (open columns). Numbers of animals are indicated by numbers at base of columns. Data in (A) from Arai & Gorski (1968); in (B), from Clemens et al. (1969).

terone can facilitate lordosis in the ovariectomized rat, an important question arises: What is the hormonal basis for sexual behavior in the intact female rat? Hardy & DeBold (1971) stress that both the intensity and duration of lordosis behavior differ between natural receptivity and that induced by exogenous hormones. They suggest that discrepancies between the dynamics of hormone replacement and the normal pattern of hormone changes in the intact animal probably explain these differences. Therefore, it is necessary to consider the hormonal pattern of the estrous cycle of the normal rat. A highly schematic representation of these changes is illustrated in Fig. 3, which is based on the reports of Uchida, Kadowaki, & Miyake (1969); Brown-Grant (1971); and Cramer & Barraclough (1971). Inasmuch as the emphasis of this discussion is not on specific hormone levels but on the pattern of release, this illustration is offered only as a qualitative summary of the temporal pattern of ovarian activity. Superimposed on this figure is the pattern of the rate of lordosis-responding throughout proestrus, as described by Hardy (1972), who also describes a "rejection quotient" that shows a pattern inverse to that of the LQ.

There are several features of potential importance that are readily

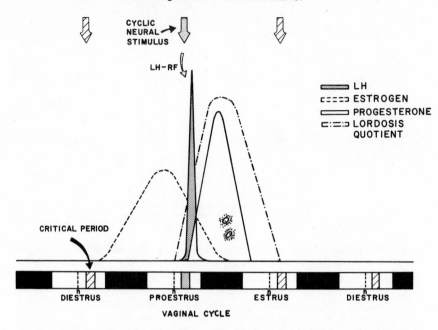

Fig. 3.   Highly schematic description of the cyclic changes in plasma LH, estrogen, and progesterone at behavioral estrus during the rat reproductive cycle. Roughly superimposed on these changes is a curve representing the rate of lordosis responding over this time period as adapted from Hardy (1972). Also indicated is the concept that the discharge of LH that results in follicular rupture (at ova) is the result of a cyclic neural stimulus that activates the release of LH-releasing factor (LH-RF) during the critical period, which begins approximately 2 hr after noon (n) on proestrus.

apparent from Fig. 3. The normal female is exposed to estrogen only for a relatively brief period during an individual estrous cycle. Estrogen concentration in the blood appears to peak before the ovulatory surge of LH begins, and the latter event is closely related temporally with an increase in plasma progesterone, which in turn correlates well with the display of lordosis behavior. If one accepts this general pattern of hormone changes, the study of Powers (1970) clearly suggests that endogenous progesterone normally plays an important role in the initiation of sexual receptivity. Powers found that acute ovariectomy performed at approximately 9 PM (colony time) on proestrus did not alter the LQ determined 6 hr later. Note that ovariectomy at this time would have been performed after the increase in plasma progesterone seen on the afternoon of proestrus. However, when ovariectomy was performed at approximately 3 PM colony time, subsequent lordosis behavior was markedly reduced. Inasmuch as ovariectomy at this time would be expected to attenuate the increase in plasma progesterone, Powers concluded that the secretion of endogenous progesterone was essential for normal female receptive behavior. This conclusion is not shared by Schwartz & Talley (1965).

It should be noted that Powers did not measure plasma steroid levels in his experiment, and strain differences or variations in the illumination schedule could alter the pattern of ovarian activity and negate his conclusions. However, as already stressed, the technique of behavioral evaluation is also critical to the interpretation of the data. Thus, although Schwartz & Talley (1965) reported that 7 out of 13 rats showing 5 day estrous cycles mated even though the ovaries had been removed prior to the release of ovulating hormone and the presumed secretion of progesterone, their observation may not actually contradict that of Powers (1970). In their study the criterion of mating behavior was the presence of vaginal sperm following overnight cohabitation with males. Even in the case of Powers' experiment, which utilized the LQ, an appropriately timed ovariectomy, although significantly reducing the rate of lordosis-responding, still permitted lordosis to occur at least 20% of the times a female was mounted. Even at this low rate of receptive behavior the persistent male would presumably ejaculate during the night. This author considers it most likely that preovulatory progesterone serves to facilitate sexual behavior in the normal female rat. Under experimental conditions exogenous estrogen alone also has this capacity. It is interesting that in the rat progesterone can also inhibit lordosis behavior (Nadler, 1970).

Specificity of Hormone Action

We have already indicated that testosterone facilitates masculine sexual behavior in the castrated male, and the ovarian hormones estrogen and progesterone facilitate lordosis behavior in the ovariectomized female. In addition to these homotypical responses, which could give rise to the probably erroneous concept of hormone-specific behavioral effects of gonadal steroids, we must consider the ability of these same hormones to facilitate heterotypical behavior. As is evident from the review of Young (1961), heterotypical behavioral responses are readily obtained. In other studies TP has been shown to facilitate very high levels of lordosis-responding as long as progesterone is also administered to ovariectomized female rats (Whalen & Hardy, 1970; Pfaff, 1970). Interestingly, TP injections alone, unlike EB, were not able to facilitate lordosis behavior in either study. In these experiments TP was administered at a dose level at least 20 times that of EB; thus it is clear that lordosis behavior is far more sensitive to estrogen than to androgen. Although these studies suggest that the neural mechanisms that control lordosis in response to hormone exposure are not specific to one steroid, another particularly interesting explanation has been proposed: Because the hypothalamus of several mammalian species, including rat, rabbit, monkey, and man can convert a small fraction of exogenous androstenedione into estrone (see Ryan, Naftolin, Reddy, Flores & Petro, 1972), and because only androgens capable of being aromatized (ring A reduction) to estrogen facilitate lordosis behavior, testosterone may normally be converted to estrogen before acting centrally (Beyer & Komisaruk, 1971).

Although the percent conversion to estrogen is very small, if sufficient androgen is administered systematically in the female rat, adequate amounts could be converted, perhaps locally at its site of action in the brain. Thus, the apparently heterotypical activation of lordosis behavior by androgen may, in fact, support the view of rigid intraneuronal hormone-specificity within the brain. The argument that only androgens that can be aromatized are effective in facilitating lordosis behavior is circumstantial and does not prove a causal relationship. However, in a most relevant experiment, Whalen, Battie, & Luttge (1972) have reported that treatment with an *anti-estrogen*, CI-628 (CN-55,945-27; Parke, Davis), successfully inhibits *androgen*-induced lordosis behavior in the female rat. Because it would be critical to show that such a compound does not also have a direct antiandrogenic activity, these investigators showed that CI-628 did not inhibit the action of exogenous TP on seminal vesicle weight in castrated male rats, although treatment with a known antiandrogen did. The most critical test would be to demonstrate that CI-628 has no central antiandrogenic potency. Whalen et al. (1972) tested the ability of CI-628 to inhibit TP-induced masculine behavior in male rats. However, their negative results are difficult to interpret, inasmuch as cyproterone acetate, a known antiandrogen, also failed to inhibit TP-induced masculine behavior (Whalen & Edwards, 1969).

Heterotypical sexual behavior can also be induced by estrogen, and in this case, it would appear that there is indeed a lack of central hormonal specificity, at least in the face of very high levels of EB. Pfaff (1970) reported that after 9–11 days of treatment with 10 μg EB/day, both male and female gonadectomized rats showed an increase in mounting behavior, and in the male, intromission was also facilitated by EB. As mounting activity, including "intromission" behavior can be displayed by the normal female, and in fact may be relatively independent of gonadal hormones (see Beach, 1968), this observation is not surprising and need not question the concepts of hormone specificity. However, in recent unpublished experiments in the author's laboratory, Paup has demonstrated that the complete pattern of male sexual behavior, including ejaculation, can be induced in the male rat following prolonged treatment (36 days) with large doses of EB (25 μg). The conversion of estrogen to androgen is not thought to occur, so the observation that eight of nine males treated with EB displayed ejaculatory behavior suggests some lack of specificity for the hormone receptors that facilitate this behavioral pattern. However, the dose of EB employed is massive, so this lack of specificity may have little physiological significance. It is interesting to note that there appears to be considerable overlap between estrogen- and androgen-concentrating neurons in the brain (Pfaff, 1971; Stumpf, 1971; Sar & Stumpf, 1972).

Although the heterotypical facilitation of components of sexual behavior can occur following hormone administration, homotypical patterns are most readily activated. Implicit in this statement is the assumption that sex differences exist with respect to the behavioral response to gonadal hormones. In a subsequent section of this chapter we will describe in detail the sex differences in sexual behavioral potential, and, moreover, consider the origin of these differences. At this point, we can state that many differences in the behavioral capacity of the adult are not the result of differences in neuronal genetic expression. On the contrary, female receptive behavior, that is, the lordosis reflex, appears to be fundamental to both the male and the female. As we shall document below in a consideration of the concept of sexual differentiation of the brain, masculine behavioral potential is most likely imposed on the developing brain by exposure to androgen at a critical stage in development, and androgen exposure definitely suppresses lordosis-response capacity.

The foregoing comments, including the concept of sexual differentiation, apply in general terms to many mammalian forms. In the guinea pig, progesterone appears to be an obligatory hormone for female sexual behavior, whereas in the ewe, progesterone must precede estrogen for behavioral estrus to occur (see Young, 1961). In the rhesus monkey and in the human, sexual behavior is not restricted to a specific period of maximum female fertility but can occur throughout the menstrual cycle as a form of social behavior. In a review of the influence of exogenous and endogenous gonadal and adrenal hormones on sexual behavior in the primate, Luttge (1971) concludes: ". . . It appears that gonadal hormones characteristically aid in the induction, maintenance, and control of heterosexual behavior in both the human and rhesus monkey, but they may not be absolutely essential for its display in all individuals."

Space does not permit a detailed discussion of this question. The reader interested in the regulation of sexual behavior in the monkey is referred to two excellent reviews: Michael, Zumpe, Keverne, & Bonsall (1972), and Goy & Resko (1972).

The Neural Control of Sexual Behavior

There is no doubt that the brain controls sexual behavior. The important questions are rather these: What areas of the brain are involved in the regulation and expression of sexual behavior? How is this behavior coordinated with gonadal activity? The use of radiolabeled steroid hormones has clearly shown that these hormones are taken up and retained in certain brain regions. Lesion studies have demonstrated that the destruction of certain neural structures totally prevents, or in some cases facilitates, sexual behavior. Similarly, the direct application of steroid hormones to specific areas of the brain can facilitate sexual behavior. Finally, the administration of several drugs likewise alters mating behavior. In keeping with our attempt to use the rat as a model system, the following discussion will review the experimental evidence for the neural control of sexual behavior in the male and female rat.

The Male

Current concepts of steroid hormone action in the brain are based on the assumption that gonadal hormones act on specific neurons, which may or may not be concentrated in specific anatomical or functional groups. Although most work in this area has involved estradiol, recent studies of the autoradiographic localization of tritiated testosterone suggest that there may be considerable overlap between the localization of neurons capable of taking up and retaining estradiol and testosterone (Pfaff, 1971; Stumpf, 1971; Sar & Stumpf, 1972). Androgen-retaining neurons were observed in the lateral septum, medial preoptic area (POA), periventricular and arcuate nuclei, ventromedial nucleus (VMN), and the amygdala. However, differences between estrogen- and androgen-concentrating neural systems do exist. The regional differences in the neuronal concentration of testosterone and the effect of competition with unlabeled hormone in these regions are less pronounced than in the case of estradiol (see McEwen & Pfaff, 1973). Moreover, the demonstrations of rather significant metabolism of androgen within the brain (Ryan et al., 1972; Massa, Stupnicka, Kniewald, & Martini, 1972; Sholiton, Jones, & Werk, 1972) raise the important question: What is the identity of the active form(s) of testosterone in these various regions of the brain? We have already considered this question in terms of hormone specificity.

The presence in the medial POA of a large concentration of androgen-retaining neurons is remarkably consistent with the demonstration that crystalline TP facilitates masculine sexual behavior when implanted in the preoptic-anterior hypothalamic area (Davidson, 1966; Lisk, 1967), and with the report that medial, but not lateral, POA lesions prevent male sexual behavior even after castration and daily injection of 500 μg TP/100 g body weight (Larsson & Heimer, 1964). Lisk (1968) similarly reported that medial POA lesions disrupted male behavior, but in his experiment, mating behavior was assessed only by counting the number of seminal copulatory plugs found on the floor of communal cages. On the basis of even less adequate behavioral evidence (in this case the display of a single mount), Dörner has proposed that the POA represents a male hypothalamic mating center in both the genetic male and female rat (Dörner, Döcke, & Hinz, 1969; Dörner, Döcke, & Moustafa, 1968a, 1968b). On the basis of the quality of the behavioral data, this conclusion must be considered only as speculation. Another experimental strategy that further documents an important role of the POA in male sexual behavior is the observation that electrical stimulation of this area facilitates copulatory behavior (Vaughan & Fisher, 1962; van Dis & Larsson, 1971). Attention is also drawn to the observation of Hillarp, Olivecrona, & Silfverskiöld (1954) that electrolytic destruction of the medial POA in either sex under ether anesthesia can be followed by a brief transient period of active mounting behavior.

Although the evidence that the medial POA is important for the display of male copulatory behavior is particularly strong, that strength should not be taken to indicate that the neural regulation of male sexual behavior is understood. Lesion and stimulation studies indicate that diverse regions of the brain play a role in this behavior. It must also be emphasized that a single lesion could disrupt the expression of sexual behavior at many different levels. Lesions could (a) suppress pituitary and hence gonadal function; (b) destroy neurons that must be acted upon by androgen; (c) interfere with appropriate integration of the "androgen stimulus" with other processes including the recognition of the presence of a responsive female; (d) disturb the normal balance of neurotransmitter input or function; and/or (e) interfere finally with the motor response necessary for the copulatory act.

On the basis of the data presented above, it is logical to conclude that the POA contains androgen receptor cells, which when activated appear to facilitate male sexual behavior. However, the cerebral cortex also appears to be essential for male copulatory behavior as determined by the suppression of such behavior following surgical removal of the cortex (Beach, 1940; Larsson, 1964), or the application of potassium chloride (KC1) to the cortex. The latter procedure induces spreading cortical depression (Larsson, 1962). Lesions of the septum have been reported not to alter male behavior (Goodman, Bunnell, Dewsbury, & Boland, 1969), whereas lesions of the amygdala produced marked, but very transient, alterations (inhibition) of certain components of male behavior (Bermant, Glickman, & Davidson, 1968).

The influence of lesions of the hippocampus (HPC) on sexual behavior of the male rat remains unclear. Kimble, Rogers, & Hendrickson (1967) reported that aspiration lesions of the dorsal HPC had no obvious effect on sexual behavior of either the male or female under endogenous gonadal hormones. Bermant et al. (1968) reported that electrolytic lesions of the dorsal HPC consistently decreased postejaculatory intervals, although ventral or combined dorsal and ventral HPC lesions were without effect. Dewsbury, Goodman, Salis, & Bunnell (1968) concluded from their analysis of the effect of aspiration lesions of the HPC that this structure is of little importance in the mediation of masculine behavior in the sexually experienced rat. They found that the only effect of near total removal of the HPC was to increase the latency to the first mount and intromission. Once initiated, however, the behavior was comparable to that of control males.

Several recent experiments implicate the medial forebrain bundle (MFB), an extensive fiber pathway interconnecting rostral forebrain, midbrain, and hypothalamus, in the regulation of male sexual behavior. Parasagittal knife cuts that severed the lateral connections of the preoptic-anterior hypothalamic area (POA-AH) with the MFB markedly inhibited male sexual behavior (Paxinos & Bindra, 1973). Knife cuts in the MFB in the frontal plane, and those placed at the level of the anterior commissure, did not disrupt male behavior, whereas cuts placed more posterior in the MFB impaired copulatory behavior (Paxinos & Bindra, 1973). Electrolytic lesions, when placed in the MFB just caudal to the POA, also virtually abolished masculine sexual behavior (Hitt, Bryon, & Modianos, 1973), as did lesions placed in the parafornical MFB near the mammillary body (Hitt, Hendricks, Ginsberg, & Lewis, 1970). Lesions of the mammillary bodies themselves, however, do not impair mating behavior (Heimer & Larsson, 1964a).

These results are consistent with the view that connections between the MFB and the medial POA-AH play an important role in male behavior. These connections could conduct information to the POA-AH, or from the POA-AH to more caudal structures. It would be tempting to conclude, as a working hypothesis, for example, that the action of androgen upon neurons in the POA-AH is transmitted via neuronal activity along the MFB to more caudal motor centers necessary for mating behavior. Although such a view is supported by the finding that electrical stimulation of the MFB in the region of the posterior hypothalamus facilitates male behavior (Caggiula & Szechtman, 1972), Caggiula (1970) suggests that such stimulation may combine with or augment stimuli that would heighten sexual arousal rather than elicit copulation directly. It should also be noted that Lisk (1967) has reported that TP implants in the mammillary region in male rats resulted in their becoming very excitable in the presence of the female, yet they did not show mounting behavior. It is possible that multiple components of the relatively diffuse system of androgen-concentrating neurons are obligatory participants in normal mating behavior.

A logical sequel to the MFB experiments would be to attempt to trace the neural substrate for masculine behavior into the midbrain. Although Goodman, Jansen, & Dewsbury (1971) found that mesencephalic reticular formation (MRF) lesions did not alter male behavior, Paxinos & Bindra (1973) reported that larger lesions produced by knife cuts in the MRF markedly disrupted copulatory behavior. In sharp contrast, however, Heimer & Larsson (1964b) observed marked facilitation of mating behavior in the male rat following extensive lesions of the junction between the diencephalon and mesencephalon.

In summary, it is obvious that the POA-AH is involved in the regulation of male sexual behavior, and may be an important, but not necessarily exclusive, site of action of androgen. The anatomical integrity of the MFB appears to be necessary for male copulatory behavior and may convey important neural information to, or away from, the POA-AH. The functional integrity of other areas of the brain, including the cortex, perhaps components of the limbic system, and the reticular formation, is also necessary for mating. How the activity of these various brain structures (and others as well) is integrated with hormone action and environmental and experiential factors to produce stereotyped male sexual behavior is a fascinating and important biological problem, but one for which we can only expect slow progress towards a solution.

The Role of Biogenic Amines in Male Behavior. Experimental manipulation of the MFB, which can alter male sexual behavior, also produces marked changes in cerebral biogenic amines (Moore & Heller, 1967; Moore, 1970). In fact, the MFB transmits aminergic fibers from their complex origin in the midbrain and brainstem to their distribution throughout the brain (Fuxe, Hökfelt, & Ungerstedt, 1970; Ungerstedt,

1971). Drug-induced manipulations in cerebral monoamine levels have produced effects that implicate these amines in the regulation of sexual behavior in the male. Gessa, Tagliamonte, Tagliamonte, & Brodie (1970) reported that parachlorophenylalanine (PCPA), a serotonin-synthesis inhibitor, which in their treatment regime reduced serotonin levels by 90% but did not alter brain catecholamines, increased the frequency at which intact males mounted other males. This response was dependent upon testosterone, because PCPA was ineffective in castrates. Da Prada, Carruba, O'Brien, Saner, & Pletscher (1972) injected 5,6-dihydroxy-tryptamine into the lateral ventricle of male rats. This procedure destroys serotoninergic nerve terminals and resulted in a 59% fall in brain serotonin and a facilitation of male–male mounting behavior. Catecholamines were only slightly decreased (by less than 8%).

Although these studies are consistent with the view that monoamines, particularly serotonin, may inhibit mounting behavior in the male, it must be indicated that in both these studies the experimental behavioral index is particularly weak. Gessa et al. (1970) "considered as *sexually excited* those animals which made at least *one attempt* to mount another male during the observation period of *three* hours." (Italics added.) In the opinion of this author one mount in a period of 3 hr is probably an insignificant observation that does not describe the behavioral state of the test animal, and which may mask actual significant findings. Gessa et al. (1970) reported, for example, that intact rats treated with both testosterone and PCPA exhibited greatly increased mounting activity, including tandem mountings. Their behavioral data, however, provide no indication of this observation. The occurrence of bizarre tandem mating is probably far more significant than the suggestion that PCPA will induce a mounting frequency that could be as low as eight mounts/day.

The importance of the method of testing for male copulatory behavior is further emphasized by several studies that have attempted to correlate drug effects on brain amines with sexual behavior of the male rat. In experiments designed, according to the authors, to test the readiness of male rats to mount females, PCPA treatment increased both the percent of the animals mounting and the mount frequency, whereas treatment with a monoamine oxidase inhibitor, pargyline, which would increase brain amines, inhibited these behaviors (Malmnäs & Meyerson, 1971). Tagliamonte, Tagliamonte, & Gessa (1971) reported that pargyline treatment inhibited, whereas PCPA treatment facilitated, male behavior as measured by the percent of animals mounting and the percent ejaculating. Following rather complete analyses of male sexual behavior, Ahlenius, Eriksson, Larsson, Modigh, & Södersten (1971) and

Dewsbury (1971) reported that the frequency of intromission was increased following PCPA or reserpine administration, respectively. Each of these experiments is consistent with the view that brain monoamines may suppress at least certain components of male sexual behavior.

On the other hand, in experiments designed to test the maximal level of male behavior, sexual satiation, no potentiation of behavior was detected following drug-induced changes in monoamines (Whalen & Luttge, 1970a; Hyyppä, Lehtinen, & Rinne, 1971). It would seem obvious that the mechanisms initiating, maintaining, and terminating sexual behavior need not be identical. Therefore, the depletion of one or several monoamines may indeed facilitate sexual behavior. Whether or not these same processes are active in the normal regulation of reproductive behavior in the male remains to be determined.

The Female

In the previous discussion we have considered how a single hormone, testosterone, may facilitate male sexual behavior. In the female the action—and probably the interaction—of two hormones, estrogen and progesterone, brings about sexual receptivity. Fortunately, the estrous cycle has been well studied, and we have a clear idea of the hormonal basis of sexual behavior in the normal animal. Even in the ovariectomized rat, the temporal characteristics of the hormonal facilitation of lordosis behavior are well established. In the following sections of this chapter we will consider both the possible central site and mechanisms of action of these two steroids.

A generally held concept is that estrogen acts at the level of the POA-AH to facilitate lordosis behavior in the female rat, although there are dissenting views. Lisk (1962) reported that implants of crystalline estradiol contained with the lumen of 27 gauge tubes restored lordosis behavior in ovariectomized rats if placed within the POA or medial anterior hypothalamic area. This paper is generally quoted as indicating the principal site of action of this hormone. When smaller amounts of estrogen (that within 30 gauge tubing) were used, the effective site of estrogen action was limited to the basal POA, anterior to the suprachiasmatic nuclei. As influential as this paper has been, the behavioral data as reported are surprisingly weak. Animals were considered sexually receptive if they displayed one lordosis in a 10 min test. In a more recent study, Ross, Claybaugh, Clemens, & Gorski (1971) confirmed that POA estrogen implants can facilitate lordosis, but the LQ rose only to a maximum of about 50. Is it possible that estrogen acts elsewhere as well?

Dörner et al. (1968b) reported, for example, that implantation of 1 μg EB in the region of the ventromedial hypothalamus (VMH) "facilitated distinct female behavior" (as determined by the display of a single lordosis within a 5 min test). Lisk (1962) and Dörner et al. (1968b) contradict each other even more directly. In Lisk's study, VMH implants were behaviorally negative, although they induced ovarian atrophy. And from the latter study, it was concluded that POA-AH implants stimulate *male* behavior (the display of at least one mount in a 5 min test with a receptive female). If we must discount the speculative hypothesis of Dörner et al., (1968a, 1968b, 1969) because of weak behavioral data, we must also seriously challenge the report of Lisk (1962) as equally speculative in terms of the data reported.

The fact that the POA contains neurons that retain radiolabeled estradiol (Pfaff, 1968; Anderson & Greenwald, 1969; Stumpf, 1970) is beautifully consistent with the view that estrogen acts at this site to facilitate lordosis behavior. However, estrogen-concentrating neurons are also found in the VMH, particularly in the arcuate nucleus. Is the VMH the site of the feedback action of estrogen as the observation that estrogen implants in this area induce gonadal atrophy would imply (Lisk, 1962)? Dörner et al. (1968b) would suggest rather that the ventromedial hypothalamic estrogen-concentrating neurons are active in sexual behavior. In addition, it is very probable that estrogen can act at the level of the POA-AH to regulate ovulation (see Gorski, 1971). Hypothalamic deafferentation studies (Halász & Gorski, 1967; Köves & Halász, 1969) clearly indicate the presence of estrogen-responsive neurons in the anterior hypothalamic area, distinctly caudal to the cells that can be identified autoradiographically. Finally, estrogen also appears to regulate food intake, presumably through a hypothalamic mechanism (Tarttelin & Gorski, 1971). It should be evident that consideration of the localization of estradiol-concentrating neurons alone cannot elucidate the site of estrogen's facilitatory action on sexual receptivity, and cannot make more valid implant studies that may have relied on the minimum of behavioral data. Estrogen can have many functions in the brain.

Several investigators have used the experimental approach of making lesions to identify the neural substrate for lordosis behavior and possibly the site of action of estrogen. Unfortunately, variations in the probable validity of the behavioral measures again confuse the issue. Clark (1942) reported that females with electrolytic lesions of the medial POA-AH refused to mate, but provided no experimental details for analysis. Law & Meagher (1958) reported, on the basis of the mean number of lordosis responses in a 10 min test, that retrochiasmatic (anterior hypothalamic (AH)) lesions eliminated lordosis behavior. This study, however, included data from only three lesioned animals, which were ovariectomized and primed with sufficient exogenous hormone to restore lordosis behavior in control animals. Interestingly, premammillary lesions appeared to facilitate sexual behavior because lordosis was observed during vaginal diestrus. Singer (1968) distinguished between lesions of the POA and of the AH. POA lesions did not alter lordosis behavior, whereas AH lesions eliminated lordosis. The behavioral criterion, however, was again merely the presence or absence of lordosis. In addition, these animals, although ovariectomized, received TP daily; EB and progesterone injections were superimposed upon androgen treatment.

Although these studies suggest that lesions of the POA and/or AH disrupt lordosis behavior, they do not provide strong evidence. Lesions of the VMH have also been reported to inhibit lordosis behavior. Unfortunately Kennedy (1964) did not publish any behavioral measurements, just the qualitative statement that mating behavior was abolished by VMN lesions. Dörner et al. (1969) reported that lesions of the VMN-arcuate complex, as well as lesions of the AH, in ovariectomized rats reduced the display of lordosis behavior. These animals were treated daily with TP, not ovarian hormones, and the behavior was evaluated as numbers of tests positive for female behavior (one lordosis within a 5 min test). Fifty of 88 tests among 22 control rats were positive for lordosis, whereas 21 of 60 tests among 12 VMN-lesioned animals were positive. The significance of such an expression of behavioral data is difficult to assess.

In spite of the general acceptance of the concept that estrogen acts in the POA-AH of the female rat to facilitate lordosis behavior, a critical analysis of the supporting data reveals that this fundamental view still requires definitive proof. At the present time it must be relegated to the status of a working hypothesis.

Implicit in this working hypothesis (as it is generally accepted) is that estrogen activates the POA (or AH) to bring about lordosis behavior. Powers & Valenstein (1972) have published an experiment that supports the reverse hypothesis, that the POA tonically inhibits lordosis behavior in the rat and that estrogen acts at the POA to reduce this inhibitory influence. They report that medial POA lesions in ovariectomized rats reduce the "mean EB threshold" for lordosis behavior. Although their behavioral measurement consisted of the calculation of a receptivity index, which takes into account the actual degree of lordosis shown by the female, the experimental design may have negated the value of the rigid behavioral test. In order to determine EB threshold the dose of EB was reduced by one-half in weekly tests until *no* behavior was observed. If experimental and control groups maintained a very low level of lordosis-responding over just the last few doses of EB, then the behavioral test criteria would have been reduced to the range where one or two lordoses per test would be considered positive! In spite of this possible criticism this experiment is still particularly important because of its almost total disagreement with the working hypothesis that is generally accepted. An unpublished experiment by Nance, Shryne, & Gorski suggests yet another possible explanation for the results of Powers & Valenstein (1972).

Bilateral lesions of the lateral septum markedly increase the behavioral responsiveness (as measured by the LQ calculated from 25-mount tests) of ovariectomized rats to EB (Fig. 4). In another group of ovariectomized rats the LQ was determined after priming with varying doses of EB. Lateral septal lesions increased behavioral sensitivity to estrogen by approximately threefold (Fig. 5). Although scattered estrogen-con-

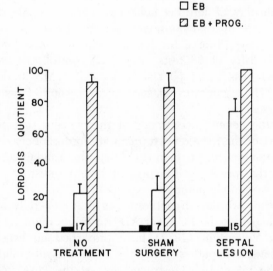

Fig. 4. Influence of septal lesions or sham surgery on lordosis behavior studied under three conditions in ovariectomized rats: (a) after no hormonal treatment (solid columns); (b) after three daily injections of 2 µg EB, then tested on day 4 (open columns); and (c) after similar EB treatment followed by 0.5 mg progesterone given 4–6 hr before testing on day 4 (shaded columns). The lordosis quotient was calculated from 25 mount tests. Behavioral scores following EB treatment in the lesioned group were significantly greater than control ($p < 0.002$) and sham ($p < 0.02$) groups. Numbers of animals per group are indicated at the base of the open columns. From unpublished data of Nance, Shryne, & Gorski.

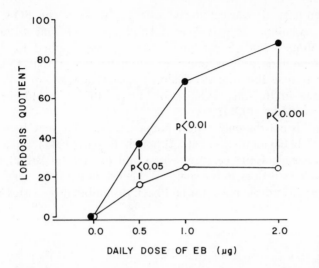

Fig. 5. Facilitation of the behavioral response of the ovariectomized female rat to estrogen by septal lesions. Eleven sham-operated animals (open circles) and 13 septal-lesioned animals (closed circles) were injected with 0.0, 0.5, 1.0, or 2.0 μg EB/day for 3 days. The lordosis quotient to 25 mounts was obtained on day 4. Progesterone was not injected. From unpublished data of Nance, Shryne, & Gorski.

centrating neurons are found in the lateral septum (Stumpf, 1970; McEwen & Pfaff, 1973), it is not likely that the influence of septal lesions is mediated through the destruction of these few cells. Septal lesions markedly change animal behavior (see Brady & Nauta, 1955), and the increased behavioral response to estrogen may be a nonspecific consequence of the elimination or reduction in a general inhibitory system. It is possible, therefore, that the lesions of Powers & Valenstein partially damaged the septum or its connections and thereby decreased the activity of a nonspecific inhibitory system, one consequence of which may be heightened sexual responsiveness.

In our consideration of the hormonal basis of lordosis, we concluded that both estrogen and progesterone normally act together to facilitate sexual receptivity. Where does progesterone act? Although it has been reported that progesterone may act in areas of the hypothalamus known to be estrogen-sensitive (Smith, Weick, & Davidson, 1969; Pasteels & Ectors, 1971) these studies involved the feedback regulation of GTH secretion. The possible site of progesterone action in facilitating lordosis behavior was studied by Ross et al. (1971), who prepared animals with double cannulae chronically implanted in various areas of the brain.

In estrogen-primed ovariectomized rats, exposure of the POA, AH, or VMH to crystalline progesterone did not alter behavior within the 2 hr observation period. Surprisingly, progesterone applied to the MRF rapidly facilitated lordosis behavior (Fig. 6). Since that time it has been shown that the mesencephalon appears to take up radiolabeled progesterone in the rat (Whalen & Luttge, 1971a,b) and the guinea pig (Wade & Feder, 1972).

The MRF is not the only extrahypothalamic site that may be important for lordosis behavior in the rat. Although Beach (1944) reported that surgical removal of the cerebral cortex did not inhibit sexual behavior in the female as it does in the male rat, he also noted behavioral changes that suggested lordosis behavior had been disinhibited by cortex removal.

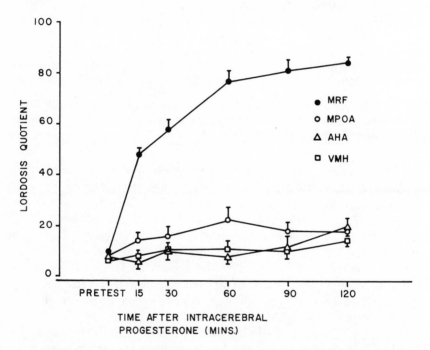

TIME AFTER INTRACEREBRAL
PROGESTERONE (MINS.)

Fig. 6.   Facilitation of lordosis behavior by the implantation of crystalline progesterone into the mesencephalic reticular formation (MRF; solid circles). Ovariectomized rats bearing permanent unilateral cannulae in the MRF, medial preoptic area (MPOA), anterior hypothalamic area (AHA), or ventromedial hypothalamus (VMH) were primed with 3 μg EB/day for 3 days. On the fourth day a pretest yielded consistently low lordosis quotients. Additional behavioral tests were performed at the indicated time intervals after the insertion of an inner cannula containing progesterone. Data from Ross et al. (1971).

In contrast, Larsson (1962) reported that cortical spreading depression induced by KC1 suppressed sexual behavior in both males and females. In a series of experiments from this laboratory the role of the cerebral cortex in lordosis behavior has been clarified. In estrogen–progesterone-primed ovariectomized rats that are receptive, the induction of spreading cortical depression by KC1 causes general depression of the animals and results in an apparent suppression of the lordosis response (Clemens, Wallen, & Gorski, 1967). However, KC1-induced spreading depression can effectively replace progesterone and markedly facilitate lordosis behavior in nonreceptive estrogen-primed ovarectomized rats (Clemens et al., 1967; Ross & Gorski, 1973). Interestingly, when accompanied by marked postural depression, the effect of KC1 on lordosis was impossible to determine. The females could not bear the weight of the mounting male and had to be scored negative for lordosis. It is probable that this postural impairment explains the above findings that KC1 suppresses lordosis. Electrical stimulation of the cerebral cortex also facilitates lordosis-responding, apparently because this procedure also induces cortical spreading depression (Ross, Gorski, & Sawyer, 1973). These studies suggest that the cerebral cortex of the female rat may tonically inhibit lordosis behavior. Because exogenous progesterone inhibits the electrical activity of the cortex, we have suggested the working hypothesis that progesterone facilitates lordosis behavior in the estrogen-primed ovariectomized rat by suppressing a cortical inhibitory system, presumably by a direct action on the MRF (Clemens et al., 1967; Ross & Gorski, 1973; Ross et al., 1973).

Recently, experimental data that appear to contradict this hypothesis have been published by Powers (1972). In this study the intracerebral application of crystalline progesterone to the VMH, but not to the MRF, is reported to facilitate lordosis. The significance of this contradiction is difficult to determine because the two progesterone-implant studies cannot be compared directly. In the study from this laboratory, ovariectomized rats were primed with a total of 6 μg EB divided over 3 days. On the fourth day animals that displayed a LQ of less than 20 unilaterally received an inner cannula containing progesterone, and were found to have an LQ of 80 1 hour later (Ross et al., 1971). In Powers' experiment ovariectomized rats received less estrogen (10 μg/kg) but as a single dose. Behavior was tested 42 hr after EB to obtain pretest scores. After this pretest progesterone was applied directly to the brain bilaterally, and in addition, 100 μg progesterone was injected subcutaneously. Six hours later (48 hr after EB) the main test was performed. Such temporal and hormonal differences in experimental design preclude direct comparison of the experiments. In addition, as we have maintained throughout this discussion, the actual method of assessing behavior is very important, and the differences between the two studies also preclude their direct comparison. Ross et al. (1971) determined the LQ to tests of 10 mounts. Powers (1972) expressed behavior in terms of a receptivity score, also over 10 mounts, but in this case each lordosis was graded in intensity (from 0 for no lordosis to 3 for maximum response). The final expression, or receptivity score, represents the mean lordosis intensity per mount. Note that a LQ of 20, the rejection level in the experiment of Ross et al., could equal any score between 0.2 and 0.6 on the Powers scale, depending on the degree of lordosis in the two responses. An LQ of 80 would range from 0.8 to 2.5. Not only is it impossible to compare these two methods of behavioral analysis, it would appear that the receptivity score introduces more variability (see also the data in Powers, 1972), which may or may not be justified biologically. In spite of the difficulty comparing these two experiments, we must entertain the concept that progesterone may act both in the MRF and VMH. Lisk & Suydam (1967) also suggest that progesterone can act in the POA to facilitate the lordosis response. Thus, although we suggest the working hypothesis that progesterone acts in the MRF, this proposal is most likely incomplete.

Mechanisms of Hormone-Induced Alterations in Behavior

Estrogen

The possible mechanism of action of estrogen on its target tissues has been greatly clarified in the case of the uterus (for reviews see Gorski, Toft, Shyamala, Smith, & Notides, 1968; Baulieu, Alberga, Jung, Lebeau, Mercier-Bodard, Milgrom, Raynaud, Raynaud-Jammet, Rochefort, Truong, & Robel, 1971; Jensen & de Sombre, 1972). In very general terms estrogen is thought to bind in the cytoplasm with characteristic estrogen-binding proteins or receptors. The steroid-receptor complex then migrates into the nucleus where it binds to an acceptor site, apparently in the nuclear chromatin, and changes genomic function. Ultimately the physiology of the target cell is changed. Because estrogen stimulates uterine growth, its action at the genomic or nuclear level is expected, but can the uterine model of estrogen action be applied to the nervous system? It has been clearly demonstrated that the processes of uptake, receptor binding, and transfer into the nucleus can and do occur in the hypothalamus (see McEwen & Pfaff, 1973). Although neuronal growth is not the result of the central action of estrogen, it is possible that this hormone's feedback and/or behavior effects are mediated by the altered production of a protein or enzyme that ultimately changes the responsiveness of the neuron, its neurotransmitter function, or its spontaneous activity. A similar change in a specific population of functionally related neurons might well change behavior. Because of the anatomical and functional complexity of the brain, however, specific knowledge as to the site of a particular action of estrogen and its temporal characteristics would be required before such possibilities can be investigated. We have already discussed the site of action of EB and have suggested that a reasonable, although far from established, working hypothesis would be that estrogen facilitates lordosis behavior at the level of the POA-AH. The temporal characteristics of estrogen action are more clearly known.

In fact, the temporal characteristics of estrogen facilitation of lordosis behavior are consistent with the hypothesis that estrogen acts by altering the fundamental biochemistry of certain neurons. After direct implantation of crystalline estrogen to the brain, behavior is facilitated only after a minimum period of 2–3 days (Lisk, 1962; Palka & Sawyer, 1966). Green, Luttge & Whalen (1970) observed that following the intravenous injection of estradiol, a period greater than 16 hr had to elapse before lordosis behavior was displayed. Arai & Gorski (1968) had earlier defined the temporal pattern of EB action with the anti-estrogen CN-55,945-27 (Parke, Davis). As illustrated in Table 1, antiestrogen effectively inhibited lordosis behavior if administered within 12 hr of EB. However, even 24 hr after EB, progesterone was unable to facilitate lordosis behavior. It appears that estrogen must be present for an extended period of time, and that after that, additional time is required before the condition of the animal is changed so that progesterone can facilitate receptivity. In the cat, Michael (1965) induced sexual receptivity with radiolabeled hexestrol and found that at the time behavior was facilitated (3 days later), no hexestrol could be detected in the brain. These studies suggest that estrogen initiates processes that culminate in behavior after the estrogen has disappeared. Although the level of radioactive estradiol in the brain decreases rapidly with time (Green, Luttge, & Whalen, 1969) significant radioactivity remains in the hypothalamus for more than 24 hr (Whalen & Luttge, 1970b). Certainly, the greatest concentration of estrogen within hypothalamic cells occurs many hours before behavior is altered.

In experiments that can only be considered preliminary because of the complex nature of the problem and the experimental approach, attempts have been made in this laboratory to investigate the possibility

Table 1   Mean Lordosis Quotients (LQ) in Ovariectomized Rats Following Administration of Anti-estrogen and Gonadal Steroids

Group	No. of Rats	Treatment[a] at Indicated Hour					30 Mount LQ[b] ± SE
		0	6	12	24	48	
1	9	EB				P	89.9 ± 2.5
2	10	EB CN[c]				P	2.0 ± 1.6[d]
3	9	EB	CN			P	2.2 ± 1.5[d]
4	9	EB		CN		P	50.1 ± 8.5[d]
5	9	EB			CN	P	82.5 ± 5.0
6	9	EB				P CN	84.2 ± 3.9
7	6	EB		P			23.8 ± 2.7[d]
8	6	EB					1.1 ± 2.7[d]

SOURCE: Data from Arai & Gorski (1968; also unpublished observations).
[a] EB, estradiol benzoate, 5 μg/kg; P, progesterone, 0.5 mg; CN, anti-estrogen CN-55, 945-27).
[b] Measured 4–6 hr after progesterone.
[c] Time of the first administration of 2 mg CN/kg by gavage; CN was administered again 24 hr later.
[d] Significantly different from Group 1, $p < 0.001$.

that estrogen facilitates lordosis behavior by altering genomic expression within hypothalamic neurons. In these studies it has been shown that the intracerebral application of actinomycin-D (Act-D), a RNA-synthesis inhibitor, will inhibit lordosis behavior (Quadagno, Shryne, & Gorski, 1971). These studies will be presented in some detail, first because they represent initial evidence of the possible mechanism of action of estrogen in a behavioral system, and second, because interpretation of these data is speculative. These data should be presented in sufficient detail to permit the reader to make his own judgment (see pp. 263–266 of Sawyer & Gorski (1971) for an example of the controversy stimulated by speculation about these data).

For this study ovariectomized female rats were injected with 3 μg EB at time zero. Control animals injected with 0.5 mg progesterone 36 hr later displayed a high LQ within 5 hr (Fig. 7). Twelve hours after EB injection, additional animals were subjected to sham surgery, acute implantation into the POA of pellets of either cocoa butter, or cocoa butter plus Act-D in varying dosages. Manipulation of the POA 12 hr after EB injection even by control procedures markedly reduced

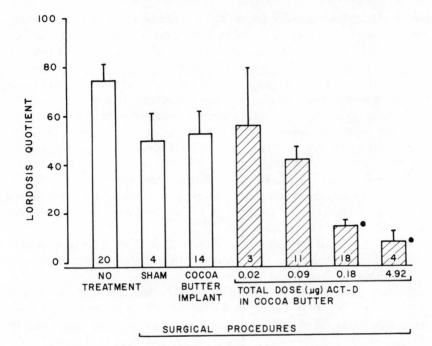

Fig. 7. Influence of the acute implantation of various amounts of actinomycin-D (Act-D; shaded columns) in the preoptic area. All animals were ovariectomized and primed with 3 μg EB at time zero, and 36 hr later with 0.5 mg progesterone. Such treatment induced a high level of sexual receptivity (no-treatment column. All surgical procedures, including sham controls, were performed 12 hr after EB injection. Asterisk indicates $p < 0.01$ vs groups receiving control implant of cocoa butter. Numbers of animals are indicated at the base of each column. Data from Quadagno et al. (1971).

the resultant LQ (attained over a 50 mount test). However, the inhibition of lordosis was only significant if at least 0.18 μg Act-D (total dose) was implanted within the bilateral cocoa butter pellets (Fig. 7). Because Act-D is a toxic substance, the inhibition of lordosis behavior could be due to nonspecific cytotoxicity or to the inhibition of a specific genomic process initiated by estrogen. The fact that many of these animals died within 2 weeks, and had massive lesions of the hypothalamus at that time, supports the first interpretation. However, these animals were in excellent health at the time of the behavioral test as judged by general appearance and motor coordination. In addition, lesions were not present at the time of the behavioral test. Thus the controversy: Was lordosis behavior inhibited because of nonspecific toxicity, or had the Act-D implant actually uncovered the fundamental step in estrogen action? Although the controversy still remains, two experiments further support the view of a more specific action of Act-D. Ho, Quadagno, Cooke, & Gorski (1973) report that at the time lordosis behavior is inhibited following Act-D implantation, the major change in ultrastructure of preoptic cells in the vicinity of the implants is a change in nucleolar morphology. A similar change in nucleolar structure has been observed as a consequence of Act-D action in other tissues (Schoefl, 1964; Recher, Briggs, & Perry, 1971). This observation merely argues against generalized cytotoxicity; nevertheless, a specific inhibition of nucleolar function would still be a rather gross effect in biochemical terms to support the argument that estrogen modifies RNA synthesis. Inhibition of nucleolar function might stop all cellular synthetic activity and eventually lead to cell death.

Note that control procedures performed 12 hr after EB injection also reduced lordosis behavior. The possibility that any perturbation of POA function during this period of presumed estrogen action might inhibit that action suggested reinvestigation of this problem with a chronic preparation. Therefore, Gorski & Terkel (1972) implanted guide cannulae into the brain of ovariectomized rats. By inserting an inner cannula it was possible to infuse Act-D in saline into the POA at different times in relation to the subcutaneous injection of EB and progesterone, and without anesthesia. In addition, it was possible to test for lordosis behavior both before and after drug infusion in tests spaced approximately 10 days apart. As is shown in Fig. 8, a total dose of 0.11 μg Act-D infused into the POA simultaneously with, or 6 hr after, EB injection significantly and reversibly inhibited lordosis behavior (50 mount tests). The reversibility of the Act-D effect is strong evidence that it is not due to general toxicity. However, lesions were still produced, although again not at the time the behavioral test was performed.

The fact that lesions are not a prerequisite for Act-D induced suppression of lordosis is indicated by the observation that the intraventricular infusion of 0.11 μg Act-D significantly and reversibly inhibits lordosis, but does not produce lesions (Fig. 9). However, the effectiveness of Act-D infused into the third ventricle suggests that this drug could have an action outside of the POA.

These studies illustrate one experimental approach to the question of the possible mechanism of action of estrogen. Although they are consistent with the concept that the alteration of behavior by estrogen is dependent upon altered genomic function, this approach can never produce conclusive evidence. It can always be argued that a suppression in genomic activity inhibits the function of another intracellular system, and that estrogen action is related specifically to that other system.

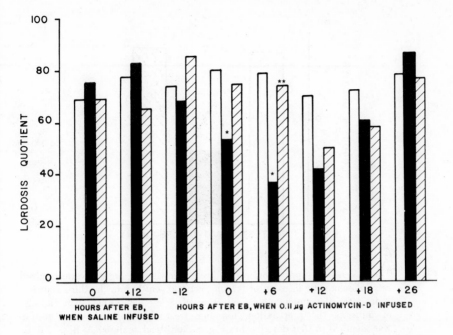

Fig. 8.   Temporal characteristics of the reversible inhibition of lordosis behavior
by intracerebral infusion of actinomycin-D. Actinomycin-D or saline was
infused into the medial preoptic area at various times with respect to
the subcutaneous injection of 3 μg EB (at time zero) in ovariectomized
rats. Since animals had permanently implanted guide cannulae, it was
possible to test for lordosis behavior (50 mount tests) both prior to (pretest;
open columns) or 10 days after (post-test; shaded columns) the drug
test (solid columns). All behavior tests were performed 4–6 hr after progesterone, which was injected 48 hr after EB. Statistical analysis: * significantly
different ($p < 0.01$) from respective pretest score; ** significantly different
($p < 0.05$) from the drug test score. The number of animals in each
group is indicated at the base of pretest columns. Data from Gorski &
Terkel (1972).

Another approach would be to show that estrogen does alter protein
synthesis within temporal restraints consistent with the behavioral effect.
Hormone-induced changes in synthetic and metabolic activity of hypothalamic regions have been reported (see Moguilevsky & Christot, 1972),
but these have not yet been correlated with behavior.

Meyerson (see pp. 263–266 in Sawyer & Gorski, 1971) also reports
preliminary results that suggest that Act-D may suppress lordosis behavior. More recently, Meyerson (1973) investigated the ability of cycloheximide, a protein-synthesis inhibitor, and of colchicine, which disrupts
microtubular function, to inhibit hormone-induced lordosis behavior. In

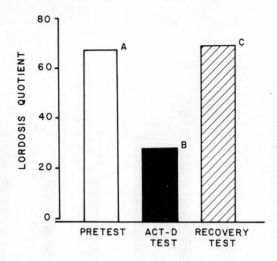

Fig. 9. The reversible suppression of lordosis behavior in eight ovariectomized rats following the infusion of 0.11 μg actinomycin-D into the third ventricle 6 hr after the subcutaneous injection of 3 μg EB. Other than the site of infusion, the preparation, hormone treatment and behavioral testing was identical to that described in Fig. 8. Statistical analysis: A–B, $p < 0.02$; B–C, $p < 0.01$; A–C, not significant. From unpublished data of Terkel, Shryne, & Gorski.

these experiments he expressed behavioral data in terms of percent of animals responding. A positive response is the display of at least two lordoses in six mounts (an LQ of at least 33). Although these agents both inhibit lordosis behavior, there is a general decrease in overt behavior as well. Meyerson (1973) argues against a nonspecific effect, however, because lordosis was unaffected if either cycloheximide or colchicine was given beyond 24 hr after EB injection, even though lordosis was tested at the time when the overt behavioral effect of these drugs was maximal. Although this study extends the list of chemical agents that interfere with lordosis behavior, the question of specificity remains. Hopefully, research of this type will indicate agents that can be studied with more sophisticated chemical techniques after the temporal pattern of their behavioral effect is established.

Progesterone

In the case of progesterone a single possible mechanism cannot be presented for strong consideration. In the chicken oviduct progesterone has been shown to modify genomic activity (O'Malley, McGuire, Kohler, & Korenman, 1969), and in the guinea pig, the progesterone-induced suppression of lordosis behavior is blocked by cycloheximide (Wallen, Goldfoot, Joslyn, & Paris, 1972). Does the facilitation of lordosis by progesterone involve an alteration in genomic function similar to that postulated for estrogen?

As indicated previously, progesterone, when applied to the MRF, markedly facilitates lordosis behavior within 15 min, perhaps too rapidly to be mediated by genomic mechanisms. This rapid effect of progesterone in the MRF suggests another possible mechanism of action, which takes into account the following observations: (a) the MRF controls cortical activity; (b) systemic progesterone induces cortical inhibition as measured by the appearance of sleep-like activity (Ramirez, Komisaruk, Whitmoyer, & Sawyer, 1967; Arai, Hiroi, Mitra, & Gorski, 1967); (c) the cortex appears to inhibit lordosis behavior (Clemens et al., 1967; Ross & Gorski, 1973; Ross et al., 1973); and (d) the MRF appears to contain progesterone-concentrating neurons (Whalen & Luttge, 1971a, 1971b). These observations suggest that progesterone acts at the MRF, presumably by rapidly changing its membrane potential or spontaneous activity, so that the cortical inhibition of lordosis behavior is suppressed or overcome, and the probability of the female lordosing in response to the mounting stimulus is increased. In unpublished observations from this laboratory, Kubo has found that the direct application of progesterone to the MRF increases its multiunit activity.

Biogenic Amines and Lordosis Behavior. In addition to a possible effect of progesterone on the electrical properties of the lordosis-regulating system, the fact that the MRF may be the site of progesterone action introduces yet another system in the possible mechanism of progesterone action: the biogenic amines. From a series of experiments Meyerson (1964a, 1964b) concluded that a serotoninergic system tonically inhibits lordosis behavior in the rat. This conclusion was based on the observation that the amine depletors reserpine or tetrabenazine facilitated lordosis behavior in estrogen-primed ovariectomized rats, whereas serotonin precursors suppressed such behavior. In addition, PCPA, which inhibits serotonin synthesis, was capable of replacing progesterone in the facilitation of lordosis behavior, just like reserpine or tetrabenazine (Meyerson & Lewander, 1970). The observation that crystalline progesterone implants in the caudal MRF rapidly facilitate lordosis behavior (Ross et al., 1971) may be relevant to this concept. Cell bodies of an ascending serotoninergic fiber system are located in the raphe nuclei of the lower brainstem (Fuxe et al., 1970; Ungerstedt, 1971).

Although in Ross's experiment the localization of highest progesterone sensitivity of the MRF was not studied, it may be that the site of progesterone action correlates specifically with the ascending serotoninergic system.

Although this hypothesis would be attractive, there is sufficient controversy over the role of monoamines in lordosis behavior to preclude its general acceptance at this time. An example of this controversy is that Segal & Whalen (1970) were unable to detect a facilitation in lordosis behavior following PCPA treatment to estrogen-primed ovariectomized rats, and in fact, observed a significant suppression of lordosis behavior when PCPA was injected into animals treated with both estrogen and progesterone. Although it is not possible to explain this discrepancy, it should be indicated that in Meyerson's experiments a female rat was termed receptive if she displayed a single lordosis. Segal & Whalen used the LQ, which may provide a better estimate of behavioral receptivity.

Another laboratory has confirmed that tetrabenazine (Ahlenius, Engel, Eriksson, & Södersten, 1972) and PCPA (Ahlenius, Engel, Eriksson, Modigh, & Södersten, 1972) facilitate lordosis behavior in estrogen-primed ovariectomized rats. In the former study, however, the authors report that a low dose of tetrabenazine (2 mg/kg), which significantly increased the LQ (to five mounts), caused a significant decrease in cerebral dopamine rather than serotonin. At higher doses tetrabenazine also lowered brain serotonin. In the second study these authors investigated the temporal pattern of amine depletion and the facilitation of lordosis behavior. PCPA induced a gradual but prolonged decline in brain serotonin and a transient decline in brain catecholamines. Although lordosis was enhanced 2–8 hr after drug injection, when amine levels were decreased, serotonin levels continued to fall. At 26 hr after drug injection, serotonin was markedly suppressed, whereas catecholamine levels had returned to normal. At this point in time, lordosis behavior was *not* facilitated in spite of the low brain serotonin.

Because one could postulate that several amines participate in the regulation of lordosis behavior in the female, it may be argued that aminergic balance is the important factor. Inasmuch as the brainstem contains the cell bodies of the several aminergic systems, it is still possible that the mesencephalic application of progesterone, and progesterone action in general, involves one or more of these systems. However, yet another explanation for the drug-induced alteration in lordosis behavior has yet to be ruled out completely. In the rat and guinea pig, ACTH administration can result in the secretion of sufficient adrenal progesterone to facilitate lordosis behavior in the ovariectomized estrogen-primed animal (Feder & Ruf, 1969). In the similarly treated mouse, reserpine also facilitates lordosis, but not after adrenalectomy (Uphouse, Wilson, & Schlesinger, 1970). Finally, it has been postulated that a central noradrenergic system tonically inhibits ACTH secretion (Ganong, 1972). It is possible, therefore, that drug-induced depletion of amines facilitates lordosis behavior by increasing the secretion of progesterone from the disinhibited adrenal. The significance of such a mechanism to the concept of a specific aminergic lordosis-inhibiting system is obvious. It should be emphasized, however, that Meyerson (1964b) reported, on the basis of the display of a single lordosis response in rats, that the facilitation of lordosis by reserpine is not altered by adrenalectomy.

Monoamine depletors have also been shown to facilitate lordosis behavior in estrogen-primed castrated males (Meyerson, 1968; Larsson & Södersten, 1971; Södersten & Ahlenius, 1972). The last-mentioned investigators suggest that catecholamine rather than serotonin depletion is responsible for this effect. Because progesterone does not ordinarily facilitate lordosis behavior in the male castrated as an adult (Clemens et al., 1970; Davidson & Levine, 1969), it does not seem likely that the effect of amine depletion in the male is mediated through adrenal progesterone.

Testosterone

In the case of testosterone action, very little is known. Androgen receptor neurons, although they may be rather coextensive with estradiol-concentrating neurons (Pfaff, 1971; Stumpf, 1971; Sar & Stumpf, 1972), appear not to have the extreme specificity of the latter (McEwen & Pfaff, 1973). In addition, testosterone appears to be actively metabolized in the brain. As discussed above, it may be that the conversion of androgen to estradiol is a fundamental step in its action within the brain.

Sexual Differentation of the Neural Control of Sexual Behavior

Although sexual behavior in the adult rat is not totally hormone-specific, the male and female are most sensitive to sex-appropriate hormones. With the possible exception of mounting behavior, which may be a component of normal female behavior (Beach, 1968; Whalen, 1968), the several components of sexual behavior appear quite sex-specific. Ejaculation and lordosis, for example, are rather exclusively exhibited by the male and female rat, respectively. Although the gonadal steroid responsivity of the POA-AH presumably plays an important role in the control of sexual behavior in both sexes, the neural substrates for ejaculation and lordosis undoubtably differ. For example, the cerebral cortex is essential for male mating behavior; in the female, the cortex may be part of an inhibitory system, the suppression of which facilitates lordosis. In the female it is also important to stress that two hormones, possibly acting on anatomically and functionally discrete systems, are normally responsible for sexual behavior. Thus, estrogen appears to act in the POA whereas progesterone may act in the midbrain. As a generalization it may be stated that in the adult the specific gonadal hormones facilitate sexual behavior by an action (of unknown mechanisms) on various neural structures and on the interaction between potentially widely dispersed neural systems.

In our consideration of the neuroendocrine regulation of mating behavior, we might well ask about the development of these complex processes. How are these sex differences established? Do the gonadal hormones play a role prior to the activation of adult behavior? Will a consideration of development clarify adult regulatory processes? We have already indicated that sexual dimorphism in brain function is the result of the process of sexual differentiation. These marked differences in brain function do not develop as a consequence of neuronal genetic expression. On the contrary, the hormone environment during a particular and limited phase of development modifies functional differentiation to the extent that the behavioral potential of the animal, at least in response to adult gonadal hormone action, is permanently changed. In the normal rat the balance of this critical period in development is postnatal, and the exposure of the brain to a testicular product, presumably testosterone, is necessary to establish the normal masculine pattern of sexual behavior.

The process of sexual differentiation of the brain has been extensively studied in the rat, hamster, and rhesus monkey, and its possible application to man has been seriously considered. Again, we shall emphasize the rat, and to put the concept of the sexual differentiation of behavioral regulation in perspective, we must emphasize that in the rat, sexual differentiation of the brain also includes those processes that lead to the suppression in the genetic male of the female pattern of cyclic regulation of GTH secretion. Consideration of the sexual differentiation of the regulation of GTH secretion is beyond the scope of this chapter, but the reader is referred to Figure 1.6 in Gorski (1971a). Note from this general summary that the POA has been considered to be the focus of the process of sexual differentiation. This view is, however, an oversimplification as indicated by Gorski (1971b).

Female Sexual Behavior

In the rat, the fact that the neural mechanisms regulating female sexual behavior, at least that behavior represented by lordosis, undergo sexual differentiation is particularly well documented. Numerous laboratories have confirmed the original observation of Grady, Phoenix, & Young (1965) that castration of the male rat on the day of birth or shortly thereafter will permit that animal when adult to lordose to the mounting stimulus at a rate that approaches or may be identical to that of the female (Feder & Whalen, 1964; Gerall, Hendricks, Johnson, & Bounds, 1967; Whalen & Edwards, 1967; Mullins & Levine, 1968b; Davidson & Levine, 1969). The male castrated as an adult, or after approximately the fifth day of life, will display lordosis behavior but only after priming with rather large doses of EB for more than a week (Davidson, 1969). The neonatally castrated male, on the other hand, exhibits high levels of lordosis-responding at doses of estrogen and progesterone also required by the normal ovariectomized female. The fact that males castrated as early as day 6 of life show only the masculine pattern of low lordosis-responding argues against the possibility that lordosis in the neonatally castrated male is a consequence only of a long postcastration interval before behavioral testing. Neonatal ovariectomy is without effect on the ability of the adult to exhibit lordosis (Lisk & Suydam, 1967).

The converse of the effect of neonatal castration on lordosis behavior potential in the male has also been demonstrated without question. The postnatal injection of TP or EB to the intact female (Barraclough & Gorski, 1962; Harris & Levine, 1965; Whalen & Nadler, 1965; Mullins & Levine, 1968a; Clemens et al., 1969, 1970) or the neonatally castrated male (Feder & Whalen, 1964; Mullins & Levine, 1968b; Hendricks, 1972) suppresses the display of lordosis behavior in response to estrogen–progesterone treatment when these animals reach adulthood. Thus, in the rat, it is particularly well demonstrated that the potential to display lordosis behavior in response to ovarian hormones is not sexually dimorphic genetically. At birth the male and female both have the potential to develop this capacity, and apparently to the same extent. When the brain develops in the presence of testicular hormone, this potential either fails to develop or is actively inhibited, a process that also appears to be stimulated by exogenous steroids even in the female (Fig. 10).

If the brain of the rat develops in the presence of testicular hormone, the inherent potential to secrete GTH cyclically is also lost. Thus, it might be concluded that sexual differentiation of GTH and of lordosis regulation are closely interrelated. Such a hypothesis would be consistent

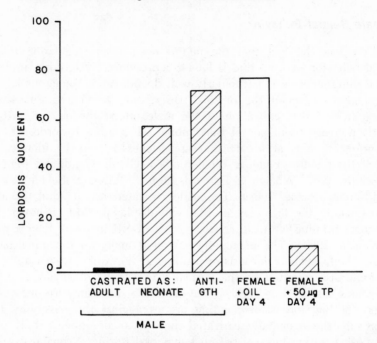

Fig. 10. Experimental data that support the concept of the sexual differentiation of the neural control of lordosis behavior in the rat. Presented are the lordosis quoteints obtained in adult gonadectomized animals after priming with EB and progesterone for the behavioral test. The classic sex difference in lordosis behavior (compare first and fourth columns) is reversed by TP injection to the neonatal female and castration or antigonadotropin treatment of the neonatal male. Data for the latter treatment from Goldman et al. (1972); other data from Quadagno et al. (1972).

with the possible action of androgen in the POA, which is an important neural center for both processes. Although the suppression of behavioral receptivity and GTH cyclicity are often coresults of exposure to androgen, several studies clearly indicate that they can be dissociated. Barraclough & Gorski (1692) first reported that rats rendered anovulatory and in persistent vaginal estrus by the injection of a low dose of TP (10 μg) would mate daily, as judged by the presence of vaginal sperm. Subsequently, this observation was confirmed by more acceptable behavioral analysis (Mullins & Levine, 1968a). Daily receptivity in the anovulatory rat could be due to an actual increase in responsiveness of the lordosis-regulating system (see below), or to the action of a tonic level of ovarian estrogen on a normal neural substrate that is ordinarily activated cyclically at proestrus.

Behavioral tests after ovariectomy and estrogen–progesterone replacement confirm that lordosis responsiveness is not necessarily suppressed by an injection of androgen sufficient to block spontaneous ovulation (Clemens et al., 1969, 1970). Data from a later study are presented in Table 2. This study was initiated because of an apparent change in sensitivity of the neonatal female to exogenous androgen, but clearly confirms the classical view that the influence of androgen on the developing nervous system is both age- and dose-dependent. The fact that GTH-control and lordosis-regulating mechanisms can be dissociated by early androgen exposure suggests that these two processes are unequally sensi-

Table 2   Influence of Various Doses of Testosterone Propionate (TP)

TP Dose (μg)	Age of Rat (days)	No. of Rats	% Rendered Anovulatory		LQ[a]
			at 45 Days of Age	at 90 Days of Age	
		12	0	0	98.0
(Oil)	2	9	0	0	89.3
	3	7	0	0	73.7
	4	3	0	0	96.0
	5	8	0	0	87.4
10	2	10	80	90	87.1
	3	8	75	88	71.3
	4	9	67	100	95.6
	5	7	14	71	77.6
30	2	8	100	100	16.5
	3	10	100	100	17.2
	4	8	88	100	70.0
	5	7	86	100	53.7
90	2	8	75	100	11.4
	3	10	100	100	36.8
	4	10	90	100	27.2
	5	10	70	90	33.2
270	2	8	100	100	25.1
	3	10	90	100	9.6
	4	10	100	100	3.2
	5	9	100	100	1.3

SOURCE: Tarttelin, Shryne, & Gorski (unpublished data).
[a] Obtained after ovariectomy and priming with EB and progesterone.

tive to androgen and/or that their temporal pattern of differentiation is dissimilar. Previous data from this laboratory (Clemens et al., 1969) indicated that the lordosis system was more sensitive to TP on days 4 or 6 of age, at a time when sensitivity of the ovulation-controlling mechanism to TP is markedly decreasing; that is, there is a definite dissimilarity in the temporal pattern of differentiation. However, the data given in Table 2 do not confirm this observation. In any case, GTH-regulating mechanisms in the female are more readily affected by postnatal exposure to TP than is the lordosis-control mechanism. The same may be true for the male rat (Goldman, Quadagno, Shryne, & Gorski, 1972.).

As indicated previously, continuous sexual receptivity in the intact anovulatory female treated neonatally with a low dose of TP could indicate that this behavioral system was actually hyperresponsive to ovarian hormones. However, several laboratories have reported that androgenization decreases behavioral responsiveness to estrogen (Gerall & Kenney, 1970; Whalen, Luttge, & Gorzalka, 1971; Hendricks, 1972), and that the normal male is also less responsive to estrogen (Davidson, 1969). This is in agreement with the several reports that estradiol uptake within the hypothalamus of the androgenized rat is diminished in comparison to that of the normal rat (Flerkó & Mess, 1968; Tuohimaa, Johansson, & Niemi, 1969; Anderson & Greenwald, 1969). Although one laboratory (Green et al., 1969; Whalen & Luttge, 1971b) suggests that this difference is due to variation in body weight between male and female, it is still generally regarded that estradiol uptake is diminished after early androgen treatment. In fact, Flerkó, Illei-Donhoffer, & Mess (1971) have reported a significant difference in uptake not related to body weight.

Experiments from the author's laboratory have suggested another explanation. It is clear that the androgenized female and the male rat, do not display levels of lordosis-responding comparable to that of the normal female when their behavior is measured after gonadectomy and brief replacement treatment with small doses of EB followed by progesterone (Fig. 10). Because in this instance two hormones have been used to prime the animals, it is impossible to assign the behavioral deficit to a specific insensitivity to either hormone. Clemens et al. (1969, 1970) argued that it might be possible to clarify the problem by comparing the behavioral responses to estrogen only. When tested in this way, the LQ of the androgenized females, and even of males castrated as adults, fell within the range of the normal females (Fig. 11). These authors therefore concluded that there is no effect of perinatal androgen on estrogen sensitivity of the lordosis response, and that the clear

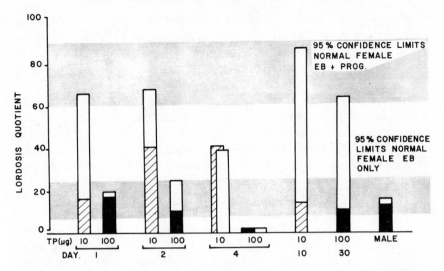

Fig. 11. The influence of 10 or 100 μg testosterone propionate (TP) administered to female rats at the indicated ages on their lordosis behavior as adults subsequent to ovariectomy and replacement treatment with EB and progesterone (open columns), or EB only (shaded and solid columns). The mean response of the male orchidectomized in adulthood, as well as the 95% confidence limits for normal ovariectomized females identically primed with ovarian hormones, are also indicated. Note that apparent estrogen sensitivity and estrogen–progesterone sensitivity varies with age and amount of TP injected. Data from Clemens et al. (1969, 1970).

behavioral deficit seen when both EB and progesterone are used to prime the animals is due to a specific insensitivity to progesterone. The fact that the male rat does not respond behaviorally to progesterone has also been shown (Davidson & Levine, 1969). If, as the experiments of Ross et al. (1971) suggest, progesterone facilitates lordosis behavior by an action at the level of the MRF, it must be concluded that androgenization may directly alter the adult function of the MRF. Study of sexual differentiation of brain function has focused on the hypothalamus, and it is quite possible that this focus is too narrow.

Clearly, the question of hormone responsiveness after androgenization is controversial. When lordosis behavior is studied after prolonged treatment with estrogen, androgenization appears to have reduced estrogen sensitivity. When lower doses of estrogen are used to induce sexual receptivity, however, androgenization appears to have decreased progesterone sensitivity. The main argument against the estrogen-sensitivity hypothesis is that prolonged treatment with EB is pharmacologic and the physiological significance of any difference in sensitivity under these circumstances is unclear. In the case of the use of physiological levels of estrogen, it is argued that the level of lordosis-responding is too low to permit meaningful interpretation of the fact that the lordosis behavior of males, and androgenized and normal females does not differ.

Although it may be that androgenization can change the sensitivity of the brain to both estrogen and progesterone, the possibility that only one of these changes is physiological should be considered. The author is of the opinion that androgenization does not alter the behavioral response to estrogen under physiological conditions. The intact androgenized rat, for example, when tested for sexual receptivity attains a LQ no different from that following ovariectomy and priming with low doses of estrogen, and progesterone administration does not change the LQ (Nance, Shryne, & Gorski, unpublished observations). Finally, the fact that androgenization need not reduce estrogen sensitivity is clearly documented by the observation that under appropriate testing conditions, the androgenized female is behaviorally significantly *more* responsive to a given dose of estrogen than is the normal female (Fig. 12).

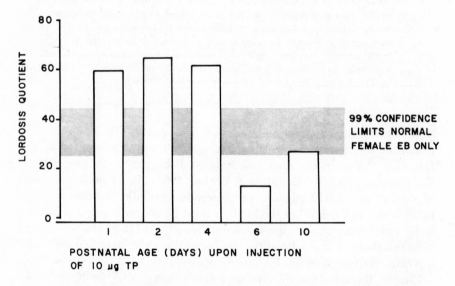

Fig. 12. Evidence for increased behavioral responsiveness to EB subsequent to treatment with 10 μg testosterone propionate (TP) at the indicated postnatal ages. The lordosis quotients illustrated are based on the last 10 mounts of a 50 mount test. All animals were ovariectomized as adults and primed for the behavioral test with EB alone. The 99% confidence limits for normal females under these conditions are also shown. Data from Clemens et al. (1969).

It is important to point out that most studies of sexual differentiation of the brain have involved the female. It has, of course, been shown that early castration of the male will produce an adult that will form corpora lutea in ovarian grafts, and that will exhibit a high level of lordosis-responding when primed with estrogen and progesterone at levels effective in the normal female. With respect to the control of GTH secretion, Gorski (1967) has provided evidence that the neural substrate for ovulation is comparable in the neonatally castrated male and the female, and Wagner (1968) has reported that the timing of the cyclic GTH release is identical as well. The dose of exogenous steroid required to suppress ovulation or lordosis behavior in the genetic male has not been determined, although the male has been shown to be sensitive to exogenous steroids (Gorski & Wagner, 1965). Undoubtedly, most experiments have involved the female because of convenience. The experimenter can administer a known amount of hormone at any postnatal age and study the functional activity on the animal's own ovary in the adult. In the case of the male, it is likely that the testes continually produce androgen from late in intrauterine life until at least several days after birth (Resko, Feder, & Goy, 1968; Miyachi, Nieschlag, & Lipsett, 1973). Therefore, study of the effect of exogenous hormone treatment in the male first requires the inhibition of the testes, either by castration of antiandrogen treatment. One antiandrogen, cyproterone acetate, has been used extensively, and its use clearly established that differentiation of sex organs, the hypothalamic control of cyclic GTH release, and lordosis behavior are androgen-dependent (Neumann & Kramer, 1967). It remains to be seen whether or not the injection of TP postnatally in the female actually reproduces the effect of testicular activity in the perinatal male.

In addition to the need for detailed study of the effects of androgen in the male, the sex in which sexual differentiation of the brain is a physiological process, consideration of the male raises another important question. What controls the critical secretory activity of the neonatal rat testes? The results of a recent study suggest that the secretion of testicular androgen that normally suppresses the ability of the male rat to exhibit high levels of lordosis-responding is dependent upon the pituitary gland (Goldman et al., 1972). When male rats were injected with antiserum against LH on days 1, 3, and 5 of life, adult testicular function appeared normal, but when castrated, these males exhibited exceptionally high levels of lordosis behavior (Fig. 10). Thus, the testicular activity that suppresses lordosis potential depends on the neonatal pituitary gland. Whether the pituitary merely maintains, or actually regulates, the secretory activity of the neonatal testes is unknown. If the latter is true, it will be interesting to learn whether or not the hypothalamus itself plays any role in this regulation, hence, in its own differentiation.

Sheridan, Zarrow, & Denenberg (1973) have suggested another explanation for masculine sexual differentiation. According to their view, high postnatal levels of GTH develop both the cyclic pattern of GTH secretion of the adult female, and female sexual receptivity. When androgen or estrogen is administered to the newborn rat, GTH secretion is inhibited (Goldman & Gorski, 1971). It is this inhibition of GTH level, and not the steroids themselves, that is responsible for masculine differentiation. As evidence for this hypothesis, Sheridan et al. (1973) report that the administration of exogenous GTH with TP attenuates the action of androgen. However, treating the intact neonatal female with large doses of exogenous GTH induces anovulatory sterility (Gorski, unpublished observation). In addition, the fact that treating the neonatal male with antigonadotropin serum leads to the retention of lordosis-behavior capacity (a phenomenon that, according to Sheridan et al., would require high levels of GTH) seems to argue against this view.

In the preceding discussion there has been no mention of male sexual behavior. The corollary of sexual differentiation applied to male behavior would state that exposure of the perinatal brain to androgen is essential to establish the male's capacity to display masculine sexual behavior. Thus, sexual differentiation in the male rat would be brought about through testosterone secretion by the testes and would consist of the suppression of the cyclic release of GTH, the suppression of lordosis responsiveness, and the induction, maturation, and/or development of masculine behavior potential. Unfortunately, it has not been possible to elucidate the latter process, at least not in the rat. Much of the confusion in the literature on this subject can be traced to the behavioral measures employed. We have already indicated how the presence of vaginal sperm, for example, can be a misleading indication of sexual receptivity, in that a poorly receptive female, if housed with an agressive male overnight, may permit sufficient intromissions to stimulate ejaculation. The quantification of male sexual behavior is also subject to important variation from laboratory to laboratory. The most valid behavioral test distinguishes between mounts, intromissions, and ejaculations, whereas the least valid test accepts the display of a single mount as indicative of normal masculine behavior. Both male and female rats mount; moreover, mounting activity in the female does not appear to be influenced by the postnatal administration of androgen (Whalen, 1968). On the other hand, Clemens & Coniglio (1971) suggested that whether or not the female displays mounting behavior (but not the mount frequency in those females that do mount) may be related to prenatal exposure to androgen. They report that the display of mounting activity by the female rat, ovariectomized and primed with TP as an adult, is directly related to the number of male fetuses carried in utero by the mother. This stimulating observation, if confirmed, would suggest that a potent factor presumably testicular in origin, may be transferred from male pups to neighboring females. A similar process, but carried out through vascular anastomoses may be the explanation for the free-martin in cattle (Jost, Vigier, & Prepin, 1972). It has also been reported in the rat that the prenatal injection of androgen can increase masculine behavior in the female (Whalen & Robertson, 1968; Nadler, 1972).

In addition to this possibility, that differentiation of masculine behavior occurs prenatally, there is another factor to be considered. The act of intromission and eventually of ejaculation requires the insertion of a normally developed and sensitive penis into the vagina of the lordosing female. In the rat the penis appears to pass through a period of development during which time it must be exposed to androgen to attain adult sensitivity to this same hormone and, therefore, adult development (Beach & Holz, 1946; Whalen et al., 1969; also see Hart, 1972). Therefore, castration of the newborn male, which appears to reduce masculine behavior of the adult as measured by intromission of ejaculation, also retards penile growth and responsiveness. The decrease in masculine behavior produced by postnatal treatment with antigonadotropin may also be due to a peripheral effect on the penis rather than a central effect (Goldman et al., 1972). It must be noted that in this case, the actual number of mounts shown by the experimental male was increased (Fig. 13). The numbers of intromissions and ejaculations, however, were significantly reduced. This example clearly indicates the flaw in measuring masculine behavior in terms of the mere appearance of mounting behavior. By this criterion, both groups of males would have been indistinguishable. In spite of this limitation about penile development, Hart (1972) concludes that the influence of neonatal androgen is necessary for the normal masculine development of the neural substrate controlling ejaculation.

Although space does not permit a comparative review of sexual differentiation, reference at this point to the hamster may be instructive. In the hamster, which is born after a relatively short gestation, the female shows very little, if any, mounting behavior. In this species the postnatal injection of TP does facilitate mounting activity (Paup, Coniglio, & Clemens, 1972). Interestingly, only testosterone, other androgens that can be converted to estrogens, and estrogen itself can facilitate neonatally the eventual adult display of mounting behavior in the female

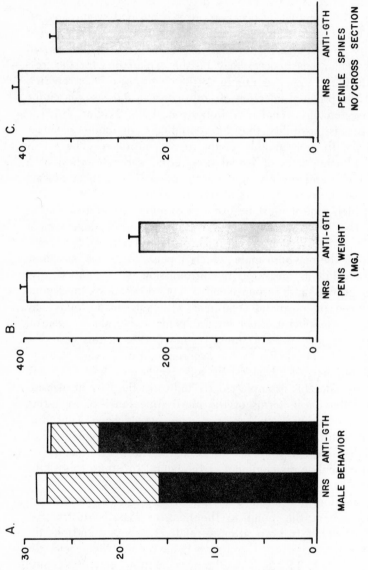

Fig. 13. Influence of neonatal treatment with normal rabbit serum (NRS) or gonadotropin antiserum (anti-GTH) on male behavior (A), and penile development (B,C) measured in gonadectomized adult males primed for 2 weeks with TP. Male behavior: numbers of intromissions (shaded portion) and of ejaculations (open portion) significantly reduced in anti-GTH treated rats; number of mounts are indicated by the solid portion of the columns in A. Penis weight (B) and number of penile spines (C) significantly reduced in anti-GTH treated males. Data from Goldman et al. (1972).

46

hamster. It is also interesting to note that the genetic male hamster will, when castrated as an adult and primed with estrogen and progesterone, display lordosis behavior (Swanson & Crossley, 1971). These authors have suggested that the male hamster normally secretes sufficient androgen neonatally to establish the male behavioral potential, and to suppress the cyclic release of GTH, but not enough androgen to inhibit the lordosis-response potential.

A significant portion of this chapter has been devoted to the sexual differentiation of behavior to emphasize the importance this concept may have for our general understanding of the neuroendocrine regulation of sexual behavior. The expression of adult mating behavior may be limited by restraints imposed perinatally. Frequently in behavioral tests a few animals perform poorly. Some of this variation may be as much a reflection of disturbances in sexual differentiation as a reflection of individual variation.

It is also likely that sexual differentiation may provide a valuable model system on which to study the possible mechanisms of hormone-induced alterations in behavior. In this respect, for example, recent experiments of Nadler (1972) appear to challenge the "classical" view that the POA is the important neural center for sexual behavior. Nadler implanted crystalline TP into various regions of the hypothalamus of the neonatal rat. Rather than POA implants, TP implants in the VMN-arcuate complex were found to eliminate lordosis behavior when these animals reached adulthood. Can these data obtained with neonatal implants of androgen help resolve the question of the site of estrogen action in facilitating adult behavior?

Although metabolic inhibitors have been used to study the mechanism of androgenization (Gorski & Shryne, 1972), or the effect of androgenization on metabolic function of the hypothalamus measured (Moguilevsky, Libertun, Schiaffini, & Scacchi, 1969), these studies have not yet reached the stage when they might be applied to the control of sexual behavior. Androgenization of the female alters weight gain, GTH pattern, and masculine and feminine behavior patterns. At this time it is impossible to correlate possible biochemical changes with any specific function. Because these effects are permanent, however, study of the perinatal effects of steroids may be particularly useful.

The concept of sexual differentiation of the brain clearly establishes that GTH and behavioral control mechanisms can be dissociated, at least in terms of their perinatal sensitivity to gonadal steroids. This fact may lead to experiments that will be able to establish the precise degree of independence and interrelation, as well as the identity of the neural substrate responsible for the regulation of GTH secretion, lordosis, and masculine sexual behavior—if indeed, these are governed by distinct neural systems.

Finally, the concept of sexual differentiation may provide insight into the understanding of human sexual behavior. Although in the human the independence of sexual behavior from gonadal hormones has reached a peak, the gonads may play an important role in establishing behavioral potentials. Current concepts of the differentiation of human psychosexual identity, so clearly summarized by Money & Ehrhardt (1972), stress that postnatal experience is the prime determiner of human sexuality. Nevertheless, prenatal hormones are involved in two important ways. Prenatal testicular hormones induce the development of masculine genitalia, and during the early years of life when psychosexual identity is formulated, the form of the genitalia dictate to a large degree sexually dimorphic social feedback from other individuals, and in this way play a major role in sexual differentiation of psychosexual identity. In their book, Money & Ehrhardt refer to several cases in which the sex of rearing, that is, phenotypic or genital sex, clearly overcame any apparent influence of the discordant genotypic and hormonal sex.

The second way in which gonadal hormones, particularly testicular androgen, influence psychosexual differentiation in the human is far more speculative. However, according to the results of a psychological study of individuals exposed prenatally to androgen for one reason or another, but raised from near birth as females, certain personality traits normally associated in high incidence only with males are frequently found in these individuals (Money & Ehrhardt, 1972). It is likely, although far from established, that the prenatal hormone environment of man alters the sensitivity of the nervous system, perhaps to subsequent hormone exposure and/or to subsequent experiential and cultural factors in a way that may lead at the extreme to frankly aberrant behavior. If the prenatal hormonal environment is in fact one of the ingredients in the recipe from which we develop our own psychosexual identity, it is likely that the full understanding of this process in man will require greater elucidation of what may be an analogous process in lower forms, that is, sexual differentiation of the brain.

Acknowledgments

The original research from the author's laboratory was supported by Grant HD-01182 from the National Institutes of Health, and by the Ford Foundation.

References

Ahlenius, S., Engel, J., Eriksson, H., Modigh, K., & Södersten, P. (1972). Importance of central catecholamines in the mediation of lordosis behaviour in ovariectomized rats treated with estrogen and inhibitors of monoamine synthesis. *J. Neural Transmission*, 33, 247–255.

Ahlenius, S., Engel, J., Eriksson, H., & Södersten, P. (1972). Effects of tetrabenazine on lordosis behaviour and on brain monoamines in the female rat. *J. Neural Transmission*, 33, 155–162.

Ahlenius, S., Eriksson, H., Larsson, K., Modigh, K., & Södersten, P. (1971). Mating behavior in the male rat treated with p-chlorophenylalanine methyl ester alone and in combination with pargyline. *Psychopharm.*, 20, 383–388.

Anderson, C. H., & Greenwald, G. S. (1969). Autoradiographic analysis of estradiol uptake in the brain and pituitary of the female rate. *Endocrinology*, 85, 1160–1165.

Arai, Y., & Gorski, R. A. (1968). Effect of anti-estrogen on steroid induced sexual receptivity in ovariectomized rats. *Physiol. Behav.*, 3, 351–354.

Arai, Y., Hiroi, M., Mitra, J., & Gorski, R. A. (1967). An influence of intravenous progesterone administration on the cortical electroencephalogram of the female rat. *Neuroendocrinology*, 2, 276–282.

Barfield, R. J., & Sachs, B. D. (1968). Sexual behavior: Stimulation by painful electrical shock to skin in male rats. *Science*, 161, 392–395.

Barraclough, C. A., & Gorski, R. A. (1962). Studies on mating behavior in the androgen-sterilized rat and their relation to the hypothalamic regulation of sexual behavior in the female rat. *J. Endocrinol.*, 25, 175–182.

Baulieu, E. E., Alberga, A., Jung, I., Lebeau, M. C., Mercier-Bodard, C., Milgrom, E., Raynaud, J. P., Raynaud-Jammet, C., Rochefort, H., Truong, H., & Robel, P. (1971). Metabolism and protein binding of sex steroids in target organs: An approach to the mechanisms of hormone action. *Rec. Progr. Horm. Res.*, 27, 351–419.

Beach, F. A. (1940). Effects of cortical lesions upon the copulatory behavior of male rats. *J. Comp. Physiol. Psychol.*, 29, 193–244.

Beach, F. A. (1944). Effects of injury to the cerebral cortex upon sexually-receptive behavior in the female rat. *Psychosom. Med.*, 6, 40–45.

Beach, F. A. (1968). Factors involved in the control of mounting behavior by female mammals. In M. Diamond (Ed.), *Perspectives in reproduction and sexual behavior*. Indiana University Press, Bloomington. Pp. 83–131.

Beach, F. A., & Holz, M. (1946). Mating behavior in male rats castrated at various ages and injected with androgen. *J. Exp. Zool.*, 101, 91–142.

Bermant, G., Glickman, S. E., & Davidson, J. M. (1968). Effects of limbic lesions on copulatory behavior of male rats. *J. Comp. Physiol. Psychol.*, 65, 118–125.

Beyer, C., & Komisaruk, B. (1971). Effects of diverse androgens on estrous behavior, lordosis reflex and genital tract morphology in the rat. *Horm. Behav.*, 2, 217–225.

Brady, J. V., & Nauta, W. J. H. (1955). Subcortical mechanisms in emotional behavior: The duration of affective changes following septal and habenular lesions in the albino rat. *J. Comp. Physiol. Psychol.*, 48, 412–420.

Brown-Grant, K. (1971). The role of steroid hormones in the control of gonadotropin secretion in adult female mammals. In C. H. Sawyer & R. A. Gorski (Eds.), *Steroid hormones and brain function.* UCLA Forum Med. Sci. No. 15. University of California Press, Los Angeles. Pp. 269–288.

Caggiula, A. R. (1970). Analysis of the copulation–reward properties of posterior hypothalamic stimulation in male rats. *J. Comp. Physiol. Psychol.,* **70,** 399–412.

Caggiula, A. R., & Eibergen, R. (1969). Copulation of virgin male rats evoked by painful peripheral stimulation. *J. Comp. Physiol. Psychol.,* **69,** 414–419.

Caggiula, A. R., & Szechtman, H. (1972). Hypothalamic stimulation: A biphasic influence on copulation of the male rat. *Behav. Biol.,* **7,** 591–598.

Clark, G. (1942). Sexual behavior in rats with lesions in the anterior hypothalamus. *Amer. J. Physiol.,* **137,** 746–749.

Clemens, L. G., & Coniglio, L. (1971). Influence of prenatal litter composition on mounting behavior of female rats. *Amer. Zool.,* **11,** 617.

Clemens, L. G., Hiroi, M., & Gorski, R. A. (1969). Induction and facilitation of female mating behavior in rats treated neonatally with low doses of testosterone propionate. *Endocrinology,* **84,** 1430–1438.

Clemens, L. G., Shryne, J., & Gorski, R. A. (1970). Androgen and development of progesterone responsiveness in male and female rats. *Physiol. Behav.,* **5,** 673–678.

Clemens, L. G., Wallen, K., & Gorski, R. A. (1967). Mating behavior: Facilitation in the female rat following cortical application of potassium chloride. *Science,* **157,** 1208–1209.

Cramer, O. M., & Barraclough, C. A. (1971). Effect of electrical stimulation of the preoptic area on plasma LH concentrations in proestrous rats. *Endocrinology,* **88,** 1175–1183.

Da Prada, M., Carruba, M., O'Brien, R. A., Saner, A., & Pletscher, A. (1972). The effect of 5,6-dihydroxytryptamine on sexual behaviour of male rats. *Eur. J. Pharmacol.,* **19,** 288–290.

Davidson, J. M. (1966). Activation of the male rat's sexual behavior by intracerebral implantation of adrogen. *Endocrinology,* **79,** 783–794.

Davidson, J. M. (1969). Effects of estrogen on the sexual behavior of male rats. *Endocrinology,* **84,** 1365–1372.

Davidson, J. M., & Levine, S. (1969). Progesterone and heterotypical sexual behavior in male rats. *J. Endocrinol.,* **44,** 129–130.

Davidson, J. M., Rodgers, C. H., Smith, E. R., & Bloch, G. J. (1968a). Stimulation of female sex behavior in adrenalectomized rats with estrogen alone. *Endocrinology,* **82,** 193–195.

Davidson, J. M., Smith, E. R., Rodgers, C. H., & Bloch, G. J. (1968b). Relative thresholds of behavioral and somatic responses to estrogen. *Physiol. Behav.,* **3,** 227–229.

Dewsbury, D. A. (1969). Copulatory behaviour of rats (*Rattus norvegicus*) as a function of prior copulatory experience. *Anim. Behav.,* **17,** 217–223.

Dewsbury, D. A. (1971). Copulatory behavior of male rats following reserpine administration. *Psychon. Sci.,* **22,** 177–179.

Dewsbury, D. A., Goodman, E. D., Salis, P. J., & Bunnell, B. N. (1968). Effects of hippocampal lesions on the copulatory behavior of male rats. *Physiol. Behav.*, **3**, 651–656.

Dörner, G., Döcke, F., & Hinz, G. (1969). Homo- and hypersexuality in rats with hypothalamic lesions. *Neuroendocrinology*, **4**, 20–24.

Dörner, G., Döcke, F., & Moustafa, S. (1968a). Homosexuality in female rats following testosterone implantation in the anterior hypothalamus. *J. Reprod. Fert.*, **17**, 173–175.

Dörner, G., Döcke, F., & Moustafa, S. (1968b). Differential localization of a male and a female hypothalamic mating centre. *J. Reprod. Fert.*, **17**, 583–586.

Edwards, D. A., Whalen, R. E., & Nadler, R. D. (1968). Induction of estrus: Estrogen–progesterone interactions. *Physiol. Behav.*, **3**, 29–33.

Feder, H. H., & Ruf, K. B. (1969). Stimulation of progesterone release and estrous behavior by ACTH in ovariectomized rodents. *Endocrinology*, **84**, 171–174.

Feder, H. H., & Whalen, R. E. (1964). Feminine behavior in neonatally castrated and estrogen-treated male rats. *Science*, **147**, 306–307.

Flerkó, B., Illei-Donhoffer, A., & Mess, B. (1971). Oestradiol-binding capacity in neural and non-neural target tissues of neonatally androgenized female rats. *Acta Biol. Acad. Sci. Hung.*, **22**, 125–130.

Flerkó, B., & Mess, B. (1968). Reduced oestradiol-binding capacity of androgen sterilized rats. *Acta Physiol. Acad. Sci. Hung.*, **33**, 111–113.

Fuxe, K., Hökfelt, T., & Ungerstedt, U. (1970). Morphological and functional aspects of central monoamine neurons. *Int. Rev. Neurobiol.*, **13**, 93–126.

Ganong, W. F. (1972). Evidence for a central noradrenergic system that inhibits ACTH secretion. In K. M. Knigge, D. E. Scott, and A. Weindl (Eds.), *Brain–endocrine interaction. Median eminence: Structure and function.* Karger, Basel. Pp. 254–266.

Gerall, A. A., Hendricks, S. E., Johnson, L., & Bounds, T. W. (1967). Evaluation of the effects of early castration in male rats on adult sexual behavior. *J. Comp. Physiol. Psychol.*, **64**, 206–212.

Gerall, A. A., & Kenney, A. McM. (1970). Neonatally androgenized females' responsiveness to estrogen and progesterone. *Endocrinology*, **87**, 560–566.

Gessa, G. L., Tagliamonte, A., Tagliamonte, P., & Brodie, B. B. (1970). Essential role of testosterone in the sexual stimulation induced by *p*-chlorophenylalanine in male animals. *Nature*, **227**, 616–617.

Goldman, B. D., & Gorski, R. A. (1971). Effects of gonadal steroids on the secretion of LH and FSH in neonatal rats. *Endocrinology*, **89**, 112–115.

Goldman, B. D., Quadagno, D. M., Shryne, J., & Gorski, R. A. (1972). Modification of phallus development and sexual behavior in rats treated with gonadotropin antiserum neonatally. *Endocrinology*, **90**, 1025–1031.

Goodman, E. D., Bunnell, B. N., Dewsbury, D. A., & Boland, B. (1969). Septal lesions and male rat copulatory behavior. *Psychon. Sci.*, **16**, 123–124.

Goodman, E. D., Jansen, P. E., & Dewsbury, D. A. (1971). Midbrain reticular formation lesions: Habituation to stimulation and copulatory behavior in male rats. *Physiol. Behav.*, **6**, 151–156.

Gorski, R. A. (1967). Localization of the neural control of luteinization in the feminine male rat (FALE). *Anat. Rec.*, **157**, 63–69.

Gorski, R. A. (1971a). Steroid hormones and brain function: Progress, principles, and problems. In C. H. Sawyer & R. A. Gorski (Eds.), *Steroid Hormones and Brain Function,* 1971. UCLA forum Med. Sci. No. 15, University of California Press, Los Angeles. Pp. 1–26.

Gorski, R. A. (1971b). Gonadal hormones and the perinatal development of neuroendocrine function. In L. Martini & W. F. Ganong (Eds.), *Frontiers in neuroendocrinology, 1971.* Oxford University Press, New York. Pp. 237–290.

Gorski, R. A., & Shryne, J. (1972). Intracerebral antibiotics and androgenization of the neonatal female rat. *Neuroendocrinology,* 10, 109–120.

Gorski, R. A., & Terkel, A. S. (1972). Inhibition of estrogen induced lordosis behavior by the intracerebral infusion of actinomycin-D. *Anat. Rec.,* 172, 318–319.

Gorski, J., Toft, D., Shyamala, G., Smith, D., & Notides, A. (1968). Hormone receptors. Studies on the interaction of estrogen with the uterus. *Rec. Progr. Horm. Res.,* 24, 45–80.

Gorski, R. A., & Wagner, J. W. (1965). Gonadal activity and sexual differentiation of the hypothalamus. *Endocrinology,* 76, 226–239.

Goy, R. W., & Resko, J. A. (1972). Gonadal hormones and behavior of normal and pseudohermaphroditic nonhuman female primates. *Rec. Progr. Horm. Res.,* 28, 707–733.

Grady, K. L., Phoenix, C. H., & Young, W. C. (1965). Role of the developing rat testis in differentiation of the neural tissues mediating mating behavior. *J. Comp. Physiol. Psychol.,* 59, 176–182.

Green, R., Luttge, W. G., & Whalen, R. E. (1969). Uptake and retention of tritiated estradiol in brain and peripheral tissues of male, female and neonatally androgenized female rats. *Endocrinology,* 85, 373–378.

Green, R., Luttge, W. G., & Whalen, R. E. (1970). Induction of receptivity in ovariectomized female rats by a single intravenous injection of estradiol-17B. *Physiol. Behav.,* 5, 137–141.

Halász, B., & Gorski, R. A. (1967). Gonadotrophic hormone secretion in female rats after partial or total interruption of neural afferents to the medial basal hypothalamus. *Endocrinology,* 80, 608–622.

Hardy, D. F. (1972). Sexual behavior in continuously cycling rats. *Behaviour,* 41, 288–297.

Hardy, D. F., & DeBold, J. F. (1971). The relationship between levels of exogenous hormones and the display of lordosis by the female rat. *Horm. Behav.,* 2, 287–297.

Hardy, D. F., & DeBold, J. F. (1972). Effects of coital stimulation upon behavior of the female rat. *J. Comp. Physiol. Psychol.,* 78, 400–408.

Harris, G. W., & Levine, S. (1965). Sexual differentiation of the brain and its experimental control. *J. Physiol.,* 181, 379–400.

Hart, B. L. (1972). Manipulation of neonatal androgen: Effects on sexual responses and penile development in male rats. *Physiol. Behav.,* 8, 841–845.

Heimer, L., & Larsson, K. (1964a). Mating behaviour in male rats after destruction of the mammillary bodies. *Acta Neurol. Scand.,* 40, 353–360.

Heimer, L., & Larsson, K. (1964b). Drastic changes in mating behavior of male rats following lesions in the junction of diencephalon and mesencephalon. *Experientia,* 20, 1–4.

Hendricks, S. E. (1972). Androgen modification of behavioral responsiveness to estrogen in the male rat. *Horm. Behav.*, **3**, 47–54.

Hillarp, N. A., Olivecrona, H., & Silfverskiöld, W. (1954). Evidence for the participation of the preoptic area in male mating behavior. *Experientia*, **10**, 224–227.

Hitt, J . C., Bryon, D. M., & Modianos, D. T. (1973). Effects of rostral medial forebrain bundle and olfactory tubercle lesions upon sexual behavior of male rats. *J. Comp. Physiol. Psychol.*, **82**, 30–36.

Hitt, J. C., Hendricks, S. E., Ginsberg, S. I., & Lewis, J. H. (1970). Disruption of male, but not female, sexual behavior in rats by medial forebrain bundle lesions. *J. Comp. Physiol. Psychol.*, **73**, 377–384.

Ho, G. K., Quadagno, D. M., Cooke, P. H., & Gorski, R. A. (1973). Intracranial implants of actinomycin-D: Effects on sexual behavior and nucleolar ultrastructure in the rat. *Neuroendocrinology*, **13**, 47–55.

Hyyppä, M., Lehtinen, P., & Rinne, U. K. (1971). Effect of *l*-Dopa on the hypothalamic, pineal and striatal monoamines and on the sexual behavior of the rat. *Brain Res.*, **30**, 265–272.

Jensen, E. V., & de Sombre, E. R. (1972). Mechanism of action of the female sex hormones. *Ann. Rev. Biochem.*, **41**, 203–230.

Jost, A., Vigier, B., & Prepin, J. (1972). Freemartins in cattle: The first steps of sexual organogenesis. *J. Reprod. Fert.*, **29**, 349–379.

Kennedy, G. C. (1964). Hypothalamic control of the endocrine and behavioural changes associated with oestrus in the rat. *J. Physiol.*, **172**, 383–392.

Kimble, D. P., Rogers, L., & Hendrickson, C. W. (1967). Hippocampal lesions disrupt maternal, not sexual, behavior in the albino rat. *J. Comp. Physiol. Psychol.*, **63**, 401–407.

Komisaruk, B. R. (1971). Induction of lordosis in ovariectomized rats by stimulation of the vaginal cervix: Hormonal and neural interrelationships. In C. H. Sawyer & R. A. Gorski (Eds.), *Steroid hormones and brain function*. UCLA Forum Med. Sci. No. 15. University of California Press, Los Angeles. Pp. 127–135.

Köves, K., & Halász, B. (1969). Data on the location of the neural structures indispensable for the occurrence of ovarian compensatory hypertrophy. *Neuroendocrinology*, **4**, 1–11.

Larsson, K. (1962). Spreading cortical depression and the mating behaviour in male and female rats. *Zeitschrift fur Tierpsychologie*, **19**, 321–331.

Larsson, K. (1963). Non-specific stimulation and sexual behaviour in the male rat. *Behaviour*, **20**, 110–114.

Larsson, K. (1964). Mating behavior in male rats after cerebral cortex ablation. II. Effects of lesions in the frontal lobes compared to lesions in the posterior half of the hemispheres. *J. Exp. Zool.*, **155**, 203–214.

Larsson, K. (1966). Individual differences in reactivity to adrogen in male rats. *Physiol. Behav.*, **1**, 255–258.

Larsson, K., & Heimer, L. (1964). Mating behaviour of male rats after lesions in the preoptic area. *Nature*, **202**, 413–414.

Larsson, K., & Södersten, P. (1971). Lordosis behavior in male rats treated with estrogen in combination with tetrabenazine and nialamide. *Psychopharm.*, **21**, 13–16.

Law, O. T., & Meagher, W. (1959). Hypothalamic lesions and sexual behavior in the female rat. *Science,* **128,** 1626–1627.

Lehrman, D. S. (1971). Experiential background for the induction of reproductive behavior patterns by hormones. In E. Tobach, L. R. Aronson, & E. Shaw (Eds.), *The biopsychology of development.* Academic Press, New York. Pp. 297–302.

Lisk, R. D. (1962). Diencephalic placement of estrodiol and sexual receptivity in the female rat. *Amer. J. Physiol.,* **203,** 493–496.

Lisk, R. D. (1967). Neural localization for androgen activation of copulatory behavior in the male rat. *Endocrinology,* **80,** 754–761.

Lisk, R. D. (1968). Copulatory activity of the male rat following placement of preoptic-anterior hypothalamic lesions. *Exp. Brain Res.,* **5,** 306–313.

Lisk, R. D., & Suydam, A. J. (1967). Sexual behavior patterns in the prepubertally castrate rat. *Anat. Rec.,* **157,** 181–190.

Luttge, W. G. (1971). The role of gonadal hormones in the sexual behavior of the rhesus monkey and human: A literature survey. *Arch. Sexual Behav.,* **1,** 61–88.

McEwen, B. S., & Pfaff, D. W. (1973). Chemical and physiological approaches to neuroendocrine mechanisms: Attempts at integration. In W. F. Ganong & L. Martini (Eds.), *Frontiers in neuroendocrinology, 1973.* Oxford University Press, New York. Pp. 267–335.

Malmnäs, C., & Meyerson, B. J. (1971). p-Chlorophenylalanine and copulatory behaviour in the male rat. *Nature,* **232,** 398–400.

Massa, R., Stupnicka, E., Kniewald, Z., & Martini, L. (1972). The transformation of testosterone into dihydrotestosterone by the brain and the anterior pituitary. *J. Steroid Biochem.,* **3,** 385–399.

Meyerson, B. J. (1964a). Central nervous monoamines and hormone induced estrus behaviour in the spayed rat. *Acta Physiol. Scand.,* **63,** Suppl. 241.

Meyerson, B. J. (1964b). Estrus behaviour in spayed rats after estrogen or progesterone treatment in combination with reserpine or tetrabenazine. *Psychopharm.,* **6,** 210–218.

Meyerson, B. J. (1968). Female copulatory behaviour in male and androgenized female rats after oestrogen/amine depletor treatment. *Nature,* **217,** 683–684.

Meyerson, B. J. (1973). Mechanisms of action of sex steroids on behavior: inhibition of estrogen-activated behavior by ethamoxytriphetol (Mer-25), colchicine and cycloheximide. *Progr. Brain Res.,* **39,** 135–147.

Meyerson, B. J., & Lewander, T. (1970). Serotonin synthesis inhibition and estrous behavior in female rats. *Life Sci.,* **9,** 661–671.

Michael, R. P. (1965). Oestrogens in the central nervous system. *Brit. Med. Bull.,* **21,** 87–90.

Michael, R. P., Zumpe, D., Keverne, E. B., & Bonsall, R. W. (1972). Neuroendocrine factors in the control of primate behavior. *Rec. Progr. Horm. Res.,* **28,** 665–706.

Miyachi, Y., Nieschlag, E., & Lipsett, M. B. (1973). The secretion of gonadotropins and testosterone by the neonatal male rat. *Endocrinology,* **92,** 1–5.

Moguilevsky, J. A., & Christot, J. (1972). Protein synthesis in different hypothalamic areas during the sexual cycle in rats: Influence of castration. *J. Endocrinol.,* **55,** 147–152.

Moguilevsky, J. A., Libertun, C., Schiaffini, O., & Scacchi, P. (1969). Metabolic evidence of the sexual differentiation of hypothalamus. *Neuroendocrinology,* 4, 264–269.

Money, J., & Ehrhardt, A. A. (1972). *Man and woman, boy and girl.* Johns Hopkins University Press, Baltimore. 311 pp.

Moore, R. Y. (1970). Brain lesions and amine metabolism *Int. Rev. Neurobiol.,* 13, 67–91.

Moore, R. Y., & Heller, A. (1967). Monoamine levels and neuronal degeneration in rat brain following lateral hypothalamic lesions. *J. Pharm. Exp. Therapeutics,* 156, 12–22.

Mullins, R. F., & Levine, S. (1968a). Hormonal determinants during infancy of adult sexual behavior in the female rat. *Physiol. Behav.,* 3, 333–338.

Mullins, R. F., & Levine, S. (1968b). Hormonal determinants during infancy of adult sexual behavior in the male rat. *Physiol. Behav.,* 3, 339–343.

Nadler, R. D. (1970). A biphasic influence of progesterone on sexual receptivity of spayed female rats. *Physiol. Behav.,* 5, 95–97.

Nadler, R. D. (1972). Intrahypothalamic exploration of androgen-sensitive brain loci in neonatal female rats. *Trans. N. Y. Acad. Sci., Ser. II,* 34, 572–581.

Neumann, F., & Kramer, M. (1967). Female brain differentiation of male rats as a result of early treatment with an androgen antagonist. In L. Martini, F. Fraschini, & M. Motta, (Eds.), *Hormonal steroids.* Excerpta Medica, Amsterdam. Pp. 932–941.

O'Malley, B. W., McGuire, W. L., Kohler, P. O., & Korenman, S. G. (1969). Studies on the mechanism of steroid hormone regulation of synthesis of specific proteins. *Rec. Progr. Horm. Res.,* 25, 105–160.

Palka, Y., & Sawyer, C. H. (1966). The effects of hypothalamic implants of ovarian steroids on oestrous behavior in rabbits. *J. Physiol.,* 185, 251–269.

Pasteels, J. L., & Ectors, F. (1971). Identical localization of oestrogen- and progesterone-sensitive hypothalamic areas. In P. O. Hubinont, R. Leroy, & P. Galand (Eds.), *Basic actions of sex steroids on target organs.* Karger, Basel. Pp. 200–207.

Paup, D. C., Coniglio, L. P., & Clemens, L. G. (1972). Masculinization of the female golden hamster by neonatal treatment with androgen or estrogen. *Horm. Behav.,* 3, 123–131.

Paxinos, G., & Bindra, D. (1973). Hypothalamic and midbrain neural pathways involved in eating, drinking, irritability, aggression, and copulation in rats. *J. Comp. Physiol. Psychol.,* 82, 1–14.

Pfaff, D. W. (1968). Uptake of ³H-estradiol by the female rat brain. An autoradiographic study. *Endocrinology,* 82, 1149–1155.

Pfaff, D. W. (1970). Nature of sex hormone effects on rat sex behavior: Specificity of effects and individual patterns of response. *J. Comp. Physiol. Psychol.,* 73, 349–358.

Pfaff, D. W. (1971). Steroid sex hormones in the rat brain: Specificity of uptake and physiological effects. In C. H. Sawyer & R. A. Gorski (Eds.), *Steroid hormones and brain function.* UCLA Forum Med. Sci. No. 15. University of California Press, Los Angeles. Pp. 103–112.

Powers, J. B. (1970). Hormonal control of sexual receptivity during the estrous cycle of the rat. *Physiol. Behav.,* 5, 831–835.

Powers, J. B. (1972). Facilitation of lordosis in ovariectomized rats by intracerebral progesterone implants. *Brain Res.*, 48, 311–325.

Powers, B., & Valenstein, E. S. (1972). Sexual receptivity: Facilitation by medial preoptic lesions in female rats. *Science*, 175, 1003–1005.

Powers, J. B., & Zucker, I. (1969). Sexual receptivity in pregnant and pseudopregnant rat. *Endocrinology*, 84, 820–827.

Quadagno, D. M., Shryne, J., Anderson, C., & Gorski, R. A. (1972). Influence of gonadal hormones on social, sexual, emergence, and open field behaviour in the rat, *Rattus norvegicus. Anim. Behav.*, 20, 732–740.

Quadagno, D. M., Shryne, J., & Gorski, R. A. (1971). The inhibition of steroid induced sexual behavior by intrahypothalamic actinomycin-D. *Horm. Behav.*, 2, 1–10.

Ramirez, V. D., Komisaruk, B. R., Whitmoyer, D. I., & Sawyer, C. H. (1967). Effects of hormones and vaginal stimulation on the EEG and hypothalamic unit activity in the rat. *Amer. J. Physiol.*, 212, 1376–1384.

Recher, L., Briggs, L. G., & Perry, N. T. (1971). A re-evaluation of nuclear and nucleolar changes induced in vitro by actinomycin-D. *Cancer Res.*, 31, 140–151.

Resko, J. A., Feder, H. H., & Goy, R. W. (1968). Androgen concentrations in plasma and testis of developing rats. *J. Endocrinol.*, 40, 485–491.

Rosenblatt, J. S. (1965). Effects of experience on sexual behavior in male cats. In F. A. Beach (Ed.), *Sex and behavior.* Wiley, New York. Pp. 416–439.

Ross, J. W., Claybaugh, C., Clemens, L. G., & Gorski, R. A. (1971). Short latency induction of estrous behavior with intracerebral gonadal hormones in ovariectomized rats. *Endocrinology*, 89, 32–38.

Ross, J. W., & Gorski, R. A. (1973). Effects of potassium chloride on sexual behavior and the cortical EEG in the ovariectomized rat. *Physiol. Behav.*, 10, 643–646.

Ross, J. W., Gorski, R. A., & Sawyer, C. H. (1973). Effects of cortical stimulation on estrous behavior in estrogen-primed ovariectomized rats. *Endocrinology*, 93, 20–25.

Ryan, K. J., Naftolin, F., Reddy, V., Flores, F., & Petro, Z. (1972). Estrogen formation in the brain. *Amer. J. Obstet. Gynecol.*, 114, 454–460.

Sar, M., & Stumpf, W. E. (1972). Cellular localization of androgen in the brain and pituitary after the injection of tritiated testosterone. *Experientia*, 28, 1364–1365.

Sawyer, C. H., & Gorski, R. A. (1971). *Steroid hormones and brain function.* UCLA Forum Med. Sci. No. 15. University of California Press, Los Angeles.

Schoefl, G. I. L. (1964). The effect of actinomycin-D on the fine structure of the nucleolus. *J. Ultrastruc. Res.*, 10, 224–243.

Schwartz, N. B., & Talley, W. L. (1965). Effect of acute ovariectomy on mating in the cyclic rat. *J. Reprod. Fertil.*, 10, 463–466.

Segal, D. S., & Whalen, R. E. (1970). Effect of chronic administration of *p*-chlorophenylalanine on sexual receptivity of the female rat. *Psychopharm.*, 16, 434–438.

Sheridan, P. J., Zarrow, M. X., & Denenberg, V. H. (1973). The role of gonadotropins in the development of cyclicity in the rat. *Endocrinology*, 92, 500–508.

Sholiton, L. J., Jones, C. E., & Werk, E. E. (1972). The uptake and metabolism of (1,2-^{3}H)-testosterone by the brain of functionally hepatectomized and totally eviscerated male rats. *Steroids*, 20, 399–415.

Singer, J. J. (1968). Hypothalamic control of male and female sexual behavior in female rats. *J. Comp. Physiol. Psychol.*, **66**, 738–742.

Smith, E. R., Weick, R. F., & Davidson, J. M. (1969). Influence of intracerebral progesterone on the reproductive system of female rats. *Endocrinology*, **85**, 1129–1136.

Södersten, P., Ahlenius, S. (1972). Female lordosis behavior in estrogen-primed male rats treated with p-chlorophenylalanine or α-methyl-p-tyrosine. *Horm. Behav.*, **3**, 181–189.

Stumpf, W. E. (1970). Estrogen-neurons and estrogen-neuron systems in the periventricular brain. *Amer. J. Anat.*, **129**, 207–218.

Stumpf, W. E. (1971). Autoradiographic techniques and the localization of estrogen, androgen, and glucocorticoid in the pituitary and brain. *Amer. Zool.*, **11**, 725–739.

Swanson, H. H., & Crossley, D. A. (1971). Sexual behavior in the golden hamster and its modification by neonatal administration of testosterone propionate. In M. Hamburgh & E. J. W. Barrington (Eds.), *Hormones in development*. Appleton-Century-Crofts, New York. Pp. 677–687.

Tagliamonte, A., Tagliamonte, P., & Gessa, G. L. (1971). Reversal of pargyline-induced inhibition of sexual behavior in male rats by p-chlorophenylalanine. *Nature*, **230**, 244–245.

Tarttelin, M. F., & Gorski, R. A. (1971). Variations in food and water intake in the normal and acyclic female rat. *Physiol. Behav.*, **7**, 847–852.

Tuohimaa, P., Johansson, R., & Niemi, M. (1969). Oestradiol binding in the hypothalamus and uterus of the androgenized rat. *Scand. J. Clin. Lab. Invest.*, **23**, Suppl. 108, 427–432.

Uchida, K., Kadowaki, M., & Miyake, T. (1969). Ovarian secretion of progesterone and 20-α-hydroxypregn-4-en-3-one during rat estrous cycle in chronological relation to pituitary release of luteinizing hormone. *Endocrinol. Jap.*, **16**, 227–237.

Ungerstedt, U. (1971). Stereotaxic mapping of the monomaine pathways in the rat brain. *Acta Physiol. Scand.*, Suppl. 367. 48 pp.

Uphouse, L. L., Wilson, J. R., & Schlesinger, K. (1970). Induction of estrus in mice: The possible role of adrenal progesterone. *Horm. Behav.*, **1**, 255–264.

Van Dis, H., & Larsson, K. (1971). Induction of sexual arousal in the castrated male rat by intracranial stimulation. *Physiol. Behav.*, **6**, 85–86.

Vaughan, E., & Fisher, A. E. (1962). Male sexual behavior induced by intracranial electrical stimulation. *Science*, **137**, 758–760.

Wade, G. N., & Feder, H. H. (1972). (1,2-^{3}H)-Progesterone uptake by guinea pig brain and uterus: Differential localization, time-course of uptake and metabolism, and effects of age, sex, estrogen-priming and competing steroids. *Brain Res.*, **45**, 525–543.

Wagner, J. W. (1968). Luteinization of ovarian transplants in gonadectomized pregnant mare's serum-primed immature male rats. *Endocrinology*, **83**, 479–484.

Wallen, K., Goldfoot, D. A., Joslyn, W. D., & Paris, C. A. (1972). Modification of behavioral estrus in the guinea pig following intracranial cycloheximide. *Physiol. Behav.*, **8**, 221–223.

Whalen, R. E. (1968). Differentiation of the neural mechanisms which control gonadotropin secretion and sexual behavior. In M. Diamond (Ed.), *Perspectives in reproduction and sexual behavior.* Indiana University Press, Bloomington. Pp. 303–340.

Whalen, R. E., Battie, C., & Luttge, W. G. (1972). Anti-estrogen inhibition of androgen induced sexual receptivity in rats. *Behav. Biol., 7,* 311–320.

Whalen, R. E. & Edwards, D. A. (1967). Hormonal determinants of the development of masculine and feminine behavior in male and female rats. *Anat. Rec., 157,* 173–180.

Whalen, R. E., & Edwards, D. A. (1969). Effects of the anti-androgen cyproterone acetate on mating behavior and seminal vesicle tissue in male rats. *Endocrinology, 84,* 155–156.

Whalen, R. E., Edwards, D. A., Luttge, W. G., & Robertson, R. T. (1969). Early androgen treatment and male sexual behavior in female rats. *Physiol. Behav., 4,* 33–39.

Whalen, R. E., & Hardy, D. F. (1970). Induction of receptivity in female rats and cats with estrogen and testosterone. *Physiol. Behav., 5,* 529–533.

Whalen, R. E., & Luttge, W. G. (1970a). p-Chlorophenylalanine methyl ester: An aphrodisiac? *Science, 169,* 1000–1001.

Whalen, R. E. & Luttge, W. (1970b). Long-term retention of tritiated estrodiol in brain and peripheral tissues of male and female rats. *Neuroendocrinology, 6,* 255–263.

Whalen, R. E. & Luttge, W. G. (1971a). Differential localization of progesterone uptake in brain. Role of sex, estrogen pretreatment and adrenalectomy. *Brain Res., 33,* 147–155.

Whalen, R. E., & Luttge, W. G. (1971b). Role of the adrenal in the preferential accumulation of progestin by mesencephalic structures. *Steroids, 18,* 141–145.

Whalen, R. E., Luttge, W. G., & Gorzalka, B. B. (1971). Neonatal androgenization and the development of estrogen responsivity in male and female rats. *Horm. Behav., 2,* 83–90.

Whalen, R. E., & Nadler, R. D. (1965). Modification of spontaneous and hormone-induced sexual behavior by estrogen administered to neonatal female rats. *J. Comp. Physiol. Psychol., 60,* 150–152.

Whalen, R. E., & Robertson, R. T. (1968). Sexual exhaustion and recovery of masculine copulatory behavior in virilized female rats. *Psychon. Sci., 11,* 310–320.

Young, W. C. (1961). The hormones and mating behavior. In W. C. Young (Ed.), *Sex and internal secretions.* Vol. II. Williams & Wilkins, Baltimore. Pp. 1173–1239.

Chapter 2

PLASTIC AND DEGENERATIVE CHANGES IN VISUAL CENTERS

EVA FIFKOVÁ

Kerckhoff Laboratories of the Biological Sciences
California Institute of Technology, Pasadena

The reactions of synaptic contacts to changes in quantity and nature of incoming impulses have become a point of interest in the last decade. Physiological and morphological approaches to these problems have been used in short- as well as in long-term experiments. The results have been reviewed by Cragg (1972) and by Raisman & Matthews (1972). This chapter will deal with structural changes in visual centers after long-term unilateral deprivation and illumination.

The visual system has been used repeatedly as a model for studies on the significance of adequate afferent stimulation for the maintenance of nervous centers. The main advantages of this system are as follows: (*a*) The sensory input, which enters mainly via the optic fibers, can be easily modified and quantified. (*b*) It is a system with minimal convergence of afferent fibers from other brain centers, which is very important, because the nonvisual afferents might reduce the effect of deprivation. (*c*) The visual influx is lateralized because of more or less complete crossing of the optic fibers in the chiasma (Polyak, 1957) in lower vertebrates and some mammals (e.g., rodents). Albino rats have been shown to be especially suitable from this point of view (Lund, 1965; Creel, Dustman, & Beck, 1970). Visual deprivation can be achieved by dark-rearing, enucleation of the eye, or suturing the lids over the eye. Because dark-rearing induces compensatory activation of other sensory modalities (Gyllensten, Malmfors, & Norrlin, 1966) and enucleation is an irreversible state, the unilateral lid-suturing became the method of choice.

Retina

The effect of lack—as well as excess—of light stimuli to the retina has been studied. Biochemical, electrophysiological, and morphological

59

changes were demonstrated in the retinae of mammals reared in the dark. A reduction of the RNA (Brattgård, 1952) and protein content (Gomirato & Baggio, 1962) of retinal ganglion cells was found after dark-rearing. Under similar conditions Rasch, Swift, Riesen, & Chow (1961) reported in a cytological study a lowering of the chromosomal, nucleolar, and cytoplasmic RNA in ganglion, bipolar, and amacrine cells. The retina contains a high concentration of cholinesterase, which is primarily located in the amacrine cells and their processes (Koelle, Wolfand, Friedenwald, & Allen, 1952; Nichols & Koelle, 1967). Liberman (1962) observed a decrease in acetylcholinesterase activity after light deprivation, and explained this finding by the decrease of RNA (shown by Brattgård, 1952; and Rasch et al., 1961), required for the enzyme synthesis. Also, monocular lid-suturing resulted in a decrease of acetylcholinesterase activity (Maraini, Carta, & Franguelli, 1969). Glow and Rose (1964), when inhibiting irreversibly the cholinesterase activity, demonstrated a decrease in the de novo synthesis of acetylcholinesterase following exclusion of light.

In electrophysiological experiments the b-wave of the electroretinogram (ERG) was found to be altered by the exclusion of light (Baxter & Riesen, 1961; Legein & van Hof, 1970; Zetterström, 1955) as well as by monocular deprivation (Cornwell & Sharpless, 1968; Ganz, Fitch, & Satterberg, 1968). All components of the ERG, including the late receptor potential, were found to be depressed after light deprivation (Hamasaki & Pollack, 1972). Sherman and Stone (1973), however, did find neither morphological nor functional changes in the retinal ganglion cells after lid-closure in kittens.

In a morphological study, Weiskrantz (1958) described a reduction in the thickness of the inner plexiform layer together with a significant decrease in the density of Müller fibers as a consequence of dark-rearing. Shrinkage of the inner plexiform layer was also observed by Rasch et al. (1961), under similar circumstances. No effect was observed on the width of the retinal layers in adult hooded rats monocularly deprived for different periods of time (Sosula & Glow, 1971). An increase in the number of amacrine contacts in the inner plexiform layer was found in the eye deprived by monocular occlusion (Sosula & Glow, 1971; Fifková, 1972a).

Whereas the effect of lack of stimulation of the retina has been studied quite extensively, far less attention has been paid to the effect of excess stimulation. Shrinkage of the receptor endings was observed by Cragg (1969a) after exposing rats reared in the dark to daylight. Light applied continuously led to a degeneration of the outer retinal layers in albino rats (Kuwabara & Gorn, 1968; Grignolo, Orzalesi, Castellazzo, & Vittone,

1969; Noell & Albrecht, 1971; O'Steen & Anderson, 1971; Reiter & Klein, 1971; Fifková, 1973). The extent of the damage was related to the period of continuous light exposure. The outer retinal layers of albino rats suffered degeneration even when the light was not applied continuously, but for long daily periods, resulting in a decrease in the number of bipolar contacts in the inner plexiform layer (Fifková, 1972b).

Materials and Methods

Fourteen-day-old albino rats were kept in rooms illuminated for 8, 11, and 16 hr per day at an intensity of 500 lux and a temperature of 25°C for 2, 4, and 6 months. The animals were fed with the usual Larsen diet. Starting from the 14th day of age, a number of the rats in the group that survived 2 months had the lids sutured over the right eye.

The eyes were fixed by perfusing the animal with glutaraldehyde, even though fixation by immersion is generally recommended for this material. Perfusion fixation should ensure effective fixation of the rat's retina, as blood capillaries are quite numerous in both plexiform layers (Cragg, 1969a). Because the reported experiments were based on a comparison of the retinae from the lid-sutured and open eyes, identical treatment of the eyes was of considerable importance. This can hardly be achieved by the dissection of unfixed eyes, but can be accomplished in perfused eyes. Rats anesthetized with urethane were perfused through the abdominal aorta with 2.5% glutaraldehyde in a 1/15 M phosphate buffer (pH 7.3, Van Harreveld & Khattab, 1968). After 15 min perfusion the eyes were removed, the occipital pole was dissected, embedded in paraffin (Paraplast–Sherwood), cut serially, and stained with methylene blue and azure II (Richardson, Jarett, & Finke, 1960). The thickness of the retinal layers was determined in sections 100 μ apart, all passing through the blind spot. In each of the sections, measurements were performed on both sides of the blind spot at intervals of 2–4 μ. The thickness of the outer and inner plexiform and nuclear layers was measured with a Zeiss oil immersion objective ($\times 1000$) and a $10\times$ ocular supplied with a scale. In the rat the ganglion cells form a single layer of cells of variable size, the continuity of which is at some places interrupted. Because of these irregularities no quantitative data on this layer were collected.

For the electron microscope examination the retinae were fixed with glutaraldehyde (in 1/15 M phosphate buffer with 1% sucrose added), which has been shown to give overall good preservation of the tissue except for the mitochondria (Dowling & Boycott, 1966). After 15 min of perfusion the eyes were removed, the occipital pole was dissected and transferred to 2% osmium tetroxide in the 1/15 M phosphate buffer and postfixed for 1.5 hr at 4°C. The tissue was washed in the phosphate buffer, dehydrated in increasing concentrations of acetone and kept in repeatedly changed 100% acetone for 1.5 hr at 4°C. After replacing the acetone with propylene oxide for 15 min the material was transferred to Epon. By this time the whole occipital pole of the eye was hard enough to permit the isolation of a strip of tissue 1 mm wide, from which blocks next to the optic nerve were prepared. This procedure ensured the comparison of identical regions, which was considered to be important because the density of different types of synapses might vary over the retina. From the block next to the optic nerve golden sections were cut, which were treated with lead citrate and examined with the electron microscope (Philips 200).

The inner plexiform layer (IPL) was photographed at a magnification of 3800 and printed at 7× enlargement to give an overall magnification of 26,600. Pictures were taken at random from the whole width of the IPL and the contacts in each field covering 56.2 μ^2 were counted. The random way of sampling is necessary, because not all components of the IPL are uniformly distributed. Impregnated as well as intravitally stained retinae (Boycott & Dowling, 1969; Brown, 1965; Cajal, 1911; Polyak, 1941) show that the preceding statement applies to amacrine cell processes as well as to ganglion cell dendrites. The tissue of the IPL appeared rather uniform, except for those parts containing large profiles of Müller cells. Rather large profiles of all tissue components are found in the innermost part of the IPL contacting the ganglion cells. Micrographs of this region of the IPL and those containing parts of Müller cells were not used for the quantitative determinations.

The number of animals, the length of daily illumination, the period of survival, as well as the treatment and the extent of the surface on which the counts were performed, are summarized in Tables 1 and 2.

Results

Description of the Normal Retina

The retina consists of a number of elements arranged in distinct layers. The outermost layers are formed by light-receptive elements, the cell bodies of which are arranged in the outer nuclear layer. The receptor terminals make synaptic contacts in the outer plexiform layer with dendrites of bipolar cells and with fibers of horizontal cells. The inner nuclear layer is formed by the cell bodies of horizontal, bipolar, and

Table 1   Material for Light Microscope Observation

Treatment Group		No. of Animals	Daily Illumination (hr)	Survival (mo)
Undeprived				
I	A	10	8	2
	B	6	8	6
II		7	11	2
III	A	10	16	2
	B	4	16	4
	C	8	16	6
Deprived				
IV		6	8	2
V		5	11	2
VI		21	16	2

Table 2   Material for Electron Microscope Observation

Treatment Group		No. of Animals	Daily Illumination (hr)	Survival (mo)	Surface of IPL (μ^2)
Undeprived					
I	A	3	8	2	25,077.00
	B	6	8	6	31,022.00
II	A	5	16	2	25,852.00
	B	4	16	4	21,187.00
	C	3	16	6	17,198.00
Deprived					
III	A	7	8	2	61,820.00
	B	8	16	2	44,398.00

amacrine elements. Processes of the last two elements make contacts between each other and with the dendrites of ganglion cells in the inner plexiform layer (IPL), which is a layer of neuropil favorable for the study of the synaptic organization under different experimental conditions.

According to the functional scheme proposed by Dowling & Boycott (1966) and Dowling & Werblin (1969), information from the receptors is brought to the IPL by bipolar cells. From these it is transferred to the dendrites or bodies of ganglion cells either directly or indirectly via amacrine cell processes. It is postulated that the complex processing of visual information is carried out by amacrine cells, which detect and amplify the relative differences in the intensity of the visual field and its configuration. Four types of contacts in the IPL are involved in this processing. Three of them are of conventional type in which two elements are involved (similar to those found e.g., in the cerebral cortex), and where an amacrine ending forms the presynaptic side. The fourth type is a complex synapse involving more than two elements (usually three) in which a bipolar ending forms the presynaptic side. The number of amacrine contacts is directly related to the functional complexity of the retina, in contrast to the number of bipolar synapses, which does not vary in species in which the functional complexity is different (Dubin, 1970).

As the electron micrographs of the inner plexiform layer have been described in a number of species (Kidd, 1962; Dowling & Boycott, 1966; Dowling & Cowan, 1966; Goodland, 1966; Cohen, 1967, Pellegrino de Iraldi & Etcheverry, 1967; Raviola & Raviola, 1967; Dowling, 1968; Witkovsky & Dowling, 1969; Dowling & Werblin, 1969; Sosula & Glow, 1970; Caley, Johnson, & Liebelt, 1972; Leure-Duprée, 1973) including the rat, the criteria used for the classification of various contacts can be briefly summarized.

Amacrine endings are presynaptic to bipolar endings, other amacrine endings, or ganglion cell dendrites. All three kinds of synapses are of the conventional type, exhibiting on the presynaptic side (amacrine) a thickening of the presynaptic membrane with accumulated synaptic vesicles. The bipolar and amacrine postsynaptic sides show a simple membrane thickening (Fig. 1a, b, c), whereas the dendritic postsynaptic side has under the membrane thickening a subsynaptic opacity, as has been observed in cortical axodendritic synapses (Fig. 1d, e). Complex types of amacrine/amacrine synapses such as serial (Kidd, 1962) and reciprocal (Dowling & Boycott, 1966) synapses were observed.

The greater electron transparency and lower concentration of synaptic vesicles (as compared with those of the bipolar endings) together with the synaptic specialization were used to identify the amacrine endings.

More amacrine/dendritic contacts than in the present material were found by Sosula & Glow (1970) in areas obtained by montages of several micrographs. This way of sampling assumes uniform distribution of all components of the IPL. If the distribution is not uniform, as is the case for amacrine processes as well as ganglion cell dendrites (Boycott & Dowling, 1969; Brown, 1965; Cajal, 1911; Polyak, 1941), then a certain limited area may not be representative of the entire IPL. Results differing from those of the random sampling used in the present material can, therefore, be expected.

Bipolar endings contact amacrine processes and ganglion cell dendrites in complex synapses called dyads (Dowling & Boycott, 1966), which

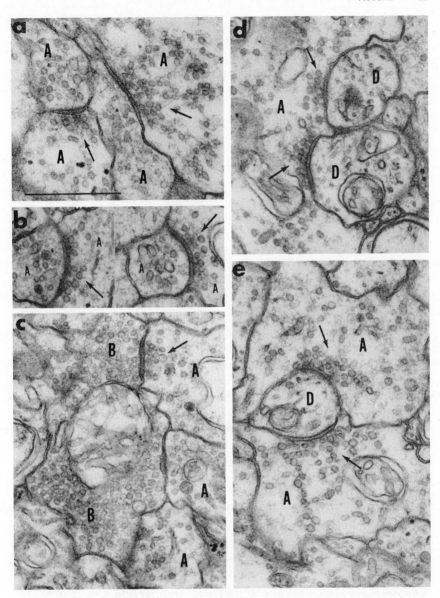

Fig. 1. Various types of conventional synapses: amacrine/amacrine (**a, b**), ama-
crine/dendritic (**d, e**), and amacrine/bipolar (**c**). Abbreviations: A, amacrine ending; B, bipolar ending; D, dendrite. The presynaptic side is indicated by an arrow. Calibration line, 0.5 μ.

exhibit on the presynaptic side (bipolar) a ribbon of electron-dense material. The postsynaptic elements are either two similar or two different profiles. The latter are an amacrine ending and a dendrite (Fig. 2a, c), the former usually two amacrine profiles (Fig. 2d, e). Occasionally two dendrites contact the bipolar ending (Fig. 2b). The last-mentioned synapses were not included in the counts. It was not always possible to identify with certainty the dendrites because of the lack of some of their characteristic components (as described below). Sometimes the postsynaptic amacrine process formed a conventional synapse with the bipolar ending in which it acted as a presynaptic structure, forming thus a two-directional connection called *reciprocal synapse* (Dowling & Boycott, 1966).

The bipolar endings were recognized by the high concentration of synaptic vesicles and the relatively darkly stained material between the vesicles (which is characteristic for the glutaraldehyde-fixed IPL (Dowling & Boycott, 1966)).

The presence of a synaptic specialization, that is, the synaptic ribbon, was necessary to identify a dyad. The first two characteristics were considered to be sufficient to identify the bipolar profile as a postsynaptic structure in an amacrine/bipolar contact, as the low electron transparency distinguishes the bipolar endings from other structures.

Sosula & Glow (1970) found fewer amacrine bipolar synapses than were found in the present experiments. Because of the relatively high transparency of bipolar endings in osmium-fixed material, Sosula & Glow had to use the presence of ribbons for the identification of a bipolar profile forming amacrine/bipolar contacts. The number of dyads and thus the number of ribbons in a bipolar ending is not high, and they may be missed by the plane of sectioning, which would account for the lower number of amacrine/bipolar contacts identified by the criteria of Sosula & Glow (1970).

Dendrites of ganglion cells appear as profiles with microtubules, granular and agranular endoplasmic reticulum, and mitochondria. No structures resembling the synaptic vesicles observed in bipolar and amacrine endings have been noticed in dendrites (Fig. 1d, e).

Changes Caused by Light and by Visual Deprivation

*The Effect of Light on Visual Receptors.** The results of measurements of the dimensions of the outer retinal layers (outer nuclear layer, ONL, outer plexiform layer, OPL) are summarized in Table 3. The rats illuminated 8 hr daily for 2 months exhibited well-preserved receptors, and were therefore taken as a control group. The numbers in Table

* Light microscopy study.

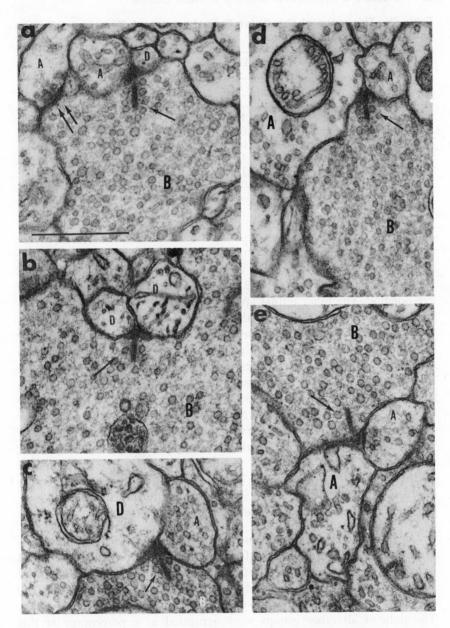

Fig. 2. Various types of complex synapses (dyads). Bipolar ending contacting an amacrine ending and a dendrite (**a, c**). Bipolar ending contacting two dendrites (**b**) and two amacrine endings (**d, e**). Single arrows point to synaptic ribbons in bipolar endings. Double arrow indicates an amacrine/bipolar synapse. Note the arrangment of the vesicles around the synaptic ribbon (**a, c,** and **d**). Calibration line, 0.5 μ.

Table 3   Thickness of the Outer Retinal Layers of Undeprived Groups under Various Light Conditions

Group		Exposure Period	OPL Thickness (μ, mean $\pm$ SE)	(% of Control)	ONL Thickness (μ, mean $\pm$ SE)	(% of Control)
I	A[a]	8 hr/2 mo	9.3 $\pm$ 0.14	100	49.1 $\pm$ 0.42	100
	B	8 hr/6 mo	7.2 $\pm$ 0.09	77.4	38.2 $\pm$ 0.23	78.0
II		11 hr/2 mo	5.4 $\pm$ 0.05	58.0	46.1 $\pm$ 0.72	95.0
III	A	16 hr/2 mo	3.4 $\pm$ 0.10	36.6	34.7 $\pm$ 0.26	71.0
	B	16 hr/4 mo	2.6 $\pm$ 0.11	28.0	25.9 $\pm$ 0.19	52.8
	C	16 hr/6 mo	1.4 $\pm$ 0.08	15.0	10.4 $\pm$ 0.30	21.2

[a] Control group.

3 indicate the mean thickness (in microns) $\pm$ standard error, and thickness as a percent of the control value in animals subjected to 8, 11, and 16 hr of daily light exposure for 2, 4, and 6 months after the physiological eye opening. The inner retinal layers did not show any significant difference and are not included in the table. As the receptors degenerate, the outer retinal layers (formed mainly by the receptors) become thinner. This decrease in the thickness is correlated with an increase in the daily illumination and with an increase in the period of exposure to various light conditions. After 2 months a relatively mild reduction in the thickness occurred in the ONL after 11 hr, as compared to the 8 hr of daily light exposure; a considerable shrinkage took place after 16 hr. The shrinkage was also correlated with the period of time spent under different illumination conditions. Six months of 8 hr illumination, for example, led to a decrease in the thickness by 22% as compared to the 2 month period. With 16 hr illumination, this value became doubled (46%). The changes in width in the outer plexiform layer were in general more severe than in the outer nuclear layer.

*The Effect of Monocular Occlusion on Visual Receptors.** The widths of the outer retinal layers in the group of animals illuminated for 8 hr with both eyes open were not different from those in the lid-sutured eyes of the group of monocularly deprived animals illuminated for the same daily period. These values were, therefore, taken as control values. The data of all other groups were expressed as a percentage of this value (Fig. 3). The results of measurements of the outer retinal layers in monocularly deprived and undeprived rats after 2 months exposure to 8, 11, and 16 hr daily illumination are summarized in Table 4.

* Light microscopy study.

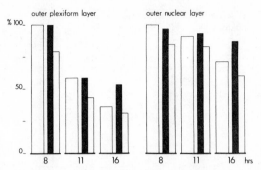

Fig. 3. Thickness of the outer retinal layers with increased daily illumination (for 2 months) expressed as a percentage of the undeprived group illuminated 8 hr for 2 months. Wide white column: open eyes of undeprived rats. Narrow black column: lid-sutured eye of monocularly deprived rats. Narrow white column: open eye of monocularly deprived rats.

A similar effect of the daily illumination as found in the undeprived group was observed in both outer layers of the open eyes in the group of monocularly deprived animals. In this group the reduction of the layers under various light conditions was always larger than in the corresponding group of undeprived animals (Fig. 3). In the closed eyes of the deprived group, milder changes were observed, especially in the outer nuclear layer, where after 16 hr of daily light exposure the thickness dropped to 87% of the control value. The plexiform layer in these eyes shrunk even more (54%) (Fig. 3, Table 4). The differences in thickness of both the outer nuclear and plexiform layers in the closed and open eye were also correlated with the length of daily light exposure. In both layers this difference was found to be 2.5 times larger after 16 hr than after 8 hr of illumination (Fig. 4). Examples of the retinae of open and lid-sutured eyes after 8 hr and 16 daily light exposure for 2 months are presented in Fig. 5.

*Effect of Light on the Synapses of the Inner Plexiform Layer (IPL)** The comparison of electron micrographs from long-illuminated retinae (longer than 8 hr per day for more than 2 months) with short-illuminated ones (8 hr per day for 2 months) did not reveal striking differences in the overall appearance of the tissues. The difference observed referred mainly to the big bipolar terminals (situated next to the ganglion cell layer) which were considerably diminished in size or absent. For reasons mentioned in the Methods section, this part of the IPL was not included in the counts, which could explain the rela-

---

* Electron microscope study.

Table 4 Comparison of Thickness of the Outer Retinal Layers of Deprived and Undeprived Groups

Group	Exposure Period	OPL Thickness (μ, mean $\pm$ SE)[a]			ONL Thickness (μ, mean $\pm$ SE)[a]		
		Closed Eye	Open Eye	Combined[a]	Closed Eye	Combined[a]	Open Eye
IV Deprived	8 hr/2 mo	9.3 $\pm$ 0.32 $p < 0.001$	7.7 $\pm$ 0.22		47.6 $\pm$ 0.62 $p < 0.001$		41.6 $\pm$ 0.42
IA Undeprived	8 hr/2 mo	p, ns	$p < 0.001$	9.3 $\pm$ 0.14	p, ns	49.1 $\pm$ 0.42	$p < 0.001$
V Deprived	11 hr/2 mo	5.4 $\pm$ 0.08 $p < 0.001$	4.0 $\pm$ 0.08		44.7 $\pm$ 0.32 $p < 0.001$		41.0 $\pm$ 0.34
II Undeprived	11 hr/2 mo	p, ns	$p \pm 0.001$	5.4 $\pm$ 0.05	p, ns	46.1 $\pm$ 0.72	$p < 0.001$
VI Deprived	16 hr/2 mo	5.0 $\pm$ 0.08 $p < 0.001$	2.9 $\pm$ 0.05		42.7 $\pm$ 0.26 $p < 0.001$		29.5 $\pm$ 0.24
IIIA Undeprived	16 hr/2 mo	$p < 0.001$	$p < 0.001$	3.4 $\pm$ 0.10	$p < 0.001$	34.7 $\pm$ 0.26	$p < 0.001$

[a] Figures for the undeprived animals did not reveal significant differences between right and left retinas; data of both sides were combined.

ABBREVIATIONS: ns, nonsignificant.

p (in the monocularly deprived groups, IV, V, VI), level of significance between closed and open eye.

p (in the undeprived groups, IA, II, IIIA), level of significance between the undeprived eyes and the closed or open eye of the deprived group.

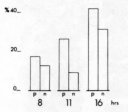

Fig. 4. Percentile difference in thickness between the outer plexiform (p) and outer nuclear (n) layers of the lid-sutured eye (taken as 100%) and the open eye of monocularly deprived rats after different periods of daily illumination for 2 months.

tively mild loss of dyads after long-illumination, as will be discussed later. The rest of the profiles did not differ from those in the control IPL, and the synaptic contacts had all characteristics observed in the controls (Figs. 6, 7). Occasionally, profiles of changed dendrites or amacrine endings were observed in the IPL without any predilection in location. The dendrites were either dark (Fig. 8a) or swollen (Fig. 8c); the amacrine endings were increased in size and contained vacuoles (Fig. 8b). In spite of these changes, the profiles retained their contacts.

The groups of rats, the number of animals in each group, the experimental conditions and the areas of the IPL in which the counts were performed, are summarized in Table 2. The results of synapse counts are shown in Table 5. Because the figures between the right and left IPL were not different, the data of both sides were combined. The numbers indicate the mean density of synapses per electron micrograph and per μ^2 of the entire IPL except for that part situated close to the ganglion cell layer (see section on Methods). There was a moderate decrease in the total synaptic density of long-illuminated retinae (not exceeding 25%) independent of the length of daily light exposure as well as of the time spent under different light conditions. From the organization of the IPL it can be assumed that different types of contacts are affected differently by the increased light exposure. Therefore the density of each synaptic type was determined separately (Table 5). Because animals that were illuminated daily for 8 hr for a period of 2 months (group IA) had the visual receptors well preserved, the synaptic density in the IPL of this group was taken as the reference value and data of all other groups were expressed as a percentage of this value (Fig. 9).

1. *Contacts of bipolar endings:* the bipolar endings form ribbon synapses (dyads) with amacrine endings and with dendrites. Their density

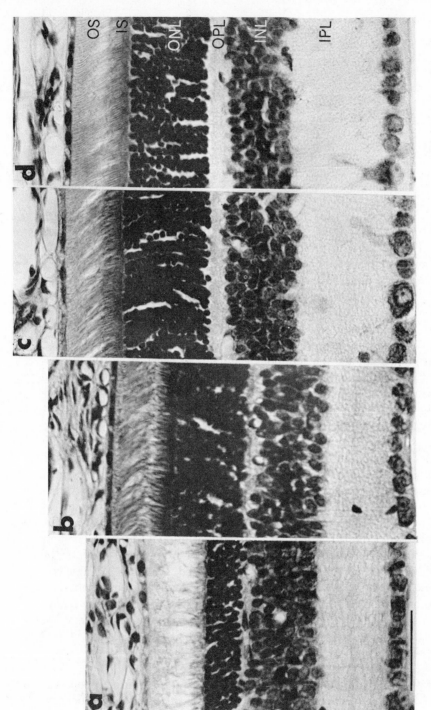

Fig. 5. Retinae of the open eye (**a**), companion lid-sutured eye (**b**) after 16 hr of daily light exposure and open eyes of the unde-prived control group (**c**, **d**) after 8 hr of daily light exposure for 2 months. Abbreviations: IS, inner segment of the light-sensitive elements; OS, outer segment; INL, inner nuclear layer; IPL, inner plexiform layer; ONL, outer nuclear layer; OPL, outer plexiform layer. Calibration line, 0.05 mm.

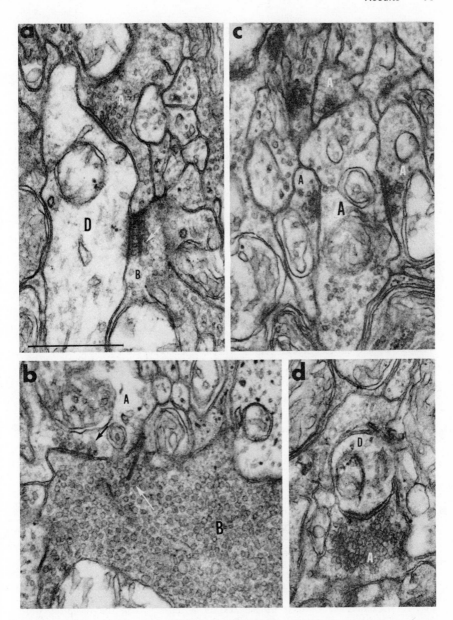

Fig. 6. Examples of synaptic contacts in the IPL of a retina in which the receptor layer was reduced to one-third. Conventional amacrine/dendritic contacts (a, d). Note the opacity on the postsynaptic side. A large amacrine ending is contacted by three small amacrine endings (c). Synaptic ribbons of the dyads are marked by white arrows (a, b). A black arrow points to a reciprocal amacrine/bipolar contact (b). Calibration line, 0.5 μ.

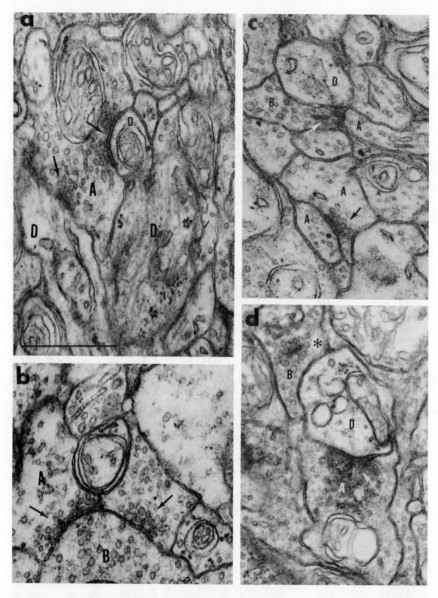

Fig. 7. Examples of contacts in the IPL of a retina where the receptors were completely destroyed. Conventional contacts: amacrine/dendritic (**a, d**), amacrine/bipolar (**b**), amacrine/amacrine (**c**), a dyad (**c**). The presynaptic sides are marked by arrows. Bipolar ending with a ribbon without any apparent postsynaptic side (**d**) is marked by an asterisk. Note the arrangement of vesicles around the ribbon. Calibration line, 0.5 μ.

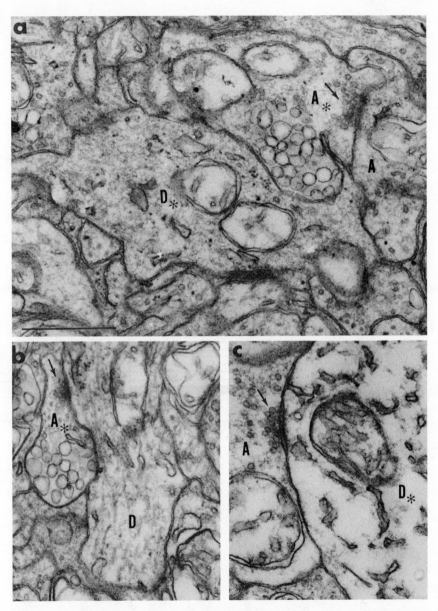

Fig. 8. Changes in the dendritic profiles (**a, c**) and amacrine endings (**a, b**) after long illumination (longer than 8 hr per day for more than 2 months) are marked by an asterisk. Dendrite in **b** seems to be normal. The altered structures retain their synaptic contacts, marked by arrows. Calibration line, 0.5 μ.

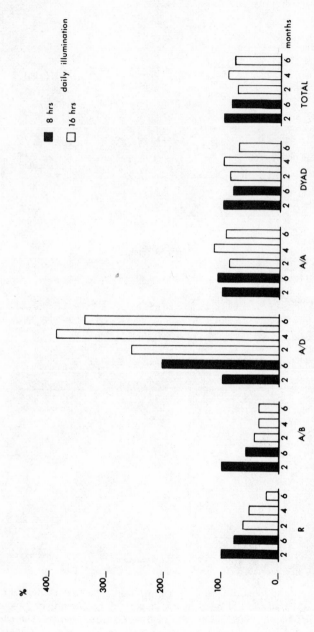

Fig. 9. Density of different synaptic contacts in the IPL (A/B, amacrine/bipolar; A/D, amacrine/dendritic; A/A, amacrine/amacrine and dyads) and the thickness of the receptor layers (R) under various light conditions expressed in percentage of the control group (illuminated daily 8 hr for 2 months).

Table 5 Synaptic Density in the IPL of Undeprived Groups I and II after Different Periods of Light Exposure

Group	Exposure Period	Total		Dyad		A/B		A/A		A/D	
		DF	D/μ²	DF	D/μ²	DF	D/μ²	DF	D/μ²	DF	D/μ²
I A	8 hr/2 mo	7.42 ± 0.14	0.1320	0.64 ± 0.03	0.0114	4.14 ± 0.17	0.0737	2.02 ± 0.08	0.0360	0.62 ± 0.02	0.0110
B	8 hr/6 mo	6.40 ± 0.10	0.1145	0.52 ± 0.03	0.0096	2.40 ± 0.06	0.0428	2.22 ± 0.05	0.0395	1.26 ± 0.04	0.0224
II A	16 hr/2 mo	5.67 ± 0.08	0.1010	0.56 ± 0.04	0.0101	1.74 ± 0.04	0.0310	1.75 ± 0.04	0.0311	1.60 ± 0.04	0.028
B	16 hr/4 mo	6.90 ± 0.13	0.1230	0.64 ± 0.08	0.0114	1.49 ± 0.08	0.0265	2.35 ± 0.06	0.0418	2.42 ± 0.07	0.0431
C	16 hr/6 mo	5.97 ± 0.11	0.1063	0.47 ± 0.05	0.0084	1.47 ± 0.06	0.0262	1.91 ± 0.06	0.0340	2.12 ± 0.06	0.0378

NOTE: Figures between the right and left retina did not reveal significant differences, therefore data of both sides were combined.

ABBREVIATIONS: D/F = density of synapses per field (±SE)
D/μ² = density of synapses per μ²
A/B = amacrine/bipolar synapse
A/A = amacrine/amacrine synapse
A/D = amacrine/dendritic synapse

was moderately decreased in all groups compared with the controls. This loss was not correlated with the length of the light exposures investigated.

2. *Contacts of amacrine endings:* the most affected synapses of this group were the amacrine/bipolar and the amacrine/dendritic contacts. The density of the former had decreased in proportion to the length of illumination, reaching its lowest value in groups IIB and C as compared to the control group IA (Table 5). On the other hand, there was a considerable increase in density of the amacrine/dendritic contacts. This increase was also proportional to the length of light exposure, and reached its maximum in groups IIB and C. Relatively small density variations were observed in the amacrine/amacrine contacts without relation to the illumination. In Fig. 9 are presented the results of the shrinking of the receptor layers and of the density of amacrine/bipolar and amacrine/dendritic contacts in relation to the length of illumination and the age of the animals.

Effect of Monocular Deprivation on Synapses of the IPL. * Two time periods were used:

1. *Eight hours daily illumination.* The results of synapse counts in seven experimental animals and three controls are summarized in Table 6. The synaptic density was 29% higher in the IPL of the lid-sutured eye of monocularly deprived rats than in the eyes of the undeprived control group. On the other hand, a lower density (by 21%) was found in the open eye of the deprived group as compared to the controls. Because the light affects various types of contacts differently, deprivation could also be expected to have a different effect on individual types of synapses. Table 7 summarizes the results of density counts of various types of contacts. Eyes subjected to monocular lid-closure exhibited a markedly higher density of the amacrine/amacrine synapses. The amacrine/bipolar showed a smaller difference, whereas the amacrine/dendritic contacts remained the same. The difference between the deprived and undeprived IPL in density of the amacrine/amacrine contacts (71.5%) was mainly due to the increase of the number of contacts in the deprived IPL. The density of the undeprived IPL did not differ from the control values. The density of the amacrine/bipolar synapses was higher (19%) in the deprived and significantly lower (by 29%) in the undeprived IPL as compared with the controls.

2. *Sixteen hours daily illumination.* The density counts were performed in eight monocularly deprived and five undeprived control animals and the results are summarized in Table 6. The density of all contacts was 23%

* Electron microscope study.

Table 6 Comparison of Synaptic Densities in the IPL of Deprived and Undeprived Groups

Group	Exposure Time	Synaptic Density		Density Compared to Control Group (%)
		D/F	D/μ^2	
IIIA	8 hr/2 mo	9.58 ± 0.11	0.1707	+29.0 (IA)
closed eye (R)		5.88 ± 0.11	0.0996	−20.6 (IA)
open eye (L)		7.42 ± 0.14	0.1320	
IA (control)	8 hr/2 mo			
IIIB	16 hr/2 mo			
closed eye (R)		6.69 ± 0.10	0.0124	+18.0 (IB)
open eye (L)		5.65 ± 0.11	0.01005	−0.5 (IB)
IB (control)	16 hr/2 mo	5.67 ± 0.08	0.1010	

NOTE: Figures for the undeprived animals did not reveal significant differences between right and left retina; data for both sides were combined.

ABBREVIATIONS: D/F = density of synapses per field (mean ± SE)
D/μ^2 = density of synapses per μ^2
R = right
L = left

higher in the IPL of the lid-sutured eye than of the companion open eye. Contrary to the findings in the 8 hr illuminated animals, the density of the undeprived 16 hr illuminated group did not differ from the density in the open eye of the deprived group. There was a 30% decrease in the total synaptic density when the deprived eye was compared with the similarly treated eye in the 8 hr illuminated group. The difference between open eyes of the monocularly deprived groups after rearing under these two different light conditions was negligible (4%).

As in the preceding groups, densities of various types of synapses were calculated separately and the results are presented in Table 7. In the 16 hr illuminated group, as in the 8 hr illuminated group, the lid-closure stimulated the formation of new amacrine contacts. This increase was, however, lower when applying long-lasting rather than short-lasting illumination. As in the 8 hr illuminated animals, there was also in the 16 hr illuminated group an increase of amacrine/bipolar contacts in the deprived eye, and no difference in the density of amacrine/dendritic synapses. The results derived from 8 and 16 hr illuminated, monocularly deprived, and undeprived animals are summarized in Fig. 10. The data from different groups are expressed as a percentage

Table 7   Comparison of Synaptic Densities of Different Contacts in the IPL of Deprived and Undeprived Groups

Group	Exposure Period	Dyad				Amacrine/Bipolar			
		D/F	D/μ^2	% of Control	p	D/F	D/μ^2	% of Control	p
Deprived									
IIIA	8 hr/2 mo								
Closed		0.52 ± 0.04	0.0093	−18.7	<0.02	4.93 ± 0.13	0.0877	+19.0	<0.0
Open		0.34 ± 0.06	0.0061	−46.8	<0.01	2.92 ± 0.00	0.0520	−29.4	<0.0
Undeprived									
IA	8 hr/2 mo	0.64 ± 0.03	0.0114			4.14 ± 0.17	0.0737		
Deprived									
IIIB	16 hr/2 mo								
Closed		0.52 ± 0.06	0.0093	−7.5	ns	2.10 ± 0.05	0.0374	+21.0	<0.0
Open		0.46 ± 0.04	0.0082	−17.0	ns	1.71 ± 0.05	0.0342	−1.8	ns
Undeprived									
IB	16 hr/2 mo	0.56 ± 0.04	0.0100			1.74 ± 0.04	0.0310		

of the values of the undeprived group reared under 8 hr daily illumination.

Discussion

The lack of light stimuli does not seem to interfere with the development of receptors. Eakin (1965) showed that rods differentiate normally and are maintained in frogs reared in the dark. Darkness can, to some extent, retard the deterioration of the dystrophic rat retina (Dowling & Sidman, 1962). Also the receptor degeneration due to the lack of vitamin A in rats is slowed down in the dark (Noell, Delmelle, & Albrecht, 1971). On the other hand, it has been shown that light, under certain circumstances, can be damaging to the visual cells. Light, at intensities ordinarily encountered, causes degeneration of the receptors of the retina of the albino rat if applied continuously for more than 7 days (Noell, Walker, Kang, & Berman, 1966; O'Steen & Anderson, 1971; Reiter & Klein, 1971; Bennett, Dyer & Dunn, 1973). It has been suggested (a) that this is the result of prolonged cell activity that the highly differen-

ʋle 7   Continued

ʋup	Exposure Period	Amacrine/Amacrine				Amacrine/Dendritic			
		D/F	D/μ^2	% of Control	p	D/F	D/μ^2	% of Control	p
prived									
IIA	8 hr/2 mo								
Closed		3.52 ± 0.09	0.0626	+74.0	<0.001	0.61 ± 0.05	0.0108	−1.5	ns
Open		2.05 ± 0.06	0.0364	+1.5	ns	0.57 ± 0.04	0.0101	−8.0	ns
deprived									
A	8 hr/2 mo	2.02 ± 0.08	0.0360			0.62 ± 0.02	0.0110		
prived									
IIB	16 hr/2 mo								
Closed		2.64 ± 0.06	0.0470	+51.0	<0.001	1.43 ± 0.05	0.0255	−11.0	<0.02
Open		2.09 ± 0.07	0.0372	+19.0	<0.01	1.39 ± 0.05	0.0248	−13.0	<0.01
deprived									
B	16 hr/2 mo	1.75 ± 0.04	0.0311			1.60 ± 0.04	0.0285		

тε: Figures of the undeprived animals did not reveal significant differences between right and
: retinas; data of both sides were combined.
вREVIATIONS: D/F = density of contacts per field
   D/μ^2 = density of contacts per μ^2

tiated receptor cannot sustain, and (b) that the essential factor controlling the cell viability is the diurnal cycle of light and darkness (Noell &
Albrecht, 1971; Noell et al., 1971). The present results show the effect
of prolonged light exposure, which caused a loss of receptors. They show,
furthermore, that light can be damaging even when not applied continuously. Under these conditions, however, the degeneration seems less
severe than after continuous illumination (Noell et al., 1966; O'Steen
& Anderson, 1971; Reiter & Klein, 1971). Such a loss of receptors can be
expected to reduce the width of those retinal layers that are formed completely or partly by the various parts of the light-sensitive elements. A
severe shrinkage of the outer retinal layers was found after prolonged
illumination.

After 2 months of 16 hr illumination, the thickness of the outer plexiform layer was decreased to one-third, and the outer nuclear layer to
two-thirds of that in control retinae (8 hr illumination). It is, however,
not only the length of the daily illumination that determines the thickness
of the outer retinal layers, but also the period of time during which
the animals are exposed to the light condition. Even a moderate illumina-

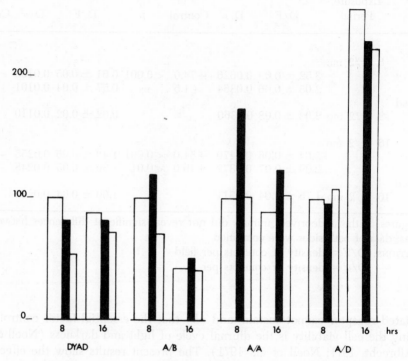

Fig. 10. Density of different synaptic contacts in the IPL of monocularly deprived and undeprived groups under 8 and 16 hr daily illumination for 2 months. The values are expressed as a percentage of the undeprived control group illuminated daily for 8 hr. Wide white column, open eyes of undeprived rats. Narrow black column, lid-sutured eye of monocularly deprived rats. Narrow white column, open eye of monocularly deprived rats. (A/B, amacrine/bipolar; A/A, amacrine/amacrine; A/D, amacrine/dendritic.)

tion of 8 hr per day caused, after 6 months, a shrinkage of the outer layers by 22%. Sixteen hours of light exposure reduced, in 4 months, the thickness to one-half; it caused, in 6 months (in some specimens), a complete loss of the receptors.

The changes in the outer plexiform layer were always more severe and occurred earlier than those in the outer nuclear layer except for the group illuminated for 8 hr for 6 months, where both layers were moderately but equally affected. This may indicate that from the whole receptor the terminal part located in the outer plexiform layer is affected earlier and more severely (after long-lasting illumination) than other components of this element. Cragg (1969a) observed a decrease in the width of receptor terminals with light exposure as short as 3 min in rats that previously had been kept in the dark.

In an electron microscope study, O'Steen, Shear, & Anderson (1972) did not find any apparent changes in the structures of the IPL in rats in which the light receptors had completely degenerated due to cyclic or constant illumination over a period of 4–6 months. Because of the similar period of exposure the present results can be compared with theirs. There is agreement as far as the general appearance of the IPL is concerned, except for the lack of big bipolar endings next to the ganglion cell layer, which is not mentioned by O'Steen et al. (1972). The changes in dendrites and amacrine endings found in the present material were not so frequent as to change noticeably the overall appearance of the IPL. A qualitative comparison of the various types of contacts from retinae in which the receptors were damaged to a different degree showed, at low magnification, no difference. Quantitative comparison, however, revealed extensive differences between the retinae with intact and degenerated receptors.

The total density of contacts in the IPL under different light conditions did not show as big a change as could be expected from the effect on the visual receptors. In the 8 hr illuminated group, a moderate decrease of the synaptic density occurred between the second and sixth months of exposure. In the group illuminated for 16 hr for 6 months the average density was lower than in the group illuminated for 8 hr for the same period of time. However, no correlation with the period of exposure was found within the 16 hr illuminated group; the lowest density was found after 2 months, the highest after 4 months exposure.

The total density does not seem to be a good indicator of the changes occurring in the IPL, as not all types of synapses react in the same way to prolonged illumination. The density of the amacrine/amacrine contacts was not affected by the length of light exposure. A small decrease in the density occurred in the dyads. This relatively mild loss of dyads is probably due to the method of sampling used. The part of the IPL adjoining the ganglion cell layer where most of the damaged big bipolar endings are situated and where the loss of dyads can be expected to be high was not included in the counts (for reasons mentioned in Methods). The amacrine/bipolar and amacrine/dendritic synapses were markedly affected by the period of illumination. Whereas the density of the former decreased with the thickness of the receptor layers, the density of amacrine/dendritic contacts increased.

Because the bipolar elements are directly connected with the receptors, one can expect that loss of the latter will affect the density of synapses of the bipolar endings (amacrine/bipolar and dyads). This decrease in density, which was correlated with the increased time of daily illumination, can therefore be considered as a transsynaptic change due to receptor damage. Similar observations were made by Cragg (1968) in the visual cortex. After the optic nerve was severed, transsynaptic changes occurred in the neurons of the visual cortex in terms of a density decrease of their axon terminals.

The relatively mild decrease in the total density contrasts with the considerable loss of amacrine/bipolar endings. This may be due to the compensatory increase of the amacrine/dendritic contacts. The amacrine endings, when partly deprived of the site of their termination (the bipolar endings) may make instead new contacts on the dendrites of ganglion cells. Such a translocation would require space on the dendritic surface for the formation of new contacts. A new formation of dendritic surface may occur to accommodate the amacrine endings.

It has been observed that a denervated region in the rat's central nervous system constitutes a strong stimulus for growth that can manifest itself either as axonal sprouting or as changes in dendritic morphology (Guth & Windle, 1970). An instance of the first case is the reoccupation of deafferented sites in septal nuclei by local terminals, described by Raisman (1969). Two main afferent systems terminate in the septal nuclei: the fimbria, carrying fibers from the hippocampus, and the medial forebrain bundle, carrying fibers from the hypothalamus. If a long-term lesion was placed in the fimbrial system, then a short-term lesion of hypothalamic fibers showed a spread of their terminals on places originally occupied by the fimbrial fibers and vice versa. A similar synaptic rearrangement occurs in the superior colliculus after long-term unilateral enucleation. Cortical or retinal fibers, homolateral to the deafferented colliculus, replace the degenerated endings (Lund & Lund, 1971; Chow, Masland & Stewart, 1973). Alteration in dendrites of anterior horn cells observed proximal to the site of hemitransection of the spinal cord is an example of the second case (Bernstein & Bernstein, 1971). The alteration manifested itself as an increase in the number of varicosities on the dendritic tree, enhancing in this way the potential synaptic sites. Transsynaptically induced rearrangement of the synaptic population was found also in the rabbit lateral geniculate after severing the optic radiation (Ralston and Chow, 1973).

The bipolar elements make direct contacts with the dendrites as well as with the cell bodies of ganglion cells, so that the transsynaptically induced degeneration in the bipolars could partially denervate the ganglion cells. Either one or both of the above-mentioned mechanisms could then trigger a process that will result in the increased number of amacrine/dendrite contacts. These are suggestions rather than explanations of what mechanism could be involved, inasmuch as the present material does not offer direct evidence for any of them.

Amacrine cells are not directly connected with the receptors, so that the loss of the latter should not affect contacts involving exclusively amacrine endings. The results agree with this assumption: the density of amacrine/amacrine contacts was not affected by the length of the daily illumination.

A correlation between the shrinkage of the outer retinal layers and the length of daily light exposure was observed in the open eye of monocularly deprived rats. After 11 and 16 hr illumination a more pronounced degeneration was observed in these eyes than in the eyes of rats with both eyes open. A shrinkage developed in this open eye even after 8 hr of daily light exposure. These data suggested that the loss of receptors observed in the retinae of the open eye of monocularly deprived rats is due to an excess of light entering this eye. One could assume that an animal that has only one eye functional keeps it open over a longer period of time than would the animal having the use of both eyes. The sutured lids protected the retinae of the deprived eyes so that no shrinkage of the outer nuclear layer developed during the 2 months of deprivation. Some scattered light, however, can be expected to reach the retina even through the sutured lids. This might account for the moderate decrease in the thickness of the outer nuclear layers of deprived eyes in the 16 hr exposed animals, as compared to the 8 hr light-exposed animals.

The pigment in the iris and chorioidea probably forms a natural protection against the deleterious effect of light. In hooded rats that have pigmented eyes no change was observed in the outer retinal layers of the open eye of monocularly deprived animals illumunated 12 hr per day (Sosula & Glow, 1971). This protection, however, is limited to a cyclic illumination schedule, since it has been shown by Noell et al. (1971) that continuous illumination even in hooded rats damages the receptors.

The light microscope data suggest that monocular lid-suturing acts in two ways on the eyes of deprived animals. Besides the effect of the deprivation on the closed eye, which is relatively mild, lid-suturing induces in the companion open eye more severe changes, which appear to be a secondary effect of the monocular lid-closure. This eye, therefore, cannot be used as a control, being itself damaged. Instead, the open eyes of undeprived animals exposed to the same light conditions as the closed eye of the monocularly deprived rats (i.e., with 8 hr of daily light exposure) should be used as controls.

In spite of the relatively small differences in the width of the receptor layers between the lid-sutured and open eye in animals illuminated for 8 hr daily for 2 months, the synapse counts in the IPL revealed considerable changes. In the open eye a decrease of contacts involving bipolar endings (dyads and amacrine/bipolars) was observed, reflecting changes in the receptors similar to those in the undeprived, long-illuminated groups. In hooded rats, in which the receptors of the undeprived eye are protected by the pigment of iris and chorioidea no damage in the light-sensitive elements has been observed and consequently no changes in the density of bipolar contacts (Sosula & Glow, 1971). In the lid-sutured eye a decreased number of dyads was observed. This reduction does not seem to be due to the damage to the receptors, so it must be of different nature than the decrease observed in the open eye. It might be caused by the disuse of the deprived eye.

Amacrine endings, because they are not directly connected with the receptors, should not be affected by the loss of the light-sensitive elements. Indeed, the density of amacrine contacts in the open eye of monocularly deprived rats did not differ from that of undeprived animals. Because amacrine cells are believed to be involved in the complex processing of visual information (Werblin & Dowling, 1969), changes in the amacrine system can be expected to occur in the closed eye, which is completely deprived of form vision. In fact, in this eye the density of amacrine/amacrine contacts was considerably increased. Similar results were reported by Sosula & Glow (1971).

Present findings indicate that visual deprivation and increased illumination affect selectively different types of contacts. The first increases the amacrine/amacrine and amacrine/bipolar contacts and decreases dyads; the second decreases dyads and amacrine/bipolar and increases amacrine/dendritic synapses. If both conditions are applied simultaneously (the 16 hr light-exposure of monocularly deprived animals) a combination of both effects occurs. The protective influence of the sutured lids is expressed by the higher density of dyads and amacrine/bipolars in the closed as compared with the open eye. The comparison of densities of amacrine/amacrine contacts in groups subjected to short- and long-lasting illumination suggests that light suppresses the formation of new contacts. This result is difficult to interpret if the amacrine/amacrine contacts are completely independent of the receptors. Therefore some indirect influence via the bipolar elements has to be assumed.

As to the significance of the effect of deprivation on the IPL one can only speculate. An increase in the density of amacrine/amacrine contacts was observed in frogs during metamorphosis and could also be induced by thyroxin administration. This increase was associated with the development of motion sensitivity and direction selective cells in the retina (Fisher, 1972). In this case the morphological change reflects the development of a new function whereas lid-suturing interferes with the normal function of the eye. Inasmuch as spontaneous firing of retinal ganglion cells increases in the dark (Somjen, 1972) and an inhibitory function has been ascribed to the amacrine cells (Dowling, 1967; Nichols & Koelle, 1967) the formation of new amacrine contacts in the lid-sutured eye could protect the retina against overactivity. The smaller increase in density of amacrine/amacrine contacts in the deprived eye with 16 hr as compared to 8 hr of illumination supports this explanation.

In addition to the activation by the light receptors via the bipolar elements, the amacrine cells can probably be activated by tecto-retinal fibers, which were identified with certainty in teleosts and elasmobranchs (Witkovsky, 1971) and in birds (Dowling & Cowan, 1966; Cowan, 1970). In mammals their existence is still under discussion (Ogden, 1968), though it seems to be confirmed by recent observations in the rabbit (Shkol'nik-Yaross, 1971; Borg & Knave, 1971). Under normal conditions the number of tectoretinal fibers in mammals may be small and therefore hard to detect. However, abnormal conditions, such as lid-suture, may trigger a mechanism of central control over the retina by increasing the number of tectoretinal fibers, which in turn may induce the formation of new amacrine contacts.

Surprisingly, few electrophysiological and biochemical data are available about the retinae of visually deprived animals. It has been shown that the b-wave of the ERG is suppressed in the deprived eye (Cornwell & Sharpless, 1968; Ganz et al., 1968). This wave is believed to be generated by the bipolar cells (Brown, 1968; Brown & Wiesel, 1961; Tomita & Torihama, 1956). Since the amacrine elements are assumed to inhibit these elements, the increased number of amacrine/bipolar contacts could account for this ERG change. If the b-wave is generated by the Müller cells as suggested by Miller & Dowling (1970), then the reduced number of Müller fibers observed after rearing in the dark (Weiskrantz, 1958) could explain the diminished amplitude of the b-wave.

A number of potential neurotransmitters have been associated with amacrine cells such as acetylcholine (Koelle et al., 1952; Pellegrino de Iraldi & Etcheverry, 1967), GABA and dopamine (Ehinger & Falck, 1971), GABA (Graham, 1972). There are data available only on the acetylcholinesterase content of the retina after dark-rearing (Glow & Rose, 1964; Liberman, 1962) and monocular lid-suture (Maraini et al., 1969).

The activity of this enzyme, which is believed to be directly related to the amount of acetylcholine in the tissue, is decreased after visual deprivation. Because of the increased number of amacrine contacts in the deprived eye, one would expect an increase of the acetylcholinesterase activity if acetylcholine were the transmitter of the amacrine contacts.

Visual Centers

The effect of modified visual impulses on the structure and function of visual centers has attracted attention since the turn of the century. Considerably more work has been done on changes induced by visual deprivation in subcortical and cortical visual centers than in the retina. Morphological, physiological, and biochemical studies were carried out on animals with and without previous visual experience. An exhaustive survey of the literature was published by Gyllensten, Malmfors, & Norrlin (1965). In morphological studies, changes in tissue volume, cell size, and density have been described since then in the lateral geniculate body connected with the deprived eye (Fifková, 1967; Maraini, Carta, Franguelli, & Santori, 1967; Fifková & Hassler, 1969; Guillery & Stelzner, 1970; Chow & Stewart, 1972). A decrease in tissue volume of the deprived visual cortex was found together with an increase in the cell density in the supragranular and granular layers (Fifková, 1967; Fifková & Hassler, 1969). With improved impregnation techniques, the attention became focused on the neuropil. The deprivation was shown to induce changes in the dendritic branching (Globus & Scheibel, 1967a; Coleman & Riesen, 1968; Fox, Inman, & Glisson, 1968) and in the number and shape of dendritic spines (Globus & Scheibel, 1967a; Valverde, 1967, 1968; Fifková, 1968, 1970a). The number of dendritic spines appears to be a sensitive index of the number of synaptic contacts. The impregnation technique visualizes only a part of the synaptic population, however. A less-restricted evaluation of the synaptic density is possible with the electron microscope. Variations were observed in the size and density of synaptic contacts in the visual cortex and lateral geniculate body of dark-reared rats (Cragg, 1967a, 1969b) and in the cortex of monocularly deprived rats (Fifková, 1970b, 1970c). Lid-closure, furthermore, induced changes in the ratios of certain specialized synaptic contacts in the superior colliculus (Lund & Lund, 1972).

The electrophysiological parameters of the deprived centers were markedly affected. The amplitude of all components of the evoked potentials in the cortex deprived by monocular eye-closure was smaller than on the opposite side (Ganz et al., 1968). Not only the specific, but also the diffuse projection was changed; a lack of response in the pre-cruciate gyrus and a modified response in the suprasylvian area were observed after visual deprivation (Glass, 1971). Some of the lateral geniculate neurons driven by the deprived eye had changes in their responses (Hamasaki, Rackensperger, & Vesper, 1972; Sherman, Hoff-mann, & Stone, 1972). The cortical neurons gave smaller and fewer responses, which were less selective and more easily fatigued (Wiesel & Hubel, 1963a; Ganz et al., 1968). The activity of neurons on the deprived colliculus superior reflected changes of the deprived cortical neurons (Wickelgren & Sterling, 1969).

Behavioral deficits induced by various types of visual deprivation were observed as well (Riesen & Aarons, 1959; Nealey & Riley, 1963; Walk, Trychin, & Karmel, 1965; Baxter, 1966; Riesen, 1966; Ganz & Fitch, 1968; Walk & Bond, 1968; Dews & Wiesel, 1970; Glass, 1971; Chow & Stewart, 1972; Slomin & Pasnak, 1972; Ganz, Hirsch, & Tieman, 1972).

Biochemical changes involved a decrease of acetylcholinesterase activity in subcortical visual centers after dark-rearing (Maletta & Timiras, 1967) as well as after monocular deprivation (Bondy & Margolis, 1969), a reduced rate of RNA synthesis (Margolis & Bondy, 1970) and a decreased incorporation of amino acids in the lateral geniculate body (Maraini et al., 1967). Light exposure following dark-rearing caused an increase in the protein and DNA synthesis (Talwar, Chopra, Goel, & D'Monte, 1966; Rose, 1972).

Material and Methods

Visual deprivation was achieved by lid-suture of the right eye in albino rats. The lid-suturing and eventual lid-opening were performed in light ether anesthesia. The number and age of the animals at the time of the operation, the length of the deprivation period and the period after reopening the eye, together with the histological technique used in the different experimental groups are summarized in Table 8.

After completion of the experiments, the animals to be used for cell staining were sacrificed under allobarbital anesthesia by perfusion through the heart with 10% formol-saline. The brains were embedded in celloidin and cut serially at 20 μ; every third section was stained with cresyl violet. From these sections, relevant parts of the brain were drawn at 40× magnification. The areas of the dorsal part of the lateral geniculate body (GLD) and the nucleus lateralis posterior (LP) were determined by planimetry. The cells were counted in 60 tissue samples

Table 8   **Experimental Data**

Group	No. of Animals	Age on Day of Eye Closure (days)	Period of Eye Closure (days)	Period after Eye Reopening (days)	Histological Technique
I A	6	14	3		Nissl
B	7	14	10		Nissl
C	6	14	10		Ramón-Moliner
D	5	14	30		Nissl
E	5	14	30		Ramón-Moliner
II A	16	14	60		Nissl
B	10	14	60		Ramón-Moliner
C	6	14	60		electron microscope
D[a]	3				electron microscope
III	6	60	90		Nissl
IV A	9	14	60	10	Nissl
B	10	14	60	30	Nissl

[a] Unoperated controls.

in the GLD and in 40 samples in the LP in each hemisphere. Each sample represented a volume of 297,680 μ^3. The area of the intracerebral course of the optic tract (OT), from its penetration into the brain until it reached the temporal cone of the lateral ventricle, was measured as well. In the superior colliculus (SC) the thickness of the stratum griseum superficiale was measured at 0.1 mm intervals in a strip of tissue measuring 0.36 $\times$ 1.0 mm, located 0.5 mm from the midline.

The thickness of the visual cortex was determined in coronal sections of the entire area 17, spaced 120 μ apart. Starting from the medial limit of the area the thickness of the cortex was measured in each section at 0.5 mm intervals. The mean values of about (140) measurements in right and left hemispheres were compared. Because of the lack of sharp cytoarchitectonic boundaries between different cortical layers in the rat's primary visual area, only the thickness of the supragranular complex (II–IV layers) and that of layers V and VI were measured separately. Cell counts were carried out in layers III and IV on tissue volumes of 297,680 μ^3 and 11,858 μ^3, respectively. Cells in 30 of such volumes of each layer were determined in each hemisphere and the mean computed. The difficulty in distinguishing neurons from glia was overcome to a certain extent by counting as neurons cells with a well-defined nucleolus. In most glial cells the nuclear chromatin is distributed in several small, irregularly shaped bodies. In layer IV, however, some small neurons also have several chromatin particles in their nuclei, as was described by Cragg (1967b). The presence of a distinct cytoplasmic fringe was used as the criterion for neurons in this layer. Although this criterion is not a sharp one, it is not believed that it affects the results, because the counting was done by one person and incidental mistakes can therefore be expected to be the same for both the deprived and the undeprived side.

For the procedure of Ramón-Moliner (1958) for spine counts, the anesthetized animals were decapitated, the brains were quickly removed and the occipital half of the hemisphere was placed in the impregnation solution. Blocks of tissues were embedded in celloidin and cut at 80 μ perpendicular to the cortical surface. Within the boundaries of the visual cortex, approximately equally impregnated pyramidal cells corresponding to class I of Globus & Scheibel (1967b) were chosen for spine counts. The shafts of the apical dendrites were divided in 50 μ long segments on which the number of spines were determined. All counts were carried out with Zeiss oil immersion objective ($\times$ 1000) and a 12.5 $\times$ ocular supplied with a graticule. Altogether 1984 segments were evaluated, 1036 on the side corresponding to the nondeprived eye, and 948 on the experimental side.

For the electron microscopy, urethane anesthetized animals were perfused with 5% glutaraldehyde in a 1/15 M phosphate buffer (pH 7.3) through the abdominal aorta. After 15 min of perfusion the skull was opened and the brain removed. Two coronal slices about 0.75 mm thick were isolated from the occipital pole of the hemisphere. From each slice one block within area 17 was dissected out. The tissue blocks were pyramid-shaped with the top pointing to the white matter and the base formed by the cortical surface. This made the orientation of the blocks for cutting possible. The material was transferred to a 2% osmic acid solution in the phosphate buffer where it remained for 2 hr at 4°C. The tissue blocks were then dehydrated for 2 hr in 100% acetone, which was changed repeatedly. After replacing the acetone with propylene oxide, the material was embedded in Maraglas (Freeman & Spurlock, 1962).

The blocks were sectioned parallel to the cortical surface. Sections 1 μ thick were cut on an LKB Ultrotome and stained with methylene blue and azure II (Richardson et al., 1960) for light microscopy. For electron microscopy, thin, golden sections treated on the grids with lead citrate and examined with a Philips (EM 200) electron microscope.

In the cerebral cortex, cut tangentially, apical dendrites appeared as oval-shaped structures grouped in bunches. These bundles of dendrites

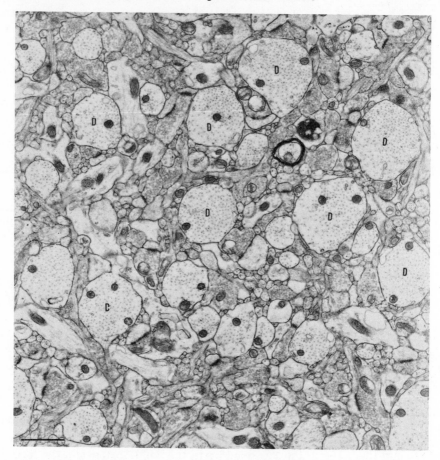

Fig. 11. Microphotograph of a bundle of apical dendrites from level 2 (see Fig.
15) of a tangentially cut visual cortex connected with the undeprived
eye. D, dendrites. Calibration line, 1 μ.

were photographed at a magnification of 3500$\times$, and printed at 8$\times$
enlargement to give an overall magnification of 28,000. Figs. 11, 12, 13,
and 14 show four of such micrographs at a magnification lower than used
for the actual counts. Regions containing the largest dendrites were
chosen. Cutting was started from the surface, and sections from the
first (molecular) layer, recognizable by the absence of neurons, were
discarded. Serial sections were cut along the whole length of the dendritic bundles up to layer V, where the thick apical dendrites arising
from the pyramidal cells in this layer disappear. Eighty sections 1 μ

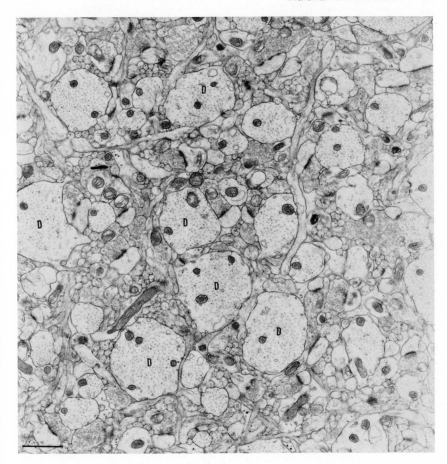

Fig. 12. Microphotograph of a bundle of apical dendrites from level 2 (see Fig.
15) of a tangentially cut visual cortex connected with the lid-sutured
eye. Calibration line, 1 μ.

thick alternated with thin sections for electron microscopy. In this way
the distance occupied by the length of apical dendrites was artificially
divided in eight levels 80 μ apart (Fig. 15). Although lid-suturing results
in a reduction of the thickness of layers II–IV of about 8% (Fifková,
1967; Fifková & Hassler, 1969), the right and left visual cortices were
cut in the same way. It is not likely that the shrinkage on the deprived
side would seriously influence the homology of the compared levels,
assuming that the reduction was not grossly different in the three layers
investigated. The differences of 6 μ for each 80 μ level is believed to

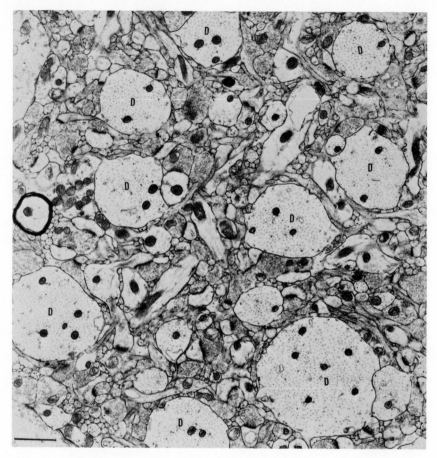

Fig. 13. Microphotograph of a bundle of apical dendrites from level 4 (see Fig. 15) of a tangentially cut visual cortex connected with undeprived eye. Calibration line, 1 μ.

be an admissible error. From each level the axodendritic synapses, including those in the neuropil and the less numerous ones on the trunks of apical dendrites, were counted in 10 electron micrographs each having an area of 64 μ^2. Right and left visual cortices were examined in nine animals, a total of 1440 fields. The criteria used for synapses were the presence of synaptic vesicles and the membrane thickening in the synaptic region. Fig. 16a demonstrates the actual magnification used for the determination of density and dimensions of the synaptic contacts. At each level the length of apposition of 100 synapses was measured,

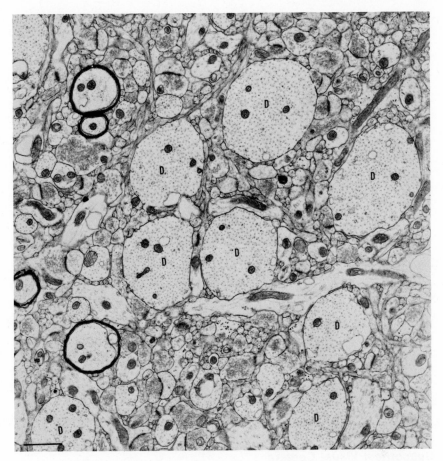

Fig. 14. Microphotograph of a bundle of apical dendrites from level 4 (see Fig. 15) of a tangentially cut visual cortex connected with the deprived eye. Calibration line, 1 μ.

on each side, so that 14,400 contacts were compared. The technique of measuring (between bars and arrows) is presented in Fig. 16b and c.

For measurements of the size of axosomatic synaptic contacts, cross-sections of neurons of any size in which the nucleus and preferably the nucleolus were visible were examined, so that the cell membrane could be expected to have been cut more or less perpendicularly. The synaptic contacts were photographed at a magnification of 8500$\times$ and printed at 6$\times$ enlargement to give an overall magnification of 51,000$\times$. Only two to three synaptic contacts per cell were found, not enough

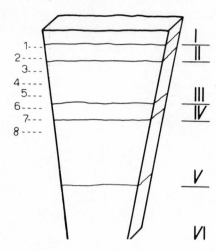

Fig. 15. Relation between cytoarchitectonic layers (I–V) of the tangentially cut visual cortex and the levels resulting from the serial cutting (1–8).

to count their density. The length of the synaptic apposition of 20–30 synapses was measured at each of the levels of the right and left visual cortices. A total of 1565 synapses were measured in experimental animals and 742 in controls.

Results

Subcortical Visual Centers

Primary and secondary visual centers were chosen according to the distinctness of their cytoarchitectonic border lines, which was a necessary prerequisite for volumetric estimations. Although many subcortical nuclei with retinal input have been described, the above criterion restricted the number to two: the dorsal part of the lateral geniculate body (GLD) and the nucleus lateralis posterior (LP). Values of these visual centers supplied by the seeing eye were taken as 100%. Table 9 summarizes the percentile differences in volumes of the deprived and undeprived lateral geniculate body and nucleus lateralis posterior.

1. Lateral geniculate body. Although in rats the GLD is not laminated, two parts differing in cell size can be distinguished. The rostral part contains mainly large neurons with large, thick-branched dendrites,

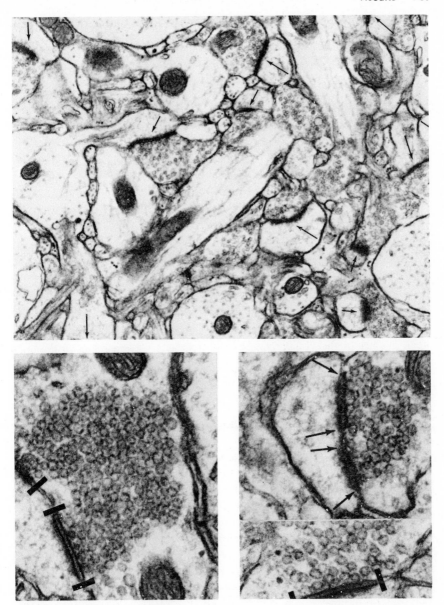

Fig. 16. Part of a cortical field at the actual magnification used for the density
counts and size measurements of axodendritic synapses (**a**). Axodendritic
contacts with marks between which length of the synaptic apposition was
measured (**b, c**). Calibration lines, 1 μ (**a**); 0.5 μ (**b, c**).

Table 9   Percentile Differences in Volume of Right and Left Visual Subcortical Centers

| Group | | Corpus Geniculatum Laterale Pars Dorsalis[a] | | | Nucleus Lateralis Pars Posterior[a] |
		Total	Rostral	Caudal	
I	A	−2.43 ± 1.72 ns			−0.10 ± 1.48 ns
	B	−11.04 ± 1.91 $p < 0.001$			−6.37 ± 4.10 ns
	D	−15.10 ± 3.47 $p < 0.02$	−3.54 ± 4.00 ns	−25.80 ± 4.80 $p < 0.02$	−12.48 ± 5.25 ns
II	A	−5.07 ± 1.2 $p < 0.01$	−1.80 ± 2.14 ns	−7.35 ± 1.88 $p < 0.01$	−3.5 ± 1.59 $p < 0.05$
III		−10.46 ± 1.18 $p < 0.001$	−7.65 ± 2.06 $p < 0.02$	−11.31 ± 3.15 $p < 0.02$	−8.23 ± 1.95 $p < 0.005$
IV	A	−10.96 ± 1.95 $p < 0.005$	−6.61 ± 4.98 ns	−10.23 ± 2.84 $p < 0.01$	−5.33 ± 2.28 $p < 0.05$
	B	−7.25 ± 0.99 $p < 0.001$	−4.50 ± 3.85 ns	−12.06 ± 1.77 $p < 0.01$	−4.71 ± 1.82 $p < 0.025$

NOTE: Values of the visual center of the right side corresponding to the open eye were taken as 100%.
[a] ns = p not significant.

whereas small neurons prevail in the caudal part. Taking this fact into account. the volumes of the rostral and caudal parts were calculated separately. The transition from one part to the other is gradual so that some uncertainty is involved in these numbers. In some groups (IA, B) the determination of the two parts of the nucleus could not be carried out, because at the ages of the test animals the large and the small elements are intermingled in a considerable part of the nucleus.

Three days of lid-closure did not change the volume of the deprived GLD; in 10 days, however, a significant decrease of its volume occurred. After 30 and 60 days of lid-suture the volumes of the deprived compared with the undeprived GLD were considerably smaller. The caudal segment of the nucleus was responsible for this difference. The cell number per unit of tissue volume was lower by 17% on the side receiving fibers from the deprived eye. The loss of cells was not equally distributed within the GLD, being greater in the caudal than in the rostral part; 22% and 14% respectively.

Fig. 17 shows the growth of the GLD from the 17th day of life (14 days before the lid-closure and 3 days after) to the 74th day (14 days

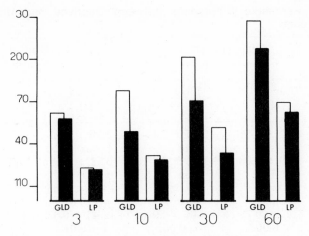

Fig. 17. Differences in mean volumes of the lateral geniculate body (GLD) and the nucleus lateralis posterior (LP) at different time periods after the lid-suturing (3, 10, 30, and 60 days). Black columns indicate structures connected with the deprived eye (8 hr daily illumination for 2 months).

before and 60 days after lid-closure). The GLD connected with the seeing eye grew continuously, whereas the GLD connected with the deprived eye was decreased in volume after 10 days of deprivation. The nucleus grew again in the period between the 10th and 60th day of deprivation. When, after the 60 day period, the eyes were reopened neither 10 nor 30 days of visual experience could revert the deficit. Similar changes also developed when the animals were allowed unobstructed vision for 60 days prior to the time the lids were sutured.

2. Nucleus lateralis posterior. Thirty days of deprivation were not long enough to cause changes in volume in this nucleus. However, a significant decrease occurred after 60 days of lid-closure. At this time also the cell density dropped by 7%. Fig. 17 shows a similar growth curve as the GLD during the 3–60 day deprivation period. The difference between the deprived and undeprived LP, once developed, did not change after the eye was reopened. Similar differences were observed when the lid-suture was performed in animals with previous visual experience.

3. Superior colliculus (SC). Because of the technical difficulties in establishing the volume of the SC, the thickness of the superficial stratum griseum was measured. No consistent asymmetry was found in monocularly deprived rats.

Table 10 Percentile Differences between Deprived and Undeprived Visual Cortices

Group	Difference in Cortex Thickness[a]		Difference in Cell Density[a]	
	Layers II–IV	Layers V–VI	Layer III	Layer IV
I A	−0.92 ± 5.86	−2.05 ± 3.17	+2.38 ± 2.90	+2.35 ± 2.42
	ns	ns	ns	ns
B	−5.58 ± 2.00	−1.38 ± 2.80	+6.82 ± 1.61	+7.25 ± 1.34
	$p < 0.02$	ns	$p < 0.005$	$p < 0.005$
D	−9.40 ± 3.22	−3.26 ± 1.66	+13.63 ± 0.63	+12.20 ± 0.30
	$p < 0.05$	ns	$p < 0.01$	$p < 0.005$
II	−7.92 ± 0.78	−4.46 ± 0.69	+12.45 ± 0.82	+11.50 ± 2.42
	$p < 0.001$	$p < 0.001$	$p < 0.01$	$p < 0.01$
III	−8.33 ± 1.28	−1.48 ± 2.10	+11.75 ± 1.98	+10.20 ± 1.75
	$p < 0.005$	ns	$p < 0.005$	$p < 0.005$
IV A	−9.63 ± 2.05	−0.56 ± 0.54	+12.68 ± 0.20	+10.85 ± 1.17
	$p < 0.005$	ns	$p < 0.001$	$p < 0.001$
B	−6.22 ± 1.20	−2.20 ± 0.20	+11.06 ± 1.39	+9.50 ± 1.38
	$p < 0.005$	$p < 0.001$	$p < 0.005$	$p < 0.005$

NOTE: Values of the visual cortices of the right side corresponding to the open eye were taken as 100%.
[a] ns = p not significant.

4. *Optic tract* (OT). The area of the intracerebral course of the OT was measured. This part is less subjected to deformation during the histological procedure than the extracerebral portion. Since the area of the optic tract has been determined—not the number of optic fibers—the oblique course of the optic fibers was not prejudicial to the calculation. No asymmetry was found.

Visual Cortex

Light Microscope Observations. The primary visual area of the rat is lacking distinct cytoarchitectonic boundaries between the cortical layers, except between layers I and II and between layers IV and V. Therefore, the thickness of the combined layers II–IV and V–VI (Table 10) was measured.

No significant right–left differences were noted in measuring the thickness of the cell layers in the visual cortex after 3 days of deprivation. The cell density remained unchanged as well. After 10 days of lid-closure, layers II–IV were significantly narrower in the deprived cortex, a difference that became somewhat greater after 30 and 60 days. The cell density

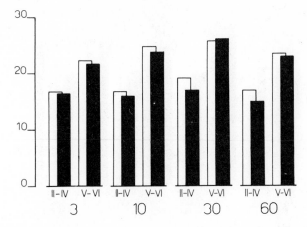

Fig. 18. Differences in the mean thickness of cortical layers II–IV and V–VI at different time periods after lid-suturing (3, 10, 30, and 60 days). Black columns indicate structures connected with the deprived eye (8 hr daily illumination for 2 months).

in the deprived cortex was increased in layers III and IV after a period of 10 days of lid-closure, and was accentuated after longer periods of deprivation (30 and 60 days).

On the side connected with the seeing eye the ultimate thickness of layers II–IV and V–VI is practically established at the 17th day of postnatal life (Fig. 18). However, the cell density in layers III and IV decreases from the 17th to the 44th day of life (Fig. 19). No further changes in cell density appear to take place after this age.

As observed for the subcortical visual centers the reopening of the eye after 60 days of deprivation did not affect the volume and density difference between the deprived and undeprived visual cortex. Previous visual experience did not prevent the development of the changes typical for unilateral eye-closure.

The groups of rats used for the impregnation technique survived the lid-suture for 10, 30, and 60 days. In the deprived and undeprived visual cortices the number of spines on the apical dendrites of layer V pyramidal cells was compared in layer IV. Because it is difficult to determine the boundaries of different layers precisely in the impregnated visual cortex, and the large pyramids are not always located at the same depth, these preparations were studied in connection with the Nissl stained material. This material used for the volumetric study showed that 54% of the whole thickness of the cortex is occupied by the complex of layers V–VI and 20% by layer IV. For each pyramidal cell (corresponding to class I of Globus & Scheibel, 1967b) that was found suitable

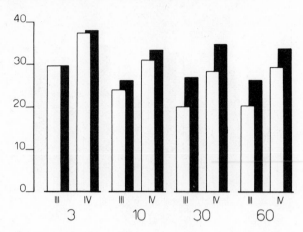

Fig. 19. Differences in the mean values of the cell density of cortical layers III and IV at different time periods after lid-suturing (3, 10, 30, and 60 days). Black columns indicate structures connected with the deprived eye (8 hr daily illumination for 2 months).

for spine counts, the position in the cortex was determined by measuring the distance from the cortical surface as well as from the white matter to the upper margin of the cell body. This measurement made it possible to decide which parts of the apical dendrite belong to layers IV and V respectively. In Fig. 20 apical dendrites from the undeprived (a, b) and deprived (c) visual cortices are shown. The spines are sparser on the deprived than on the control side. The mean number of spines per segment (50 μ long) and the percentage difference between the deprived and undeprived visual cortex are given in Table 11. The mean quantitative deficit for the entire measured length of the dendrites was lower in case of 10 day deprivation (17%) than in the case of 30 or 60 days standing, 28% respectively. It has been shown that normally the number of spines increases until the 44th day of life. No similar increase has been observed on the deprived neurons.

Electron Microscope Observations. The group of rats used for electron microscopy was kept for 60 days after lid-suture. The density of axodendritic synapses was determined as well as the length of synaptic apposition of axodendritic and axosomatic contacts.

1. Axodendritic contacts

   a. Density. The results of the synapse counts are summarized in Table 12. The numbers indicate the mean density of synapses per electron micrograph, over the whole length of the apical dendrites up to

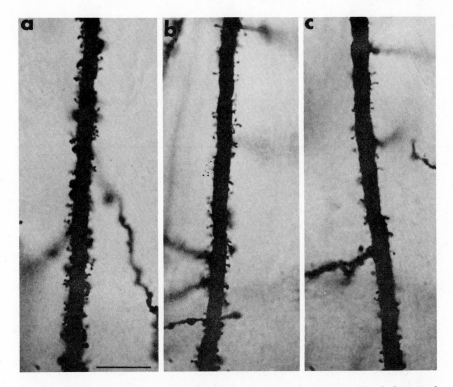

Fig. 20. Shafts of apical dendrites of V layer pyramids in layer IV of the visual cortex connected with the seeing eye (**a, b**) and with the deprived eye (**c**). Calibration line, 20 μ.

the layer of large pyramidal cells (layer V). Taking the density of contacts in the cortex connected with the seeing eye as 100%, the percent differences between the deprived and undeprived cortex are given. The mean density of synapses of the visual cortex supplied by the lid-sutured

Table 11   Difference in Spine Number between the Deprived and Undeprived Visual Cortex after Various Periods of Deprivation

Group		Period of Deprivation (days)	No. of Segments		Mean No. of Spines/Segment		Difference (%)
			Undeprived	Deprived	Undeprived	Deprived	
I	C	10	208	176	45.66 ± 1.15	38.01 ± 1.00	16.8
I	E	30	119	71	52.49 ± 1.09	37.77 ± 1.09	28.0
II	B	60	709	701	51.29 ± 0.62	37.09 ± 0.65	27.6

Table 12   Mean Density of Axodendritic Synapses, Mean Length of Apposition of Axodendritic and Axosomatic Synapses in the Deprived (Left) and Undeprived (Right) Visual Cortex, and in Controls

	Experimental Animals						Controls		
	I	II	III	IV	V	VI	I	II	III
Axodendritic synapses									
D/F[a]									
Right	32.7 ± 0.7	32.7 ± 0.8	26.4 ± 0.7	28.8 ± 0.5	28.4 ± 0.7	25.0 ± 0.7	29.3 ± 0.7	23.6 ± 0.7	26.7 ± 0.6
Left	23.5 ± 0.3	27.6 ± 0.7	25.0 ± 0.7	22.0 ± 0.5	21.7 ± 0.6	19.7 ± 0.7	29.3 ± 0.7	23.6 ± 0.6	27.1 ± 0.9
Difference, %	−27.0	−17.0	−5.0	−24.0	−23.6	−21.3	0	0	+4.0
p	<0.001	<0.001	<0.3	<0.001	<0.001	<0.001	ns[b]	ns[b]	ns[b]
Size									
Right	5.1 ± 0.10	5.2 ± 0.10	6.2 ± 0.09	5.1 ± 0.08	5.5 ± 0.09	5.3 ± 0.09	5.9 ± 0.10	5.1 ± 0.09	5.0 ± 0.07
Left	5.8 ± 0.10	5.7 ± 0.07	6.1 ± 0.10	6.1 ± 0.09	5.6 ± 0.09	6.2 ± 0.10	6.2 ± 0.09	5.1 ± 0.09	5.0 ± 0.09
Difference, %	+11.4	+9.7	−1.5	+12.0	+2.0	+11.7	<0.05	0	0
p	<0.001	<0.001	<0.5	<0.001	<0.05	<0.001	+5.0	ns[b]	ns[b]
Axosomatic synapses									
Size									
Right	13.9 ± 0.5	15.2 ± 0.5	12.9 ± 0.4	13.4 ± 0.3	13.6 ± 0.5	15.1 ± 0.5	13.2 ± 0.4	12.7 ± 0.4	12.6 ± 0.4
Left	9.8 ± 0.4	10.0 ± 0.2	13.8 ± 0.4	10.0 ± 0.5	10.6 ± 0.3	11.0 ± 0.4	14.9 ± 0.4	12.8 ± 0.4	11.4 ± 0.4
Difference, %	−29.5	−33.7	+6.0	−25.0	−22.0	−26.7	+11.3	+1.0	−9.7
p	<0.001	<0.001	<0.2	<0.001	<0.001	<0.001	<0.01	<0.1	<0.5

[a] Density of synapses per field.
[b] Not significant.

eye of all experimental animals was 20% lower than on the side supplied by the seeing eye. In all experiments but one (III) the differences are highly significant. In the unoperated control animals no right–left difference was present.

The serial sectioning of the cortex allowed a more detailed analysis of the loss of synapses with respect to the various cytoarchitectonic layers (Fig. 15). The distance between the surface of layer II and layer V was artificially divided into eight levels, which were 80 μ apart. The mean synaptic densities of all experimental animals were calculated separately for each of the levels. The results for the undeprived and deprived visual cortex of both experimental and control animals are summarized in Table 13. The percentile differences were calculated with respect to the side connected with the seeing eye, which was again taken as 100%. Whereas the density difference in levels 1–6 (cortical layers II, III, IV) of deprived and undeprived visual cortex is statistically significant no such difference could be established for levels 7 and 8. Right and left cortices did not differ in the group of unoperated animals. A gradual decrease in density of contacts occurs from the upper to lower levels in the experimental as well as in the control material.

The densities in the deprived and undeprived cortices of experimental animals were compared with those of unoperated controls. The synaptic density of the undeprived cortex differed from the controls only in the second cortical layer (levels 1, 2) where the density was increased (Fig. 21).

b. Size of synaptic contacts. The average length of synaptic apposition expressed in arbitrary units and the percentile difference between the synapses in the monocularly deprived and undeprived control groups are given in Tables 12 and 13. In four out of six experiments this value was significantly larger on the side connected with the seeing eye. When calculating the size of contacts for each of the above-mentioned eight levels in these four experiments, the difference was significant for levels 1–5 (cortical layers II and III). In experiment V in which the average right–left difference was not significant, levels 1–3 showed significant differences. The negative results in experiment III, which also failed to show a significant difference in synapse density between the deprived and undeprived cortex, seem to point to parallel development of changes in size and density of the axodendritic synaptic contacts.

In comparing the length of synaptic contacts of the experimental and control rats the contacts in the cortex (layers II and III) connected with the seeing eye of the unilaterally sutured group were not only smaller than those of the cortex supplied by the deprived eye but also smaller than the synapses from the control unoperated group (Fig. 21).

Table 13 Mean Density of Axodendritic Synapses and Mean Length of Apposition of Axodendritic and Axosomatic Contacts at Different Cortical Levels on the Undeprived (right) and Deprived (left) side.

Cortical Levels	II		III			IV		V
Layers	1	2	3	4	5	6	7	8
Axodendritic D/F[a]								
Experiment								
Right	32.9 ± 0.9	35.5 ± 0.8	29.7 ± 0.9	31.2 ± 0.8	28.4 ± 0.9	26.6 ± 0.6	23.3 ± 0.7	23.3 ± 0.8
Left	24.2 ± 0.9	26.6 ± 0.9	24.5 ± 0.7	25.4 ± 0.7	24.6 ± 0.7	21.8 ± 0.6	21.8 ± 0.8	20.5 ± 0.7
Difference, %	−25.3	−25.3	−14.5	−17.9	−13.4	−18.1	−6.5	−12.0
p^b	< 0.01	< 0.001	< 0.01	< 0.01	< 0.02	< 0.01	< 0.2	< 0.1
Control								
Right	26.4 ± 0.9	28.4 ± 1.0	29.8 ± 1.0	29.0 ± 0.7	27.5 ± 0.6	25.2 ± 0.6	25.1 ± 0.7	24.5 ± 0.8
Left	29.1 ± 1.0	33.2 ± 1.0	30.3 ± 0.9	29.7 ± 0.7	28.6 ± 0.9	24.8 ± 0.7	23.4 ± 1.0	19.5 ± 0.7
Difference, %	+10.0	+11.7	+1.5	−2.5	+3.8	−1.8	−7.0	−20.9
p^b	ns	ns	ns	ns	ns	ns	ns	< 0.05
Size								
Experiment								
Right	5.0 ± 0.1	4.8 ± 0.1	5.0 ± 0.1	5.4 ± 0.1	5.5 ± 0.1	6.0 ± 0.1	4.9 ± 0.1	5.0 ± 0.1
Left	6.0 ± 0.1	5.7 ± 0.1	6.0 ± 0.1	6.1 ± 0.1	6.0 ± 0.1	6.1 ± 0.1	5.0 ± 0.1	5.2 ± 0.1
Difference, %	+12.0	+11.9	+12.0	+11.3	+9.0	+1.8	+2.7	+4.0
p^b	< 0.001	< 0.05	< 0.01	< 0.1	< 0.05	ns	ns	ns
Control								
Right	5.4 ± 0.1	5.3 ± 0.1	5.3 ± 0.1	5.4 ± 0.1	5.7 ± 0.1	5.8 ± 0.1	5.7 ± 0.1	6.1 ± 0.1
Left	5.3 ± 0.1	5.4 ± 0.1	5.4 ± 0.1	5.7 ± 0.1	5.5 ± 0.1	6.0 ± 0.1	6.0 ± 0.1	6.4 ± 0.1
Difference, %	−2.7	+2.0	+2.0	+5.5	−3.5	+3.5	+5.2	+5.0
p^b	ns	ns	ns	ns	ns	ns	ns	ns

Axosomatic
Size

Experiment								
Right	13.9 ± 0.4	13.6 ± 0.6	12.9 ± 0.6	13.8 ± 0.6	14.5 ± 0.6	13.8 ± 0.6	13.7 ± 0.4	13.6 ± 0.4
Left	11.9 ± 0.5	10.9 ± 0.5	11.0 ± 0.5	10.2 ± 0.4	9.8 ± 0.5	10.9 ± 0.4	11.4 ± 0.5	10.6 ± 0.5
Difference, %	−14.6	−19.7	−14.5	−26.7	−32.5	−20.8	−17.3	−21.5
p [b]	< 0.05	< 0.05	< 0.05	< 0.01	< 0.01	< 0.02	< 0.02	< 0.01
Control								
Right	11.8 ± 0.8	13.2 ± 0.6	12.9 ± 0.6	13.3 ± 0.6	11.0 ± 0.7	12.3 ± 0.5	13.2 ± 0.7	12.8 ± 0.5
Left	13.7 ± 0.8	13.3 ± 0.9	13.5 ± 0.7	12.0 ± 0.9	12.7 ± 0.7	12.9 ± 0.6	11.6 ± 0.4	13.3 ± 0.7
Difference, %	+11.6	+0.3	+4.5	−9.1	+11.6	+4.6	−12.0	−4.0
p [b]	ns	ns	ns	ns	ns	ns	ns	ns

NOTE: The values for each cortical level are the means calculated from six experiments and three controls.

[a] Density of synapses per field.

[b] ns = p not significant.

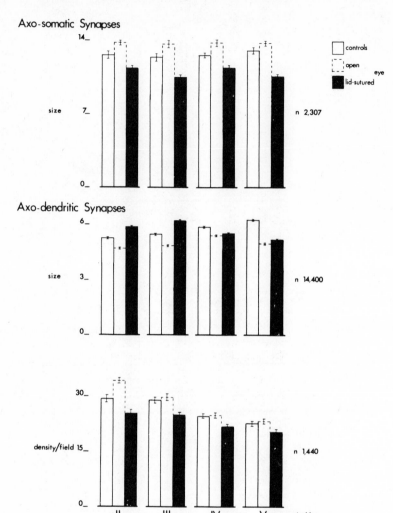

Fig. 21. The size of axosomatic contacts and the density and size of axodendritic contacts in cortical layers II, III, and IV. Solid-line columns indicate values from the undeprived control group; dashed-line columns, values from the cortex connected with the seeing eye; black columns, values from the cortex connected with the lid-sutured eye.

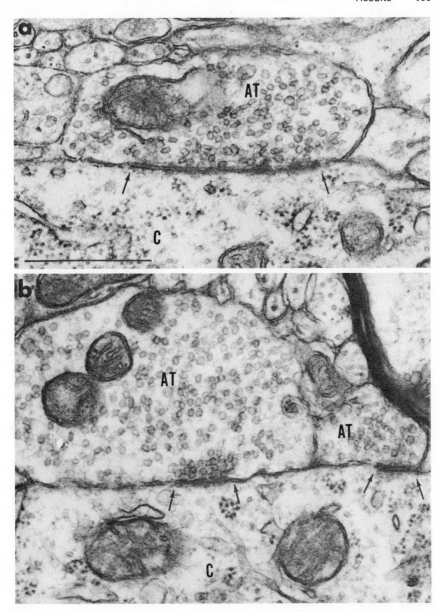

Fig. 22. An axosomatic contact with flattened vesicles (a) and two axosomatic contacts with spherical vesicles (b). AT, axon terminal; C, cytoplasma. Calibration line, 0.5 μ.

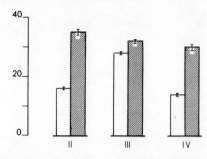

Fig. 23. Percentile difference in the size of synaptic contacts in layers II, III, and IV of the visual cortex connected with the seeing and deprived eyes (8 hr daily illumination for 2 months). White columns, synapses with flattened vesicles; shaded columns, synapses with sperhical vesicles.

2. Axosomatic contacts. The mean length of these synaptic contacts was again expressed in arbitrary units. For the calculation of the percentile difference the side connected with the seeing eye was taken as 100%. The results after 2 months of monocular deprivation are given in Table 12. In all experiments but one (III) the synapses connected with the lid-sutured eye were significantly smaller than those connected to the open eye, the average difference being −23%. In one control (I) the synapses were found larger on the left side, in the second (II) there was no right–left difference and in the third (III) the contacts were smaller on the left side. When calculating the mean size of the contacts from all experimental and control animals separately for each of the eight levels, significantly smaller contacts were found at all levels of the deprived cortex. The changes seem therefore not to be confined to any cytoarchitectonic cortical layer (Table 13).

With respect to the unoperated controls the size of the axosomatic contacts was, in all layers studied (II, III, IV), decreased in the deprived cortex and increased on the undeprived side (Fig. 21).

About 85% of the total population of the measured axosomatic synapses was found to contain flattened vesicles, and the remaining 15%, spherical vesicles. The possibility was considered that synaptic contacts with flattened and spherical vesicles are not affected in the same way by visual deprivation. The synapses with flattened (Fig. 22a) and spherical (Fig. 22b) vesicles were therefore measured separately. The length of the contacts with spherical vesicles were more seriously affected by the deprivation than those with flattened vesicles. Whereas the contacts with flattened vesicles in the layers II and IV were smaller by 16% and 14% respectively, contacts with spherical vesicles differed by 35% and 29%.

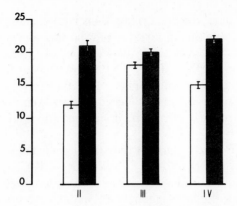

Fig. 24. The percentage of contacts with spherical vesicles in layers II, III, and IV of the visual cortex connected with the seeing eye (white columns), and in the cortex connected with the deprived eye (black columns). Light conditions, 8 hr daily illumination for 2 months.

This difference in the size reduction of synapses with spherical and flattened vesicles is statistically significant. In layer III there was no difference between the two types, the contacts with flattened vesicles being reduced by 18% and those with spherical vesicles by 20% (Fig. 23). The percentage of contacts containing spherical vesicles was significantly higher on the deprived side in layers II and IV indicating a larger reduction of the terminals with flattened vesicles. The results are summarized in Fig. 24.

Discussion

From the volume measurements and cell density counts it can be concluded that the GLD and visual cortex supplied by the deprived eye are severely changed, whereas the superior colliculus and optic tract are not affected. These changes are probably not degenerative in nature, for degenerative changes after unilateral enucleation cause an obvious volume decrease of the relevant lateral geniculate body and superior colliculus with moderate changes in the visual cortex (Tsang, 1936).

Marked histological changes in the GLD after monocular lid-suturing were shown by Wiesel & Hubel (1963b), Kupfer & Palmer (1964), Guillery & Stelzner (1970) and Guillery (1972, 1973) in kittens. The same method did not yield as severe structural changes in rats as in kittens. The changes in rats became apparent by quantitative comparison only. Since rats have thinner eyelids than kittens, more light can be expected to reach the retina of rats through the closed eyelids. This assumption is favored by the results of Wiesel & Hubel (1963b) who observed moderate changes in the GLD by using translucent occluders, and no changes by suturing the still thinner nictitating membrane. Species difference might also be involved. The higher the animals' position in the phylogenetical scale, the greater their susceptibility may be to the experimental treatment.

The rostral and caudal parts of the lateral geniculate body were differently affected by deprivation. The two parts differ in cell size (larger cells rostrally) and cell density. The layers of large cells of the lateral geniculate body in higher mammals are mainly concerned with the perception of light independent of wavelength (De Valois & Jones, 1961; Hassler, 1966). Considering the rostral part of the rat's lateral geniculate body as a homolog of these layers, the milder changes in the rostral than in the caudal part observed are in agreement with the incomplete light deprivation achieved by the lid-closure. An alternate explanation, however, would be that small cells participate more in the integrative processes, which are affected by the deprivation of pattern vision rather than of brightness discrimination.

Guillery & Stelzner (1970) put forward an interesting theory, according to which unilateral visual deprivation in kittens disfavors the geniculate neurons receiving input from the deprived eye in competition for the synaptic surfaces on binocular cortical neurons. The growth becomes inhibited in those parts of the deprived laminae of the GLD that are homotopic to the undeprived ones and project to the same group of cortical neurons. It is not probable that this explanation holds true for the reported findings in albino rats, which have very few uncrossed optic fibers (Lund, 1965; Guillery, Amorn, & Eighmy, 1971), hence not many cortical neurons are driven by both eyes (Montero, Brugge, & Beitel, 1968; Creel, Dustman, & Beck, 1970). To this point are relevant the experiments of Chow, Masland and Stewart (1973), who tested for function homolateral retinal fibers sprouting in the superior colliculus denervated by enucleation of the contralateral eye. These sprouts could not have been activated either by visual or electrical stimulation.

Although the LP plays a role in the integration of visual information, the postdeprivation changes in it are relatively mild and can be demonstrated by quantitative evaluation only. This can be explained by the influence of nonvisual afferents terminating in this structure.

No lateralized effect of monocular lid-suture has been observed in the thickness of the superficial stratum griseum of the colliculus superior. The electron microscope revealed more contacts with spherical than with flattened vesicles in the upper layers of the deprived superior colliculus, without differences in the total density of contacts (Lund & Lund, 1972). Since light stimuli are mainly directed to this structure and the sutured lids do not deprive the eye completely of light, these results are not surprising even though in the rat half of the optic fibers are distributed to the colliculus superior (Hayhow, Sefton, & Webb, 1962). In line with this explanation is the failure to find alterations in the retinocollicular pathway by deprivation (Wickelgren & Sterling, 1969). Changes after unilateral eye-closure in the collicular neurons reported by the latter authors were secondarily induced from the deprived visual cortex; the changes disappeared after the cortex had been removed.

Morphological changes due to lid occlusion were demonstrated in layers II–IV of the deprived cortex of a number of experimental animals (Berger, 1900; Gyllensten et al., 1965; Umrath, 1965). No obvious anatomical changes were seen by Wiesel & Hubel (1963a), but functional deficits were uncovered in the cat's deprived visual cortex. In this species most cortical neurons have binocular input, which may explain that no major structural changes can be observed with the light microscope. In albino rats, where most of the cortical neurons are monocularly driven (because of the nearly complete crossing of optic fibers), the effect of monocular lid closure is lateralized and can therefore be more easily demonstrated, especially if quantitative methods are employed. The commissural fibers connect the "second" (Lund & Lund, 1970) visual area (area occipitalis lateralis 18a of Krieg's classification, 1946), but not the primary one (area 17) which was under investigation, so that the laterality of its input remained undisturbed.

The specific location of changes in the supragranular (II and III) and granular (IV) layers is in agreement with the terminal distribution of the geniculocortical tract. According to the classical view the main site of the termination of visual fibers is layer IV and the lower part of layer III (Cajal, 1911; Lorente de Nó, 1949; Nauta & Bucher, 1954; Polyak, 1957). In addition to this distribution, terminals were also demonstrated in the supragranular layers (II and especially in the layer III, Kruger & Malis, 1964; Rose & Malis, 1964; Globus & Scheibel, 1967a,c; Hubel & Wiesel, 1969). According to the present state of knowledge the axons of GLD neurons terminate on the dendrites of layer IV stellate neurons, basal dendrites of layer III pyramids, and apical dendrites of layer V pyramids (Valverde, 1967, 1968, 1970) prevalently on dendritic spines (Garey & Powell, 1971). All three structures become affected after experimental manipulation of the visual input, which results in decrease of afferent impulses.

The volume of layers II–IV in the deprived cortex was more reduced than that of the infragranular layers (V–VI). Together with this decrease there was an increase in the cell density in layers III and IV, but the density in layer V remained unchanged. These findings contrast with the changes in the GLD where the decreased volume was accompanied by a decrease in cell density. Dark-reared animals exhibited a decrease in nuclear diameter and "internuclear" material in layers II–IV without a marked change in layers V and VI (Gyllensten et al., 1965).

Besides the reduction in the cell density there are a number of other factors that can influence the volume of a structure, for example, the decreased size of perikarya, dendrites, axons and their terminals, and glia. Such changes would reduce the volume of a structure without changing the total number of neurons, thus increasing the number per unit of tissue volume. The present data on the decreased volume and increased cell density in layers III and IV can be considered as indirect evidence for a decrease in dendritic arborization. Fewer dendrites as well as smaller dendritic length of stellate cells in layer IV have been observed as a consequence of dark-rearing (Coleman & Riesen, 1968). Enucleation and dark-rearing caused an alteration of orientation of the dendrites of pyramids in layer III and stellate cells in layer IV. Instead of their normal branching in layer IV they direct their dendrites out of this layer mainly to layers III and II (Valverde, 1968, 1970; Ruiz-Marcos & Valverde, 1970). On the other hand, Globus & Scheibel (1967a), under similar conditions, were unable to find quantitative differences in the branching of stellate neurons; they observed, however, a greater range of variation in the dendritic length. If there is any justification for comparing lid-suturing with rearing in an impoverished environment (both should result in diminished stimulation) then Holloway's results (1966) should be mentioned. Under impoverished conditions he found evidence for diminished branching of stellate neurons in the second layer.

Since their discovery by Cajal (1891), the dendritic spines have been shown to be functional units. Electron microscopy showed them to be sites of synaptic contacts essentially similar to other dendritic synapses (Gray, 1959). Their organization can be expected to reflect the organization of the axon terminals contacting them. A reduced number of spines (by 28%) on the apical dendrites of layer V pyramids at the niveau of layer IV has been observed in the cortex connected with the lid-sutured eye. A larger effect (39%) was observed in dark-reared mice (Valverde, 1967). By contrast Globus & Scheibel (1967a) found in dark-raised rabbits pathologically changed spines but no decrease in number. The deprivation period used by Globus & Scheibel (1967a) was, however, much shorter and the way of spine counting was different from those used in the preceding communications.

The results of the spine counts suggested a quantitative study of the contacts on apical dendrites with the electron microscope. This turned out not to be feasible because large distances of dendrites are devoid of synapses as was observed by Colonnier (1968) and confirmed in the present investigation. Therefore the density of contact in the neuropil was estimated (see Method). Semiserial sectioning of the cortex permitted a more detailed analysis of the synaptic changes with respect to the cortical layers.

A decrease in the density of axodendritic contacts was observed in all layers examined, and was more severe in layers II and III as compared to layer IV. This could be explained by assuming a more severe loss of optic radiation fibers for the superficial layers (II and III) than for the deeper one (IV). Alternately, assuming a uniform loss of optic radiation fibers, this difference could indicate that the main site of termination of the optic radiation is in the neuropil of layers II and III the secondary site in that of layer IV. Only a small percentage (about 5%) of the afferent fibers from the GLD contribute to the total population of synaptic contacts in the visual cortex (cat and monkey, Cragg, 1968; Garey & Powell, 1971), most of them forming contacts with dendritic spines. The 20% decrease in the density of axodendritic contacts observed in the present experiments suggests that the nongeniculate terminals are also affected by deprivation.

Keeping in mind that the undeprived eye and possibly the related visual cortex are not adequate controls for the deprived side in monocularly deprived animals, a comparison between the former and the undeprived control group has been carried out. The cortex connected with the open eye in the monocularly deprived group did not differ from the undeprived controls except for the second layer where the synaptic density was increased. An enhanced stimulation has been postulated for the undeprived eye, and this could have induced formation of new synaptic contacts. Light has been shown to cause an increase of the number of synapses in the GLD of rats that were originally dark-reared and then brought into the light (Cragg, 1969b). The results are supported by findings derived from experiments dealing with the rearing in an enriched environment, which implies extensive sensory stimulation resulting in an increased branching of dendrites of pyramidal as well as stellate neurons (Volkmar & Greenough, 1972). Inasmuch as these branches occur on the higher-order dendrites, which are mainly located in the cortical layers II and I, the prevalent location of the higher synaptic density in the second layer would not be surprising.

The deprived cortex exhibited an increase in size of the axodendritic contacts in the supragranular layers but no change in the granular layer. The restriction of this change to layers II and III may be explained by the findings of Valverde (1968, 1970) and of Ruiz-Marcos & Valverde (1970). After enucleation or dark-rearing the dendrites of stellate neurons and the basal dendrites of layer III pyramids reorient themselves from the granular layer (IV) where (due to the decreased afferentation) no adequate connections can be offered, to the layers where such connections are still available (i.e., supragranular layers II and III). Because of the reduced afferent input and the consequent loss of axodendritic contacts (20%) the remaining axonal endings spread themselves over the vacated places on the dendritic surfaces. The affected dendrites could also act as partially deafferented structures that attract other axon terminals in terms of synaptic relocation as was described by Raisman (1969) and discussed in detail in the first part. Axons forming the enlarged terminals might be of geniculate or extrageniculate origin. In the first case they could be either the less-affected axons from the deprived geniculate cells driven by the open eye. This idea, originally postulated by Ganz et al. (1968) for kittens (which have a considerable number of uncrossed optic fibers), is not likely for albino rats, where the crossing of optic fibers is nearly complete. The question of extrageniculate fibers forming enlarged contacts will be discussed in the context of axosomatic contacts.

When comparing the size of axodendritic contacts in the unoperated control group with those of the undeprived side of the monocularly sutured group, smaller contacts were found in the latter. As was suggested above, the stimulation of the undeprived eye might be increased and might induce formation of new contacts, which are of smaller size. Smaller synapses were shown to develop in the GLD of rats after they were transferred from dark to light (Cragg, 1969b). By changing the complexity of the environment, variation in density and size of cortical axodendritic contacts has also been observed (Møllgaard, Diamond, Bennett, Rosenzweig, & Lindner, 1971).

Decreased afferentation by unilateral lid suture causes a reduction in the size of axosomatic synapses in all layers studies (II, III, IV). Layers II and IV contain mainly stellate and granular cells, whereas in layer III pyramidal neurons dominate. In the tangentially cut cortex it is not always possible to distinguish between pyramidal and stellate neurons, so that in the way of sampling used (see Method) contacts of all types of elements must have been involved. Although direct termination of visual afferents on the cell bodies of stellate neurons was described (Colonnier, 1967) such terminations are not numerous (about

2%) according to Garey & Powell (1971). One has, therefore, to assume that most of the contacts which were found to be reduced in size, were of extrageniculate origin.

Lid closure acted differently on the dimensions of axosomatic and axodendritic contacts; the former ones became smaller, the latter bigger. The difference could point to the existence of two projecting systems from different sources in terms of geniculate and extrageniculate origins. The axodendritic contacts are in general believed to mediate excitation and the axosomatic inhibition (Walberg, 1968 for review; Benevento & Ebner, 1971; Garey & Powell, 1971). These axodendritic synapses which increase in size may be of geniculate origin and those axosomatic which decrease in size may be of extrageniculate origin. According to the scheme of interaction of inhibition and excitation proposed by Watanabe, Konishi, & Creutzfeld (1966) and Benevento, Creutzfeld, & Kuhnt (1972), the excitation coming from the GLD is modified by intra-cortical inhibition, since the latency of inhibition is always longer than that of excitation. A direct inhibitory pathway from the GLD is not considered probable.

It has been shown that the ability of visual impulses to excite structures in the visual pathways is diminished by deprivation. This finding can be partly explained by the decreased density of axodendritic contacts. The deficiency could be compensated for either by an increase in the size of the remaining excitatory axodendritic contacts, and/or by a decrease of the inhibitory influence by diminishing the size of axosomatic synapses. Present data indicate that both changes take place. Similar observations were made by Cragg (1968). After optic tract lesion the density of contacts (the axodendritic and axosomatic contacts were not mentioned separately) in the visual cortex was decreased and their size increased. Subsequent lesion of the GLD showed that relatively few of the enlarged contacts are of geniculate origin.

The size of axosomatic contacts was not only decreased in the deprived cortex, but also increased in the undeprived one with respect to the unoperated controls. This observation could be explained by a more intense stimulation from the undeprived eye. It has been suggested above, that this eye receives more light. Overstimulation might be prevented by increased inhibition caused by the growth of axosomatic contacts.

Most of the axosomatic contacts in the present material had flattened vesicles; only about 15% had spherical vesicles. The opinions vary considerably as to the significance of the shape of vesicles. Evidence has been presented that the vesicle morphology is determined by the osmolarity of the buffer used in the fixative and that the vesicles differ in their reaction to the same osmotic conditions (Valdivia, 1971). This explains the presence of axon terminals with spherical and flattened vesicles in the same preparation. It is now a generally accepted view that the synaptic vesicles contain chemical transmitters. Therefore attempts have been made to relate the shape of synaptic vesicles to the enclosed transmitter, suggesting for the contacts with spherical vesicles an excitatory, for those with flattened vesicles an inhibitory function (Uchizono, 1965; Bodian, 1966; Lund & Westrum, 1966; Westrum, 1966). The number of cases in which the function of the synapse is known show, however, that such a generalization is not justified (Walberg, 1968), especially not if the findings in the motor endplate (Korneliussen, 1972) relating the morphology of vesicles to the functional state of a given synapse can be also extended to the brain centers.

In the deprived cortex the size of the synapses with spherical vesicles was more reduced than the size of contacts with flattened vesicles. Synapses in the superior colliculus with spherical vesicles belong to axons of extrinsic, mainly retinal, origin (Lund & Lund, 1972), whereas contacts with flattened vesicles belong to axons of intrinsic neurons. If the same scheme applies to the visual cortex, then the axon terminals with spherical vesicles would originate from GLD neurons. Because of the postulated excitatory function of the cortical afferents from the GLD their contacts should then be excitatory. It is conceivable that this type of synapse is more severely affected by the lack of adequate stimulation than the intrinsic type with flattened vesicles. More contacts with spherical vesicles were found in the deprived cortex of the present material. Inasmuch as the uncrossed fibers are negligible in the albino rat, sprouting of some of the deprived geniculate axon terminals may have occurred. Such a new formation of excitatory axosomatic contacts might be another way to compensate for the lost axodendritic contacts. The resulting activity of the deprived visual cortex is decreased anyway, so this compensation is either not sufficient or the newly formed synapses are silent, nonfunctioning contacts. An explanation of this discrepancy may follow from the results of Chow and Spear (1974) and Van Sluyters and Stewart (1974). These authors have shown that the changes caused by monocular deprivation in the lateral geniculate as well as in the visual cortex are less far reaching in the rabbit than in the cat. The monocular respective binocular character of the visual pathways of these two species provides an explanation. While certain morphological and functional changes are caused by unilateral deprivation in both monocular and binocular pathways, a competitive process in the latter further disadvantages cortical and geniculate neurons receiving input from the deprived eye. The question of nonoperative synapses is discussed in detail by Cragg (1972). At present there are no criteria known by which an inoperative synapse (if existing) could be distinguished from the functioning ones. The change that turns an active synapse to an inactive one might occur at the molecular level, not accessible to the present electron microscopy.

The altered ERG shows that deprivation affects the first steps in the visual process (Ganz et al., 1968; Hamasaki & Pollack, 1972). Subsequently changed electrophysiological parameters were observed in the deprived visual centers. The optic fibers from the deprived eye failed to drive 50% of the GLD neurons in a normal way: their firing rate was lower and their latency was prolonged as compared with units from the undeprived GLD (Hamasaki et al., 1972; Hamasaki & Winters, 1973). Furthermore it has been shown that deprivation affects prevalently those GLD neurons that are activated by fast-conducting optic fibers (Sherman et al., 1972). It can therefore be expected that the cortical neurons connected with the abnormally reacting geniculate cells respond in an abnormal way as well. Few cortical neurons could be driven from the deprived eye, the amplitude of their responses was smaller, and they were more easily fatigued. The same applied to the evoked responses (Wiesel & Hubel, 1963a; Ganz et al., 1968; Glass, 1971; Yinon & Auerbach, 1973). The altered unit activity suggests that the abnormality resides at the synaptic junctions. Decreased synaptic density in the GLD as well as in the visual cortex (after dark-rearing and monocular deprivation) could partly explain the decreased activation, which cannot be compensated for by the increased size of the synaptic contacts. These experiments demonstrated an altered function of visual centers when they are stimulated via the deprived eye. No data available on the reaction of these centers to impulses coming via other than visual pathways (in the case of the visual cortex, e.g., intracortical or callosal fibers). Such data could give important information about the functional properties of the modified and newly formed synapses.

In addition to the changes in the deprived cortex there were electron microscope changes also in the cortex supplied by the seeing eye. It would be tempting to attribute them to enhanced stimulation of the functional eye, before the light induced degeneration of the retinal receptors develops. Changes in the undeprived cortex were in an opposite direction to the changes in the deprived cortex, for which decreased stimulation was postulated. No valid interpretation of changes in the deprived cortex can be made from the data obtained in albino rats as they may result from the transsynaptic effect of the degenerating retina. The observation of Yinon & Auerbach (1973), who also found the undeprived cortex in monocularly sutured rats to be changed as compared to the controls, is of interest here.

The question of how far the changed nature of an input can alter the maturation of a structure and how far it affects the already mature structure should be considered in this context. According to the findings here reported previous visual experience for the time and at the period of the rat's life explored in the present experiments does not diminish the effect of unilateral deprivation on the visual centers as visualized with the light microscope. Changes of the same magnitude were observed in the lateral geniculate body and visual cortex of animals that had been allowed unobstructed vision for 6 weeks before the eye was closed (2-month-old animals) as in rats who never had visual experience. Similar results were noted by Gyllensten et al. (1965), who examined the visual centers of mice kept in the dark either from birth or from the fourth month of age. Changes in the size and density of synaptic terminals were found by Cragg (1969b) in the lateral geniculate body of rats kept in the dark from the fourth week of age on. Increased density of amacrine contacts was observed in the retina of rats with monocular occlusion from the third month of age (Sosula & Glow, 1971). Plastic changes in the visual cortex were furthermore observed in adult mice after an eye removal (Valverde, 1968) and in the lateral geniculate of adult rabbits after the visual cortex has been undercut (Ralston and Chow, 1973). Other brain centers of adult rats, such as septum, yielded plastic changes as well (Raisman, 1969). However, Burke & Hayhow (1968) found that the responses of the lateral geniculate neurons to physiological stimuli in cats raised in the dark over a period of 2 years after initial exposure to diurnal light conditions, were no different from those of controls who were never deprived; neither were histological changes observed in such animals. Wiesel & Hubel (1963b), Hubel & Wiesel (1970), and Dews & Wiesel (1970) stated that lid-suturing in adult cats was without any effect. In kittens the extent of damage was related to a period of susceptibility. The visual system would start to react to deprivation at the age of 1 month, reaching the maximum in the second and disappearing around the third month. During the period of high susceptibility, in the fourth and fifth weeks, eye-closure for a period as short as 6 days was enough to reduce the number of cells that could be driven by the deprived eye to a small fraction of normal (Hubel & Wiesel, 1970; Blakemore & Van Sluyters, 1974). There has been no evidence whether there is a similar period of susceptibility to deprivation in rats. Visual deprivation will apparently cause changes at any period of the animal's life and the development of these changes will expand over a longer period of time. It seems likely that species differences exist, and that these are related to the extent to which plasticity is retained during and after maturation.

The observed differences are permanent at least for the periods of time studied. In the present experiment reopening of the eye following 2 months of lid-closure caused no recovery in the deprived visual centers. The anatomical changes found 10 and 30 days after reopening of the eye were entirely comparable to those seen in animals sacrificed immediately after 2 months of deprivation. The deficit in the number of spines on the apical dendrites of pyramidal cells (caused by dark-rearing) never reached normal values after the animals were subsequently placed under diurnal dark-light conditions (Valverde, 1971). These data are in contrast with the observed plastic changes in adult rats induced by deprivation. A longer period of time may be needed for recovery which would be detected by the light microscope. However, Blakemore and Van Sluyters (1974) demonstrated not only a period of sensitivity to the effect of monocular deprivation as Hubel and Wiesel (1970) did, but also a similar period of sensitivity for the reversal of these effects by reverse lid-suturing which ends at the fourth month of the kittens' age. Partial recovery in the structure can be therefore expected. Information on this topic would be of a great theoretical and practical value as a morphological correlate of the partly recovered function. Results obtained with the light microscope do not, however, exclude the possibility of a recovery at the ultrastructural level. Cragg (1969b) described in the lateral geniculate body of rats raised in the dark (until weaning) an increase in the density of geniculate synapses after exposure to daylight. The same author (1967a) observed an increase in the size of axon terminals in the upper half of the visual cortex of dark-raised rats as early as 3 hr after light exposure. Wiesel & Hubel (1965) found only a very limited capacity for recovery from the effects of visual deprivation in kittens. After 3-15 months of exposure to light no improvement in the morphology of the lateral geniculate was seen and many cortical neurons gave abnormal responses to visual stimuli.

Conclusions

The experiments discussed above are examples of the induction of structural changes in the synaptic arrangement in brain centers by altering the input. Plastic reactions of retinal and cortical synapses are the result of a long-term change in afferent stimulation. The described experiments create, however, unnatural conditions comparable to certain pathological states, but probably not occurring under physiological circumstances. Any intervention that modifies the afferent stimuli might, in addition to its own effect, mobilize the ability of the nervous tissue to react to the experimentally induced changes. If the synaptic pattern is changed in one way by the experimental procedure, the compensatory mechanism might change it in another way. The ability of nervous cells to divide and so replace the damaged units ceases in the early stages of development, so the dendrites and axon terminals are the only excitable structures capable of reaction. Translocation of dendrites occurs together with displacement of certain types of contacts, new contacts are formed, some of the remaining increase in size, some decrease, and so on. Taking into account the precise arrangement of the connections of brain centers necessary for the function of the nervous system it is obvious that the above-listed changes induce disorder. Electrophysiological data indicate that the resulting function of the centers affected by deprivation and secondary compensatory processes is defective. How far the appropriate connections can be reformed after normal connections are reestablished is not yet clear.

The accumulated experimental data are, for the time being, too fragmentary. More information of the biochemical and physiological properties of the modified and newly formed contacts have to be available to permit any valid conclusion as to the cause of the observed morphological changes in the synaptic contacts.

Acknowledgments

The author expresses her gratitude to Dr. A. Van Harreveld for the critical reading of the manuscript, and to Miss Ruth E. Estey and Mrs. Jane Sun for valuable technical assistance.

This investigation was carried out in part at the Institute of Physiology of the Czechoslovak Academy of Sciences, Prague, Czechoslovakia, at the Max Planck-Institute for Brain Research in Frankfurt/Main, Germany, and at the California Institute of Technology, Pasadena, California, where it was supported by a grant from the National Science Foundation (GB 6698) and by a grant from the U.S. Public Health Service (NS 09493).

References

Baxter, B. L. (1966). Effect of visual deprivation during postnatal maturation on the electroencephalogram of the cat. *Exp. Neurol.*, 14, 224–237.

Baxter, B. L., & Riesen, A. H. (1961). Electroretinogram of the visually deprived cat. *Science*, 134, 1626–1627.

Benevento, L. A., Creutzfeld, D. D., & Kuhnt, U. (1972). Significance of intracortical inhibition in the visual cortex. *Nature, New Biol.* 238, 124–126.

Benevento, L. A., & Ebner, F. A. (1971). The contribution of the dorsal lateral geniculate nucleus to the total pattern of thalamic terminations in striate cortex of the Virginia opossum. *J. Comp. Neurol.*, 143, 243–260.

Bennett, M. V., Dyer, R. F., & Dunn, J. (1973). Visual dysfunction after long-term continuous light exposure. *Exp. Neurol.* 40, 652–660.

Berger, H. (1900). Experimentell-anatomische Studien über die durch den Mangel optischer Reize veranlassten Entwicklungshemmungen in Occipitallappen des Hundes und der Katze. *Arch. Psychiat. Nervenkr.*, 33, 521–567.

Bernstein, J. J., & Bernstein, M. E. (1971). Axonal regeneration and formation of synapses proximal to the site of lesion following hemisection of the rat spinal cord. *Exp. Neurol.*, 30, 336–351.

Blakemore, C., & Van Sluyters, R. C. (1974). Reversal of the physiological effects of monocular deprivation in kittens: Further evidence for a sensitive period. *J. Physiol.* (London) 237, 195–216.

Bodian, D. (1966). Electron microscopy: Two major synaptic types on spinal motoneurones. *Science,* 151, 1093–1094.

Bondy, S. C., & Margolis, F. L. (1969). Effects of unilateral visual deprivation on the developing avian brain. *Exp. Neurol.*, 25, 447–457.

Borg, E., & Knave, B. (1971). Long-term changes in the ERG following transection of the optic nerve in the rabbit. *Acta Physiol. Scand.*, 83, 277–281.

Boycott, B. B., & Dowling, J. E. (1969). Organization of the primate retina: Light microscopy. *Phil. Trans. Roy. Soc. B.*, 255, 109–184.

Brattgård, S. O. (1952). The importance of adequate stimulation for the chemical composition of retinal ganglion cells during early postnatal development. *Acta Radiol.*, Suppl. 96, 1–30.

Brown, J. E. (1965). Dendritic fields of retinal ganglion cells of the rat. *J. Neurophysiol.*, 28, 1091–1100.

Brown, K. T. (1968). The electroretinogram: Its components and their origins. *Vision Res.*, 8, 633–677.

Brown, K. T., & Wiesel, T. N. (1961). Localization of origins of electroretinogram components by intraretinal recording in the intact cat eye. *J. Physiol. (Lond.)*, 158, 257–280.

Burke, W., & Hayhow, W. R. (1968). Disuse in the lateral geniculate nucleus in the cat. *J. Physiol. (Lond.)* 194, 495–519.

Cajal, S. R. (1891). Sur la Structure de De'corce cerebral de quelque mammiteres. *La Cellule,* 17, 1–54.

Cajal, S. R. (1911). *Histologie du systeme nerveaux de l'homme et des vertebres* Vol. 2, Paris. A. Maloine, pp. 316–319.

Caley, D. W., Johnson, C., & Liebelt, R. A. (1972). The postnatal development of the retina in the normal and rodless CBA mouse: A light and electron microscopic study. *Amer. J. Anat.*, 133, 179–212.

Chow, K. L., Masland, R. H., & Stewart, D. L. (1973). Spreading of uncrossed retinal projection in superior colliculus of neonatally enucleated rabbits. *J. comp. Neurol.* 151, 307–322.

Chow, K. L., & Spear, P. D. (1974). Morphological and functional effects of visual deprivation on the rabbit visual system. *Exp. Neurol.* 42, 429–447.

Chow, K. L., & Stewart, D. L. (1972). Reversal of structural and functional effects of long-term visual deprivation in cats. *Exp. Neurol.*, 34, 409–433.

Cohen, A. I. (1967). An electron microscopic study of the modification by monosodium glutamate of the retinas of normal and "rodless" mice. *Amer. J. Anat.*, 120, 319–356.

Coleman, P. D., & Riesen, A. H. (1968). Environmental effects on cortical dendritic fields: I. Rearing in the dark. *J. Anat.*, 102, 363–374.

Colonnier, M. (1967). The fine structural arrangement of the cortex. *Arch. Neurol. (Chicago)*, 16, 651–657.

Colonnier, M. (1968). Synaptic patterns on different cell types in different laminae of the cat visual cortex. An electron microscope study. *Brain Res.*, 9, 268–287.

Cornwell, A.Ch., & Sharpless, S. K. (1968). Electrophysiological retinal changes and visual deprivation. *Vision Res.*, 8, 389–401.

Cowan, W. M. (1970). Centrifugal fibres to the avian retina. *Brit. Med. Bull.*, 26, 112–118.

Cragg, B. G. (1967a). Changes in the visual cortex on first exposure of rats to light. *Nature*, 215, 251–253.

Cragg, B. G. (1967b). The density of synapses and neurons in the motor and visual areas of the cerebral cortex. *J. Anat.*, 101, 639–654.

Cragg, B. G. (1968). Are there structural alterations in synapses related to functioning? *Proc. Roy. Soc. B.*, 171, 319–323.

Cragg, B. G. (1969a). Structural changes in naive retinal synapses detectable within minutes of first exposure to daylight. *Brain Res.*, 15, 79–96.

Cragg, B. G. (1969b). The effects of vision and dark-rearing on the size and the density of synapses in the lateral geniculate nucleus measured by electron microscopy. *Brain Res.*, 13, 53–67.

Cragg, B. G. (1972). Plasticity of the synapses. In G. H. Bourne (Ed.), *The structure and function of nervous tissue*. Vol. IV. Academic Press, New York. pp. 1–60.

Creel, D. J., Dustman, R. E., & Beck, E. C. (1970). Differences in visually evoked responses in albino versus hooded rats. *Exp. Neurol.*, 29, 298–309.

De Valois, R. L., & Jones, A. E. (1961). Single-cell analysis of the organization of the primate color-vision system. In, *The visual system: Neurophysiology and psychophysics*. R. Jung & H. Kornhuber (Eds.), Springer, Berlin. pp. 178–191.

Dews, P. B., & Wiesel, T. N. (1970). Consequence of monocular deprivation on visual behaviour in kittens. *J. Physiol. (Lond.)*, 206, 437–455.

Dowling, J. E. (1967). The site of visual adaptation. *Science*, 155, 273–279.

Dowling, J. E. (1968). Synaptic organization of the frog retina: An electron microscopic analysis comparing the retinas of frogs and primates. *Proc. Roy. Soc. B.*, 170, 205–228.

Dowling, J. E., & Boycott, B. B. (1966). Organization of primate retina: Electron microscopy. *Proc. Roy. Soc. B.*, 166, 80–111.

Dowling, J. E., & Cowan, W. M. (1966). An electron microscope study of normal and degenerating centrifugal fibre terminals in the pigeon retina. *Z. Zellforsch. Mikroscop. Anat.*, 71, 14–28.

Dowling, J. E., & Sidman, R. L. (1962). Inherited retinal dystrophy in the rat. *J. Cell Biol.,* **14,** 72–110.

Dowling, J. E., & Werblin, F. S. (1969). Organization of the retina of the mudpuppy, *Necturus maculosus.* I. Synaptic structure. *J. Neurophysiol.,* **32,** 315–338.

Dubin, M. W. (1970). The inner plexiform layer of the vertebrate retina: A quantitative and comparative electron microscopic analysis. *J. Comp. Neurol.,* **140,** 479–506.

Eakin, R. M. (1965). Differentiation of rods and cones in total darkness. *J. Cell Biol.,* **25,** 162–165.

Ehinger, B., & Falck, B. (1971). Autoradiography of some suspected neutrotransmitter substances: Gaba, glycine, glutamic acid, histamine, dopamine and L-dopa. *Brain Res.,* **33,** 157–172.

Fifková, E. (1967). The influence of unilateral visual deprivation on optic centers. *Brain Res.,* **6,** 763–766.

Fifková, E. (1968). Changes in the visual cortex of rats after unilateral deprivation. *Nature,* **220,** 379–381.

Fifková, E. (1970a). The effect of unilateral deprivation on visual centers in rats. *J. Comp. Neurol.,* **140,** 431–438.

Fifková, E. (1970b). The effect of monocular deprivation on the synaptic contacts of the visual cortex. *J. Neurobiol.,* **1,** 285–294.

Fifková, E. (1970c). Changes of axosomatic synapses in the visual cortex of monocularly deprived rats. *J. Neurobiol.,* **2,** 61–71.

Fifková, E. (1972a). Effect of visual deprivation and light on the synapses of the inner plexiform layer. *Exp. Neurol.,* **35,** 458–469.

Fifková, E. (1972b). Effect of light and visual deprivation on the retina. *Exp. Neurol.,* **35,** 450–457.

Fifková, E. (1973). Effect of light on the synaptic organization of the inner plexiform layer of the retina of albino rats. *Experientia.* **29,** 851–854.

Fifková, E., & Hassler, R. (1969). Quantitative morphological changes in visual centers in rats after unilateral deprivation. *J. Comp. Neurol.,* **135,** 167–178.

Fisher, L. J. (1972). Changes during maturation and metamorphosis in the synaptic organization of the tadpole retina inner plexiform layer. *Nature,* **235,** 391–392.

Fox, M. W., Inman, O., & Glisson, S. (1968). Age differences in central nervous effects of visual deprivation in the dog. *Develop. Psychobiol.,* **1,** 48–54.

Freeman, J. A., & Spurlock, B. O. (1962). A new epoxy embedment for electron microscopy. *J. Cell Biol.,* **13,** 437–443.

Ganz, L., & Fitch, M. (1968). The effect of visual deprivation on perceptual behavior. *Exp. Neurol.,* **22,** 638–660.

Ganz, L., Fitch, M., & Satterberg, J. A. (1968). The selective effect of visual deprivation on receptive field shape determined neurophysiologically. *Exp. Neurol.,* **22,** 614–637.

Ganz, L., Hirsch, H. V. B., & Tieman, S. B. (1972). The nature of perceptual deficits in visually deprived cats. *Brain Res.,* **44,** 547–568.

Garey, J. L., & Powell, T. P. S. (1971). An experimental study of the termination of the geniculo-cortical pathway in the cat and monkey. *Proc. Roy. Soc. B.,* **179,** 41–63.

Glass, J. D. (1971). Photically evoked potentials in cat neocortex altered by visual pattern deprivation. *Brain Res.*, 30, 207–210.

Globus, A., & Scheibel, A. B. (1967a). The effect of visual deprivation on cortical neurons: A Golgi study. *Exp. Neurol.*, 19, 331–345.

Globus, A., & Scheibel, A. B. (1967b). Pattern and field in cortical structure: The rabbit. *J. Comp. Neurol.*, 131, 155–172.

Globus, A., & Scheibel, A. B. (1967c). Synaptic loci on visual cortical neurons of the rabbit: The specific afferent radiation. *Exp. Neurol.*, 18, 116–131.

Glow, P. H., & Rose, S. (1964). Effects of light and dark on the acetylcholinesterase activity of the retina. *Nature*, 202, 422–423.

Gomirato, G., & Baggio, G. (1962). Metabolic relationships between the neurons of the optic pathway in various functional conditions. *J. Neuropathol. Exp. Neurol.*, 21, 634–644.

Goodland, H. (1966). The ultrastructure of the inner plexiform layer of the retina of *Cottus bubalis*. *Exp. Eye Res.*, 5, 198–200.

Graham, L. T., Jr. (1972). Intraretinal distribution of GABA content and GAD activity. *Brain Res.*, 36, 476–479.

Gray, E. G. (1959). Axo-somatic and axo-dendritic synapses of the cerebral cortex: An electron microscope study. *J. Anat.*, 93, 420–433.

Grignolo, A., Orzalesi, N., Castellazzo, R., & Vittone, P. (1969). Retinal damage by visible light in albino rat. *Ophthalmologica*, 157, 43–59.

Guillery, R. W., Amorn, C. S., & Eighmy, B. B. (1971). Mutants with abnormal visual pathways: An explanation of anomalous geniculate laminae. *Science*, 174, 831–832.

Guillery, R. W. (1972). Binocular competition in the control of geniculate cell growth. *J. comp. Neurol.* 144, 117–130.

Guillery, R. W. (1973). The effect of lid suture upon the growth of cells in the dorsal lateral geniculate nucleus of kittens. *J. comp. Neurol.* 148, 417–422.

Guillery, R. W., & Stelzner, D. J. (1970). The differential effects of unilateral lid closure upon the monocular and binocular segments of the dorsal lateral geniculate nucleus in the cat. *J. Comp. Neurol.*, 139, 413–422.

Guth, L., & Windle, W. F. (1970). The enigma of central nervous regeneration. *Exp. Neurol.*, 28, Suppl. 5, 1–43.

Gyllensten, L., Malmfors, T., & Norrlin, M. L. (1965). Effect of visual deprivation on the optic centers of growing and adult mice. *J. Comp. Neurol.*, 124, 149–160.

Gyllensten, L., Malmfors, T., & Norrlin, M. L. (1966). Growth alteration in the auditory cortex of visually deprived mice. *J. Comp. Neurol.*, 126, 463–470.

Hamasaki, D. S., & Winters, R. W. (1973). Intensity-response functions of visual deprived LgN neurons of cats. *Vision Res.* 13, 925–936.

Hamasaki, D. I., & Pollack, J. G. (1972). Depression of the late receptor potential and the ERG by light deprivation in cats. *Vision Res.*, 12, 835–842.

Hamasaki, D. I., Rackensperger, W., & Vesper, J. (1972). Spatial organization of normal and visually deprived units in the lateral geniculate nucleus of the cat. *Vision Res.*, 12, 843–854.

Hassler, R. (1966). Comparative anatomy of the central visual systems in day- and night-active primates. In R. Hassler & H. Stephan (Eds.), *Evolution of the forebrain*. Thieme, Stuttgart. pp. 419–434.

Hayhow, W. R., Sefton, A., & Webb, G. (1962). Primary optic centers of the rat in relation to the terminal distribution of the crossed and uncrossed optic nerve fibers. *J. Comp. Neurol.*, **118**, 295–322.

Holloway, R. L., Jr. (1966). Dendritic branching: Some preliminary results of training and complexity in rat visual cortex. *Brain Res.* **2**, 393–396.

Hubel, D. H., & Wiesel, T. N. (1969). Anatomical demonstration of columns in the monkey striate cortex. *Nature*, **221**, 747–750.

Hubel, D. H., & Wiesel, T. N. (1970). The period of susceptibility to the physiological effects of unilateral eye closure in kittens. *J. Physiol.* (*Lond.*), **206**, 419–436.

Kidd, M. (1962). Electron microscopy of the inner plexiform layer of the retina in the cat and the pigeon. *J. Anat.* (*Lond.*), **96**, 179–187.

Koelle, G. B., Wolfand, L., Friedenwald, J. S., & Allen, R. A. (1952). Localization of specific cholinesterase in ocular tissues of the cat. *Amer. J. Ophthalmol.*, **35**, 1580–1584.

Korneliussen, H. (1972). Ultrastructure of normal and stimulated motor endplates. *Z. Zellforsch. Mikroscop. Anat.*, **130**, 28–57.

Krieg, W. J. S. (1946). Connections of the cerebral cortex. I. The albino rat. A. Topography of cortical areas. *J. Comp. Neurol.*, **84**, 221–275.

Kruger, L., & Malis, L. S. (1964). Distribution of afferent and efferent fibers in the cerebral cortex of the rabbit revealed by laminar lesions produced by heavy ionizing particles. *Exp. Neurol.*, **10**, 509–524.

Kupfer, C., & Palmer, P. (1964). Lateral geniculate nucleus: Histological and cytochemical changes following afferent denervation and visual deprivation. *Exp. Neurol.*, **9**, 400–409.

Kuwabara, T., & Gorn, R. (1968). Retinal damage by visible light. An electron microscopic study. *Arch. Ophthalmol.*, **79**, 69–78.

Legein, C. P. J. J. M. M. & Van Hof, M. W. (1970). The effect of light deprivation on the electroretinogram of the guinea pig. *Pflüg. Arch.*, **318**, 1–6.

Leure-Duprée, A. E. (1973). Observation on the synaptic organization of the retina of the albino rat: A light and electron microscopic study. *J. comp. Neurol.* **153**, 149–178.

Liberman, R. (1962). Retinal cholinesterase and glycolysis in rats raised in darkness. *Science*, **135**, 372–373.

Lorente de Nó, R. (1949). Cerebral cortex: Architecture, intracortical connections, motor projections. In *Fulton's physiology of the nervous system*. Oxford University Press, London. pp. 288–330.

Lund, J. S., & Lund, R. D. (1970). The termination of callosal fibers in the paravisual cortex of the rat. *Brain Res.*, **17**, 25–45.

Lund, J. S., & Lund, R. D. (1972). The effects of varying periods of visual deprivation on synaptogenesis in the superior colliculus of the rat. *Brain Res.*, **42**, 21–32.

Lund, R. D. (1965). Uncrossed visual pathways of hooded and albino rats. *Science*, **149**, 1506–1507.

Lund, R. D., & Lund, J. S. (1971). Synaptic adjustment after deafferentation of the superior colliculus of the rat. *Science*, **171**, 804–807.

Lund, R. D., & Westrum, L. E. (1966). Synaptic vesicle differences after primary formalin fixation. *J. Physiol.* (*Lond.*), **185**, 7–9.

Maletta, G. J., & Timiras, P. S. (1967). Acetylcholinesterase activity in optic structures after complete light deprivation from birth. *Exp. Neurol.*, **19**, 513–518.

Maraini, G., Carta, F., & Franguelli, R. (1969). Metabolic changes in the retina and the optic centres following monocular light deprivation in the new-born rat. *Exp. Eye Res.*, **8**, 55–59.

Maraini, G., Carta, F., Franguelli, R., & Santori, M. (1967). Effect of monocular light-deprivation on leucine uptake in the retina and the optic centres of the newborn rat. *Exp. Eye Res.*, **6**, 299–302.

Margolis, F. L., & Bondy, S. C. (1970). Effect of unilateral visual deprivation by eyelid suturing on protein and ribonucleic acid metabolism of avian brain. *Exp. Neurol.*, **27**, 353–358.

Miller, R. F., & Dowling, J. E. (1970). Intracellular responses of the Müller (glial) cells of mudpuppy retina: Their relation to *b*-wave of the electroretinogram. *J. Neurophysiol.*, **33**, 323–341.

Møllgaard, K., Diamond, M. C., Bennett, E. L., Rosenzweig, M. R., & Lindner, B. (1971). Quantitative synaptic changes with differential experience in rat brain. *Int. J. Neurosci.*, **2**, 113–128.

Montero, V. M., Brugge, J. F., & Beitel, R. E. (1968). Relation of the visual field to the lateral geniculate body of the albino rat. *J. Neurophysiol.*, **31**, 221–236.

Nauta, W. J. H., & Bucher, V. M. (1954). Efferent connections of the striate cortex in the albino rat. *J. Comp. Neurol.*, **100**, 257–286.

Nealey, S. M., & Riley, D. A. (1963). Loss and recovery of discrimination of visual depth in dark-reared rats. *Amer. J. Psychol.*, **76**, 329–332.

Nichols, C. W., & Koelle, G. B. (1967). Acetylcholinesterase: Method for demonstration in amacrine cells of rabbit retina. *Science*, **155**, 477–478.

Noell, W. K., & Albrecht, R. (1971). Irreversible effects on visible light on the retina: Role of vitamin A. *Science*, **172**, 76–80.

Noell, W. K., Delmelle, M. C., & Albrecht, R. (1971). Vitamin A deficiency effect on retina: Dependence on light. *Science*, **172**, 72–76.

Noell, W. K., Walker, V. S., Kang, B. S., & Berman, S. (1966). Retinal damage by light in rats. *Invest. Ophthalmol.*, **5**, 450–473.

Ogden, T. E. (1968). On the function of efferent retinal fibers. In C. von Euler, S. Skoglund, & U. Söderberg (Eds.), *Structure and function of inhibitory neuronal mechanisms*. Pergamon Press, Oxford. Pp. 89–109.

O'Steen, W. K., & Anderson, K. V. (1971). Photically evoked responses in the visual system of rats exposed to continuous light. *Exp. Neurol.*, **30**, 525–534.

O'Steen, W. K., Shear, Ch.R., & Anderson, K. V. (1972). Retinal damage after prolonged exposure to visible light. A light and electron microscopic study. *Amer. J. Anat.*, **134**, 5–22.

Pellegrino de Iraldi, A., & Etcheverry, G. J. (1967). Granulated vesicles in retinal synapses and neurons. *Z. Zellforsch. Mikroscop. Anat.* **81**, 283–296.

Polyak, S. L. (1941). *The retina*. University of Chicago Press, Chicago. Pp. 297, 309, 321.

Polyak, S. L. (1957). In H. Klüver (Ed.), *The vertebrate visual system*. University of Chicago Press, Chicago. Pp. 1390.

Pysh, J. J., & Wiley, R. G. (1972). Morphologic alterations of synapses in electrically stimulated superior cervical ganglia of the cat. *Science,* **176,** 191–193.

Raisman, G. (1969). Neuronal plasticity in the septal nuclei of the adult rat. *Brain Res.,* **14,** 25–48.

Raisman, G., & Matthews, M. R. (1972). Degeneration and regeneration of synapses. In G. H. Bourne (Ed.), *The structure and function of nervous tissue.* Vol. IV. Academic Press, New York. Pp. 61–104.

Ramón-Moliner, E. (1958). A tungstate modification of the Golgi–Cox method. *Stain Technol.,* **33,** 19–29.

Ralston, III, H. J., & Chow, K. L. (1973). Synaptic reorganization in the degenerating lateral geniculate nucleus of the rabbit. *J. comp. Neurol.* **147,** 321–350.

Raviola, G., & Raviola, E. (1967). Light and electron microscopic observations on the inner plexiform layer of the rabbit retina. *Amer. J. Anat.,* **120,** 403–426.

Rasch, E., Swift, H., Riesen, A. H., & Chow, K. L. (1961). Altered structure and composition of retinal cells of dark-reared mammals. *Exp. Cell Res.,* **25,** 348–363.

Reiter, R. J., & Klein, D. C. (1971). Observations on the pineal gland, the harderian glands, the retina, and the reproductive organs of adult female rats exposed to continuous light. *J. Endokrinol.,* **51,** 117–125.

Richardson, K. C., Jarett, L., & Finke, E. H. (1960). Embedding in epoxy resins for ultrathin sectioning in electron microscopy. *Stain Technol.,* **35,** 313–323.

Riesen, A. H. (1966). Sensory deprivation. In E. Stellar & J. M. Sprague (Eds.), *Progress in physiological psychology.* Vol. 1. Academic press, New York. Pp. 117–147.

Riesen, A. H., & Aarons, L. (1959). Visual movement and intensity discrimination in cats after early deprivation of pattern vision. *J. Comp. Physiol. Psychol.,* **52,** 142–149.

Rose, S. P. R. (1972). Changes in the amino acid pools in the rat brain following first exposure to light. *Brain Res.,* **38,** 171–178.

Rose, J. E., & Malis, L. S. (1964). Geniculate connections in the rabbit. I. Retrograde changes in the dorsal lateral geniculate body after destruction of cells in various layers of the striate cortex. *J. Comp. Neurol.,* **125,** 95–120.

Ruiz-Marcos, A., & Valverde, F. (1970). Dynamic architecture of the visual cortex. *Brain Res.,* **19,** 25–39.

Sherman, S. M., Hoffmann, K.-P., & Stone, J. (1972). Loss of specific cell type from dorsal lateral geniculate nucleus in visually deprived cats. *J. Neurophysiol.,* **35,** 532–541.

Sherman, S. M., & Stone, J. (1973). Physiological normality of the retina in visually deprived cats. *Brain Res.* **60,** 224–230.

Shkol'nik-Yarros, E. G. (1971). *Neurons and interneuronal connections of the central visual system.* Plenum Press, New York. Pp. 239–245.

Slomin, V., Jr., & Pasnak, R. (1972). The effects of visual deprivation on the depth perception of adult and infant rats and adult squirrel monkeys (*Saimiri sciurea*). *Vision Res.,* **12,** 623–626.

Somjen, G. (1972). *Sensory coding in the mammalian nervous system.* Appleton-Century-Crofts, New York.

Sosula, L., & Glow, P. H. (1970). A quantitative ultrastructural study of the inner plexiform layer of the rat retina. *J. Comp. Neurol.*, **140**, 439–478.

Sosula, L., & Glow, P. H. (1971). Increase in number of synapses in the inner plexiform layer of light deprived rat retinae: Quantitative electron microscopy. *J. Comp. Neurol.*, **141**, 427–452.

Talwar, G. P., Chopra, S. P., Goel, B. K., & D'Monte, B. (1966). Correlation of the functional activity of the brain with metabolic parameter—III. Protein metabolism of the occipital cortex in relation to light stimulus. *J. Neurochem.*, **13**, 109–116.

Tomita, T., & Torihama, Y. (1956). Further study on the intraretinal action potentials and on the site of ERG generation. *Jap. J. Physiol.*, **6**, 118–136.

Tsang, Y. (1936). Visual centers in blinded rats. *J. Comp. Neurol.*, **66**, 211–262.

Uchizono, K. (1965). Characteristics of excitatory and inhibitory synapses in the central nervous system of the cat. *Nature*, **207**, 642–643.

Umrath, K. (1965). Histologische Veränderungen im Gehirn von Tieren nach Ausschaltung von Augen durch Vernähen der Lider oder durch Extirpation. *Z. Biol.*, **115**, 99–118.

Valdivia, O. (1971). Methods of fixation and morphology of synaptic vesicles. *J. Comp. Neurol.*, **142**, 257–274.

Valverde, F. (1967). Apical dendritic spines of the visual cortex and light deprivation in the mouse. *Exp. Brain Res.*, **3**, 337–352.

Valverde, F. (1968). Structural changes in the area striata of the mouse after enucleation. *Exp. Brain Res.*, **5**, 274–292.

Valverde, F. (1970). The Golgi method. A tool for comparative structural analysis. Contemporary Research Methods in Neuroanatomy. In W. J. H. Nauta & S. O. E. Ebbesson (Eds.), Springer-Verlag, New York, Heidelberg, Berlin. Pp. 12–31.

Valverde, F. (1971). Rate and extent of recovery from dark rearing in the visual cortex of the mouse. *Brain Res.*, **35**, 1–11.

Van Harreveld, A., & Khattab, F. I. (1968). Perfusion fixation with glutaraldehyde and post-fixation with osmium tetroxide for electron microscopy. *J. Cell Sci.*, **3**, 579–594.

Van Sluyters, R. C., & Stewart, D. L. (1974). Binocular neurons of the rabbit's visual cortex: Effects of monocular sensory deprivation. *Exp. Brain Res.* **19**, 196–204.

Volkmar, F. R., & Greenough, W. T. (1972). Rearing complexity affects branching of dendrites in the visual cortex of the rat. *Science*, **176**, 1445–1447.

Walberg, F. (1968). Morphological correlates of postsynaptic inhibition processes. In C. von Euler, S. Skoglund, & U. Söderberg (Eds.), *Structure and function of inhibitory mechanisms*. Pergamon Press, Oxford. Pp. 7–14.

Walk, R. D., & Bond, E. J. (1968). Deficit in depth perception of 90-day-old dark-reared rats. *Psychon. Sci.*, **10**, 383–384.

Walk, R. D., Trychin, S., Jr, & Karmel, B. Z . (1965). Depth perception in the dark-reared rat as a function of time in the dark. *Psychon. Sci.*, **3**, 9–10.

Watanabe, S., Konishi, M., & Creutzfeld, O. D. (1966). Postsynaptic potentials of the cat's visual cortex following electrical stimulation of afferent pathways. *Exp. Brain Res.*, **1**, 272–283.

Weiskrantz, L. (1958). Sensory deprivation and the cat's optic nervous system. *Nature*, 181, 1047–1050.

Werblin, F. S., & Dowling, J. E. (1969). Organization of the retina of the mudpuppy, *Necturus maculosus*. II. Intracellular recording. *J. Neurophysiol.*, 32, 339–355.

Westrum, L. E. (1966). Synaptic contacts on axons in the cerebral cortex. *Nature*, 210, 1289–1290.

Wickelgren, B. G., & Sterling, P. (1969). Effect on the superior colliculus of cortical removal in visually deprived cats. *Nature*, 224, 1032–1033.

Wiesel, T. N., & Hubel, D. H. (1963a). Single-cell responses in striate cortex of kittens deprived of vision in one eye. *J. Neurophysiol.*, 26, 1003–1017.

Wiesel, T. N., & Hubel, D. H. (1963b). Effects of visual deprivation on morphology and physiology of cells in the cat's lateral geniculate body. *J. Neurophysiol.*, 26, 978–993.

Wiesel, T. N., & Hubel, D. H. (1965). Extent of recovery from the effects of visual deprivation in kittens. *J. Neurophysiol.*, 28, 1060–1072.

Witkovsky, P. (1971). Synapses made by myelinated fibers running to teleost and elasmobranch retinas. *J. Comp. Neurol.*, 142, 205–222.

Witkovsky, P., & Dowling, J. E. (1969). Synaptic relationships in the plexiform layers of carp retina. *Z. Zellforsch. Mikroscop. Anat.*, 100, 60–82.

Yinon, U., & Auerbach, E. (1973). Deprivation of pattern vision studied by visual evoked potentials in the rat cortex. *Exp. Neurol.* 38, 231–251.

Zetterström, B. (1955). The effects of light on the appearance and development of the electroretinogram in newborn kittens. *Acta Physiol. Scand.*, 35, 272–279.

Chapter 3

BEHAVIORAL DEVELOPMENT, ENVIRONMENTAL DEPRIVATION, AND MALNUTRITION

ROBERT R. ZIMMERMANN
Central Michigan University

CHARLES R. GEIST
University of Montana

LARRY A. WISE
Texas Wesleyan University

Introduction and History of the Problem

The paucity of information, both empirical and theoretical, concerning the effects of nutrition on behavioral development stands in sharp contrast to the interest philosophers and scientists have shown toward the role of other forms of environmental manipulations on the ontogeny of behavior. From the first observations of the pecking behavior of young chicks reared for a short time with hoods covering their heads (Spalding, 1873), to far more sophisticated contemporary studies, investigators have sought answers to both empirical and theoretical questions regarding the ontogeny and phylogeny of'behavior by enhancing or restricting the stimulus conditions of an organism during development. It would be beyond the scope of this paper to provide a comprehensive list of the extent of these efforts, but a sampling of the field should suffice. The investigations have included attempts to evaluate almost all aspects of development, such as emotion (Ader, 1959; Denenberg, 1964; Levine, 1959; Riesen, 1961), learning (Angermeier, Phelps, & Reynolds, 1967; Denenberg & Bell, 1960; Forgays & Forgays, 1952; Forgus, 1955; Gill, Reid, & Porter, 1966; Krech, Rosenzweig, & Bennett, 1962; Levine & Nelzel, 1963; Nyman, 1967; Rosenzweig, 1966; Thompson & Heron, 1954; Wilson, Warren, & Abbott, 1965), motivation (Berkson, Mason, & Saxon, 1963; Mason & Green, 1962; Menzel, 1963; Sackett, 1965, 1967; Woods,

Fiske, & Ruckelshaus, 1961), perception (Fantz, 1965; Ganz, 1968; Hebb, 1937a, 1937b, 1949; Held & Hein, 1963; Melzack, 1961, 1962; Riesen 1959; Walk, Gibson, & Tighe, 1957), and social behavior (Cross & Harlow, 1965; Harlow & Harlow, 1962; Mason, Davenport, & Menzel, 1968; Scott, 1958; Scott & Marston, 1950).

Prior to the advent of European ethology into contemporary American psychology, the bulk of the interpretations of the research findings was that ontogenetic experience—deprived or enriched—was the primary factor responsible for the development of normal learning abilities, perception, and social behavior. This interpretation, favoring the role of ontogenetic experience over the phylogenetic determinants in behavioral development, was rapidly assimilated into American psychological theory and practice, as these interpretations were highly consistent with the zeitgeist of naive behaviorism so prevalent from the 1930s to the early 1950s. Investigators went as far as rearing animals such as chimpanzees in their homes in competition with their children (Kellogg & Kellogg, 1933), or in place of their children (Hays, 1951) to demonstrate the enhancement of the behavioral capacities by proper environmental manipulation.

As American psychologists brought European ethology into the laboratory, it soon became evident that behavioral development was the result of a highly complex interaction between ontogenetic variables and phylogenetic factors. The role of hereditary factors as limiting conditions for the development of certain behaviors was more readily accepted.

Of all the many potential environmental variables that were investigated both before and after the ethological revolution in American psychology, few people considered nutrition as an important factor. Indeed, the only role nutrition played in contemporary behavioral research with animals was as a medium for inducing the organism to act. With the probable exception of primate research, most investigators manipulated the nutritional status of the organism in order to ensure that the behavior desired by the experimenter would appear with some regularity and reliability. It was standard procedure to place an animal on limited feeding schedules that would control weight gain, or the animal would be allowed food for only a short period each day, followed by an extensive (23 hr) food deprivation prior to testing. Nutritional status was a constant in the American experimental psychology equation. The bulk of the data used to support or negate the theories of learning in the prime of the Guthrie–Hull–Tolman controversies was collected employing undernourished rats.

The manipulation of diet as a variable influencing the behavior of an organism was usually concerned with the motivating properties of deprivation. Little if any effort was made to evaluate the role of nutrition on the development or functioning of the primary processes of learning, perception, or social behavior. When nutritional factors were manipulated for their own sake, the research was usually directed toward evaluating the effects of altering some aspects of a homeostatic mechanism on the behavior associated with the maintenance of the homeostatic drives. The major research thrust was directed toward creating specific hungers for compounds, essential elements of a normal diet, or vitamins and searching for behavior distinctive to that specific hunger (Young, 1955). The results of the behavioral studies in which nutritional status functioned as the primary independent variable tended to support the concept that only motivational mechanisms associated with the specific deprivations were altered and that many of these deviations were transient. Some long-term effects of food deprivation early in development have been reported, such as changes in food consumption and eating habits (Barnes, Neely, Kwong, Labadan, & Frankova, 1968; Elliott & King, 1960; Marx, 1952), increased hoarding behavior (Hunt, 1941; Wolfe, 1939), and increases in operant rates (Mandler, 1958). But studies concerned specifically with the effects of nutritional conditions on the process of learning (Anderson & Smith, 1926, 1932; Biel, 1938; Ruch, 1932) reported little or no reduction in learning ability as a result of infantile nutritional deprivation.

Research at the human level was no more encouraging than the results of animal studies. Extensive programs with human subjects placed on highly controlled starvation diets failed to reveal any changes in human behavior that could not be accounted for on the basis of temporary fatigue or motivational variables produced by the conditions of starvation (Guetzkow & Bowman, 1946; Keys, Brozek, Henschel, Michelson, & Taylor, 1950). Few if any permanent changes in intellectual, perceptual, or social functioning were detected in cases of rather severe manipulations of nutritional conditions. The apparent lack of interest in nutrition as a variable of importance in psychological functioning was the result of the accumulation of negative results over a period of years.

Rebirth of the Problem—Observations of Human Behavior

By the early 1960s information that implicated chronic malnutrition as a primary source of behavioral and intellectual retardation (Cravioto & Robles, 1963, 1965; Stoch & Smythe, 1963) began to accumulate from medical studies in underdeveloped countries. These reports had both political and social implications that were rapidly publicized by the press, radio, and television. The United States launched a drive on hunger, and a press release from the White House (during the Johnson administration) stated quite directly that malnutrition produced mental retardation in children, even though no research uncontaminated with economic and social variables existed at the time to support this rather dramatic statement. As sophistication in behavioral and social research improved in the study of behavior and malnutrition, it became evident that socioeconomic factors were present in the populations that were studied, and these factors could readily account for most of the behavioral deficits reported (Cravioto, 1968; Monckeberg, 1968; Stoch & Smythe, 1968).

In a review of the literature current at the time, Eichenwald & Fry (1969) came to the conclusion that there was ample evidence to indicate that malnutrition was a factor influencing neural development and psychological functioning if it occurred during a specific period of development. These authors emphasized the need for additional research at all levels of inquiry from the biochemical to the sociocultural if the role of nutrition in mental development were to be identified.

A survey of the nutrition field studies that controlled for some of the cultural and economic variables affecting mental development (Pollitt, 1972) tends to support the analysis of Eichenwald & Fry (1969). It appears that behavioral deficiencies persisted in children who had a history of malnutrition during the first year of life (nutritional marasmus), and such children did not achieve normal intellectual or psychological functioning; but children with a history of malnutrition during the second and third years (kwashiorkor) tended to recover.

Rebirth of the Problem—Studies in Lower Animals

With the accumulation of suggestive evidence that human intellectual performance was influenced by a history of early malnutrition, experimental psychologists and nutritionists began to take a new look at the relationship between behavior changes and nutritional deprivation. The research in this area between 1950 and 1970 has been reviewed by Levitsky & Barnes (1973) but will be summarized here. Studies that reported deficiencies in learning as a result of malnutrition early in life all suffered from methodological shortcomings. First, the authors failed to consider the incentive value of food reward to the malnourished animals (Cowley & Griesel, 1959, 1963; Rajalakshimi, Govindarajan, & Ramakrishnan, 1965). Second, no report was made regarding the asymptote of learning or the criterion, so that it is not known whether the animals failed to learn the problem or were merely slow learners (Cowley & Griesel, 1959, 1962, 1963; Ottinger & Tanabe, 1970). Third, learning and performance variables were not clearly differentiated (Caldwell & Churchill, 1966, 1967; Simonson & Chow, 1970). Finally, when aversive stimuli were used to control behavior, the potential overreaction, or incapacitating reaction to the aversive stimulation may have produced the deficits (Barnes, Cunnold, Zimmermann, Simmons, MacLeod, & Krook, 1966; Barnes, Moore, & Pond, 1970; Cowley & Griesel, 1962; Frankova & Barnes, 1968b; Guthrie, 1968; Wise & Zimmermann, 1973a). The last-mentioned criticism is supported by the analysis of the reactivity of rats with a history of early malnutrition to aversive stimuli (Levitsky & Barnes, 1970). These authors report that the animals with a history of malnutrition respond with greater vigor to a loud noise, increased passive avoidance to electric shock, and increased operant rates to avoid electrical stimulation as compared to well-fed controls.

In an attempt to overcome some of these methodological difficulties, two studies were conducted in which rats with a history of protein–calorie malnutrition were tested on a Hebb–Williams closed-field maze task (Hebb & Williams, 1946) for water reward. Protein-deficient rats and rehabilitated animals were inferior to adequately nourished controls, and length of the recovery period, 7 or 27 weeks, had no differential effect on performance (Zimmermann & Wells, 1971). Further, the error scores of animals with a history of malnutrition were only significantly different from control animals when the groups were reared under conditions of environmental deprivation (Wells, Geist, & Zimmermann, 1972). That these performance differences were probably the result of motivational factors and not learning per se is suggested by the recent research of Geist (1973). Rats reared in enriched or impoverished environments and receiving either protein-deficient or adequate diets early in life showed a diet $\times$ environment interaction when tested in a water maze with the temperature at 35°C. When the water temperature was reduced to 15°C, the main effects of both environment and nutrition disappeared, as well as interaction components.

Although learning ability may not be affected by early protein–calorie malnutrition, it is quite evident that emotional and motivational factors are consistently altered. Pigs and rats with a history of malnutrition demonstrate an overreactivity to noxious stimulation as measured by trials to extinction in a classical conditioning apparatus (Barnes et al., 1970). Similarly, Cowley & Griesel (1964) reported that rats malnourished at an early age exhibit decreased locomotion and increased defecation in an open field test, a standard procedure for determining emotionality in the rat (Denenberg, 1969), as well as increased latency to leave the home cage and suppression of movement following a loud noise.

Guthrie (1968) and Frankova & Barnes (1968a) reported a reduction in rearing responses or vertical activity for nutritionally rehabilitated rats examined in an open field situation. Barnes (personal communication) has shown that protein-deficient pigs will avoid entering that portion of a test room that contains a novel stimulus. In an open field test in which movement was recorded automatically, rats rehabilitated from early malnutrition exhibited suppressed activity in the presence of a novel stimulus as compared to normally fed controls (Zimmermann & Zimmermann, 1972).

The pattern of hyperemotionality and overreactivity to stimulation exhibited by animals that have suffered from protein–calorie malnutrition is not unlike the behavior patterns observed in animals reared under conditions of environmental isolation of stimulus deprivation. Levitsky & Barnes (1973) have gone as far as to call this a "striking" similarity, and have suggested that the mechanism underlying these behavior changes may be similar. The results of the investigations by Frankova (1968), Levitsky & Barnes (1972), and Wells et al., (1972) are consistent with this speculation, as in all cases behavioral deficiencies were enhanced when both dietary and environmental deprivations were manipulated simultaneously.

In addition to the above studies, it should be noted that in most, if not all, of the research with rats, the standard living condition for the animal was the typical 24.45 × 18.10 × 18.42 cm cage. Hebb (1947) demonstrated that the typical laboratory rearing condition for rats was, in fact, a highly isolated and stimulus-depriving environment. Thus, most of the studies reporting behavioral deficiencies as a result of early dietary manipulation have inadvertently confounded the primary independent variable of nutrition with environmental deprivation.

Studies with lower organisms such as the pig and rat can play an important role in evaluating the effects of early deprivation on adult animal performance, as well as provide critical information on how protein–calorie deprivation affects metabolic and other physiological systems. However, the limited behavioral repertoire and rapid development of these organisms precludes the analysis of complex behavior that might be altered during malnutrition. An animal having an extended developmental period and a behavioral system that changes as a function of age would provide a more detailed analysis of the effect of protein–calorie malnutrition on the emergence, integration, and organization of behavioral capacities. The infant rhesus monkey possesses these desirable characteristics and is highly adaptable to laboratory procedures. The remaining portion of this chapter will describe a program designed to evaluate the development of learning, motivation, perception, and social behavior in the rhesus monkey under various conditions of malnutrition and social experience.

An Experimental Investigation of the Development of Behavior of Rhesus Monkeys Raised on Protein-Deficient Diets

Experimental Groups, Normative Procedures, Physiological Measures, Activity, Food Consumption, and Food Preferences

During a period of 4 years 62 laboratory-born rhesus monkeys (*Macaca mulatta*) were introduced into a program designed to evaluate the relationship between behavioral development, protein–calorie malnutrition, and social rearing conditions. All the animals were separated from their mothers at 90 days of age and maintained on a liquid diet of Prosobee (Blomquist & Harlow, 1961) and vitamin sandwiches (Sidowski & Lockard, 1966). The animals were weaned from the liquid diet to solid foods between 90 and 120 days of age according to the procedures described by Zimmermann (1969a). The solid-food diets were either Purina monkey chow or a purified mixture compounded at the laboratory containing 25% casein as the sole source of dietary protein (Geist, Zimmermann, & Strobel, 1972).

The infants were assigned to groups according to the age at which they began the prepared diets and the social conditions under which they were to be reared. Groups were matched as closely as possible for age, and, although it was recognized that sex would be an important variable, the small number of births each year at the laboratory precluded producing groups matched for sex.

The dietary groups consisted of animals receiving the 25% high-protein diet (HP) or 3.5% or 2.0% low-protein diet (LP). The specific dietary regimen for the low-protein animals, either 3.5% or 2.0% protein, was manipulated according to the weight gain of the animals. If a particular monkey gained weight during the previous week it was fed the 2.0% protein diet. If, however, an animal lost weight it was provided with the 3.5% protein diet.

The social rearing conditions consisted of the following three types. First, those animals receiving daily social experience (DSE), in which the monkeys were housed in individual cages, but were placed in a large social playroom measuring 243.84 × 228.60 × 203.20 cm, and containing perches, bars, and chains, 3–5 days each week for 1–1.5 hr per day. Second, the social isolates (ISO), which were housed in individual cages, received no social experience for 1 year, and then were placed in the social playroom 1 day a month for a period of 1–1.5 hr. Third, the socially enriched animals (ENR), which were housed as a group in a large cage measuring 152.40 × 73.66 × 182.88 cm and provided social experience in the playroom 3–5 days each week after the animals were 1 year of age.

The experiments were initiated by introducing the 3.5% low-protein diet to a group of four monkeys 380 days of age who had lived in social isolation for the first year of life. Each of these animals was tested on curiosity, learning, and manipulation tasks, both prior to and subsequent to the introduction of the protein-deficient diet. A group of four monkeys approximately 400 days of age was purchased from the Oregon Regional Primate Research Center, and maintained on Purina monkey chow. This group functioned as age controls in the social experiments for the 380 day low-protein animals. Procedures of dietary preparation, feeding schedules, and blood-serum analysis were standardized with the aid of these groups. The second group of animals was 210 days of age at the introduction of the dietary regimes, six animals being assigned to the 3.5% low-protein diet and four to the high-protein diet. All these monkeys received testing on learning and manipulation tasks both before and after the initiation of the purified diets. A third group of animals began the diets at 120 days of age, and of these five animals were assigned to the low-protein group and four animals to the high-protein group. No testing was conducted on these animals prior to the introduction of the dietary regimes. All the aforementioned animals received daily social experience, and the groups were designated as follows: 380-LP-DSE, $N = 4$; 400-HP-DSE, $N = 4$; 210-LP-DSE, $N = 6$; 210-HP-DSE, $N = 4$; 120-LP-DSE, $N = 5$; and 120-HP-DSE, $N = 4$.

All the remaining groups were introduced to the purified diets at 120 days of age, and were divided into the two types of social experience described above as the social isolates (ISO) and the socially enriched group (ENR). The groups were then designated as follows: 120-LP-ISO, $N = 7$; 120-HP-ISO, $N = 6$; 120-LP-ENR, $N = 4$; and 120-HP-ENR, $N = 4$. The animals in each of these groups received no social testing until 1 year of age.

Physiological reactions to the low-protein diets were evident within the first 30 days. Reductions in blood-serum albumin and total protein appeared in the animals within the first 1 or 2 months following the introduction of the protein-deficient diets and the rate of weight gain was immediately suppressed (Geist et al., 1972). These results are similar

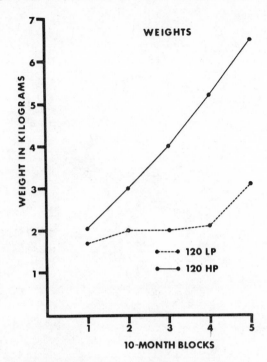

Fig. 1. Mean weight of groups 120-LP-DSE (broken line) and 120-HP-DSE (solid line) in 10 month blocks over 50 months.

to those described by Ordy, Samorajski, Zimmermann, & Rady (1966). The differences in weight gain are illustrated in Fig. 1, which depicts the average weights of the 120-LP-DSE group and the 120-HP-DSE group over a period of 50 months. Note that the malnourished animals did gain weight during the last 10 months of the protein-deficient diet, at a time when this group was being fed the 2.0% low-protein diet. There is considerable variation in these basic measures in response to the diets deficient in protein. Some animals lose weight on the 3.5% low-protein diet and some gain weight.

Approximately 5% of the animals receiving the protein-deficient diets develop clinical signs of kwashiorkor, including edema of the extremities and face; brittle, depigmented, and sparse hair; "flaky paint rash" on the body and extremities and "moist groin rash" of the genitals; hypoalbuminemia; and hypoproteinemia. Fig. 2 presents a monkey, 1 1/2 years old, from the 120-LP-DSE group exhibiting the early signs of kwashiorkor, and a normal subject approximately 120 days of age. The

Fig. 2. Early signs of kwashiorkor in the young monkey. Note the edema. On the right is a 18-month-old low-protein-raised monkey. On the left is a normal 120-day-old infant monkey.

identical malnourished subject is shown 2 months later in Fig. 3. At this time the animal was in a terminal state of health, and death ensued of lobar pneumonia and the severely debilitated state of the organism. The onset of this condition is now controlled by providing the animals with additional protein at the first sign of clinical symptomatology.

Food intake was measured by periodically sampling the food remaining in the drop-pans at the end of 16 hr of ad libitum feeding, air drying the food that was not consumed, and weighing the sample. Animals equated with respect to age and size showed little difference in food consumption across dietary and social regimes. The monkeys receiving the protein-deficient diets, as well as older animals, consumed more

than younger and adequately nourished animals. However, when the ratio of food consumed per gram body weight was calculated, no group differences were found to be significant (Geist et al., 1972).

Hillman & Riopelle (1971) reported that adult monkeys deprived of protein did not demonstrate a preference for high-protein foods in a food-preference test. Early observations that low-protein-reared monkeys showed a greater affinity for reinforcements employed in test situations when compared to the high-protein subjects suggested that malnourished animals might prefer high- to low-protein foods. Because the diets compounded at the laboratory were color coded as to casein content by the addition of food coloring (25% = green, 3.5% = yellow, 2.0% = red), it was quite simple to provide the animals with a preference task.

The subjects were placed in a cage that had one wall containing eight clear Plexiglas windows, which could be opened by pulling on

Fig. 3. Same experimental animal as in Fig. 2 (right), 2 months later. Note the severe edema.

a small knob. A small piece of colored diet or a novel toy was placed behind each window, and the animal merely had to open the window in order to secure the item. The 120-LP-DSE and the 210-LP-DSE groups and the corresponding high-protein controls were tested in this apparatus. The high-protein-reared animals exhibited no preference; however, both of the low-protein-reared groups selected significantly more 25% green diet by the end of the first nine trials of the first day of testing. Additionally, the malnourished groups selected significantly fewer toys than the respective control animals. After five days of testing under these conditions, the colors of the 25% green diet and the 2.0% red diet were reversed. The animals were tested for an additional 10 days in the apparatus for nine trials each day. The high-protein-reared animals once again did not show a preference. The low-protein subjects initially selected more of the 2.0% green diet than the 25% red diet. However, by the time the animals had been tested for 6 days, a reversal of preference had developed, but the malnourished animals still selected significantly fewer toys than controls. It should be mentioned that the daily ration of food for the protein-deprived groups remained the 2.0% red diet. Therefore, it would appear that young monkeys maintained on diets deficient in protein do, in fact, demonstrate the ability to discriminate and select high-protein foods and do not respond positively to novel objects (Peregoy, Zimmermann, & Strobel, 1972).

Because one of the traditional clinical signs of protein–calorie malnutrition in the human infant is lethargy, the activity of the high- and low-protein animals was monitored with two devices. In one test a $76.20 \times 76.20 \times 76.20$ cm cage was equipped with light-sensitive cells at each corner, 38.10 cm from the bottom of the cage. As the animal moved across or around the cage the beam of light would be broken and the relays would activate a counter. Activity records from 125 1 hr sessions were recorded from the low-protein monkeys in the 380-LP-DSE, 210-LP-DSE, and the 120-LP-DSE groups, as well as the 210-HP-DSE and the 120-HP-DSE groups. No significant group differences were found (Geist et al., 1972). The second device employed for measuring activity was a large running wheel capable of accommodating animals up to 3 years of age and similar in design to the activity wheels employed in rat research. Animals from the various treatment groups were placed in this apparatus for 1 hr intervals approximately every third day for a period of 1 year. Again no significant differences emerged between the high- and low-protein groups.

It appears that there are significant physiological changes in blood chemistry shortly following the introduction of the protein-deficient dietary regimes. Food preferences for the high-protein diet do develop, but these changes are not reflected in an alteration of general activity.

Curiosity, Manipulation, and Responses to Novelty

Curiosity, or investigatory behavior, is one of the most persistent forms of goal directed behavior that is found in the normal developing rhesus monkey (Mason, Harlow & Rueping, 1959), and is probably characteristic of all primates. However, decreased investigatory behavior has been identified as one of the consistent features of protein-calorie malnutrition in children (Jelliffe & Welbourn, 1963). In an attempt to evaluate the impact of protein malnutrition on this behavior in developing monkeys, animals in the 380-LP-DSE, 210-LP-DSE, 120-LP-DSE, 210-HP-DSE and 120-HP-DSE groups were tested on a variety of investigatory tasks.

In preliminary investigations with the 380-LP-DSE group, the subjects were tested in a visual curiosity box in which responses were recorded to door openings that permitted the animal to view the remainder of the group in a large cage. Following the introduction of the low-protein diet the door-opening responses decreased, particularly to long fixed ratios of reinforcement (Zimmermann & Strobel, 1969). These results could not be replicated with the 210-LP-DSE group and the test was discontinued. The failure to find consistent differences in this measure may have been a function of the experimental test situation. That is, the animals were only deprived of normal visual stimulation during the 1 hr test period. Longer periods of deprivation, however, may have yielded different results.

Mason et al. (1959) demonstrated that infant monkeys will respond to chains and ropes suspended in the cage by pulling and touching them for no other source of reinforcement than the mere act of responding. In order to examine this form of motivation in the malnourished animals, chains were hung in the home cage for groups 380-LP-DSE, 210-LP-DSE, 120-LP-DSE, 210-HP-DSE, and 120-HP-DSE. The chains were attached to mechanical counters and an excursion of approximately one-half inch was sufficient to activate the counters. The chains were present in the cages 24 hr a day and the counters were read and reset each afternoon. At the end of 10 days, bright shiny objects (cookie cutters) were attached to the chains. These remained on the chains for 10 additional days, at which time chains without the objects were reinstated for 20 days.

The 380-LP-DSE, 210-LP-DSE, and 210-HP-DSE groups were tested on the chain-pulling task prior to the introduction of the diets and again 30 days following initiation of the diets. Both malnourished groups exhibited a reduction in chain-pulling responses following the introduction of the low-protein diet. The 120-LP-DSE group also showed significantly lower chain-pulling scores at the end of 30 days on the dietary regimes when compared to the 120-HP-DSE group. The introduction of objects on the chains further suppressed the chain-pulling responses of the malnourished groups. In comparison, the 120-HP-DSE and 210-HP-DSE groups increased in the rate of responding to the objects on the chains. Fig. 4 shows the net change in responses for the chain only and chain-plus-object condition for the 210-LP-DSE, 120-LP-DSE, 210-HP-DSE, and 120-HP-DSE groups.

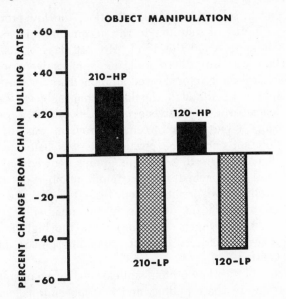

Fig. 4. Net change in response rate to the presence of the cookie cutters on the chains for groups 210-LP-DSE, 120-LP-DSE, 210-HP-DSE. and 120-HP DSE.

Another form of manipulative behavior that normal rhesus monkeys engage in for nothing more than extrinsic reinforcement is manipulation or disengagement of mechanical puzzles (Harlow, 1950). The same subjects that participated in the chain-pulling experiment were used for this test. Each subject was placed in a cage measuring 69.96 × 45.72 × 67.20 cm, one wall of which consisted of either 12 mechanical hook-and-hasp problems (two-puzzle) or 12 pin, hook, and hasp problems (three-puzzle). The cages were wired so that contact with the metal portions of the puzzle would activate a counter. Thus, frequency of contact, as well as the total number of puzzle units opened in a 1 hr period, could be recorded.

In the two-puzzle task, the three low-protein groups opened significantly fewer puzzles than the two high-protein controls, but there were no differences in contacts. The animals were then transferred to the three-puzzle problem and, although the low-protein groups again opened fewer puzzles, the group differences were not reliable (Strobel & Zimmermann, 1971). Following 200 days of testing under these conditions, reinforcement in the form of a sugar-coated piece of cereal was placed in a small food well behind the hasp. This enabled the subject to receive reward for puzzle solutions. In this situation, the low-protein animals increased the number of solutions to the maximum of 12 and the high-protein animals approached this level. After 10 days of 100% reinforcement, extinction was introduced and the animals were tested for 80 additional days. All the groups showed an immediate decrease in contacts and puzzle solutions. Although the low-protein subjects exhibited the most rapid decrease in responsiveness, the differences were not found to be significant. A partial reinforcement program was then instituted in which a different one of the puzzle units was baited each day. At the end of 70 days of testing, all the groups showed an increase in performance and approached the maximum number of solutions. An extinction procedure was reintroduced for 80 days. The low-protein groups showed a significant decrease in the number of puzzle units opened and in total contacts. In comparison, the high-protein groups remained near their reinforced level of responding (Aakre, Strobel, Zimmermann, & Geist, 1973).

The behavior of the low-protein animals in a free-operant response in the home cage, in chain pulling, and in a more formal puzzle-testing situation indicates that this form of extrinsic motivation is lowered following protein–calorie malnutrition. However, it appears that this behavior can be manipulated through the introduction of intrinsic sources of motivation such as food incentives. It is interesting to note that the reduction of curiosity and manipulatory behavior is also characteristic of the rhesus monkey reared in social isolation from either the mother or peers (Sackett, 1965).

Casual observation of the malnourished monkeys in the home cage when the objects were introduced into the chain-pulling experiment, and the avoidance of toys in the food-preference task suggested that these animals had an aversion or fear of novelty. Some of the animals had to be forced into the home cage following the introduction of the chain-pulling objects. It was also apparent that the low-protein monkeys were more disturbed by the appearance of strangers in the laboratory than were the high-protein animals. The malnourished monkeys behaved very much like the motherless monkeys described by Harlow and Seay (1966) in that they clutched themselves, rocked back and forth, screamed, and exhibited the fear grimace characteristic of the isolated infant even at 3 years of age.

In contrast, the high-protein animals would demonstrate the typical threat response, charging the front and rattling the cage, at the appearance of a stranger. In addition, the low-protein subjects were difficult to adapt to test conditions and generally required a week or more of adaptation when compared to the high-protein controls.

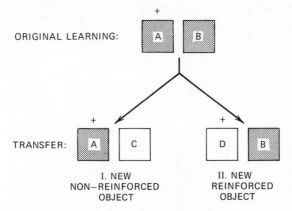

Fig. 5.   Paradigm of test for the presence of neophobia in the malnourished monkey. Neophobic reaction = significant A responses in I, and significant B responses in II. Neophilic reaction = significant C responses in I, and significant D responses in II.

These monkeys would become extremely agitated and excited with the introduction of each new problem into a learning set or oddity learning task. As a result of these observations, two experiments were designed to test the hypothesis that the developing malnourished monkey had an aversion to novel or strange stimuli (neophobia).

In the first experiment the 210-LP-DSE and the 210-HP-DSE groups were trained on a series of 50 six-trial learning-set problems. The problems were repeated in the same sequence for 10 repetitions, at which time learning had reached a level of 80–90% correct responses over the six trials (Zimmermann, 1969b). On the 11th repetition the problems were altered as diagrammed in Fig. 5. On 25 of the 50 problems the original positive stimulus was replaced with a new or novel object. For the remaining 25 problems the original negative stimulus was replaced by a new or novel object. It is well known that most infant monkeys are attracted to novel stimuli and commit the response shift error by responding to the negative stimulus after a series of correct responses (Harlow, 1959). Thus, normal monkeys have a slight propensity towards being neophilic. Under the new conditions of novel stimulation in the discrimination problems, the low-protein animals exhibited significant avoidance of the novel stimulus, decreasing from 90% correct on trial one to 40% correct. In comparison, the high-protein monkeys made significantly more responses to the new stimuli as can be seen in Fig. 6 (Zimmermann, Stroble, & Maguire, 1970).

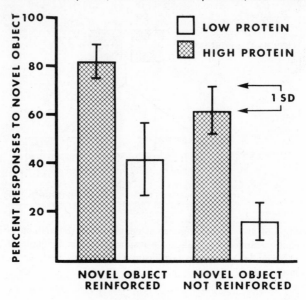

Fig. 6.   Percent responses to novel object by high, and low-protein-raised animals.

In the second experiment the 210-LP-DSE, 120-LP-DSE, 210-HP-DSE, and 120-HP-DSE animals were placed in a vertical tunnel composed of wire mesh and measuring 243.84 cm in height and 30.48 cm in diameter (Fig. 7). The subjects were taught to shuttle to the top of the apparatus and then to return to the bottom to secure reinforcement. Following shuttle training, six novel objects were suspended from the top of the cylinder in various positions. Twelve sessions, each lasting 10 min, were conducted with these objects, after which 18 additional sessions were presented to allow the animals to become familiar with the previously novel stimuli. Changes in the number of reinforcements secured under these two conditions are shown in Fig. 8. The high-protein subjects actually increased in the securing of reinforcements with a novel object present, whereas the low-protein subjects decreased. Observations recorded on a checksheet in 15 sec intervals also indicated that the low-protein animal made significantly more emotional and avoidance responses to the stimuli, whereas the high-protein subjects made significantly more approaches and contacts to the objects, as shown in Fig. 9 (Strobel, 1972).

The results of these two experiments confirm, in a quantitative manner, the qualitative observations made of the behavior of the low-protein animals. The malnourished monkeys show a significant change in behav-

Fig. 7.   Vertical tunnel for studying effects of novel stimuli on a learned operant.

ior when new or novel objects are introduced into a familiar situation. The reduced responding to the novel objects in the chain-pulling experiment, and the avoidance of toys in the food-preference task by low-protein animals, added to the findings described above demonstrate that following protein–calorie malnutrition rhesus monkeys are overreactive to novelty and find new stimulation aversive.

Learning Tasks

With the exception of the 400-HP-DSE group and the 380-LP-DSE group, all the animals began adaptation to the Wisconsin General Test Apparatus between 90 and 120 days of age. This period of adaptation required 1–2 weeks and prepared the subjects to begin formal discrimination and other learning tasks by the time each reached 120 days of

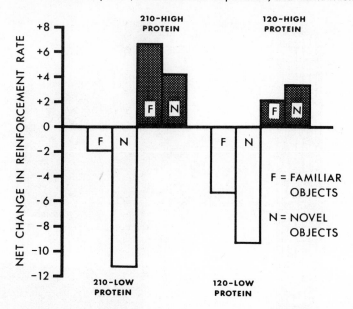

Fig. 8. Net change in reinforcement rate for groups 210-LP-DSE, 120-LP-DSE, 210-HP-DSE, and 120-HP-DSE in the vertical tunnel in the presence of novel and familiar objects.

age. The typical sequence of testing a monkey on a two-choice discrimination problem is shown in Fig. 10. The experimenter places a reinforcement in a small food well located on the delivery tray, covers it with an object, and places a different object over the empty food well. This procedure is performed while the monkey remains behind an opaque screen. With the objects in place, the experimenter lowers a one-way viewing screen, raises the opaque partition in front of the animal, and pushes the delivery tray forward in order for the animal to make a response. Only one response is permitted, after which the screen in front of the subject is lowered and a new trial begun.

A variety of different types of learning tasks can be examined with the aid of the Wisconsin General Test Apparatus, such as delay response, learning sets, oddity problems, reversal learning, and pattern string tasks, as well as a multitude of perceptual tasks, stimulus generalization problems, and visual discrimination problems. In one of the studies concerning the effects of malnutrition on complex learning in the monkey, protein-deprived animals proved to be more efficient in the memorization of 100 different discrimination problems and had higher learning set scores than controls fed a standard monkey diet. This difference was

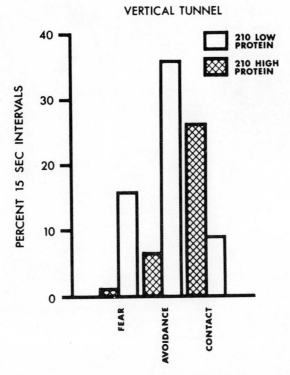

Fig. 9. Percent of 15 sec intervals in which fear, avoidance, or contact behavior was observed for the 210-HP-DSE and 210-LP-DSE.

attributed to the greater incentive value of obtaining a food reinforcement by the malnourished subjects (Zimmermann, 1969b).

Since this original effort, protein-malnourished monkeys have been subjected to a large number of different learning tasks. The 380-LP-DSE animals were presented with a series of discrimination learning and reversal learning problems both prior to and following the introduction of the low-protein diets. No measurable change in performance was detected for the pre-dietary and post-dietary conditions (Zimmermann, 1973). The 210-LP-DSE, 120-LP-DSE, 210-HP-DSE, and 120-HP-DSE animals were tested on 50 six-trial discrimination problems, which were repeated until the animals had achieved 80% correct or better on trial one. After reaching this criterion level the animals were not tested for a period of 3 months on any learning problems. At that time the 50 six-trial problems were repeated to determine the capacity of long-term memory. The high- and low-protein animals did not differ in original

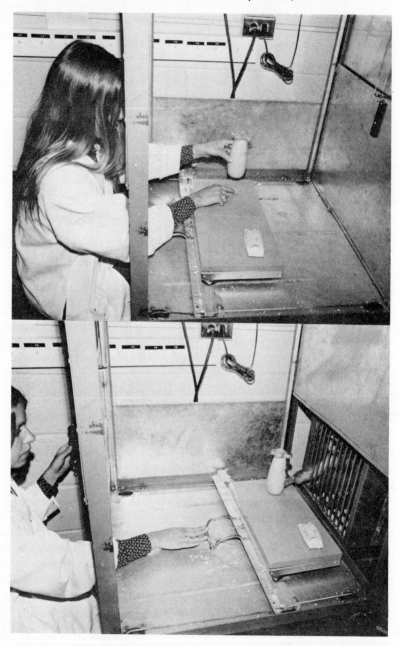

Fig. 10. Wisconsin General Test Apparatus procedure. In upper picture the experimenter baits the well with the monkey behind screen on the right. Lower picture. Opaque screen is raised and tray pushed forward so that monkey can make response.

learning, learning set, or retention as long as the high-protein groups were mildly deprived of the daily food ration and provided with high-incentive reinforcements such as grapes or raisins. If the high-protein animals were not deprived or if sugar-coated cereal was provided as the reinforcement, the performance of these subjects decreased significantly below that of the low-protein groups.

Because of the motivational differences between the malnourished animals and the controls in the traditional learning tasks, aversive stimulation was employed. In a preliminary investigation it was found that the low-protein monkeys had a lower threshold for electric shock than the high-protein subjects. Further, maladaptive responses were made by the low-protein groups to the electrical stimulation (Wise & Zimmermann, 1973a). The response to a mild electric shock by the normal rhesus monkey is usually directed toward the source of the stimulation; the normal monkey will bite the shocking-grid floor, bridge from one wall to the other above the source of stimulation, or lift one foot at a time in order to avoid or reduce the shock intensity. The malnourished animals in the 380-LP-DSE and 210-LP-DSE groups, on the other hand, exhibited diffuse responses such as defecating and screaming at the onset of shock. Often the animals would clutch themselves and fall into a fetal-like position and remain in that position until they were removed from the apparatus. Thus, it was not possible to investigate complex learning by applying electrical stimulation because of the aberrant behavioral responses of the low-protein subjects.

It is possible to train the malnourished monkeys not to make certain autoerotic responses such as compulsive penis sucking by shocking them instrumentally while they are making this response, and then applying classical conditioning procedures to generalize the avoidance response to the home cage and testing situation. Several of the malnourished animals developed such responses and had to be conditioned in order to become suitable subjects for testing in the curiosity, learning, and manipulation tasks (Stoffer, Zimmermann, & Strobel, 1973).

To overcome the difficulties encountered with aversive electrical stimulation, an apparatus was designed in which animals would receive a short but intense blast of compressed air if an incorrect choice was made in a two-choice discrimination problem. The apparatus was adapted to the Wisconsin General Test Apparatus and an investigation of the development of learning set with aversive reinforcement was initiated. The 210-LP-DSE, 120-LP-DSE, 210-HP-DSE, and 120-HP-DSE groups were tested on a series of problems which were learned to a criterion. All animals showed an improvement in performance across problems, demonstrating the formation of a learning set. Nutritional status was not a significant variable (Stoffer & Zimmermann, 1973).

A series of studies was designed to evaluate the role of stimulus discriminability and stimulus complexity on the development of learning and transposition along a stimulus continuum (Zimmermann, 1970). The 380-LP-DSE, 210-LP-DSE, 120-LP-DSE, 400-HP-DSE, 210-HP-DSE, and 120-HP-DSE groups were trained to discriminate a series of stimuli that differed in brightness, size, or brightness and size. All groups of animals showed superior learning and transposition to stimuli with multiple dimensions. The low-protein animals, however, made significantly more errors as the stimuli deviated further from the central tendency of the stimulus continuum, as well as when the differences between the stimuli became smaller (Figs. 11 and 12).

All animals were then trained to discriminate between a series of boxes, which were as small as a 2.54 cm cube and increased in size to a 7.62 cm cube. Multidimensional objects were then presented to the animals in which pairs of these stimuli had been ranked to stimulate the sizes of the boxes in order that the only consistent stimulus cue for the discrimination would be size. The low-protein-reared monkeys had significantly lower transfer scores than the high-protein animals. Failure to generalize or transfer effectively in this test may have been the result of a failure to establish a strong response to the original

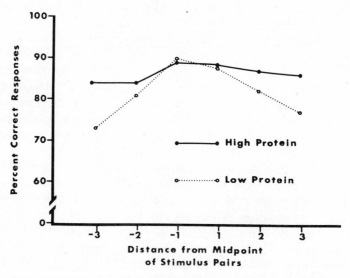

Fig. 11. Percent correct responses for high- and low-protein-raised animals to transposition stimuli as a function of distance from the midpoint of the continuum.

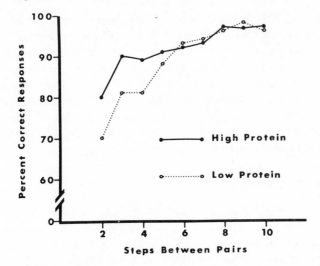

Fig. 12. Percent correct responses to transposition stimuli as a function of discriminable steps between pairs of stimuli.

cue (Ganz, 1968), or it may have been a result of the neophobia that these animals display.

Each of the animals employed in the above tasks was then tested on a series of delay-response problems in which delays of from 0 to 120 sec were used according to the standard delay-response procedure. Neither diet nor age was a significant factor in this investigation.

The 210-LP-DSE, 120-LP-DSE, 210-HP-DSE, and 120-HP-DSE groups were tested on a series of problems in which they had to select the middle-size object among three objects that were presented across a size continuum in a six-trial learning set paradigm. The high-protein animals were deprived of food to the equivalent of 10% body weight prior to initiation of the study. After being tested on 56 problems there was no sign of learning in any group. Five problems were selected from the small end, middle, and large end of the continuum and the animals were tested on these five trios, six trials per trio, until each had been presented 10 times. Under these conditions all the animals learned and, once again, no differences were found as a function of diet. After learning to discriminate these five trios, selecting the middle stimulus each time, the animals were tested for transfer of training to the remaining 51 trios employed in the original learning task. All groups showed significant savings in transferring to these problems independent of age and dietary regime.

A series of 400 six-trial oddity problems was then presented with the replication of the above results. Malnutrition does not appear to have a significant effect on reducing discrimination performance on any task with the exception of that of transposition. This reduction of performance can probably be attributed to emotional or motivational factors and not to cognitive or learning factors per se. Such findings are consistent with those reported by Harlow, Harlow, Schiltz, & Mohr (1968), that rhesus monkeys reared in social isolation are not inferior in learning tasks to monkeys reared in a group setting.

Studies in Attention

Before an animal can learn to discriminate between two stimuli it must first learn how and where to look for the discriminative cue. That is, the organism must detect and select the critical stimulus dimension that the experimenter has presented in the discrimination learning task. This ability to localize and select the critical cue has been termed the process of attention. Some theorists localize this ability in some type of central process (Sutherland & Mackintosh, 1971), whereas others conceive of it in more behavioral terms, calling the process an observing response (Wyckoff, 1952). Regardless of the location or name of the process, all but the most devout behaviorists appear to agree that there is some type of behavior that precedes and acts as a selection mechanism in the discrimination learning process of visual organisms.

Stollnitz (1965) has applied the notion of the presence of an observing response to explain the development of learning sets in monkeys in which the stimuli possess an inherent organization that breaks the typical stimulus response contiguity, producing less efficient learning set formation. He hypothesizes that on each new problem the monkey must learn to make a new observing response. Since attentional mechanisms have been identified as being variables affecting the discrimination performance in the mentally retarded (Zeaman & House, 1963), it appeared logical to view this variable as a potential source of behavioral deficiency in the malnourished monkey.

The simplest procedure for producing a stimulus response discontiguity in discrimination learning set tasks in the Wisconsin General Test Apparatus is to attach stimulus objects to thin Masonite plaques 7.62 cm square and painted a neutral gray. In doing this the point at which the monkey places his fingers to move the object is in spatial discontiguity with the discriminable stimulus object. Distances as small as 0.50–0.75 in. can reduce the efficiency of color discrimination learning (Schuck, 1960; Schuck, Polidora, McConnell, & Meyer, 1961).

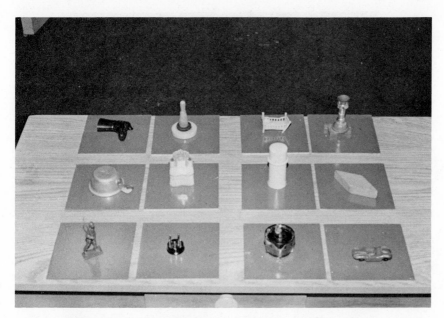

Fig. 13.   Discrimination stimuli mounted on plaques for study in reversal learning.

Two groups of animals that had been placed either on the 3.5% low-protein diet or the 25% high-protein diet at 90 days of age were tested
on a discrimination learning task. Six different discrimination problems
and six reversal problems in which the discriminable stimuli were
mounted on 7.62 × 7.62 cm gray Masonite plaques were learned to a
criterion (Fig. 13). Under these conditions the groups did not differ
in the number of errors that were made to achieve criterion in learning
the discrimination. However, the low-protein animals made significantly
more errors in reaching criterion on the reversal problems. That a difference appeared in the reversal task and not in the original learning problems probably reflects the greater difficulty of the reversal problems. Rumbaugh & Pournelle (1966) have demonstrated that reversal learning and
the speed with which primates learn reversal problems differentiates
the different classes of primates, whereas simple discrimination learning
does not.

In order to achieve a more direct test of the hypothesis that the
low-protein monkeys were deficient in tasks requiring an attentional
or observing response, the stimuli in Fig. 14 were constructed. In one
set of stimuli the discriminative cue was located in the center of a
gray field, whereas in the other set the discriminative cue was located

Fig. 14. Stimuli prepared to test the effect of locus of cue and stimuli area on reversal learning in high- and low- protein animals.

on the border with the gray field in the center. The total area of the discriminable cue was varied from 100% of the area of the stimulus card to 5% of the total area. As the total area of the centrally located cue is diminished, the discontiguity between where the monkey places his fingers when making a response and the locus of the cue is increased, as can be seen in Fig. 15.

The 210-LP-DSE, 120-LP-DSE, 210-HP-DSE, and 120-HP-DSE groups were tested with these stimuli. Each pair was presented for 216 trials

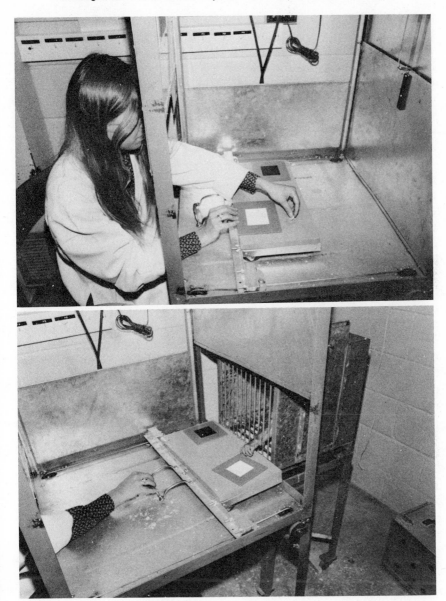

Fig. 15. Wisconsin General Test Apparatus. Upper picture, baiting the stimuli. Lower, response of the animal. Note the position of the animal's fingers.

and the order of presentation was randomized using a 6×6 Latin Square. Half the animals were tested on the stimuli with central cues and the other half were tested with peripheral cues. The high- and low-protein animals did not differ in the rate of learning, but the performance was superior in those groups learning the discrimination with cues on the periphery. On the reversal learning task, however, the low-protein animals were significantly inferior to the high-protein subjects when the cue was reduced to less than 50% of the total area of the square (Strobel, 1972).

The above findings, were encouraging, and the same groups were then tested on a conditional discrimination problem. A stimulus located in the center of a two-choice discrimination board of the Wisconsin General Test Apparatus signaled the presence of reinforcement in the right or left food well (Fig. 16). This procedure required an even greater degree of observing or attentional responses than did the previous study. The organism had to look specifically at the center stimulus in order to solve the problem.

Seven of the nine malnourished animals failed to learn this discrimination problem to a criterion of 80% correct after 2100 trials. In contrast, all the high-protein subjects achieved criterion by 1300 trials. Observations of the animals indicated that the malnourished groups were not attending to the stimulus card, but were looking from side to side at the boards covering the two food wells. Most of the high-protein animals developed specific motor responses to the central stimuli, such as touching it, or, in two cases, tracing the shape of the figure in a crude fashion (Strobel, 1972).

Another type of discrimination of perceptual task thought to be controlled to a large extent by attentional factors is the detection or identification of embedded or hidden figures. Ten stimuli (shown in Fig. 17) were designed to test the ability of the control and malnourished animals to detect hidden and embedded figures. Identical subjects to those employed in conditional learning were taught to discriminate the square from the triangle in a simple two-choice discrimination task. After reaching a criterion of learning they were tested for transfer of training. Thirty trials of each pair were presented for 10 days, during which time the stimulus card containing the originally learned square or triangle was rewarded.

The high-protein animals transferred to all of the stimuli at an above-chance level in the first 5 days of testing to each stimulus and improved in performance to an 80% level in the second 5 days of testing. The malnourished animals not only failed to transfer to the stimuli at a level significantly above chance in the first 5 days of testing, but also

Fig. 16. Stimuli used for condition learning study. Reinforcement is located under one of the flat covers to the right or the left of the stimulus. Cue indicates location of reinforcement.

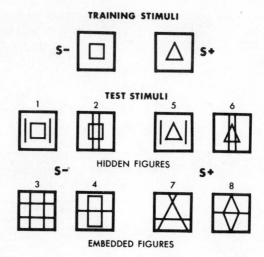

Fig. 17. Stimuli used in studies of transfer of training to hidden and embedded figures.

failed to improve during the last 5 days. That the decrease in performance was not the result of a loss of learning to the original stimulus pair was evident, as test trials with this pair of stimuli during the transfer testing did not reveal any group differences (Strobel, 1972).

The final task selected to evaluate further the apparent deficiency of attention mechanisms in protein-deprived monkeys can be described as a reward-directed task. In all the preceding experiments, the reinforcement was concealed behind or under an object of some type. In the pattern string task the reward is in sight of the organism and the problem solution merely requires the organism to pull the correct string to which the reward has been attached.

The 210-LP-DSE, 120-LP-DSE, 210-HP-DSE, and 120-HP-DSE groups were approximately 4 years of age at the time this experiment was begun and should have been mature enough to solve the problem efficiently. The patterns shown in Fig. 18 were employed in the sequence parallel, pseudo-crossed, and crossed for 400 trials each. This sequence was selected because it has been found to produce the maximum amount of negative transfer to the crossed pattern (Zimmermann, unpublished research). It should be noted that the parallel and pseudo-crossed patterns can be solved merely by pulling on the string that is closest to the reinforcement. The crossed pattern, on the other hand, requires

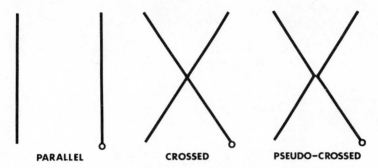

PARALLEL   **CROSSED**   **PSEUDO-CROSSED**

Fig. 18.   Pattern strings problems.

the animal to go away from the locus of reward, thereby breaking the contiguous relationship. The crossed-string problem presents a case of reinforcement-response discontiguity.

No significant differences were found between the high- and low-protein groups on the parallel or pseudo-cross problem. In the crossed pattern, however, the low-protein monkeys fell considerably below chance level of responding in the first 100 trials and barely achieved chance performance after 400 trials. The high-protein animals appeared to drop the negative transfer effects from the pseudo-crossed problem immediately and showed the normal adult learning curve (Fig. 19).

The depressed performance of the malnourished monkeys on these series of tasks, all of which require some type of attention, detection, or scanning response, stands in sharp contrast to the performances achieved on other learning tasks. Such findings are consistent with the reports by Klein, Gilbert, Canosa, & DeLeon (1969). They found that children with a history of malnutrition did not differ from control subjects on discrimination learning tasks, but were inferior in tasks requiring attention, such as repeating a rapid tapping sequence or identifying the embedded figures. These deficiencies were attributed to attentional mechanisms rather than to more central processes such as learning or cognition, because the children could follow the tapping sequence if it was presented more slowly and could point out the embedded figures if they were originally shown to them. The evidence suggests that malnutrition may not produce deficiencies in cognitive or learning tasks per se. However, if these tasks require selective attentional mechanisms, the performance of malnourished organisms probably would be inferior to organisms reared on adequate diets.

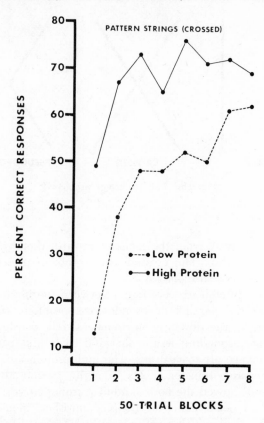

Fig. 19.   Results of pattern strings test.

Social Behavior

At the initiation of the experiments in malnutrition and behavior, monkeys raised on both high- and low-protein diets were placed in a large cage with the other members of their age and diet group to provide them with social experience so that they might develop normal sexual behavior in order to produce the next generation of experimental animals. The social cage also functioned as the stimulus for the subject in the visual exploration box. At first, no systematic observations were made of these animals in the social cage, but it soon became obvious to the most naive observer that the animals receiving the low-protein diet were not socializing in the same manner as the high-protein controls. The low-protein animals would sit around and gaze at the room for long periods of time, or manipulate parts of the cage, whereas the high-protein animals would engage in numerous and extended bouts of play behavior.

Systematic observations of the 210-LP-DSE and 210-HP-DSE groups were begun, and three classes of behavior were recorded: social interactions, actions directed toward objects or the cage, and nonobject or staring and gazing actions. Duration and frequency measures of these behaviors were recorded on an Esterline Angus recorder over a period of several months. Analysis of these data revealed that the high-protein animals spent significantly more time in social interactions and significantly less time in both nonsocial behaviors than the low-protein animals (Zimmermann & Strobel, 1969).

A more systematic study of social behavior with these same groups of animals was completed and reported in detail in Zimmermann, Steere, Strobel, & Hom (1972). The subjects were observed in a large playroom over a period of 2 years. This study revealed that the low-protein animals showed significantly *less* sexual behavior, play behavior, and grooming behavior, and significantly *more* nonsocial and aggressive behavior than the high-protein controls. The aggressive behavior often took the form of brutality and at times the observation of the low-protein group had to be terminated in order to prevent serious injury to one of the animals.

Hyperaggression has also been observed in rhesus monkeys that have been reared in social isolation, and it has been suggested that one of the factors contributing to the appearance of this behavior is the instability of dominance roles inherent in the social organization of these deprived groups (Mason, 1960, 1961b). Although dominance roles were not quantified in our observations, it appeared that the high-protein animals had a more stable social hierarchy than the malnourished animals. A series of experiments was designed to test the hypothesis that the low-protein animals had less stable dominance relationships than the high-protein animals.

In the first study (Wise, Zimmermann & Strobel, 1973) six groups of animals (380-LP-DSE, 210-LP-DSE, 120-LP-DSE, 400-HP-DSE, 210-HP-DSE, and 120-HP-DSE) were observed under two different social conditions in the playroom. In one test, dominance/aggression and subordinate/submission interactions were recorded using the system developed by Locke, Locke, Morgan, & Zimmermann (1964). In the second test subjects competed for food reward. The animal securing the most reinforcements during the test session was considered to be the most dominant. Within-group comparisons were made with all members of that particular age and diet group, and between-group comparisons were made by placing individual subjects from each of the age groups in the playroom with four members of the opposite diet group.

In general the larger, high-protein-raised animals in all age groups were dominant over the smaller, low-protein-raised animals in the social-interaction measures. Reversals of dominance did occur on occasion in comparisons between the 120-LP-DSE and 120-HP-DSE groups. At the time of testing some of the animals in this low-protein group were approximately the same size as the high-protein animals. In the food-competition task, the high-protein animals in groups 400-HP-DSE and 210-HP-DSE were not significantly dominant over their low-protein agemates, and the 120-LP-DSE group secured significantly more food rewards than the 120-HP-DSE group.

Although it was not possible to equate each group for sex, it was possible to extract some information concerning sex differences by pooling all male and all female scores across all groups. On the whole the males were significantly more dominant than the females, but there may have been a more complex interaction between sex, diet, and type of test. The females maintained on the high-protein diet had extremely low dominance scores in the food-competition task, but the low-protein-raised females were the most competitive animals on this task.

These results are consistent with previous findings (Angermeier, Phelps, Murray, & Howansteine, 1968), in which it was found that when weight differences between competing animals approach 1000 g the larger animal is consistently dominant. The failure of the larger animals to remain dominant in the food-competition test is not consistent with the notion that dominance in the rhesus monkey is a unitary trait across deprivation conditions (Maroney & Leary, 1957; Maroney, Warren, & Sinha, 1959).

In a second study (Wise & Zimmermann, 1973b) the 210LP-DSE, 120-LP-DSE, 210-HP-DSE, and 120-HP-DSE groups were subjected to competitive tasks in two appetitive tests and a shock-avoidance test. In the first appetitive task, two animals (within and between diet groups, but within age group) were placed in a standard test cage of a Wisconsin General Test Apparatus and competed for food reinforcements that were delivered on a single-well test tray. In the second appetitive test, the animals were placed in an apparatus called the Parallel Competition Box. Metal cages were placed approximately 30.48 cm apart, and the animals were prevented from reaching out of the front of the cage by a Plexiglas guillotine door. A tray containing a reinforcement was pushed between the cages, the Plexiglas doors were raised simultaneously, and the animals competed for the food. In both tests, dominance was defined in terms of the number of reinforcements secured by a particular animal.

In the avoidance task, animals were paired in all combinations of subjects within age groups and across diet groups in a chamber containing a grid floor that could be electrified. Upon the onset of a signal one of the two animals was permitted to escape through a door at the end of the chamber and the remaining animal was trapped and received a 1 sec electric shock at the termination of the signal.

As was found in the previous study on food competition, the animals raised on low protein were successful in outcompeting the adequately fed age-mates in both food-competition tasks. But when the incentive to exert dominance was escape or avoidance of electric shock, the high-protein-raised animals were significantly more dominant. In terms of consistency of dominance within diet and age groups on the three tasks, the low-protein groups had low correlations in the range of .20 to .40, whereas the high-protein subjects had correlations in the range of .80 between tasks. Again, sex differences could not be controlled experimentally. They were evaluated statistically by summing across groups and combining all female and all male scores. Contrary to the finding in the earlier study (Wise & Zimmermann, 1973b) the females did not outcompete the males in food-competition tasks, but in the avoidance task the females did avoid more shocks than did the males.

These experiments make it evident that the dominance relationships in protein-malnourished groups of rhesus monkeys are unstable and that the appearance of behavioral dominance is under the influence of incentive value and conditions of deprivation. In order to test the role of incentive value and food deprivation in the determination of dominance in a food competition, a study was designed in which the type of incentive and degree of food deprivation were manipulated.

The 120-LP-DSE and 120-HP-DSE groups were tested in all possible combinations of pairs of animals, within and between diet groups, in the Wisconsin General Test Apparatus for food reward. On each test day a different incentive was used; raisins, Froot Loops cereal, or bits of high- or low-protein diet, and testing continued until each pair of animals had been tested on two 10-trial test sessions on each of the four incentives and under four different deprivation conditions. The following deprivation conditions were used: (a) both low- and high-protein animals on standard feeding, with testing conducted just prior to daily feeding; (b) the low-protein animals on normal diets, and the high-protein animals receiving one-half of their daily ration, with testing just prior to feeding; (c) low-protein animals on normal feeding and the high-protein animals pre-fed for 3 hours prior to testing; and (d) low-protein animals pre-fed 3 hours prior to testing and high-protein animals maintained on normal feeding, with testing just prior to daily feeding.

Statistical comparison of the groups revealed that the low-protein animals significantly outcompeted the high-protein animals in all conditions except when the high-protein monkeys were deprived of half their daily ration and when the incentive was raisins or the red-colored low-protein bits. The manipulation of incentive and deprivation conditions appeared to have very little effect on the ability of the low-protein animals to compete against the much larger high-protein control animals. It is possible that the deprivation conditions were not sufficiently severe, or the incentives did not have high enough value to alter the dominance in these animals. However, these results might more accurately represent the attitude of the high-protein monkeys toward food rather than the apparent dominance of the low-protein monkeys. It has been our experience with the high-protein monkeys that they do not work consistently for food reinforcement of any kind in the Wisconsin General Test Apparatus or in operant conditioning experiments until they have been deprived of at least half their daily ration for a week; then they only respond consistently to high-incentive value reinforcements such as grapes, raisins, or banana-flavored pellets.

In the final study of the relationships between diet, rearing conditions, and social organization, the 120-LP-ISO, 120-LP-ENR, 120-HP-ISO, and 120-HP-ENR groups were observed on three different social tasks: two food-competition tasks and one observation test in which one animal from a diet and rearing group was placed in the social playroom while the remaining animals in that group were in small cages on the floor of the room (Wise, 1973). The measure of dominance in the food competition tasks was the number of reinforcements that each of the animals was able to secure in tests in the Wisconsin General Test Apparatus and the Parallel Competition Box with another member of its diet and social group. The frequency with which a particular subject altered his role from one of subordinate (securing less than five reinforcements) to one of dominant (securing six or more reinforcements) was recorded as a reversal. The extent of the reversal was computed as the difference between the number of reinforcements secured under the subordinate conditions and the number secured under the dominant condition.

In the playroom test, the preference of the operator monkey for the other monkeys caged in the room was measured by the frequency and duration that the animal entered an area 20 cm from one of the cages. The sum of these scores over a 5 min observation was called the sociability score. The frequency and duration that a particular animal in one of these cages was approached was also recorded and the sum of these scores was called the approachability score.

An analysis of variance comparing the two diet and social groups across both food competition tasks revealed that the low-protein animals in both groups had significantly more reversals and significantly greater reversals of dominance than the high-protein groups, and that social rearing conditions had no significant effect on these measures. A more detailed analysis of the diet effect revealed that most of the variance between groups was contributed by the extremely large number of reversals and the large extent of the reversals by the 120-LP-ENR group.

An analysis of variance of the sociability and approachability measures in the playroom indicated that the 120-HP-ENR group had the highest frequency score on both measures. The 120-HP-ENR and 120-LP-ENR groups had significantly longer durations of sociability and approachability scores than the two groups raised in social isolation. The socially isolated groups did not differ from one another on any of the measures. The fact that the 120-HP-ENR group had the highest scores on these measures, while the 120-LP-ISO group consistently had the lowest scores, probably contributed to the significant diet by rearing condition interaction.

The correlation matrix of the measures taken in the Parallel Competition Box, the Wisconsin General Test Apparatus, the sociability frequency and duration, and the approachability frequency and duration are shown in Table 1. With the small number of subjects per group, only correlations of .90 and above are significant, but one can detect systematic similarities and differences across these comparisons. The socially enriched groups show higher correlations between the Parallel Competition Box and the Wisconsin General Test Apparatus than the socially isolated groups. The animals in the 120-HP-ENR and 120-LP-ISO groups tend to approach and stay near those animals that they dominated in the Parallel Competition Box and the Wisconsin General Test Apparatus. The 120-HP-ENR and 120-LP-ISO are avoided by animals that they dominated in the Wisconsin General Test Apparatus and the Parallel Competition Box.

In general, the 120-HP-ENR and 120-LP-ISO groups appear to respond to their peers in the preference test in much the same manner. Both of these groups show high sociability and low approachability scores for the animals they are dominant over in the two food-competition tasks. Taking the different measures of dominance in this experiment into consideration, it appears that the 120-HP-ENR and the 120-LP-ISO groups have the most social stability as compared to the 120-HP-ISO and the 120-LP-ENR groups. The probable source of this relationship is best understood when the behavior of these groups in the free activity in the social playroom is taken into consideration. The 120-LP-ISO group is the most aggressive in this social test, while the 120-HP-ENR group

Table 1   Correlation Matrix of Test Measures

	Parallel Competition Box (PBC)				Wisconsin General Test Apparatus (WGTA)			
	SEHP	SELP	SIHP	SILP	SEHP	SELP	SIHP	SILP
WGTA (1)	.98	.91	.68	.88				
Soc. Fre. (2)	.92	.37	−.47	.87	(2) .85	−.27	.25	.55
Soc. Dur. (3)	.67	.70	.95	.80	(3) .88	.76	.49	.41
App. Fre. (4)	−.37	.73	.62	−.57	(4) −.49	.49	.07	−.14
App. Dur. (5)	−.37	.09	−.06	−.59	(5) .47	−.20	−.47	−.15

ABBREVIATIONS SEHP, socially enriched high protein group.
SELP, socially enriched low protein group.
SIHP, socially isolated high protein group.
SILP, socially isolated low protein group.

is the least aggressive. The latter group probably approaches as normal an environment for young monkeys as can be organized in a laboratory, and as such, the identification and recognition of the dominant animal in a social situation by subordinate animals is probably acquired through mechanisms that do not require direct or contact aggression. Stable dominance relationships can be maintained through subordination responses (displacement, presenting, etc.) by the submissive animal to visual signs and gestures of dominance by the aggressive animal (Mason, 1970). In the case of the 120-LP-ISO group the subordinate animal fails to recognize the dominance signs given by the aggressive animal and fails to give the appropriate submission response; or the aggressive animal fails to respond to the submission response and an aggressive and often painful encounter ensues. The subordinate animal in this case learns to avoid the dominant animal through a series of negatively reinforcing social encounters. Thus, both the 120-HP-ENR and 120-LP-ISO groups maintain a rather stable dominance hierarchy, and the dominant animal is avoided in the preference test by both groups, but as the result of rather different reinforcement histories.

The relationships among social condition, dietary condition, dominance, and social stability in the developing rhesus monkey is highly complex. Generalizations such as "social isolation produces greater social

ıble 1   continued

	Sociability Frequency (Soc. Fre.)				Sociability Duration (Soc. Dur.)				Approachability Frequency (App. Fre.)			
	SEHP	SELP	SIHP	SILP	SEHP	SELP	SIHP	SILP	SEHP	SELP	SIHP	SILP
ˈGTA												
ıc.												
ˈe.												
ıc.	(6)											
ur.	.75	.38	−.71	.98								
ɔp.	(7)				(9)							
ˈe.	.06	.15	−.93	−.83	−.84	.73	.83	−.91				
ɔp.	(8)				(10)				(11)			
ur.	−.34	.87	−.77	−.87	−.87	.47	.25	.99	.99	.56	.74	.99

instability," or "low-protein diets produce less social stability" are not supported. Rather, one has to look at the social consequences of each of the variables. The 120-LP-ENR animals are highly motivated for food, and appear to be uninhibited by the prospect of potential injury from other animals and are highly competitive in both food-competition tests. This competition results in frequent reversals and the potential social cues that signify dominance are not transferred to the preference test. The behavior of the 120-HP-ISO group is very similar to that described by Mason (1970) of animals reared in social isolation. These animals do not seem to learn the appropriate social responses, nor do they have the ability to respond to the social cues given by other animals (Mason, 1970). Thus, both of these groups have the most fluid, or unstable, social structure. The 120-LP-ISO and 120-HP-ENR animals learn to recognize and respond to the cues that indicate dominance and they avoid approaching the animal that dominated them in the food-competition tasks, thus demonstrating the highest social stability.

Rosenblum (1961) demonstrated that young rhesus monkeys develop relatively normal social and sexual behavior if they are permitted peer–peer social experience for approximately 20 min per day during the first 2 years of life. The observations described earlier in this report (Zimmermann et al., 1972) indicate that, under similar conditions, rhesus monkeys reared on a low-protein diet and socialized daily during the first two years of life develop patterns of social behavior different from those of control animals reared on a normal diet and receiving daily social experience. The patterns of aggression, lack of play behavior, and the preponderance of nonsocial activities exhibited by the monkeys raised on low-protein diets is very similar to the behavioral patterns exhibited by rhesus monkeys raised in social isolation during their first year of life (Harlow, 1965a, 1965b; Mason, 1960, 1970; Sackett, 1968a). It is possible that the daily social experience was not sufficient for animals reared on the low-protein diet to develop normal social responses. The role of social rearing conditions and dietary regimes on the development of social behavior in the rhesus monkey was evaluated in an experiment in which three different levels of social experience were orthogonal to two levels of diet.

Six groups of at least four monkeys each were formed in which each animal was separated from the mother at 90 days of age, and began the experimental diets at 120 days of age. The three social conditions were daily social experience (DSE), social isolation for the first year of life (ISO), and group living (ENR). The usual protein diets of 25% (HP) and 3.5% (LP) were assigned to the particular social group so that the following groups were formed: 120-LP-ISO, 120-HP-ISO, 120-LP-DSE, 120-HP-DSE, 120-LP-ENR, and 120-HP-ENR. As mentioned earlier, the isolated groups (ISO) remained in their living cages without peer–peer social contact until they were 1 year of age, at which time they were placed in the social playroom for 1–1.5 hr 1 day a month. The groups designated as the daily social experience group (DSE) were placed in the social room for 1–1.5 hr 3–5 days a week beginning at 120 days of age. The groups assigned to the group living (ENR) rearing condition lived as groups in large cages and were placed in the playroom for daily social experience after they were 1 year of age. Because the previous study (Zimmerman et al., 1972) had demonstrated that it was possible to discriminate the high- from the low-protein animals using five categories of behavior, the final procedure developed in that study was followed in the experiment described below.

Subjects from one of the six groups were placed in the social playroom and were separated from the observer by a one-way plastic screen. The five categories of behavior that were observed and recorded were as follows: (1) Social aggressive interactions or behavior, which included approach, contact, mouthing, biting, chewing and grabbing, and pulling without reciprocity between the aggressor and aggressee. The animal aggressed against appeared to be motivated by fear. Also included in this category were chase, escape, submission, and brutality, which was characterized by one animal jumping on another animal, pulling hair out, biting, and pulling of the skin. (2) Social tactile contact or behavior, in which the animals mutually came into physical contact, sat quietly in a group, groomed, or mounted one another. (3) Social approach play, that is, characterized by the animals chasing, running, jumping, rough-and-tumble play with mutual participation. It did not appear motivated by fear and included active approach, mouthing, and biting with reciprocity. (4) Object-oriented (nonsocial) behavior, consisting of chain-pulling and chewing, licking or chewing wood, bars, and other cage parts. (5) Undirected behavior (nonsocial), which involved sitting, standing, or pacing without visible direction, self-clutching and self-stimulation.

Observations were recorded by the observer using a hand-held box containing five typewriter keys attached to microswitches. When the key was depressed, a counter was activated for a frequency count, and a clock was activated for a measure of duration in seconds. Each animal was observed for 5 min and at the end of each observation the cumulative frequency and duration recorded on the counters and clocks were entered into the data log and the counters and clocks reset for the next 5 min observation. The order of observation was randomized for each daily session and the cumulative duration measured were converted to percent of total time for each behavior category, as there was some variation in the 5 min observation interval.

The data selected for analysis were the 12 monthly observations taken during the second year of life of the 120-HP-ISO and 120-LP-ISO groups and 12 samples taken from each corresponding month of the daily observations of the 120-HP-ENR, 120-LP-ENR, 120-HP-DSE, and 120-LP-DSE groups. The frequency and duration measures for the five categories of behavior were subjected to an analysis of variance for independent groups with unequal subject numbers (Winer, 1971). Table 2 shows the mean and p values for each behavior category for frequency and duration.

The results may be summarized as follows:

1. Social aggression interaction. (a) Frequency: the low-protein groups are significantly more aggressive than the high-protein groups. The 120-LP-ISO animals are the most aggressive and the 120-HP-ENR are the least aggressive. The animals who were socialized daily did not differ significantly from the enriched groups, but the isolate groups were more aggressive than the groups socialized daily. This pattern

Table 2 Frequency and Duration Measures for Social and Diet Groups

Diet Group/Activity	Frequency of Activity[a,b]			Duration of Activity[a,b]		
	ISO	DSE	ENR	ISO	DSE	ENR
Social Aggression						
Low protein	1.42	.96	.88	4	5	7
High protein	.76	.22	.11	4	2	1
p	.05	ns	.01	ns	ns	.01
Tactile contact						
Low protein	.65	1.05	3.40	7	9	36
High protein	.55	1.21	2.90	9	22	30
p	.05	.05	ns	.05	.01	ns
Approach play						
Low protein	.92	1.42	1.50	14	16	19
High protein	2.11	3.15	3.92	32	36	41
p	.01	.05	.01	ns	ns	ns
Nonsocial, object-oriented						
Low protein	3.40	1.94	2.11	37	31	17
High protein	2.93	1.85	2.09	28	22	15
p	.05	ns	ns	ns	ns	ns
Nonsocial, non-object-oriented						
Low protein	3.03	2.47	2.31	38	29	17
High protein	2.96	1.82	1.91	27	18	13
p	.05	ns	.05	.05	.01	.05

[a] ISO = social isolation.
DSE = daily social experience.
ENR = group living.
[b] Values given are mean and *p*; *p* values in italic.

of means produced a significant diet $\times$ social condition interaction. (*b*) Duration: the only source of significant variance on this measure was diet. The low-protein animals engaged in significantly longer aggressive interactions.

2. Tactile contact. Diet had no measurable effect on this category of behavior in either frequency or duration, but social rearing conditions were significantly different in both measures. The socially enriched groups had the highest frequency and duration scores, the isolates the lowest, and the animals socialized daily were midway between these two groups. This particular category is probably contaminated with behaviors that would normally be classified as self-clutching in the 120-LP-ENR group. This group of animals tended to show the choo-choo effect described by Harlow & Harlow (1962). These animals maintained an infantile clinging response to one another, which tended to inflate this particular category for this group (Fig. 20). Mutual clinging was almost

Fig. 20. 120-LP-ENR group in social room. Example of mutual clutching.

completely absent in the 120-HP-ENR group, but they did spend considerable time near, touching, and grooming one another. This qualitative difference between the 120-LP-ENR and 120-HP-ENR groups was not brought out in the quantitative measures.

3. Approach play. (*a*) Frequency: the high-protein groups engaged in significantly more play behavior than did the low-protein groups, and the social conditions are ordered from highest to lowest on this measure: enriched, daily, and isolate. The diet $\times$ social condition interaction was also significant. The extremely low score by the 120-LP-ISO group probably contributed to this significant source of variance. (*b*) Duration: the high-protein groups spent significantly longer time in this activity than did the low-protein groups.

4. Object-oriented (Nonsocial). (*a*) Frequency: the isolate groups had a significantly higher score on this measure than the daily social groups but did not differ from the enriched groups. (*b*) Duration: the low-protein groups spent significantly more time orienting toward inanimate objects than did the high-protein groups.

5. Non-object-oriented actions (nonsocial). Both frequency and duration measures showed the same pattern in this category of behavior. The low-protein animals had a greater frequency and duration than the high-protein animals. The isolate groups had a significantly greater frequency and duration than either of the other groups.

The pattern of behavior shown by the 120-LP-DSE and 120-HP-DSE groups was very similar to that shown by the 210-LP-DSE and 210-HP-DSE groups in the earlier experiment, and for the most part their behavior was midway between the performance of the isolated and that of the enriched social groups. The combination of a low-protein diet and social isolation during the first year of life appears to create an animal that is very similar to animals raised under extreme social isolation (Mason, 1960, 1970; Harlow, 1965a, 1965b; Sackett, 1968a). This particular combination produces a group of animals in which the consequences of most of the social interactions is active aggression on the part of the dominant animal. Summing the mean frequency of the three social interaction categories and computing the percent of social interactions that were aggressive in this group reveals that 54% of the social interactions were aggressive in nature. The same analysis for the HP-ENR group revealed a 2% frequency of aggression. It is interesting to note that the variable of high- and low-protein diet appears to have its greatest effect on the appearance of aggressive behavior, whereas grooming and other forms of tactile behavior are apparently under the control of social rearing conditions.

The social behavior patterns of the 120-LP-ISO group are the most deviant or abnormal, and the social behavior of the 120-HP-ENR group approaches the behavioral description of infant monkeys raised under conditions that simulate the normal ecology of the developing rhesus monkey (Sackett, 1968b), and the groups under other combinations of diet and social conditions fall between these two extremes.

The experiments on dominance, social stability, and social interaction, clearly demonstrate that the variables of protein malnutrition and social experience are synergistic in terms of the development of social behavior patterns in small groups of young monkeys. Low-protein diets administered early in life apparently contribute to the development of behavior that is maladaptive in social interactions and social inexperience appears to exaggerate this effect. In the experiments described, extensive social experience early in life did not eliminate, although it might have modulated, the deviant behavior patterns associated with chronic protein malnutrition. The relationship between the development of social behavior in the monkey and the factors of diet and social experience is highly complex. Certain behaviors appear to be altered more by diet, while others appear to be under the control of social variables. These results must be considered preliminary and a more detailed analysis of the alteration of specific behavior patterns under a variety of social and dietary conditions is essential if we are going to unravel the subtle behavioral interactions that evolve under the influence of these variables.

Malnutrition and Other Forms of Deprivation

Zimmermann et al. (1972) speculated that protein malnutrition might interfere with the normal development of social behavior in the monkey in much the same manner as perceptual or social isolation. As such we would expect that the malnutrition condition would interact with social rearing conditions because it would be operating through a process or mechanism that is identical with, or highly similar to, those processes or mechanisms that are operating to produce behavioral deficiencies in the perceptually or socially deprived monkey.

Levitsky & Barnes (1973) have also speculated that malnutrition early in the life of the rat and pig probably operated through the same mechanism as stimulus deprivation, in producing emotional differences between normal and malnourished animals. They cite the similarities between the emotional responsiveness and overreactivity of malnourished animals and animals raised under stimulus deprivation conditions as evidence for this speculation. These authors suggest that a factorially designed experiment in which diet and environmental rearing conditions are varied

Table 3 Behavioral Abnormalities Detected in Protein–Calorie Malnourished Monkeys and Monkeys Raised under Social Isolation or Perceptual Impoverishment

Behavior	Malnutrition Experiments	Isolation or Impoverishment Experiments
First year		
1. Self-clutching, crouching, rocking	Zimmermann & Strobel, 1969; Zimmermann et al., 1972, 1974	Harlow, 1950; Harlow & Zimmermann, 1959; Mason, 1970
2. Reduced response to complex stimuli	Zimmermann & Strobel, 1969; Strobel & Zimmermann, 1971	Bernstein & Mason, 1962; Sackett, 1965; Mason, 1961a
3. Greatly increased self sucking, self-directed oral activity	Stoffer et al., 1973; Zimmermann et al., 1973, 1974	Cross & Harlow, 1965; Benjamin, 1961
Age 1–2 years		
1. Almost no sexual behavior	Zimmermann et al., 1972	Foley, 1934; Harlow, 1965a, 1965b
2. Maintenance of infantile responses	Zimmermann et al., 1972, 1974	Foley, 1934
3. Greatly reduced self and social grooming	Zimmermann et al., 1972, 1974	Mason, 1960; Foley, 1935
4. Autoeroticism	Stoffer et al., 1973	Cross & Harlow, 1965
5. Catatonic contractions	Stoffer et al., 1973; Wise & Zimmermann, 1973a	Cross & Harlow, 1965
6. Aversion to novel stimuli	Zimmermann & Strobel, 1969; Strobel, 1972 Strobel & Zimmermann, 1972	Mason & Green, 1962
Age 2 years to puberty		
1. Minimum sexual behavior	Zimmermann et al., 1972, 1973	Mitchell, 1970

2. Low rate of grooming	Zimmermann et al., 1972	Mitchell, 1970
3. Hyperaggressiveness in social situations	Zimmermann et al., 1972, 1973, 1974	Foley, 1935; Mason, 1960; Mason, 1961; Sackett, 1968a,b;
4. Dominance relationships unstable	Wise & Zimmermann, 1973b; Wise, 1973	Mitchell & Clark, 1968; Mason, 1963a
5. Low level of play behavior	Zimmermann and Strobel, 1969; Zimmermann et al., 1972	Mitchell et al., 1966
6. High fear or arousal	Wise & Zimmermann, 1973a,b; Zimmermann & Strobel, 1969, 1970	Mitchell et al., 1966; Mitchell & Clark, 1968; Mason, 1970
7. Idiosyncratic or bizarre movements	Stoffer et al., 1973; Wise & Zimmermann, 1973a; Strobel, 1972	Mitchell et al., 1966
8. Decreased exploratory behavior and aversion to novel stimuli	Zimmermann & Strobel, 1970; Strobel & Zimmermann, 1972; Aakre et al., 1973 Strobel & Zimmermann, 1972 Strobel, 1972	Sackett, 1968b
9. No deficits in discrimination learning, delay response, oddity, etc.	Zimmermann et al., 1974	Rowland, 1964; Harlow et al., 1968
10. Apparent poor stimulus control in generalization tasks	Zimmermann, 1970; Strobel, 1972	Ganz, 1968

181

orthogonally would produce a significant interaction between diet and environment so that the detrimental effects of social isolation would be exaggerated when combined with malnutrition. This expectation has been confirmed in our last social experiment.

In Table 3, the behavioral abnormalities that appear as a result of social restriction, social isolation, or impoverished perceptual environments that are comparable to the behavioral deficiencies found in our studies with malnourished monkeys are listed. The mere frequency of the similarities are impressive and suggest that the proposal linking the outcomes of early sensory and social deprivation with protein–calorie malnutrition may not be far afield.

Sackett (1968b) has proposed a theory of the effects of early experience on primates that would provide a primary underlying mechanism for mediating the syndrome seen in malnourished and stimulus-deprived monkeys. He describes this mechanism as an inhibitory process that permits the developing organism to stop making innate and learned infantile emotional and maladaptive responses that would interfere with normal associative learning, and the ability to adjust to stimulus change. A breakdown or failure to develop the appropriate inhibitory responses would produce an animal that was unable to modify its behavior in the face of stimulus change, and would persist in stereotyped, and over-reactive emotional responses to intense or noxious stimulation.

The development of a system of inhibitory responses to momentary stimulation is essential if the animal is going to learn new responses to variations in stimulation. Sackett (1968b) likens this process to an information-analyzing system in which the inhibitory process allows information concerning new stimulation to act as a feedback system for informing the organism about the function and consequences of the new stimulus setting. Animals that do not have this inhibitory system are unable to assimilate any of this new information, because they are incapable of attending to the new properties of the incongruous stimulation except in the innate and learned behavior patterns that they used in response to less complex stimuli or to stimuli that were familiar.

One experiment was conducted at our laboratory to test this theoretical analysis. It was hypothesized that low-protein-reared monkeys, which tend to overreact to novel stimulation, would demonstrate disinhibition of delay to the introduction of stimulation during a delay period in which the animal had learned to inhibit responses. The normal monkey, on the other hand, would show a suppression effect, or no effect of the extraneous stimulation on the inhibited behavior.

Low- and high-protein-raised monkeys were trained to press a lever on a fixed-interval schedule of 2 min duration for food pellet rewards in an operant chamber. After conditioning had stabilized so that few, if any, responses were emitted during the first minute of the interval, a loud whistle-like noise was introduced during that time interval. The low-protein-reared monkeys showed a significant increase in responses during the first minute interval, but the signal had no effect, or a suppressing effect, on the response rate of the high-protein-reared animals.

Whether or not protein malnutrition and environmental deprivation are producing behavioral changes through the same underlying mechanism is academic and more detailed experimental analysis and testing of theories such as Sackett's are required to validate some of the hypotheses he has developed. The primary findings of our own research are that protein–calorie malnutrition has a major effect on the development of motivation and emotional systems in the rhesus monkey. Learning in situations that would demand the inhibition or control of motivational and emotional responses would be deficient and the organism would be unable to develop its full cognitive, intellectual, and social potential.

Even though the primary mechanisms underlying intellectual development are not directly altered by protein–calorie malnutrition, it is clear that a developing primate that finds new things or sudden changes in the environment aversive, has reduced curiosity and manipulatory motivation, cannot cope with discontiguities in stimulus-response events in an efficient manner, is hyperreactive to stimulation, makes persistent maladaptive responses to aversive stimulation, and is incapable of forming stable social relationships except through aggressive actions, would be at a serious disadvantage in the highly complex and competitive niche in which most primates find themselves.

Acknowledgments

This research was supported in part by the Nutrition Foundation Grant 401 and the National Institutes of Child Health and Human Development Grant RPI-HD-04863. This chapter was written while the senior author was completing the last 90 days of his appointment at the University of Montana. The studies on social development could not have been completed without the diligent and persevering efforts of Mrs. Wanda Gordon. Others who contributed significant time and effort to the project were: Ray Guest, Ed Shea, Dave Strobel, Gerry Stoffer, Bea Aaker, Tom Cleveland, Tim Fredrickson, and students too numerous to mention.

References

Aakre, B., Strobel, D. A., Zimmermann, R. R., & Geist, C. R. (1973). Reactions to intrinsic and extrinsic reward in protein malnourished monkeys. *Percept. Motor Skills*, **36**, 787–790.

Ader, R. (1959). The effects of early experience on subsequent emotionality and resistance to stress. *Psychol. Mono.*, 73, (2, Whole, No. 472).

Anderson, J. E., & Smith, A. H. (1926). The effect of quantitative stunting upon maze learning in the white rat. *J. Comp. Psychol.*, 6, 337–359.

Anderson, J. E., & Smith, A. H. (1932). Relation of performance to age and nutritive condition in the white rat. *J. Comp. Psychol.*, 13, 409–446.

Angermeier, W. F., Phelps, J. B., Murray, S., & Howansteine, J. (1968). Dominance in monkeys: Sex differences. *Psychon. Sci.*, 12, 344.

Angermeier, W. F., Phelps, J. B., & Reynolds, H. H. (1967). The effects of differential early rearing upon discrimination learning in monkeys. *Psychon. Sci.*, 8, 379–380.

Barnes, R. H. (1972). Experimental studies in animals: Physiological and behavioral correlates of malnutrition. *In* W. M. Moore, M. M. Silverberg, and M. S. Reid (Eds.), *Nutrition, growth, and development of North American Indian children*. Dept. of Health, Education, and Welfare Publ. No. (NIH) 72–26, Washington, D. C. Pp. 121–128.

Barnes, R. H., Cunnold, S. R., Zimmermann, R. R., Simmons, H., MacLeod, R. B., & Krook, L. (1966). Influences of nutritional deprivations in early life on learning behavior of rats as measured by performance in a water maze. *J. Nutr.*, 89, 399–410.

Barnes, R. H., Moore, A. U., & Pond, W. G. (1970). Behavioral abnormalities in young adult pigs caused by malnutrition in early life. *J. Nutr.*, 100, 149–155.

Barnes, R. H., Neely, C. S., Kwong, E., Labadan, B. A., & Frankova, S. (1968). Postnatal nutritional deprivations as determinants of adult behavior toward food, its consumption and utilization. *J. Nutr.*, 96, 467–476.

Barnes, R. H., Reid, I. M., Pond, W. G., & Moore, A. U. (1968). The use of experimental animals in studying behavioral abnormalities following recovery from early malnutrition. *In* R. A. McCance & E. M. Widdowson (Eds.), *Calorie deficiencies and protein deficiencies*. Little, Brown, Boston. Pp. 277–285.

Behar, M. (1968). Prevalence of malnutrition among preschool children of developing countries. In N. S. Scrimshaw & J. E. Gordon (Eds.), *Malnutrition, learning, and behavior*. MIT Press, Cambridge. Pp. 30–41.

Benjamin, L. S. (1961). The effect of frustration of the nonnutritive sucking of the infant rhesus monkey. *J. Comp. Physiol. Psychol.*, 54, 700–703.

Berkson, G., Mason, W. A., & Saxon, S. V. (1963). Situation and stimulus effects of stereotyped behaviors of chimpanzees. *J. Comp. Physiol. Psychol.*, 56, 786–792.

Bernstein, S., & Mason, W. A. (1962). The effects of age and stimulus conditions on the emotional responses of rhesus monkeys: Responses to complex stimuli. *J. Genet. Psychol.*, 101, 279–298.

Biel, W. C. (1938). The effect of early inanition upon maze learning in the albino rat. *Comp. Psychol. Monogr.*, 15, 1–33.

Blomquist, A. J., & Harlow, H. F. (1961). The infant rhesus monkey program at the University of Wisconsin Primate Laboratory. *Proc. Animal Care Panel*, II, 57–64.

Brockman, L. M., & Ricciuti, H. N. (1971). Severe protein–calorie malnutrition and cognitive development in infancy and early childhood. *Develop. Psychol.*, 4, 312–319.

Caldwell, D. J., & Churchill, J. A. (1966). Learning impairment in rats administered a lipid free diet during pregnancy. *Psychol. Rep.* **19,** 99–102.

Caldwell, D. J., & Churchill, J. A. (1967). Learning in the progeny of rats administered a protein deficient diet during the second half of gestation. *Neurology,* **17,** 95–99.

Canosa, C. A., Solomon, R. L., & Klein, R. E. (1973). The intervention approach: The Guatemala study. In W. M. Moore, M. M. Silverberg, & M. S. Read (Eds.), *Nutrition, growth and development of North American Indian children,* Dept. of Health, Education and Welfare Publ. No. (NIH) 72-26, Washington, D. C. Pp. 185–199.

Chase, H. P., & Martin, H. P. (1970). Undernutrition and child development. *New Engl. J. Med.,* **282,** 933–939.

Coursin, D. B. (1965). Effect of undernutrition on CNS function. *Nutr. Rev.,* **23,** 65.

Cowley, J. J., & Griesel, R. D. (1959). Some effects of low protein diet on a first filial generation of white rats. *J. Genet. Psychol.,* **95,** 187–201.

Cowley, J. J., & Griesel, R. D. (1962). Pre- and post-natal effects of a low protein diet on the behavior of the white rat. *Psychol. Afr.,* **9,** 216–225.

Cowley, J. J., & Griesel, R. D. (1963). The development of a second generation of low protein rats. *J. Genet. Psychol.,* **103,** 233–242.

Cowley, J. J., & Griesel, R. D. (1964). Low-protein diet and emotionality in the albino rat. *J. Genet. Psychol.,* **104,** 89–98.

Cravioto, J. (1968). Nutritional deficiencies and mental performance in childhood. In D. C. Glass (Ed.), *Environmental influences.* Rockefeller University Press, New York. Pp. 3–51.

Cravioto, J., & Robles, B. (1965). Evolution of adaptive and motor behavior during rehabilitation from kwashiorkor. *Amer. J. Orthopsychiat.,* **35,** 449–464.

Cravioto, J., & Robles, B. (1963). The influence of protein–calorie malnutrition on psychological test behavior. In G. Blix (Ed.), *Mild–moderate forms of protein–calorie malnutrition.* Almqvist & Wiksells, Uppsala, Sweden, Pp. 115–125.

Cross, H. A., & Harlow, H. F. (1965). Prolonged and progressive effects of partial isolation on the behavior of macaque monkeys. *J. Exp. Res. Personality,* **1,** 39–49.

Denenberg, V. H. (1964). Critical periods, stimulus inputs and emotional reactivity: A theory of infantile stimulation. *Psychol. Rev.,* **71,** 335–351.

Denenberg, V. H. (1969). Open field behavior in the rat: What does it mean? *Ann. N.Y. Acad. Sci.* **159,** 852–859.

Denenberg, V. H., & Bell, R. W. (1960). Critical periods for the effects of infantile experience on adult learning. *Science,* **131,** 227–228.

Denenberg, V. H., & Karas, G. G. (1960). Interactive effects of age and duration of infantile experience on adult learning. *Psychol. Rep.,* **7,** 313–322.

Eichenwald, H. F., & Fry, P. C. (1969). Nutrition and learning. *Science,* **163,** 644–649.

Elliott, O., & King, J. A. (1960). Effect of early food deprivation upon later consummatory behavior in puppies. *Psychol. Rep.,* **6,** 391–400.

Fantz, R. L. (1965). Ontogeny of perception. In A. M. Schrier, H. F. Harlow,

& R. Stollnitz (Eds.), *Behavior of nonhuman primates.* Vol. 2. Academic Press, New York. Pp. 365–404.

Foley, J. P. (1934). First year development of a rhesus monkey (*Macaca mulatta*) reared in isolation. *J. Genet. Psychol.,* 45, 39–105.

Foley, J. P. (1935). Second year development of a rhesus monkey (*Macaca mulatta*) reared in isolation during the first eighteen months. *J. Genet. Psychol.,* 47, 73–97.

Forgays, D. B., & Forgays, J. W. (1952). The nature of the effect of free environment experience in the rat. *J. Comp. Physiol. Psychol.,* 45, 322–328.

Forgus, R. H. (1955). Early visual and motor experience as determiners of complex maze learning ability under rich and reduced stimulation. *J. Comp. Physiol. Psychol.,* 48, 215–220.

Frankova, S. (1968). Nutritional and psychological factors in the development of spontaneous behavior in the rat. In N. S. Scrimshaw & J. E. Gordon (Eds.), *Malnutrition, learning and behavior.* MIT Press, Cambridge. Pp. 312–323.

Frankova, S., & Barnes, R H. (1968a). Effect of malnutrition in early life on avoidance conditioning and behavior of adult rats. *J. Nutr.,* 96, 485–493.

Frankova, S., & Barnes, R. H. (1968b). Influence of malnutrition in early life on exploratory behavior of rats. *J. Nutr.,* 96, 477–484.

Fuller, J. L. (1968). Experiential deprivation and later behavior. *Science,* 158, 1645–1652.

Ganz, L. (1968). Generalization behavior in the stimulus deprived organism. In G. Newton & S. Levin (Eds.), *Early experience and behavior.* Charles C Thomas, Springfield, Ill. Pp. 364–441.

Geist, C. R. (1973). Performance of rats raised on low protein diets in a water maze. *Papers, Proc. Montana Psychol. Assoc.*

Geist, C. R., Zimmermann, R. R., & Strobel, D. A. (1972). Effect of protein–calorie malnutrition on food consumption, weight gain, serum proteins, and activity in the developing rhesus monkey (*Macaca mulatta*). *Lab. Anim. Sci.,* 22, 369–377.

Gill, J. H., Reid, L. D., & Porter, P. B. (1966). Effect of restricted rearing on Lashley Strand performance. *Psychol. Rep.,* 19, 239–244.

Gluck, J. P., & Harlow, H. F. (1971). The effects of deprived and enriched rearing conditions on later learning: A review. In L. E. Jarrard (Ed.), *Cognitive processes of nonhuman primates.* Academic Press, New York. Pp. 102–120.

Griffiths, W., & Senter, R. (1954). The effect of protein deficiency on maze performance of domestic Norway rats. *J. Comp. Physiol. Psychol.,* 47, 41–43.

Guetzkow, H. S., & Bowman, P. H. (1946). *Men and hunger.* Brethen Publishing House, Elgin, Ill.

Guthrie, H. A. (1968). Severe undernutrition in early infancy and behavior in rehabilitated albino rats. *Physiol. Behav.,* 3, 619–623.

Harlow, H. F. (1950). Learning and satiation of response in intrinsically motivated complex puzzle performance by monkeys. *J. Comp. Physiol. Psychol.,* 43, 289–294.

Harlow, H. F. (1959). Learning set and error factor theory. In S. Koch (Ed.), *Psychology: A study of a science.* Vol. II. McGraw-Hill, New York. Pp. 492–537.

Harlow, H. F. (1965a). The effects of early social deprivation on primates. *Tire a Part, Symposium Bel Air II, Desafferentation Experimentales at Cliniques.* George & Co., Geneva, Switzerland. Pp. 66–77.

Harlow, H. F. (1965b). Total social isolation in monkeys. *Proc. Nat. Acad. Sci.*, **54**, 90–97.

Harlow, H. F., & Harlow, M. K. (1962). Social deprivation in monkeys. *Sci. Amer.*, **207**, 136–146.

Harlow, H. F., & Harlow, M. K. (1965). The affectional systems. In A. M. Schrier, H. F. Harlow, & F. Stollnitz (Eds.), *Behavior of nonhuman primates*. Vol. 2. Academic Press, New York. Pp. 405–448.

Harlow, H. F., Harlow, M. K., Schiltz, K. A., & Mohr, M. K. (1968). The effect of early adverse and enriched environments on the learning ability of rhesus monkeys. In L. E. Jarrard (Ed.), *Cognitive processes of nonhuman primates*. Academic Press, New York. Pp. 121–148.

Harlow, H. F., & Seay, B. (1966). Mothering in motherless mother monkeys. *Brit. J. Soc. Psychiat.*, **1**, 63–69.

Harlow, H. F., & Zimmermann, R. R. (1959). Affectional responses in the infant monkey. *Science*, **130**, 421–432.

Hays, C. (1951). *The ape in our house*. Harper, New York.

Hebb, D. O. (1937a). The innate organization of visual acuity. I. Perception of figures by rats reared in total darkness. *J. Genet. Psychol.*, **51**, 101–126.

Hebb, D. O. (1937b). The innate organization of visual acuity. II. Transfer of responses in the discrimination of brightness and size by rats reared in total darkness. *J. Comp. Psychol.*, **24**, 277–299.

Hebb, D. O. (1947). The effects of early experience on problem solving at maturity. *Amer. Psychol.*, **2**, 306–307.

Hebb, D. O. (1949). *The organization of behavior*. Wiley, New York.

Hebb, D. O., & Williams, K. A. (1946). Method of rating animal intelligence. *J. Genet. Psychol.*, **34**, 59–65.

Held, R., & Hein, A. (1963). Movement produced stimulation in the development of visually guided movement. *J. Comp. Physiol. Psychol.*, **56**, 872–876.

Hillman, N. M., & Riopelle, A. J. (1971). Acceptance and palatability of foods by protein-deprived monkeys. *Percept. Motor Skills*, **33**, 918.

Hunt, J. McV. (1941). The effects of infant feeding frustration upon hoarding in the albino rat. *J. Abnormal Soc. Psychol.*, **36**, 338–360.

Jelliffe, D. B., & Welbourn, H. F. (1963). Clinical signs of mild–moderate protein–calorie malnutrition of early childhood. In G. Blix (Ed.), *Mild–moderate forms of protein–calorie malnutrition*. Almqvist & Wiksells, Uppsala, Sweden. Pp. 12–29.

Kellogg, W. N., & Kellogg, L. A. (1933). *The ape and the child*. McGraw-Hill, New York.

Keys, A., Brozek, J., Henschel, A., Michelson, O., & Taylor, H. (1950). *The biology of starvation*. University of Minnesota Press, Minneapolis.

Klein, R. E., Gilbert, O., Canosa, C., & DeLeon, R. (1969). Performance of malnourished children in comparison with adequately nourished children. *Papers Ann. Meet. Amer. Assoc. Advance. Sci., December 1969.*

Krech, D., Rosenzweig, M. R., & Bennett, E. L. (1962). Relations between brain chemistry and problem solving among rats raised in enriched and impoverished environments. *J. Comp. Physiol. Psychol.*, **55**, 801–807.

Levine, S. (1959). The effects of differential infantile stimulation on emotionality at weaning. *Can. J. Psychol.*, **13**, 243–247.

Levine, S., Chevalier, J. A., & Korchin, S. J. (1956). The effects of shock and handling in infancy on later avoidance learning. *J. Personal.*, **24**, 475–493.

Levine, S., & Welzel, A. (1963). Infantile experiences, strain differences, and avoidance learning. *J. Comp. Physiol. Psychol.*, **56**, 879–881.

Levitsky, D., & Barnes, R. (1970). Effects of early protein–calorie malnutrition on animal behavior. *Nature*, **225**, 468–469.

Levitsky, D. A., & Barnes, R. H. (1972). Nutritional and environmental interaction in the behavioral development of the rat: Long term effects. *Science*, **176**, 68–71.

Levitsky, D., & Barnes, H. (1973). Malnutrition and animal behavior. In D. J. Kallen (Ed.), *Nutrition, development, and social behavior*, U.S. Dept. of Health, Education, and Welfare, Publ. No. (NIH) 73-242, Washington, D. C. P. 3–14.

Locke, K. D., Locke, E. A., Morgan, G. A., & Zimmermann, R. R. (1964). Dimensions of social interactions among infant rhesus monkeys. *Psychol. Rep.*, **15**, 339–349.

Mandler, J. M. (1958). Effects of early food deprivation on adult behavior in the rat. *J. Comp. Physiol. Psychol.*, **51**, 513–517.

Maroney, R., & Leary, R. (1957). A failure to condition submission in monkeys. *Psychol. Rep.*, **3**, 472.

Maroney, R. J., Warren, J. M., & Sinha, M. M. (1959). Stability of social dominance hierarchies in monkeys (*Macaca mulatta*). *J. Soc. Psychol.*, **50**, 285–293.

Marx, M. H. (1952). Infantile deprivation and adult behavior in the rat: Retention of increased rate of eating. *J. Comp. Physiol. Psychol.*, **45**, 43–49.

Mason, W. A. (1960). The effects of social restriction on the behavior of rhesus monkeys: I. Free social behavior. *J. Comp. Physiol. Psychol.*, **53**, 582–589.

Mason, W. A. (1961a). Effects of age and stimulus characteristics on manipulatory responsiveness of monkeys raised in a restricted environment. *J. Genet. Psychol.*, **99**, 301–308.

Mason, W. A. (1961b). The effects of social restriction on the behavior of rhesus monkeys. III. Dominance tests. *J. Comp. Physiol. Psychol.*, **54**, 694–699.

Mason, W. A. (1963a). The effects of environmental restriction on the social development of rhesus monkeys. In C. H. Southwick (Ed.), *Primate social behavior*. D. Van Nostrand, Princeton. Pp. 161–173.

Mason, W. A. (1963b). Social development of rhesus monkeys with restricted social experience. *Percept. Motor Skills*, **16**, 263–270.

Mason, W. A. (1970). Motivational factors in psychosocial development. In W. J. Arnold & M. M. Page (Eds.), *Nebraska symposium on motivation*. University of Nebraska Press, Lincoln. Pp. 35–68.

Mason, W. A., Davenport, R. K., & Menzel, E. W. (1968). Early experience and the social development of rhesus monkeys and chimpanzees. In G. Newton and S. Levine (Eds.), *Early experience and behavior*. Charles C Thomas, Springfield, Ill. Pp. 440–480.

Mason, W. A., & Green, P. H. (1962). The effects of social restriction on the behavior of rhesus monkeys: IV. Responses to novel environment and to an alien species. *J. Comp. Physiol. Psychol.*, **55**, 363–368.

Mason, W. A., Harlow, H. F., & Rueping, R. (1959). The development of manipulatory responsiveness in the infant rhesus monkey. *J. Comp. Physiol. Psychol.,* **52,** 555–558.

Melzack, R. (1961). The perception of pain. *Sci. Amer.,* **204,** 41–49.

Melzack, R. (1962). Effects of early perceptual restriction on simple visual discrimination. *Science,* **137,** 978–979.

Menzel, E. W., Jr. (1963). The effects of cumulative experience on responses to novel objects in young isolation reared chimpanzees. *Behavior,* **21,** 1–12.

Meyer, D. R., Treichler, F. R., & Meyer, P. M. (1965). Discrete-trial training techniques and stimulus variables. In A. Schrier, H. Harlow, & F. Stollnitz (Eds.), *Behavior of nonhuman primates, Modern research trends.* Academic Press, New York. Pp. 1–49.

Meyers, W. J. (1962). Critical period for the facilitation of exploratory behavior in infantile experience. *J. Comp. Physiol. Psychol.,* **55,** 1099–1101.

Mitchell, G. D. (1970). Abnormal behavior in primates. In L. N. Rosenblum (Ed.), *Primate Behavior Vol. I.* Academic Press, New York. Pp. 195–249.

Mitchell, G. D., & Clark, D. L. (1968). Long-term effects of social isolation in nonsocially adapted rhesus monkeys. *J. Genet. Psychol.,* **113,** 117–128.

Mitchell, G. D., Raymond, E. J., Ruppenthal, G. C., & Harlow, H. F. (1966). Long-term effects of total social isolation upon behavior of rhesus monkeys. *Psychol. Rep.,* **18,** 567–580.

Monckeberg, F. (1968). Effect of early marasmic malnutrition on subsequent physical and psychological development. In N. S. Scrimshaw & J. E. Gordon (Eds.), *Malnutrition, learning, and behavior.* MIT Press, Cambridge. Pp. 269–278.

Nyman, A. J. (1967). Problem solving in rats as a function of experience at different ages. *J. Genet. Psychol.,* **110,** 31–39.

Ordy, J. M., Samorajski, T., Zimmermann, R. R., & Rady, P. M. (1966). Effects of postnatal protein deficiency on weight gain, serum proteins, enzymes, cholesterol, and liver ultrastructure in a subhuman primate (*Macaca mulatta*). *Amer. J. Pathol.,* **48,** 769–791.

Ottinger, D. R., & Tanabe, G. (1972). Maternal food restriction: Effects on offspring behavior and development. *Develop. Psychol.,* **2,** 7–9.

Peregoy, P. L., Zimmermann, R. R., & Strobel, D. A. (1972). Protein preference in protein malnourished monkeys. *Percept. Motor Skills,* **35,** 495–503.

Pollitt, E. (1972). Behavioral correlates of severe malnutrition in man. In W. M. Moore, M. M. Silverberg, & M. S. Reid (Eds.), *Nutrition, growth, and development of North American Indian children.* Dept. of Health, Education, and Welfare Publ. No. (NIH) 76–26, Washington, D. C. Pp. 151–166.

Rajalakshimi, R., Govindarajan, K. R., & Ramakrishnan, C. V. (1965). Effect of dietary protein content on visual discrimination learning and brain biochemistry in the albino rat. *J. Neurochem.,* **12,** 261–271.

Riesen, A. H. (1959). Plasticity of behavior: Psychological aspects. In H. F. Harlow & C. N. Woolsey (Eds.), *Biological and biochemical basis of behavior.* University of Wisconsin Press, Madison. Pp. 425–450.

Riesen, A. H. (1961). Excessive arousal effects of stimulation after early sensory deprivation. In P. Solomon, P. E. Kubzansky, P. H. Liederman, J. H. Mendelson,

R. Trumbull, & D. Wexler (Eds.), *Sensory deprivation*. Harvard University Press, Cambridge. Pp. 34–40.

Rosenblum, L. A. (1961). The development of social behavior in the rhesus monkey. Unpublished doctoral dissertation. University of Wisconsin.

Rosenzweig, M. R. (1966). Environmental complexity, cerebral change, and behavior. *Amer. Psychol.*, **21**, 321–332.

Rowland, G. L. (1964). The effect of total social isolation upon learning and social behavior in rhesus monkeys. Unpublished doctoral dissertation. University of Wisconsin.

Ruch, F. L. (1932). The effect of inanition upon maze learning in the white rat. *J. Comp. Psychol.*, **14**, 321–329.

Rumbaugh, D. M., & Pournelle, M. E. (1966). Discrimination-reversal skills of primates: The reversal-acquisition ratio as a function of phyletic standing. *Psychon. Sci.*, **4**, 45–46.

Sackett, G. P. (1965). Manipulatory behavior in monkeys reared under different levels of early stimulus variation. *Percept. Motor Skills*, **20**, 985–988.

Sackett, G. P. (1967). Response to stimulus novelty and complexity as a function of rats' early rearing experience. *J. Comp. Physiol. Psychol.*, **63**, 369–375.

Sackett, G. P. (1968a). Abnormal behavior in laboratory reared rhesus monkeys. In M. W. Fox (Ed.), *Abnormal behavior in animals*. Saunders, New York. Pp. 293–331.

Sackett, G. P. (1968b). Innate mechanisms, rearing conditions and a theory of early experience effects in primates. In M. R. Jones (Ed.), *Miami symposium on the prediction of behavior: Effects of early experience*. University of Miami Press, Miami, Fla. Pp. 11–53.

Schuck, J. R. (1960). Pattern discrimination and visual sampling by the monkey. *J. Comp. Physiol. Psychol.*, **53**, 251–255.

Schuck, J. R., Polidora, V. J., McConnell, D. C., & Meyer, D. R. (1961). Response location as a factor in primate pattern discrimination. *J. Comp. Physiol. Psychol.*, **54**, 543–545.

Scott, J. P. (1958). Critical periods in the development of social behavior in puppies. *Psychon. Med.*, **20**, 42–54.

Scott, J. P., & Marston, M. V. (1950). Critical periods affecting normal and maladjustive social behavior in puppies. *J. Genet. Psychol.*, **77**, 25–60.

Sidowski, J. B., & Lockard, R. B. (1966). Some preliminary considerations in research. In J. B. Sidowski (Ed.), *Experimental methods and instrumentation in psychology*. McGraw-Hill, New York. Pp. 3–32.

Simonson, M., & Chow, B. F. (1970). Maze studies on progeny of underfed mother rats. *J. Nutr.*, **100**, 685–690.

Spalding, D. A. (1873). Instincts: With original observations on young animals. *MacMillans Magazine*, **27**, 282–293.

Stoch, M. B., & Smythe, P. J. (1963). Does undernutrition during infancy inhibit brain growth and subsequent intellectual development? *Arch. Dis. Child.*, **38**, 546.

Stoch, M. B., & Smythe, P. J. (1968). Undernutrition during infancy, and subsequent brain growth and development. In N. S. Schrimshaw & J. E. Gordon (Eds.), *Malnutrition, learning, and behavior*. MIT Press, Cambridge. Pp. 278–288.

Stoffer, G., & Zimmermann, R. R. (1973). Development of avoidance learning sets in normal and malnourished monkeys. *Behav. Biol.*, **9**, 695–705.

Stoffer, G. R., Zimmermann, R. R., & Strobel, D. A. (1973). Punishment of oral–genital self-stimulation in young rhesus monkeys. *Percept. Motor Skills*, **36**, 199–202.

Stollnitz, F. (1965). Spatial variables, observing responses, and discrimination learning sets. *Psychol. Rev.*, **72**, 247–261.

Strobel, D. A. (1972). Stimulus change and attentional variables as factors in the behavioral deficiency of malnourished developing monkeys (*Macaca mulatta*). Unpublished doctoral dissertation. University of Montana.

Strobel, D. A., & Zimmermann, R. R. (1971). Manipulatory responsiveness in protein-malnourished monkeys. *Psychon. Sci.*, **24**, 19–20.

Strobel, D. A., & Zimmermann, R. R. (1972). Responsiveness of protein deficient monkeys to manipulative stimuli. *Develop. Psychobiol.*, **5**, 291–296.

Sutherland, N. S., & Mackintosh, N. J. (1971). *Mechanisms of animal discrimination learning.* Academic Press, New York.

Thompson, W. R., & Heron, W. (1954). The effect of restricting early experience on problem solving capacity of dogs. *Can. J. Psychol.*, **8**, 17–31.

Van Hooff, J. A. R. A M. (1962). Facial expressions in higher primates. In J. Napier & N. A. Barnical (Eds.), *Symposia of the Zoological Society of London,* No. 10, The primates. The Zoological Society of London, London. Pp. 103–104.

Walk, R. D., Gibson, E. J., & Tighe, T. J. (1957). Behavior of light and dark reared rats on a visual cliff. *Science,* **126**, 80–81.

Wells, A. M., Geist, C. R., & Zimmermann, R. R. (1972). The influence of environmental and nutritional factors on problem solving in the rat. *Percept. Motor Skills,* **35**, 235–244.

Wilson, M., Warren, J. M., & Abbott, L. (1965). Infantile stimulation, activity and learning by cats. *Child Develop.*, **36**, 843–853.

Winer, B. J. (1971). Statistical principles in experimental design. McGraw-Hill, New York.

Wise, L. (1973). The effects of social experience, protein deprivation, and social coalitions on social dominance of rhesus monkeys. Unpublished doctoral dissertation. University of Montana.

Wise, L. A., & Zimmermann, R. R. (1973a). Shock thresholds of low and high protein reared rhesus monkeys. *Percept. Motor Skills,* **36**, 674.

Wise, L. A., & Zimmermann, R. R. (1973b). The effects of protein deprivation on dominance as measured by shock avoidance competition and food competition. *Behav. Biol.,* **9**, 317–329.

Wise, L. A., Zimmermann, R. R., & Strobel, D. A. (1973). Dominance measurement of low and high protein reared rhesus macaques. *Behav. Biol.,* **8**, 77–84.

Wolfe, J. B. (1939). An exploratory study of food storing in rats. *J. Comp. Psychol.,* **28**, 97–108.

Woods, P. J. (1961). The effects of free and restricted environmental experience on problem solving behavior in the rat. *J. Comp. Physiol. Psychol.,* **52**, 399–402.

Woods, P. J., Fiske, A. S., & Ruckelshaus, S. (1961). The effects of drives conflicting with exploration on the problem solving behavior of rats reared in free and restricted environments. *J. Comp. Physiol. Psychol.,* **54**, 167–169.

Wyckoff, L. B., Jr. (1952). The role of observing responses in discrimination learning: Part 1. *Psychol. Rev.,* 59, 431–442.

Young, P. T. (1955). The role of hedonic processes in motivation. In M. R. Jones (Ed.), *Nebraska symposium on motivation.* University of Nebraska Press, Lincoln. Pp. 193–237.

Zeaman, D., & House, B. J. (1963). The role of attention in retardate discrimination learning. In N. Ellis (Ed.), *Handbook of mental deficiency.* McGraw-Hill, New York. Pp. 159–223.

Zimmermann, R. R. (1969a). Early weaning and weight gain in infant rhesus monkeys. *Lab. Anim. Care,* 19, 644–647.

Zimmermann, R. R. (1969b). Effects of age, experience and malnourishment on object retention in learning set. *Percept. Motor Skills,* 28, 867–876.

Zimmermann, R. R. (1970). Stimulus discriminability and transposition sets in young monkeys. *Midwestern Psychol. Assoc. May 1970, Cincinnati.*

Zimmermann, R. R. (1973). Reversal learning in the developing malnourished rhesus monkey. *Behav. Biol.,* 8, 381–390.

Zimmermann, R. R., & Geist, C. R. (1973). A highly palatable and easy to make diet for producing protein–calorie malnutrition in the rhesus monkey. *Lab. Primate Newsletter,* 11, 1–3.

Zimmermann, R. R., Geist, C. R., Strobel, D. A., & Cleveland, T. J. (1973). Attention deficiencies in malnourished monkeys. *Symposia of the Swedish Nutrition Foundation.* Vol. XII.

Zimmermann, R. R., Steere, P. L., Strobel, D. A., & Hom, H. L. (1972). Abnormal social development of protein-malnourished rhesus monkeys. *J. Abnormal Psychol.,* 80, 125–131.

Zimmermann, R. R., & Strobel, D. A. (1969). Effects of protein–calorie malnutrition on visual curiosity, manipulation and social behavior in the infant rhesus monkey. *Proc. 77th Ann. Convention Amer. Psychol. Assoc.* Pp. 241–242.

Zimmermann, R. R., Strobel, D. A., & Maguire, D. (1970). Neophobic reactions in protein malnourished infant monkeys. *Proc. 78th Ann. Convention Amer. Psychol. Assoc.* Pp. 187–188.

Zimmermann, R. R., Strobel, D. A., Steere, P., & Geist, C. R. (1974). Behavior and malnutrition in the rhesus monkey. In L. Rosenblum (Ed.), *Primate behavior.* Vol. 4. Academic Press, New York. In Press.

Zimmermann, R. R., & Torrey, C. C. (1965). Ontogeny of learning. In A. M. Schrier, H. F. Harlow, & F. Stollnitz (Eds.), *Behavior of nonhuman primates.* Vol. 2. Academic Press, New York. Pp. 405–448.

Zimmermann, R. R., & Wells, A. M. (1971). Performance of malnourished rats on the Hebb–Williams closed-field maze learning task. *Percept. Motor Skills,* 33, 1043–1050.

Zimmermann, R. R., & Zimmermann, S. J. (1972). Responses of protein malnourished rats to novel objects. *Percept. Motor Skills,* 35, 319–321.

Chapter 4

ELECTRICAL STIMULATION OF THE BRAIN: EFFECTS ON MEMORY STORAGE

PAUL E. GOLD, STEVEN F. ZORNETZER, AND JAMES L. MCGAUGH

University of California, Irvine

The experimental demonstration of retrograde amnesia (RA), most often using electroconvulsive shock (ECS), provides a useful tool with which to study the neurobiological bases of memory. A basic assumption guiding early research in the area was that electroconvulsive shock produced a "neural storm" that interfered with memory storage processes. However, relatively little research was done to relate the concept of neural storm to meaningful neurobiological events. Many investigators have begun to examine the neurobiological bases of retrograde amnesia. The questions these experimenters are asking have always been central to the problem of memory disruption. In fact, the application of memory disruption techniques to the study of the biological nature of memory storage processes was recognized in very early studies in the area (Zubin & Barrera, 1941; Russell & Nathan, 1946; Gerard, 1949; Duncan, 1949). However, the original problem was for a time ignored while most retrograde amnesia research centered on interpretations of the phenomenon. Currently, the hypothesis is generally accepted that posttrial treatments act by influencing memory storage processes that continue for some time after training. Alternative hypotheses are discussed elsewhere (McGaugh & Dawson, 1971; McGaugh & Herz, 1972).

In this chapter, we will review those studies examining the original question of the neurobiology of retrograde amnesia, and the possible implications of the studies for the nature of memory storage processes. First, we will examine the effects on memory of different ECS parameters. Using this information as a base, we will look at various neural correlates of RA, in an attempt to find the conditions necessary for the production of RA. Finally, we will consider the problem of locating neural structures and circuits involved in memory disruption. Briefly then, the research questions are: What alterations in neural activity are necessary for the production of RA, and where must these alterations occur in the brain?

ECS as a Variable

Early studies of retrograde amnesia generally used arbitrary ECS parameters; therefore, the importance of these parameters passed unnoticed. This early research was apparently guided by the assumption that one ECS intensity—or even one amnesic treatment—was as effective as another. Undoubtedly, the assumption is responsible for many of the discrepant results reported. Unfortunately, this assumption still explicitly governs some current amnesia research (e.g., Miller & Springer, 1973).

Two major effects of varying the severity of an amnesic treatment are now clear. First, when a constant training–treatment interval is used, more intense treatments produce more amnesia. Second, the length of the training–treatment interval during which a treatment is effective (the RA gradient) is longer when more intense treatments are used.

Several experiments have examined the roles of ECS current intensity and duration on effectiveness of RA production in rats and mice (Jarvik & Kopp, 1967; Dorfman & Jarvik, 1968a,b; Weissman, 1963; Haycock & McGaugh, 1973; Buckholtz & Bowman, 1972; Alpern & McGaugh, 1968). In each of these studies, a general rule was seen: Within some range, the amnesic effectiveness of ECS is related to the severity of the treatment. The lowest intensity sufficient to produce RA was 3 mA using transcorneal ECS in mice and 17 mA using transpinnate ECS in rats.

In typical amnesia studies, rats receive transpinnate ECS (35 mA or more) and mice receive transcorneal ECS (10 mA or more). The effectiveness of the two modes of ECS administration was first systematically compared by Dorfman & Jarvik (1968a), who determined the intensities necessary to produce RA in mice using both transpinnate and transcorneal ECS. With both types of ECS administration, increased current intensity led to an increase in amnesic effectiveness, but transcorneal ECS produced RA at intensities lower than those required using transpinnate ECS.

Assuming that ECS acts as gross electrical stimulation of the brain, the reasons for the differences between transcorneal and transpinnate ECS may simply be physical. Transcorneal ECS may be a more effective amnesic treatment than transpinnate ECS because transcorneal ECS has a path of low impedance to the brain via the optic tract, whereas transpinnate ECS has a higher impedance pathway to the brain, having to pass skin, muscle, and the skull. Hayes (1950) and Ruch & Driscoll

(1968) demonstrated that the skull shunts a considerable amount of current away from the brain during ECS administration.

The amnesia studies discussed thus far examined the minimal (threshold) ECS intensity necessary to produce RA when the training–ECS interval is kept constant. The degree of amnesia produced by a treatment decreases as the training–treatment interval increases. This phenomenon, termed a retrograde amnesia gradient, has wide empirical support (see Glickman, 1961; McGaugh, 1966; McGaugh & Dawson, 1971; McGaugh & Herz, 1972). Such findings indicate that the susceptibility of memory storage processes to disruption decreases with time after training (see McGaugh & Dawson, 1971). Recent evidence indicates that as the training–ECS interval increases, the minimal intensity that will produce RA is elevated. Using two ECS levels, Miller (1968) observed that the RA gradient is extended when higher intensity ECS is used. Haycock & McGaugh (1973) obtained comparable results in mice, using transcorneal ECS at various intensities; in addition, Cherkin (1969) reported analogous findings, in chicks, using different doses of the convulsant gas, flurothyl, to produce amnesia.

Similar results are also obtained using direct brain stimulation. By varying the intensity of direct cortical stimulation, RA gradients were obtained which ranged from 5 sec to 240 min (Fig. 1; Gold, Macri, & McGaugh, 1973a; Gold, McDonald, & McGaugh, 1973). By examining the minimal stimulation intensity necessary to produce RA at different training–treatment intervals, it becomes clear that the minimal intensity that produces RA increases with time after training (Fig. 1). Thus, an RA gradient describes the time course of memory susceptibility to disruption for a particular treatment.

The increase in RA threshold continues for at least an hour after training; the upper limit has not yet been defined. When a time interval is found after which further increases in stimulation intensity do not produce RA, we will have to consider whether the limit is a property of the memory processes themselves, or whether the limit is determined by the maximal degree of neural disruption that can be produced short of permanently debilitating the organism. This type of logic reveals a very important shift in emphasis, which characterizes the new type of memory disruption studies. No longer should we assume that our results tell us only about memory processes; they tell us as much about our amnesic treatments. Consideration of the biological effects of treatments is the new direction the research has taken. The next section examines some of the biological events that result from amnesic treatments and considers the degree to which these events are related to amnesia.

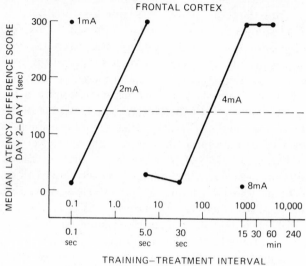

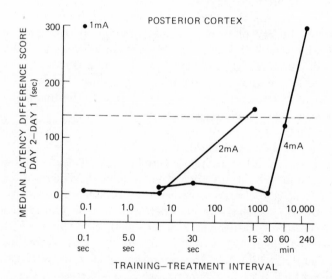

Fig. 1. Median retention score (day 2 minus day 1) for crossing into the shock compartment. All median latencies less than 140 sec (dotted line) are significantly lower (indicating RA) than latencies for animals receiving footshock only (median = 300 sec). Note that the lengths of the retrograde amnesia gradients vary directly with the intensity of the stimulation. From Gold, Macri, & McGaugh, 1973a.

Correlates of RA

As a first step toward understanding the mechanisms underlying memory disruption, it is important to determine those treatment parameters that are effective in disrupting memory. It is not surprising that there are intensities below which ECS does not produce RA. A natural subsequent research step involves identifying different neurobiological consequences of those stimulation parameters that do and do not produce RA. An experimental paradigm that seems well suited for studying neural correlates of RA is to determine first the threshold intensity for the behavioral phenomenon—the amnesia—and then to find neural alterations that have similar thresholds. On the completion of this type of experiment, one can conclude that at the RA threshold, a second event (or several events) may occur. Those animals that display this event are also the animals that exhibit RA; that is, there is a correlate of RA.

Behavioral Convulsions

The most obvious consequence of ECS administration is the behavioral convulsion. Woodbury & Davenport (1952) reported a direct relationship between transpinnate ECS current intensity and the intensity of the behavioral convulsion. A behavioral convulsion is generally classified as either a clonic convulsion, which involves rhythmic muscular twitches, or a tonic–clonic convulsion, which involves initial extension of all limbs, with the rigidity decreasing as the animals then enter the clonic portion of the convulsion.

In the first experimental attempt to find a correlate of RA, Weissman (1963) examined the behavioral convulsion pattern. In this experiment, Weissman found that at rather low ECS intensities, near the threshold for tonic–clonic convulsive patterns, those animals that showed the tonic–clonic response were more likely to be amnesic than were those that had only clonic convulsions. In an extension of the study, Weissman (1964) found a much more complex relationship between behavioral convulsion pattern and RA. A high ECS current intensity was used, which was sufficient to produce maximal behavioral convulsions in approximately 80% of the animals. Convulsion pattern was related to RA only at footshock (FS)–ECS intervals between 5 and 20 min. At shorter and longer FS–ECS intervals, the behavioral convulsion pattern did not predict the occurrence of RA. However, an interaction between the FS–ECS interval and the behavioral convulsion increased the complexity of these results. The percentage of animals that had tonic–clonic convulsions increased with an increase in FS–ECS intervals. Apparently, recent FS attenuates the behavioral convulsion produced by ECS. This finding has been confirmed and further analyzed (Pinel, 1971; Gold & McGaugh, 1972).

The Weissman results provide something of a paradox. At low ECS intensities, the severity of the convulsion pattern predicts whether a given animal will have amnesia, but this is not true at high ECS intensities. However, there may be two factors that determine whether or not an ECS produces a tonic–clonic convulsion pattern, only one of which is related to amnesia. First, when low-intensity ECS is administered, the current that actually reaches the central nervous system may be insufficient to produce a tonic–clonic convulsion pattern. A second reason that a tonic–clonic convulsion may not appear is because of an arousal blockade of the full convulsion pattern (Weissman, 1964; Pinel, 1971; Gold & McGaugh, 1972). In this second case, the current is sufficient to produce a tonic–clonic convulsion in unaroused animals but not in all aroused animals (i.e., following footshock). There may then be two populations of clonic convulsions that can be observed: type I, the result of insufficient current reaching the brain, and type II, the result of a physiological block of the convulsion pattern. Gold & McGaugh (1972) have shown that there is very little change in the nature of the cortically recorded seizures following ECS in animals with and without preceding FS, even though the convulsion pattern is changed. Consequently, assuming that brain seizures are related to RA, amnesia may not occur after a type I clonic convulsion but RA should occur following a type II clonic convulsion. This may be in fact what Weissman (1963, 1964) has demonstrated. Confirmation of this hypothesis awaits physiological recordings of the neural response to ECS at intensities near the RA threshold. The hypothesis predicts that, using weak transpinnate ECS, the neural response to the stimulation will be more severe in animals that have tonic–clonic convulsions than in those that have only clonic convulsions; furthermore, the different neural responses will be related to the production of RA.

It is important to note that the correlation between tonic–clonic convulsions and RA can be interpreted in either of two ways. First, the convulsion pattern may be an indicant of the amount of current reaching brain structures. A correlation between convulsion patterns and RA may simply reflect the fact that convulsion pattern and RA covary coincidentally but not causally. Alternatively, it is possible that the behavioral convulsion pattern is a phenomenon causally related to the RA; that is, the RA may be produced by the behavioral convulsion (Lewis &

Maher, 1965). This second possibility was tested by administering post-trial ECS to mice first placed under ether anesthesia (McGaugh & Alpern, 1966; Zornetzer & McGaugh, 1971a,b; McGaugh & Zornetzer, 1970; Zerbolio, 1971). Although ether treatment completely blocks the behavioral convulsion to ECS, the treatment does not block production of RA. Essman (1968) has reported similar results. Convulsive doses of pentylenetetrazol produced RA in mice whether or not the behavioral convulsion was pharmacologically blocked by lidocaine. Tonic–clonic convulsions are also not a necessary condition for RA in rats when brain stimulation is administered through skull screw electrodes (Gold, Farrell, & King, 1971). The results of these studies clearly indicate that behavioral convulsions are not necessary for the production of RA using ECS, direct brain stimulation, or convulsant drugs. On the basis of the findings described here, we can then rule out one biological correlate of RA as a causal agent for the production of the amnesia.

Brain Seizures

A second biological consequence of ECS is a brain seizure. Under a variety of conditions, brain seizures are correlated with the production of RA. However, there are also several instances in which brain seizures are an insufficient condition for amnesia. Furthermore, particularly when the amnesic treatment is low-level subcortical stimulation, brain seizures may not be necessary in order to produce RA; experiments that fall in this last category are discussed in the localization section which follows.

Several experiments with Swiss-Webster mice—an outbred strain—provide evidence suggesting that brain seizure activity and subsequent RA may be closely linked (McGaugh & Zornetzer, 1970; Zornetzer & McGaugh, 1971a,b). In the first of this series of experiments (McGaugh & Zornetzer, 1970) transcorneal ECS (15 mA, 200 msec) resulted in RA for a step-through inhibitory avoidance task in both unanesthesized and lightly etherized mice. This level of ECS current also produced cortical afterdischarge activity in both groups of mice. Mice more deeply anesthetized with ether developed neither RA nor afterdischarge activity following this same current level of ECS (Fig. 2). In a subsequent experiment (Zornetzer & McGaugh, 1971a), using both untreated mice and mice lightly anesthetized with controlled levels of ether, thresholds for transcorneal ECS-produced cortical afterdischarge activity and RA were compared. In nonetherized mice both the brain seizure threshold and the RA threshold were below the threshold for behavioral convulsions. In lightly etherized mice both the brain seizure and RA thresholds were significantly elevated (from approximately 2.5 mA in unanesthetized

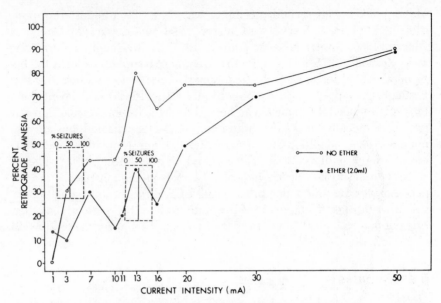

Fig. 2. The percentage of mice with RA varies directly with the intensity of transcorneal ECS in both unanesthetized and etherized mice. However, higher ECS current intensities are required for producing RA in the ether condition; higher intensities are also required for producing brain seizures. The brain seizure threshold range is indicated for both unanesthetized and ether-treated mice. From Zornetzer & McGaugh, 1971a.

mice to approximately 13.5 mA in etherized mice). Equating brain seizure threshold ranges for both untreated and etherized animals resulted in nearly identical RA-current intensity gradients (Fig. 3). In these instances, amnesia for an inhibitory avoidance response is closely associated with the production of cortical afterdischarge activity. Thus, under these conditions, ECS current results in RA (and brain seizures) in unanesthetized mice, whereas mice protected with ether have no amnesia (and no brain seizures) at the same ECS current intensity. Thus, current *per se* delivered to brain does not result in RA. Rather, the response of the brain to the current is the important determinant of RA. One neural response closely related to subsequent RA seems to be cortical afterdischarge activity.

Similar studies performed on inbred mice (DBA/2J and C57/BL6) suggest that the brain seizure–RA relationship is not always precise (Van Buskirk & McGaugh, in preparation). In both of the inbred strains, brain seizure thresholds and RA thresholds were closely related in unanesthetized animals. Also, in both of the inbred strains, light ether

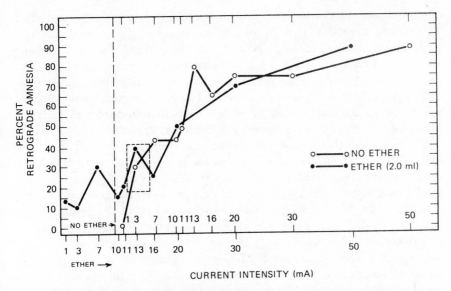

Fig. 3. When the brain seizure thresholds are equated for unanesthetized and ether-treated mice, the ECS intensity–RA curves under the two conditions are very similar. From Zornetzer & McGaugh, 1971a.

anesthesia increased the brain seizure thresholds and also the RA thresholds. To this point, these newer results are consistent with the Zornetzer & McGaugh studies discussed previously. However, in the inbred strains, the brain seizure and RA thresholds do *not* coincide when the animals are anesthetized. In both cases, the RA threshold far exceeds the brain seizure threshold. With etherized C57/BL6 mice, ECS intensities as high as 90 mA did not produce RA although brain seizures were produced. Thus, under ether anesthesia, brain seizures are not a sufficient condition for producing RA in these animals.

Conversely, in ether anesthetized outbred mice, it is possible under some conditions to produce RA *without* brain seizures. In an experiment conducted by Zornetzer & McGaugh (1971b), electrode-implanted mice were trained to avoid footshock following a light conditioned stimulus (CS) in a one-way shuttle-avoidance apparatus. Following the first training session (25 trials massed practice) all mice were lightly anesthetized with diethyl ether and administered different levels of transcorneal ECS. Difference scores, obtained by comparing errors made on a second massed practice training session with errors made during the first session, revealed that significant RA resulted at current levels below that required to produce cortical afterdischarge activity. Greater RA resulted from administration of current sufficient to produce afterdischarge activity. These data suggest that memories of some learning situations may be particularly susceptible to ECS-produced disruption; that is, in some situations, ECS may produce RA without also producing brain seizures.

A number of studies have investigated the suggestion that brain afterdischarge activity is also closely associated with RA in rats. These studies attempted to correlate an ECS- or brain stimulation-produced electrophysiological change with memory disruption. Zornetzer & McGaugh (1970) reported that afterdischarge activity elicited by immediate posttrial bilateral stimulation of frontal cortex in rats resulted in RA. The results of this study indicated that 3.0 mA delivered to the frontal cortex produced a degree of RA equivalent to that produced by 50 mA delivered transpinneally. Electrophysiological recordings of cortical afterdischarge activity revealed that direct frontal cortex stimulation resulted in longer afterdischarges than those produced by transpinneal stimulation. In a subsequent study (Zornetzer & McGaugh, 1972) rats receiving frontal cortex stimulation at a level just below brain seizure threshold did not develop RA. In contrast, rats that had slightly lower brain seizure thresholds developed both cortical seizure activity and RA after receiving the same amount of current to the frontal cortex. These studies further implicate posttrial afterdischarge activity in memory disruption.

Vardaris & Gehres (1970) also reported finding a relationship between cortical afterdischarge activity elicited by direct cortical stimulation and RA. Vardaris & Gehres further reported that rats having atypical brain seizure patterns (see Chorover & DeLuca, 1969) following stimulation also had atypical RA, that is, their performance deviated from their group medians, in the direction of either more or less RA. Their data suggest that post-ECS EEG activity associated with poor RA was of two types: either a brief afterdischarge resembling the seizure pattern seen with threshold stimulation (see Zornetzer & McGaugh, 1970; Gold & McGaugh, 1973a) or no seizure activity.

Generally, a second EEG abnormality follows the primary afterdischarge activity; a variable period of postictal depression occurs. This depression is generally widespread and is associated with a behaviorally quiescent (though often hyperexcitable) animal. Postictal depression does not appear to be necessary for the production of RA. McGaugh & Zornetzer (1970) administered the same intensity transcorneal ECS to mice lightly anesthetized with diethyl ether and to nonetherized mice. Electrocorticographic (ECoG) records indicated that nonetherized mice developed postictal depression following the afterdischarge, but etherized mice did not have postictal depression following the afterdischarge. However, both groups developed equivalent RA, suggesting that postictal depression did not contribute to the ECS-produced RA.

The effectiveness of cortical stimulation as an amnesic treatment has recently been extended in several respects to include comparisons of frontal and posterior cortex RA thresholds using different inhibitory avoidance tasks. These studies provide evidence that the brain sei- zure–RA correlation is not always precise. In particular, training variables exert a great influence on the minimal stimulation intensity necessary to produce RA using cortical stimulation. Of course, if RA thresholds vary under different behavioral conditions, neural correlates of amnesia also vary. Gold, Bueno, & McGaugh (1973) compared frontal and poste- rior cortex RA thresholds using various behavioral conditions and inhibi- tory avoidance tasks. In tasks in which animals are water-deprived before avoidance training, the frontal cortex RA threshold is lower than if the animals are not water-deprived prior to training (Zornetzer & McGaugh, 1972; Gold, Bueno, & McGaugh, 1973). In tasks in which animals are pretrained to drink or are simply given daily exposure to the avoidance apparatus prior to training (familiarization), the posterior cortex threshold is higher than it would be in the absence of the pretraining experience (Fig. 4) (Gold & McGaugh, 1973a; Gold, Bueno, & McGaugh, 1973). There are, then, situations in which the frontal cortex RA threshold is higher than that of posterior cortex, and other cases in which the reverse is true. Throughout these studies, cortical seizure patterns and thresholds are unchanged in different tasks. In all the behavioral situ- ations studied, the lowest stimulation intensity that produces RA is above the brain seizure threshold. These findings indicate that with either frontal or posterior cortex stimulation, brain seizures are a necessary but not always sufficient condition for RA. Although the nature of the interaction between task variables and RA thresholds (and hence neural correlates of RA) is not known, the added complexity suggested by these results is clear.

These results were certainly not obvious at the outset. Fortunately, there seems to be some consistency to the variables that affect frontal and posterior cortex RA thresholds. Further analysis of the interactions between water deprivation, familiarization, and brain seizure involve- ment in amnesia may help to explain a great deal about the biological nature of memory disruption. We do not yet know, for example, whether the changes seen in RA thresholds reflect differences in memory processes or differences in the neural alterations produced by the treatments, which do not appear in the brain seizure patterns.

Earlier, we described studies that demonstrated that cortical RA thresholds increase as the training–treatment interval increases (Gold, Macri, & McGaugh, 1973a; Gold, McDonald, & McGaugh, 1973). These findings also indicate that there is not one neural correlate of RA common to all situations. On the contrary, there must be *many* neural correlates,

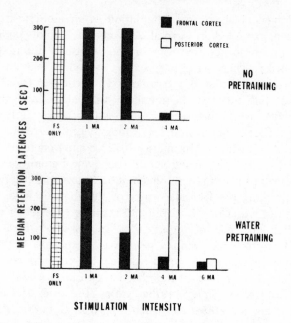

Fig. 4.   Retention latencies of rats under different behavioral conditions after receiving frontal or posterior cortex stimulation. Retrograde amnesia thresholds for frontal and posterior cortex vary with the behavioral conditions. Under conditions of no water deprivation or pretraining exposure to the apparatus (upper graph), the frontal cortex RA threshold is lower than that of posterior cortex. However, when rats are water-deprived and pretrained to drink prior to inhibitory avoidance training, the frontal cortex RA threshold is higher than that of posterior cortex. Data from Gold, Bueno, & McGaugh, 1973.

as any change in the RA threshold implies a change in the correlate of amnesia.

There is also a methodological problem that should be considered here. RA gradients can be altered arbitrarily by changing the retention criterion. In an inhibitory avoidance task, this criterion is usually a high latency to perform a response. Table 1 shows that it is possible to alter the length of this RA gradient by changing the cutoff latency in an inhibitory avoidance task (Schneider, Kapp, Aron, & Jarvik, 1969).

These experimenter-produced "changes" in the results of RA gradient studies also operate in studies of RA thresholds and correlates. Consider the experiment in Fig. 5 (Gold, Bueno, & McGaugh, 1973). In this experiment, median retention latencies varied directly with the intensity of the cortical stimulation. Frontal cortex RA thresholds and brain seizure

Table 1 Effect of Cutoff Latencies on Apparent Efficacy of ECS

Type of Shock	Cutoff Latency (sec)	Training–ECS Interval		
		10 sec	1 hr	6 hr
Transpinnate (rats)				
	600	RA	RA	Ret
	300	RA	RA	Ret
	30	RA	Ret	Ret
Transcorneal (rats)				
	600	RA	RA	RA
	300	RA	RA	RA
	30	RA	Ret	Ret
Transcorneal (mice)				
	600	RA	RA	Ret
	300	RA	Ret	Ret
	30	RA	Ret	Ret

SOURCE: Schneider et al., 1969.

thresholds were correlated when a 300 sec cutoff latency was used. If a 50 or 100 sec cutoff were used, brain seizures would not have been found to be the "correlate" of memory disruption. This alteration of RA thresholds and gradients is entirely in the hands of the experimenter. It does not reflect a neurobiological process. Yet, such arbitrary designations seriously influence the interpretation of memory disruption studies. One solution to the problem is to titrate the motivational level so that the median latency of the footshock control group falls below the cutoff latency. Even this has certain limitations, as generalizations from the data to other motivational levels (requiring higher cutoff latencies) may not be warranted. RA thresholds are themselves influenced by motivational levels (Zornetzer & McGaugh, 1972).

An obvious implication of the above experiments is that the problem of finding neurobiological correlates of RA is not an easy one. The correlate is influenced by: (*a*) the training conditions; (*b*) the particular brain site stimulated; (*c*) the training–treatment interval; and (*d*) the measure of retention. This list is undoubtedly incomplete but it emphasizes the fact that it is improbable that there is *one* correlate of RA. This is an important finding for understanding the neurobiological bases of memory disruption, although certainly it is not as satisfying as being able to point to brain seizures (or "neural storms" for that matter) as the cause of RA.

In studying the relationship between brain seizures and RA, the experiments in this section used brain stimulation methods intended to affect

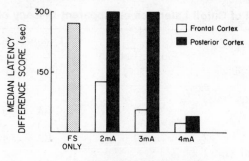

Fig. 5. Retention latencies of rats that received frontal or posterior cortex stimulation after training on an inhibitory avoidance task. Note that the RA threshold for frontal cortex stimulation is 2mA. However, if a lower cutoff latency had been used (e.g., 100 sec), the threshold would have been 3mA. By choosing an arbitrary cutoff latency, the experimenter can alter the apparent RA thresholds. From Gold, Bueno, & McGaugh, 1973.

large neuronal populations; that is, ECS or brain stimulation using skull screw electrodes. The brain seizures that result from such stimulation are widespread (unpublished findings). However, we do not know whether it is necessary to alter the activity of large areas of the brain in order to produce RA. The next issue we will discuss is whether direct stimulation of certain brain regions is particularly effective in disrupting memory.

Localization

The findings of several studies suggest that localized stimulation of some particular brain region either prior to, during, or after a learning experience interferes with later performance of the learned response. We will refer to these studies as *localization* studies, although it is not yet clear exactly what is localized. A description of two reasons for doing these studies will help explain some different interpretations of the meaning of localization data.

The first rationale is to attempt to find those brain regions involved in memory storage processing. The main assumption behind this interpretation is that if we find neural structures or circuits in which electrical stimulation is a particularly effective amnesic treatment, we have located the neural structures in which the engram would have been stored. This rationale is further based on the belief that direct brain stimulation produces transient, localized neural alterations that interfere with memory storage processing. Given these assumptions, the use of posttrial direct brain stimulation of particular neural structures provides an exciting new approach with the potential of solving the old problem of neural localization of the engram (see Boring, 1950, pp. 683–688; Lashley, 1950).

A second rationale for doing localization studies is more specifically related to finding the neurobiological basis of RA. This line of reasoning underlying localization research is to locate neural systems involved in memory disruption (as opposed to finding structures involved directly in memory storage), a rationale we prefer at this time because it is more conservative. Retrograde amnesia studies provide direct evidence about memory *disruption*, not storage. Any statements regarding memory storage processes that are based on amnesia studies are merely inferential (see McGaugh & Dawson, 1971). This second rationale, then, makes no prior assumptions about localized effects of brain stimulation or about the biological bases of the amnesia produced. Of course, once data are obtained indicating that a particular neural system is involved in memory disruption, the phenomenon must be analyzed in terms of why that disruption occurred. Many explanations are possible. First, the most obvious interpretation is that memory storage processes were directly disrupted by the electrical current, as described for the first rationale. Alternatively, processes that support memory storage events may be disrupted, by altering arousal levels or hormonal levels, for example.

Finally, the possibility must be considered that stimulation of different structures will produce RA for different reasons. Whichever reasons one favors for performing localization studies, it seems likely that these studies will increase our understanding of the neurobiological basis of retrograde amnesia, and in doing so, can be expected to add to our understanding of the biological bases of memory storage processes.

Methodological and Conceptual Problems

We outlined above two types of reasoning that lead to attempts at localizing neural structures or systems in which electrical stimulation produces memory disruption. There are certain methodological and conceptual considerations common to both rationales that must be recognized. We will discuss some of the methodological issues before turning to conceptual problems.

First, as Schwartzbaum & Gustafson (1970) recently pointed out, it is necessary to ensure that there can be no cross-talk between the footshock and brain stimulation circuits when using a task involving footshock. This can be accomplished by isolating all electrode leads from ground during footshock. It is also necessary to isolate the grid floor from ground during brain stimulation so that the effects of brain stimulation on behavior will not be due to peripheral stimulation (inadvertent footshock). In some instances we have found that even these precautions are insufficient. Footshock administered to an animal with hippocampal electrodes may produce brain seizures if the cable connected to the leads is shielded, even if the shielding is itself isolated from ground. The ungrounded shield can apparently exert a capacitative influence on the electrode leads, providing a shunt for the FS circuit, thus stimulating neural tissue.

A second point, at times disregarded in localization studies, is the need for comparisons to be made between stimulated and implanted control animals. Deficits in avoidance performance may result from the tissue damage that occurs during electrode implantation. This has been observed in animals with electrodes placed in the brainstem reticular formation (Denti, McGaugh, Landfield, & Shinkman, 1970), hippocampus (Landfield, Tusa, & McGaugh, 1973), septum (Gold, Macri, & McGaugh, 1973c), and caudate nucleus (Gold, 1970).

Third, several precautions are necessary before brain stimulation can be said to have produced the behavioral differences as a result of retrograde amnesia. By definition, demonstration of RA requires that the amnesia stimulation be administered after the training trial. However, in itself this is insufficient evidence of RA. It is also necessary to demonstrate that the brain stimulation does not have motivational properties that might produce behavioral changes in the same direction as RA. Thus, a one-trial inhibitory avoidance task is applicable when the stimulation is either neutral or aversive. In this case, the animal would be punished by two aversive stimuli (brain stimulation and footshock, for example). This should increase the degree of avoidance behavior rather than decrease it. Conversely, a one-trial appetitive task is appropriate when brain stimulation is either neutral or rewarding. Here the learned response is approach behavior, and again, brain stimulation, if rewarding, should summate with the reinforcement in the task, potentiating the behavioral response rather than interfering with it. These procedures decrease the possibility that motivational consequences of the brain stimulation will produce behavioral changes that resemble RA. In either of these cases, a behavioral change in the direction of RA is opposite that which would be predicted by the motivational component of the brain stimulation. Generally, these limitations may be overcome easily by the use of controls that demonstrate that the results are not due to motivational properties of the stimulation.

Fourth, it is essential that a retrograde amnesia gradient be demonstrated. This provides another approach to the question of reinforcing properties of the brain stimulation producing behavior that looks like, but is not, RA. As the time between the training trial and the brain stimulation is increased, the probability of observing conditioning to reinforcing brain stimulation declines rapidly (Lenzer, 1972). In addition, the gradient is also a necessary condition for the demonstration of RA on other grounds. Without the gradient, proactive effects on the test trial, rather than retroactive effects on memory, cannot be discounted.

Fifth, particularly when relatively high levels of brain stimulation are used, it is necessary to control for specificity and current spread. To accomplish any degree of specificity, it is first necessary to find brain regions in which stimulation is an effective amnesic agent, and second and equally important, to find brain regions that are ineffective. One approach to this problem is to stimulate regions near the effective site and show that they are ineffective. For example, if stimulation of dorsal hippocampus is an effective amnesic agent, then an appropriate control might be stimulation of the overlying cortex. Of course, it is difficult to provide all controls of this nature. It is in this regard that the greatest difficulties in performing a localization study are confronted.

Here, we begin to make a transition from purely methodological considerations to logical difficulties. Many studies have shown that hippocampal stimulation, generally above brain seizure threshold, is sufficient to produce RA. These will be discussed in detail below. Because the hippocampus is a particularly popular structure in these studies, it may be useful to describe a hypothetical study in which RA was produced by hippocampal stimulation. This description has as its goal an explanation of the logical limitations of such a study. Assume that attention was given to most of the methodological considerations listed above—although this in fact makes the study atypical—and that implanted controls were included, a gradient was determined, and the stimulation reliably produced hippocampal seizures. Such a study might concluded that hippocampal seizures produce RA. However, such a conclusion is only weakly supported by the data. Consider the following problems with the interpretation: (*a*) If the hippocampus is stimulated with intense stimulation parameters, several other structures may be directly or indirectly stimulated; (*b*) If EEGs were recorded from electrodes in other structures, these regions might also show brain seizures. This could occur either as a result of the brain stimulation or may be indirectly produced by propagation of the hippocampal afterdischarge to other structures. Unless otherwise demonstrated, it is perhaps most conservative to assume that the brain seizure was rapidly propagated to many neural structures, any one of which might be involved in the memory disruption. (*c*) Even when seizures are not observed in a distant structure it is likely that some abnormal input, which may be sufficient to produce RA, is being propagated to that structure. (*d*) Supraseizure stimulation of these other structures may also be sufficient to produce RA. The complexities of providing a well-designed localization experiment should now be readily apparent. Given the restrictions described above, it can be seen that simply stimulating one structure in the hope of observing RA is not sufficient.

Alternatively, one might stimulate many neural structures in order to find the structure that has the lowest RA threshold. However, before this can be accepted as a localization study, it is first necessary to relate the stimulation parameters to the seizure thresholds because of the large differences in the brain seizure thresholds at various brain sites. It may also prove necessary to test each structure with a wide range of stimulation parameters, because in different structures different types of stimulation may be most effective.

Within this methodological and conceptual framework it is now possible to examine critically the many attempts to perform localization studies and to determine to what extent they have met their goals. We therefore turn to a survey of those experiments that have examined the amnesic effects of posttrial stimulation of subcortical brain sites.

Diffuse Systems

In early studies, Mahut (1962; 1964) examined the effectiveness of stimulation of cortex, tegmentum, and midline thalamus in disrupting memory. Using stimulation parameters just below threshold for a motor response, posttrial midline thalamic stimulation appeared to produce RA for maze learning. The same stimulation did not produce an amnesic effect when delivered to the cortex or tegmentum. This experiment addressed itself to many of the localization criteria described earlier: operated controls were included, an RA gradient was obtained, and the absence of rewarding and punishing effects of the stimulation was examined. In a later study, using cats, Wilburn & Kesner (1972) found that posttrial 7 Hz stimulation of the nonspecific thalamic system results in RA. The stimulation was effective in producing RA at training–treatment intervals of 4 sec and 5 min. These experiments certainly need to be replicated with attention devoted to the nature of the physiological response of the brain to the stimulation.

Glickman (1958) found that rats that received stimulation of the mesencephalic reticular formation (MRF) after training were impaired in their later performance compared to unoperated control animals. However, Denti et al. (1970) reported that stimulated animals in fact displayed retention superior to that of operated controls although they were inferior to an unoperated control group. This is one of the clearest demonstrations of the need for operated control groups.

In contrast, Kesner & Conner (1972) obtained no effect of posttrial MRF stimulation on performance 256 sec or 24 hr later, although there was a performance deficit 64 sec after initial training and stimulation. They interpret this result as evidence for selective disruption of short-term memory processes without an effect on long-term memory processing. These results are very interesting and need to be expanded to determine whether the effect is due to a proactive influence of MRF stimulation on behavior 64 sec later. It would also be important to determine whether the particular time course of the effect is influenced by stimulation parameters in a manner analogous to the previously described relationship between cortical stimulation parameters and RA gradients (Gold, Macri, & McGaugh, 1973a).

In summary, results obtained with MRF stimulation include memory facilitation, interference, and transient interference. Hopefully, the difference in behavioral results will be resolved by experimental examination of methodological differences. An example of the direction new studies might take comes from the observation that those experiments that obtained memory facilitation used long-duration stimulation trains compared to the train durations used in memory interference experiments.

Caudate

Studies involving posttrial caudate stimulation provide the most extensive evidence that memory disruption does not require brain seizure involvement. In addition, caudate stimulation disrupts memory in a wide variety of tasks and in several species. In this respect, the phenomenon enjoys wider generality than that seen with other structures. Continuous low-level stimulation of the caudate interferes with learning when the stimulation is delivered concomitantly with the learning situation (Rosvold & Delgado, 1956). Thompson (1958) first examined the retroactive effects of posttrial caudate stimulation on memory. After cats were trained to perform a reversal task, they received posttrial bilateral stimulation of the caudate. The retroactive interference increased as a function of increases in current intensity, frequency, pulse duration, and stimulation-train duration. The basic design of this experiment is appealing, because each animal served as its own control, eliminating the need for implanted controls. Furthermore, considerable data could be generated from each animal.

Wyers, Peeke, Williston, & Herz (1968) reported that posttrial bilateral single-pulse stimulation of the caudate nucleus, as well as the ventromedial hippocampus, resulted in RA for an inhibitory avoidance response. Although no EEG records were taken, it is very unlikely that such stimulation resulted in afterdischarge activity. Wyers et al. (1968) investigated the memory-impairing effects of single-pulse stimulation on a number of other brain structures. The data suggest that the caudate nucleus and the ventral hippocampus were the only structures of those tested in which stimulation reliably produced retrograde amnesia. Haycock, Deadwyler, Sideroff, & McGaugh (1973) recently replicated the amnesic effect of caudate stimulation on inhibitory avoidance training. Furthermore, Wyers & Deadwyler (1971) demonstrated that these effects appear to be time-dependent. In animals amnesic for a prior training experience, caudate stimulation produced RA for a second training trial if the stimulation followed the trial by 30 sec but not if 15 min elapsed between the trial and stimulation.

Caudate stimulation has also been shown to interfere with acquisition of food-rewarded maze learning in rats (Peeke & Herz, 1971). Stimulation delivered either after each choice point in the maze (Lashley III) or following each trial resulted in impaired acquisition. Furthermore, the results of this study suggest that multiple-pulse stimulation of the caudate is a more effective amnesic treatment than is single-pulse stimulation. Caudate stimulation also disrupts extinction of a water-motivated task in rats (Herz & Peeke, 1971), and disrupts retention of one-trial inhibitory avoidance and appetitive task in mice (Zornetzer, Chronister, & Ross, 1973).

However, not all attempts to obtain RA with subseizure-intensity stimulation of the caudate nucleus have been successful. Gold & King (1972) and Gold, Macri, & McGaugh (1973c) using inhibitory avoidance tasks, and Herz (1972) using a taste-aversion paradigm, have reported failures to obtain amnesia with caudate stimulation. Nonetheless, the potential generality of caudate-stimulation-produced RA indicates that further analysis of this effect may provide important information about the neurobiology of memory storage processes.

Hippocampus

The association between the hippocampus and memory processes developed from varied experimental approaches including human clinical data (Penfield & Milner, 1958), localized pharmacological and chemical manipulations (Avis & Carlton, 1968; Flexner, Flexner, & Stellar, 1963; Kapp & Schneider, 1971), lesions (Hostetter, 1968), brain puncture (Bohdanecka, Bohdanecky, & Jarvik, 1967), and recording of neurophysiological correlates of learning (Olds, 1969). With this background suggesting a role for the hippocampus in memory, it is not surprising that many experimenters have examined the effects of posttrial hippocampal stimulation on memory. Because of the low seizure threshold for hippocampal stimulation (see Green, 1960), brain seizures are common in these studies. For example, hippocampal stimulation (Kesner & Doty, 1968; Lidsky & Slotnick, 1970; Hirano, 1965; Shinkman & Kaufman, 1972; Barcik, 1970; Vardaris & Schwartz, 1971) and inferotemporal lobe stimulation (Levine, Goldrich, Pond, Livesey, & Schwartzbaum, 1970) have been reported to produce RA when the stimulation is intense enough to produce brain seizures.

Potentially as interesting is the fact that there appear to be certain conditions under which similar seizure-eliciting stimulation of the hippocampus does *not* produce RA. In cats, Kesner & Doty (1968) found that seizure-eliciting hippocampal stimulation did not produce RA in all animals. They suggested that it may be necessary for the after discharge to propagate to the amygdala in order to disrupt memory. However, in many instances, cortically elicited brain seizures do not produce RA (Gold & McGaugh, 1973a; Gold, Macri, & McGaugh, 1973a; Gold, Bueno, & McGaugh, 1973) even though the seizures do propagate to both the amygdala and hippocampus (unpublished data). It is possible that propagated brain seizures are not as disruptive as direct stimulation of a particular brain structure.

In contrast, several studies have suggested that hippocampal stimulation may produce RA in the absence of brain seizures, Wyers et al. (1968) report that single-pulse posttrial stimulation of the ventral hippocampus disrupts inhibitory avoidance memory in rats. This result has recently been confirmed by Zornetzer et al. (1973) in mice; in addition, EEGs taken immediately after the stimulation revealed that no brain seizures occurred.

Kesner & Conner (1972) found that high-frequency stimulation of the dorsal hippocampus also produces amnesia. Unfortunately, EEGs were not taken after the stimulation to determine whether seizures occurred. Shinkman & Kaufman (1972) report some RA following a 90 sec train of hippocampal stimulation. EEGs were taken following the stimulation and no brain seizures were reported. However, brain seizures frequently last less than 90 sec; therefore, it is not possible to conclude that seizures did not occur.

In a recent experiment, Zornetzer et al. (1973) found that stimulation of dorsal hippocampus produced RA in the absence of brain seizures. However, the effective electrode placements were very specific. RA was seen only in animals that had electrodes implanted in bilaterally symmetrical regions of the dentate gyrus. Even in these animals, the magnitude of RA was small. In animals that had brain seizures, the symmetry appeared to be less critical.

There is therefore some evidence that hippocampal stimulation produces RA under very specific conditions in the absence of brain seizures. There is more evidence that brain seizures elicited from the hippocampus produce RA. However, even this effect is apparently not a general phenomenon.

Parenthetically, it is interesting to note that Flynn & Wasman (1960) found that animals could learn on the basis of events that were presented *during* hippocampal afterdischarges. As Flynn & Wasman point out, it is difficult to fit such data into a context of the hippocampus being uniquely involved in memory disruption.

Amygdala

Experiments using many different methods suggest that the amygdala plays a role in fear-motivated learning (see Goddard, 1969; Kaada, 1972). Posttrial amygdala stimulation apparently produces RA without brain seizures, although this is not true in all situations. Lidsky, Levine, Kreinick, & Schwartzbaum (1970) reported that bilateral subseizure-threshold electrical stimulation of the amygdala in rats failed to produce RA in a lick-suppression task. RA was produced when stimulation was sufficiently intense to elicit widespread afterdischarge activity.

In contrast, even with afterdischarge activity that involved the amygdala, retention deficits for a conditioned suppression task were not seen in monkeys (Levine et al., 1970). Afterdischarges initiated in inferotemporal cortex (and which then spread to the amygdala) did interfere with retention in this study. Furthermore, this effect was modality specific; that is, a visual CS, but not an auditory CS, was subject to posttrial inferotemporal cortex-induced memory impairment. In contrast to the results of Levine et al. (1970), Reitz & Gerbrandt (1971) did not find an amnesic effect of posttrial inferotemporal lobe seizures upon visual discrimination learning in the monkey. These authors reported that inferotemporal-induced seizures interfered with discrimination learning only if the electrical stimulation accompanied the presentation of the visual CS. Posttrial stimulation did not impair memory. The apparent discrepancy between these two studies suggests that further investigation is needed.

Recently, we found that posttrial bilateral stimulation of the amygdala disrupted retention of an inhibitory avoidance task (Gold, Macri, & McGaugh, 1973b, 1973c). EEGs were taken from the cortical electrodes during and immediately after the stimulation, and from amygdala elec-

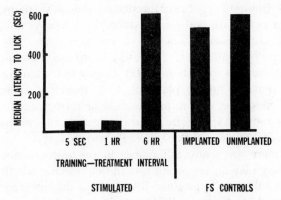

Fig. 6.   Retention latencies of rats that received bilateral subseizure amygdala stimulation after inhibitory avoidance training. This treatment effectively produced RA if delayed 1 hr after training but not 6 hr after training.
From Gold, Marcri, & McGaugh, 1973b.

trodes immediately after the stimulation. A highly significant degree
of RA was produced even though there were no brain seizures (Fig.
6). This stimulation was effective when administered either 5 sec or
1 hr after training but not 6 hr after training. Implanted control animals
showed no deficit. Furthermore, in this situation, stimulation of the dorsal
hippocampus, caudate, septum, dorsomedial thalamus, cerebellum, and
hypothalamus did not produce RA. The study suggests that there are
"cold spots" relative to the amygdala under these experimental conditions. Other studies also suggest that low-level amygdala stimulation
may produce RA in the absence of brain seizures (Ilyutchenok & Vinnitsky, 1971; McDonough & Kesner, 1971).

There is some question about whether the stimulation must be bilateral
or whether unilateral stimulation is sufficient. McDonough & Kesner
(1971) found that posttrial bilateral stimulation of the corticomedial
amygdala produces RA without brain seizures in cats. However, unilateral
stimulation was ineffective unless the contralateral amygdala had been
previously lesioned. Stimulation was effective in producing RA even if
administered 60 min after training. McDonough & Kesner conclude that if
either amygdala is left undisturbed, interference with memory storage
processes does not occur.

However, some experiments suggest that unilateral stimulation of the
amygdala may be sufficient to interfere with retention. Goddard (1964)
reported that continuous unilateral electrical stimulation of the amygdala
resulted in a learning deficit in rats for fear-motivated learning. Similarly,

Bresnahan & Routtenberg (1972) reported that a small but significant degree of memory disruption was produced by low-level unilateral stimulation of the corticomedial nucleus of the amygdala. The task was a multitrial step-down inhibitory (passive) avoidance task. Brain stimulation was administered to each animal just prior to training and whenever the rat was standing on the platform. It is, therefore, difficult to know whether the effect was due to anterograde or retrograde amnesia. However, the anatomical specificity of the effective site of stimulation to the corticomedial nucleus of the amygdala was striking.

Although there are many differences in the experiments, stimulation parameters may play an important role in determining whether unilateral stimulation is sufficient to produce RA. Perhaps the discrepancy between the McDonough & Kesner (1971) results and those of Bresnahan & Routtenberg (1972) and Goddard (1964) is the result of differences in the nature of the stimulation parameters used. McDonough & Kesner used a relatively brief (5 sec) train of biphasic square wave stimulation; Routtenberg and Goddard used long trains of stimulation totaling several minutes.

An experiment by Gold & McGaugh (1973b) provides direct support for this explanation. Five seconds after training on an inhibitory avoidance task, rats received a 10 sec or 30 sec train of unilateral amygdala stimulation. On a retention test the next day, both stimulation conditions produced RA, but more RA was observed with the longer duration stimulation. Thus, it seems that the duration of the stimulation train is an important variable in producing RA with low-level unilateral amygdala stimulation.

A review of the amygdala studies suggests that there appear to be many conditions under which brain seizures are not necessary in order for amygdala stimulation to produce RA. On the other hand, other studies suggest that brain seizures are required. Important species differences, task differences, type of brain stimulation, and reward contingencies create major difficulties in assessing the meaning of the conflicting results reported in these studies. Nonetheless, posttrial subseizure stimulation of the amygdala is in some cases an extremely effective treatment for producing RA.

Cortex

An extensive analysis of cortical stimulation and RA was given in the earlier section concerning correlates of RA, and these studies are therefore not included here. However, another method potentially useful in localization studies is the posttrial lesion technique described by

Hudspeth & Wilsoncroft (1969). RA for an inhibitory avoidance response was produced by posttrial electrocoagulation of frontal cortex in mice and an RA gradient was demonstrated. EEG records did not indicate postlesion cortical seizure activity or other EEG abnormalities. No subcortical recording was made, however. The lesion effect appears to be somewhat localized; a similar posttrial lesion, made in what Hudspeth & Wilsoncroft (1969) refer to as "motor cortex," did not result in RA. In addition, low-level electrical stimulation of frontal cortex did not result in RA. Hudspeth & Wilsoncroft (1969) interpret their data as suggesting that the lesion per se, that is, the localized neural damage, is associated with RA. An alternative explanation is that posttrial anodal polarization of frontal cortex, for a relatively long period of time (20 sec) following learning, results in RA. Albert (1966) has reported finding both facilitation and impairment of memory with cortical polarization in rats.

The posttrial lesion method offers promise, but must be used with caution. Glick & Greenstein (1972) recently found that posttrial and frontal anteromedial and frontal stab wounds result in RA in mice. Posterior-medial and occipital cortex stab wounds had no effect. On the basis of these data, they suggest that the cortex is involved in memory storage processes. However, it is also possible that there are widespread neurophysiological consequences to the cortical stab wounds. Physiological responses to the trauma may in turn produce the RA by mechanisms that are unrelated to the localization question. Support for the latter interpretation comes from data reported by Hudspeth (1973). In this experiment, Hudspeth recorded electrophysiological abnormalities that were present even hours after cortical stabs similar to those made by Glick & Greenstein (1972). These methodological problems with the posttrial lesion procedure must be examined carefully to avoid difficulties of interpretation.

Conclusions

In an effort to understand the neurobiological nature of retrograde amnesia, many experimenters have begun examining the importance of the parameters of amnesic treatments, using both localized electrical stimulation of the brain and gross stimulation (e.g., ECS), and the effectiveness of low-level electrical stimulation of specific brain regions. Knowing the effective and ineffective parameters is, of course, important in attempting to relate the neural consequences of the stimulation to the production of amnesia. The results of these studies enable us to define some of the important variables (e.g. certain task variables and training–treatment interval) that influence neural correlates of RA. In addition, it now seems clear that low-level electrical stimulation of specific brain regions can produce RA without brain seizures, although the conditions under which these results can be obtained are not well-defined. These findings lead to a new conclusion regarding the neurobiology of memory disruption: a single correlate of RA cannot exist.

Perhaps we ask too much of our methods when we hope to find *one* neural correlate or effective brain region that fits the results obtained with many different learning situations and many different disruptive treatments. It may be useful to examine a correlate or a particularly effective stimulation site in detail even when we do not find generality for the phenomenon. For example, in a large number of situations, brain seizures are very closely related to RA. We know some of the conditions under which the relationship holds best, but we do not yet understand the mechanism by which seizures disrupt retention. There may be clues hidden in the limited generality of the phenomenon, which will assist in understanding the neurobiological bases of the behavioral deficits.

One must keep in mind the possibility that memory disruption need not be a unitary concept. It may be possible to interfere with memory storage processes in many different ways. Caudate stimulation and ECS may have very different modes of actions, which independently produce the same behavioral effect—amnesia. It is possible that with one treatment we interfere with a transient short-term memory system that is necessary for the production of long-term memory. Using another treatment, we may interfere more directly with the production of long-term memory.

Still another alternative is that RA may result from interference with tonic processes that provide an optimal state in which permanent memory storage will occur. There are certainly many changes in neural activity that continue after training, and these changes may be necessary for memory storage processes to proceed normally. To illustrate this hypothesis, one can imagine that a decrease in arousal level soon after avoidance training may weaken later retention of that task. Also, various hormonal changes occur after avoidance training; for example, ACTH levels change (DeWied, Van Delft, Gispen, Weijnen, & Van Wimersma Greidanus, 1972). It is possible that some amnesic agents produce RA by disrupting these supportive neural activities. For example, RA produced by subseizure stimulation of the amygdala may be a consequence of nonspecific effects of amygdala stimulation. Amygdala stimulation produces autonomic responses, arousal changes, and emotional changes (see Kaada, 1972). If we intervene and compensate for these effects, it may be possible to counteract the amnesic effectiveness of amygdala stimulation. It should be emphasized, however, that even if we find areas of the brain in which normal activity supports memory storage processes indirectly, as in the above examples, we have identified a very important feature of memory processes. Stating that such activity merely supports memory processes is perhaps inappropriate; it might be better to accept the view that all these features are in fact part of a memory process.

This discussion emphasizes the point that localization studies of the sort reported here are at best searching for regions well-suited for producing memory disruption. It is a separate though related concern as to whether those structures in which electrical stimulation most readily disrupts memory are also the structures which are the most promising regions in which to search for correlates of memory storage processes. We must question the assumption that if a neural site is well-suited for memory disruption, it is therefore a site of memory storage processes.

Indeed, we must question whether it is reasonable to believe that such a site exists. Historically, theoretical views about the localization of memory engrams have ranged from individual memories stored in individual cortical cells (Konorski, 1967) to believing that much of the brain is involved in storing the information pertaining to any single type of learning (Franz, 1912; Lashley, 1950; John, 1972). The localization studies described in this review have frequently been interpreted as supporting a middle view: Memories are stored in those brain regions in which electrical stimulation is particularly effective in disrupting memory. However, the alternative explanation described above suggests that memory disruption may, at least in some cases, reflect disruption of neural or hormonal influences that provide an optimal state for memory storage. Clearly, this hypothesis does not require the conclusion that if stimulation of a discrete brain region produces RA, that region then represents the site of an engram. At this stage of research, we must be cognizant of our assumptions and wary of overinterpreting the data provided by these experiments. Nonetheless, studies of neural correlates of RA and of those neural regions in which electrical stimulation readily produces RA have already led to the identification of some important behavioral and physiological variables that influence the production of amnesia. Continued efforts of this type can be expected to further our understanding of the neurobiological nature of retrograde amnesia.

References

Albert, D. J. (1966). The effects of polarizing currents on the consolidation of learning. *Neuropsychologia*, 4, 65–77.

Alpern, H. P., & McGaugh, J. L. (1968). Retrograde amnesia as a function of duration of electroshock stimulation. *J. Comp. Physiol. Psychol.*, **65**, 265–269.

Avis, H. H., & Carlton, P. L. (1968). Retrograde amnesia produced by hippocampal spreading depression. *Science*, **161**, 73–75.

Barcik, J. D. (1970). Hippocampal afterdischarges and conditioned emotional response. *Psychon. Sci.*, **20**, 297–299.

Bohdanecka, M., Bohdanecky, Z., & Jarvik, M. E. (1967). Amnesic effects of small bilateral brain puncture in the mouse. *Science*, **157**, 334–336.

Boring, E. G. (1950). *A history of experimental psychology* (2nd ed.). Appleton-Century-Crofts, New York. Pp. 683–688.

Bresnahan, E., & Routtenberg, A. (1972). Memory disruption by unilateral low-level, sub-seizure stimulation of the medial amygdaloid nucleus. *Physiol. Behav.*, **9**, 513–525.

Buckholtz, N. S., & Bowman, R. E. (1972). Incubation and retrograde amnesia studies with various ECS intensities and durations. *Physiol. Behav.*, **8**, 113–117.

Cherkin, A. (1969). Kinetics of memory consolidation: Role of amnesic treatment parameters. *Proc. Nat. Acad. Sci.*, **63**, 1094–1101.

Chorover, S. L., & DeLuca, A. M. (1969). Transient change in electrocorticographic reaction to ECS in the rat following footshock. *J. Comp. Physiol. Psychol.*, **69**, 141–149.

Denti, A., McGaugh, J. L., Landfield, P., & Shinkman, P. (1970). Facilitation of learning with posttrial stimulation of the reticular formation. *Physiol. Behav.*, **5**, 659–662.

DeWied, D., Van Delft, A. M. L., Gispen, W. H., Weijnen, J. A. W. M., & Van Wimersma Greidanus, Tj. B. (1972). The role of pituitary–adrenal system hormones in active avoidance condition. In S. Levine (Ed.), *Hormones and behavior*. Academic Press, New York.

Dorfman, L. F., & Jarvik, M. E. (1968a). Comparative amnesic effects of transcorneal and transpinnate ECS in mice. *Physiol. Behav.*, **3**, 815–818.

Dorfman, L. F., & Jarvik, M. E. (1968b). A parametric study of electroshock-induced retrograde amnesia in mice. *Neuropsychologia*, **6**, 373–380.

Duncan, C. P. (1949). The retroactive effect of electroshock on learning. *J. Comp. Physiol. Psychol.*, **42**, 32–44.

Essman, W. B. (1968). Retrograde amnesia in seizure-protected mice: Behavioral and biochemical effects of pentylenetetrazol. *Physiol. Behav.*, **3**, 549–552.

Flexner, J. B., Flexner, L. B., & Stellar, E. (1963). Memory in mice as affected by intracerebral puromycin. *Science*, **141**, 57–59.

Flynn, J. P., & Wasman, M. (1960). Learning and cortically evoked movement during propagated hippocampal afterdischarges. *Science*, **131**, 1607–1608.

Franz, S. I. (1912). New phrenology. *Science*, **35**, 321–328.

Gerard, R. W. (1949). Physiology and psychiatry. *Amer. J. Psychiat.*, **106**, 161–173.

Glick, S. D., & Greenstein, S. (1972). Amnesia following cortical damage in mice. *Behav. Biol.*, **7**, 573–583.

Glickman, S. (1958). Deficits in avoidance learning produced by stimulation of the ascending reticular formation. *Can. J. Psychol.*, **12**, 97–102.

Glickman, S. E. (1961). Perseverative neural processes and consolidation of the memory trace. *Psychol. Bull.*, **58**, 218–233.

Goddard, G. V. (1964). Amygdaloid stimulation and learning in the rat. *J. Comp. Physiol. Psychol.*, 58, 23–30.

Goddard, G. V. (1969). Analysis of avoidance conditioning following cholinergic stimulation of amygdala in rats. *J. Comp. Physiol. Psychol.*, 68, 1–18.

Gold, P. E. (1970). Localization of a memory system for passive avoidance learning. Unpublished doctoral dissertation. University of North Carolina, Chapel Hill.

Gold, P. E., Bueno, O. F., & McGaugh, J. L. (1973). Training and task-related differences in retrograde amnesia thresholds determined by direct cortical stimulation of the cortex in rats. *Physiol. Behav.*, 11, 57–63.

Gold, P. E., Farrell, W., & King, R. A. (1971). Retrograde amnesia after localized brain shock in passive avoidance learning. *Physiol. Behav.*, 7, 709–712.

Gold, P. E., & King, R. A. (1972). Caudate stimulation and retrograde amnesia: Amnesia threshold and gradient. *Behav. Biol.*, 7, 709–715.

Gold, P. E., McDonald, R., & McGaugh, J. L. (1973). Direct cortical stimulation: A further study of treatment intensity effects on retrograde amnesia gradients. *Behav. Biol.*, 10, 485–490.

Gold, P. E., & McGaugh, J. L. (1972). Effect of recent footshock on brain seizures and behavioral convulsions induced by electrical stimulation of the brain. *Behav. Biol.*, 7, 421–426.

Gold, P. E., & McGaugh, J. L. (1973a). Relationship between amnesia and brain seizures in rats. *Physiol. Behav.*, 10, 41–46.

Gold, P. E., & McGaugh, J. L. (1973b). In preparation.

Gold, P. E., Macri, J., & McGaugh, J. L. (1973a). Retrograde amnesia gradients: Effects of direct cortical stimulation. *Science*, 179, 1343–1345.

Gold, P. E., Macri, J., & McGaugh, J. L. (1973b). Retrograde amnesia produced by subseizure amygdala stimulation. *Behav. Biol.*, 9, 671–680.

Gold, P. E., Macri, J., &·McGaugh, J. L. (1973c). Amnesia produced by low-level subcortical stimulation. In preparation.

Green, J. D. (1960). The hippocampus. In *Handbook of physiology, Section 1: Neurophysiology*. Vol. II. American Physiological Society, Washington, D. C.

Haycock, J. W., Deadwyler, S. A., Sideroff, S. I., & McGaugh, J. L. (1973). Retrograde amnesia and cholinergic systems in the caudate–putamen complex and dorsal hippocampus of the rat. *Exp. Neurol.*, 41, 201–213.

Haycock, J. W., & McGaugh, J. L. (1973). Retrograde amnesia gradients as a function of ECS-intensity. *Behav. Biol.*, 9, 123–127.

Hayes, K. J. (1950). The current path in electric convulsion shock. *Arch. Neurol. Psychiat.*, 63, 102–109.

Herz, M. J. (1972). Brain stimulation and the production of retrograde amnesia. Papers Amer. Psychol. Assoc. 80th Ann. Convention, Honolulu.

Herz, M. J., & Peeke, H. V. S. (1971). Impairment of extinction with caudate nucleus stimulation. *Brain Res.*, 33, 519–522.

Hirano, T. (1965). Effects of functional disturbances of the limbic system on the memory consolidation. *Jap. Psychol. Res.*, 7, 171–182.

Hostetter, G. (1968). Hippocampal lesions in rats weaken the retrograde effect of ECS. *J. Comp. Physiol. Psychol.*, 66, 349–353.

Hudspeth, W. J. (1973). Brain damage and retrograde amnesia: An electrographic control. *Behav. Biol.*, **8**, 131–135.

Hudspeth, W. J., & Wilsoncroft, W. E. (1969). Retrograde amnesia: Time-dependent effects of rhinencephalic lesions. *J. Neurobiol.*, **1**, 221–232.

Ilyutchenok, R. Y., & Vinnitsky, I. M. (1971). Influence of high-frequency stimulation of the amygdaloid complex on memory in rats. *Jurnal Visshchei Deyatelnosti*, **21**, 1220–1222.

Jarvik, M. E., & Kopp, R. (1967). Transcorneal electroconvulsive shock and retrograde amnesia in mice. *J. Comp. Physiol. Psychol.*, **64**, 431–433.

John, E. R. (1972). Statistical versus switchboard theories of memory. *Science*, **177**, 850–864.

Kaada, B. R. (1972). Stimulation and regional ablation of the amygdaloid complex with reference to functional representation. In B. E. Eleftheriou (Ed.), *The neurobiology of the amygdala*. Plenum Press, New York. Pp. 205–282.

Kapp, B. S., & Schneider, A. M. (1971). Selective recovery from retrograde amnesia produced by hippocampal spreading depression. *Science*, **173**, 1149–1151.

Kesner, R. P., & Conner, H. S. (1972). Independence of short- and long-term memory: A neural system approach. *Science*, **176**, 432–434.

Kesner, R. P., & Doty, R. W. (1968). Amnesia produced in cats by local seizure activity initiated from the amygdala. *Exp. Neurol.*, **21**, 58–68.

Konorski, J. (1967). *Integrative activity of the brain*. University of Chicago Press, Chicago.

Landfield, P. W., Tusa, R. J., & McGaugh, J. L. (1973). Effects of posttrial hippocampal stimulation on memory storage and EEG activity. *Behav. Biol.*, **8**, 485–505.

Lashley, K. S. (1950). In search of the engram. *Symp. Soc. Exp. Biol.* **4**, 454–482.

Lenzer, I. I. (1972). Differences between behavior reinforced by electrical stimulation of the brain and conventionally reinforced behavior: An associative analysis. *Psychol. Bull.*, **78**, 103–118.

Levine, M. S., Goldrich, S. G., Pond, F. J., Livesey, P., & Schwartzbaum, J. S. (1970). Retrograde amnestic effects of inferotemporal and amygdaloid seizures upon conditioned suppression of lever-pressing in monkeys. *Neuropsychologia*, **8**, 431–442.

Lewis, D. J., & Maher, B. A. (1965). Neural consolidation and electroconvulsive shock. *Psychol. Rev.*, **72**, 225–239.

Lidsky, T. I., Levine, M. S., Kreinick, C. J., & Schwartzbaum, J. (1970). Retrograde effects of amygdaloid stimulation on conditioned suppression (CER) in rats. *J. Comp. Physiol. Psychol.*, **73**, 135–149.

Lidsky, A., & Slotnick, B. N. (1970). Electrical stimulation of hippocampus and electroconvulsive shock produce similar amnestic effects in mice. *Neuropsychologia*, **8**, 363–369.

McDonough, J. H., & Kesner, R. P. (1971). Amnesia produced by brief electrical stimulation of amygdala or dorsal hippocampus in cats. *J. Comp. Physiol. Psychol.*, **77**, 171–178.

McGaugh, J. L. (1966). Time-dependent processes in memory storage. *Science*, **153**, 1351–1358.

McGaugh, J. L., & Alpern, H. P. (1966). Effects of electroshock on memory: Amnesia without convulsions. *Science*, **152**, 665–666.

McGaugh, J. L., & Dawson, R. G. (1971). Modification of memory storage processes. In W. K. Honig & P. H. R. James (Eds.), *Animal Memory.* Academic Press, New York. Pp. 215–242.

McGaugh, J. L., & Herz, M. J. (1972). *Memory consolidation.* Albion Publishing Co., San Francisco.

McGaugh, J. L., & Zornetzer, S. (1970). Amnesia and brain seizure activity in mice: Effects of diethyl ether anesthesia prior to electroshock stimulation. *Commun. Behav. Biol., 5,* 243–248.

Mahut, H. (1962). Effects of subcortical electrical stimulation of learning in the rat. *J. Comp. Physiol. Psychol., 55,* 472–477.

Mahut, H. (1964). Effects of subcortical electrical stimulation on discrimination learning in cats. *J. Comp. Physiol. Psychol., 58,* 390–395.

Miller, A. J. (1968). Variations in retrograde amnesia parameters of electroconvulsive shock and time of testing. *J. Comp. Physiol. Psychol., 66,* 40–47.

Miller, R. R., & Springer, A. D. (1973). Amnesia, consolidation, and retrieval. *Psychol. Rev., 80,* 69–79.

Olds, J. (1969). The central nervous system and the reinforcement of behavior. *Amer. Psychol., 24,* 114–132.

Peeke, H. V. S., & Herz, M. J. (1971). Caudate nucleus stimulation retroactively impairs complex maze learning in the rat. *Science, 173,* 80–82.

Penfield, W., & Milner, B. (1958). Memory deficit produced by bilateral lesions in the hippocampal zone. *AMA Arch. Neurol. Psychiat., 79,* 475–497.

Pinel, J. P. J. (1971). Disruption of ECS-induced seizures in rats by antecedent footshock. *Commun. Behav. Biol., 6,* 79–85.

Reitz, S. L., & Gerbrandt, L. K. (1971). Pre- and posttrial temporal lobe seizures in monkeys and memory consolidation. *J. Comp. Physiol. Psychol., 74,* 179–184.

Rosvold, H. E., & Delgado, J. M. R. (1956). The effect on delayed-alternation test performance of stimulating or destroying electrical structures within the frontal lobes of the monkey's brain. *J. Comp. Physiol. Psychol., 49,* 365–372.

Ruch, S. H., & Driscoll, D. A. (1968). Current distribution in the brain from surface electrodes. *Anes. Anal. Current Res. 47,* 717–723.

Russell, W. R., & Nathan, P. W. (1946). Traumatic amnesia. *Brain, 69,* 280–300.

Schneider, A. M., Kapp, B., Aron, C., & Jarvik, M. E. (1969). Retroactive effects of transcorneal and transpinnate ECS on step-through latencies of mice and rats. *J. Comp. Physiol. Psychol., 69,* 506–509.

Schwartzbaum, J. S., & Gustafson, J. W. (1970). Peripheral shock, implanted electrodes and artifactual interactions: A renewed warning. *Psychon. Sci., 20,* 49–50.

Shinkman, P. G., & Kaufman, K. P. (1972). Posttrial hippocampal stimulation and CER acquisition in the rat. *J. Comp. Physiol. Psychol., 80,* 283–292.

Thompson, R. (1958). The effect of intracranial stimulation on memory in cats. *J. Comp. Physiol. Psychol., 51,* 421–426.

Van Buskirk, R. B., & McGaugh, J. L. (1973). Retrograde amnesia and brain seizure activity in mice: Strain differences. In preparation.

Vardaris, R. M., & Gehres, L. D. (1970). Brain seizure patterns and ESB-induced amnesia for passive avoidance. *Physiol. Behav., 5,* 1271–1275.

Vardaris, R. M., & Schwartz, K. E. (1971). Retrograde amnesia for passive avoidance produced by stimulation of dorsal hippocampus. *Physiol. Behav., 6,* 131–135.

Weissman, A. (1963). Effect of electroconvulsive shock intensity and seizure pattern on retrograde amnesia in rats. *J. Comp. Physiol. Psychol.,* **56,** 806–810.

Weissman, A. (1964). Retrograde amnesic effects of supramaximal electroconvulsive shock on one-trial acquisition in rats: A replication. *J. Comp. Physiol. Psychol.,* **57,** 248–250.

Wilburn, M. W., & Kesner, K. P. (1972). Differential amnestic effects produced by electrical stimulation of the caudate nucleus and nonspecific thalamic system. *Exp. Neurol.* **34,** 45–50.

Woodbury, L. A., & Davenport, V. D. (1952). Design and use of a new electroshock seizure apparatus, and analysis of factors altering seizure threshold and pattern. *Arch. Int. Pharmacodyn. Ther.,* **92,** 97–107.

Wyers, E. J., & Deadwyler, S. A. (1971). Duration and nature of retrograde amnesia produced by stimulation of caudate nucleus. *Physiol. Behav.,* **6,** 97–103.

Wyers, E. J., Peeke, H. V. S., Williston, J. S., & Herz, M. J. (1968). Retroactive impairment of passive avoidance learning by stimulation of the caudate nucleus. *Exp. Neurol.,* **22,** 350–366.

Zerbolio, D. J. (1971). Retrograde amnesia: The first post-trial hour. *Commun. Behav. Biol.,* **6,** 25–30.

Zornetzer, S. F. (1972). Brain stimulation and retrograde amnesia in rats: A neuro-anatomical approach. *Physiol. Behav.,* **8,** 239–244.

Zornetzer, S. F., Chronister, R. B., & Ross, B. (1973). The hippocampus and retrograde amnesia: Localization of some positive and negative memory disruption sites. *Behav. Biol.,* **8,** 507–518.

Zornetzer, S. F., & McGaugh, J. L. (1970). Effects of frontal brain electroshock stimulation on EEG activity and memory in rats: Relationship to ECS-produced retrograde amnesia. *J. Neurobiol.,* **1,** 379–394.

Zornetzer, S. F., & McGaugh, J. L. (1971a). Retrograde amnesia and brain seizures in mice. *Physiol. Behav.,* **7,** 401–408.

Zornetzer, S. F., & McGaugh, J. L. (1971b). Retrograde amnesia and brain seizures in mice: Further analysis. *Physiol. Behav.,* **7,** 841–845.

Zornetzer, S. F., & McGaugh, J. L. (1972). Electrophysiological correlates of frontal cortex-induced retrograde amnesia. *Physiol. Behav.,* **8,** 233–238.

Zubin, J., & Barrera, S. E. (1941). Effect of electric convulsive therapy on memory. *Proc. Soc. Exp. Biol. Med.,* **48,** 596–597 (abstract).

Chapter 5

A BIOCHEMICAL APPROACH TO LEARNING
AND MEMORY: FOURTEEN YEARS LATER

JOHN GAITO

York University

In the fall of 1959, the author, being interested in possible chemical and neurological aspects of brain function, read two excellent articles by Crick (1954, 1957) in *Scientific American*. It was immediately apparent to him that modification of DNA in the brain might provide the mechanism whereby heredity and environment would interact in behavior. A theoretical paper that discussed this possibility was prepared, and was accepted by *Psychological Review* in early 1960 and published in 1961. This was one of the first papers with a detailed set of hypotheses in an area of research and theory labeled *molecular psychology* (Gaito, 1962), *molecular psychobiology* (Gaito, 1966, 1971), or *molecular neurobiology* (Schmitt, 1967). Although this theoretical formulation now appears to be a simple and naive one, nevertheless it helped in the development of this area. Now, it is interesting to look back and to review the developments during this period, and shortly before.

History

Stage 1: About 1950

At a symposium held during the 1963 meeting of the Midwestern Psychological Association, and at a conference held 1 year later at Kansas State University, the author referred to Ward Halstead as the "Father of Molecular Psychobiology." Although a number of individuals suggested the possible involvement of proteins in memory at about the same time (e.g., Gerard, 1953), it seems appropriate to credit Halstead with the initiation of this area because his theoretical presentations, during the 1948 meeting of the American Psychological Association and

225

in published form (Katz & Halstead, 1950; Halstead, 1951), were the first detailed theoretical descriptions, and they anticipated the formulations of later individuals. Halstead spoke of nuclear proteins being modified during experience and forming the basis for recording experience. His ideas were developed during the period in which the chemical substance of the gene was considered to be protein. However, if he had developed his ideas a few years later, when it was obvious that DNA was the genetic material, he would have stated that DNA and/or RNA were modified during experience, formulations that were offered a few years later by other theorists, such as Hydén (1959), Gaito (1961), and Dingman & Sporn (1961).

Stage 2: About 1958 to 1963–1964

Halstead had set the stage for the development of molecular psychobiology, but it was not until about a decade later that further developments in research and theory occurred. During this interim period, research had firmly established that DNA was the chemical substance of the gene. Thus theorists and researchers interested in learning and memory began to concern themselves with DNA and its sister molecule, RNA. Furthermore, even though Halstead can be considered the originator of molecular psychobiology, he did not directly influence any of the stage 2 researchers and/or theorizers. Rather, the influence came from molecular biology.

One of the first individuals to conduct research with RNA was Cameron (beginning about 1958). His effort was on an applied aspect, the administration of yeast RNA or DNA to elderly humans in an attempt to improve their memory and their overall functioning (Cameron & Solyom, 1961). These yeast RNA experiments seem logically to lead to later "transfer experiments" by McConnell and many others.

About 1958, John and colleagues conducted research using ribonuclease, the enzyme that degrades RNA; the effects of intraventricular injections into trained cats were investigated (1958 unpublished work, cited by John, 1967). Later research used ribonuclease with regenerating planarians (Corning & John, 1961).

Another early researcher was Hydén. Although Hydén had begun analyzing the chemical aspects of RNA in biological experiments during the 1940s, he did not relate RNA to learning and memory until about 1958. His theory of RNA modification in learning was promulgated in 1959; his first research effort analyzing the quantities of RNA and RNA base ratios in trained and untrained animals was described in 1962.

The "transfer experiment" began during this period. McConnell and his group injected RNA from trained and untrained planarians into naive recipients and reported successful transfer results (Zelman, Kabat, Jacobson, & McConnell, 1963). These experiments were a continuation of the regeneration and cannibalism experiments with planarians (McConnell, Jacobson, & Kimble, 1959; McConnell, 1962).

Other early research was by Dingman & Sporn (1961) and Chamberlain, Rothschild, & Gerard (1963)—with 8-azaguanine—and Flexner, Flexner, & Stellar (1963)—with puromycin—to determine the effects of chemicals on behavior.

The author's interest in molecular psychobiology developed in response to the Crick articles, as has been indicated above. Because of lack of adequate equipment and facilities, the author's research did not begin until 1963, in the Microbial Genetics and Virology Laboratory at Kansas State University, with an attempt to determine if base amounts in brain DNA change as a result of experience (Gaito, 1966). In 1964, the research effort was transferred to the Molecular Psychobiology Laboratory at York University (Gaito, Koffer, & Mottin, 1965).

During this early period, theories of RNA modification were presented by Hydén (1959), Dingman & Sporn (1961), Cameron (1963), and McConnell (1963). DNA modification was suggested by Gaito (1961). All these individuals at first had Instructive Models (change of structure of existing molecules) as opposed to Selective Models (release of existing molecules or release of potential molecules). The latter were suggested first by Briggs & Kitto (1962) and Smith (1962).

At this stage, some theoretical ideas were published in journals, the ones indicated above as well as Dingman & Sporn (1964), Gaito (1963), and Gaito & Zavela (1964). Other ideas were not published, or appeared in informal print, such as McConnell's *Worm Runners Digest,* a number of dittoed and mimeographed articles and notes that were circulated to a small group of interested individuals, and in symposia (e.g., at the Midwestern Psychological Association meetings in 1962, 1963; at Kansas State University, 1964).

The terms "memory molecule" (Gaito, 1963) and "tape recorder molecule" (McConnell, 1963) were introduced into the literature at this time. Unfortunately, there are great misconceptions concerning these terms. Many people assume that the implication is that "memory" is in the molecule and does not require neurological functioning. Such an idea is fallacious. The meaning is that a specific molecule codes for a potential experiential event but that it is actualized only in a complex functioning organism via synaptic junctions, and so on. Even in the authors' first paper (Gaito, 1961), he maintained that the chemical approach (an intracellular one) complemented the intercellular synaptic approach.

Superficially there appears to be conflict between the synaptic hypothesis and the ideas presented here. However, this need not be the case. The synaptic hypothesis allows for changes to occur elsewhere in nerve cells but concentrates on the synaptic changes effecting learning and memory. On the other hand the present viewpoint agrees that changes occur at the synapse but stresses the modification in the genic, or by-products of the genic, material; the synaptic changes are preliminary in nature. Furthermore, it is probable that both mechanisms are involved in learning and memory. (p. 291)

Few, if any, individuals in this area (other than popular-science writers) believe that memory is maintained within a single molecule distinct from a functioning nervous system. Unfortunately, even some individuals within molecular psychobiology are guilty of such misconceptions. It is rather interesting that Ungar (1970) criticizes memory-molecule or tape-recorder-molecule ideas of others, but then offers his own memory molecule, *scotophobin*, which leads to dark-avoidance in an animal (Ungar, 1972a,b).

Another misconception is that the memory molecule is one that is shaped by environmental stimuli, the old Instructive Model idea. The memory molecule notion can fit into either an Instructive Model or a Selective Model. Both deal only with a molecule that codes for *potential behavior* via a complex set of intracellular and intercellular events (in the same way that DNA provides a genetic code or "genetic memory molecule" for potential characteristics such as eye color, hair color, range of intellectual functioning, etc.). Unfortunately, researchers do not always read carefully the ideas presented by others.

Stage 3: About 1964 to the Present

Soon the field rapidly expanded. The "transfer researchers," influenced by McConnell's planaria work (and possibly indirectly via the yeast RNA experiments of Cameron), became numerous; for example, Ungar & Oceguerra-Navarro, (1965), and Jacobson's group at UCLA (Babich et al., 1965). Probably many individuals entering molecular psychobiology at this time were attracted to this work. Most laboratories attempted some research of this nature, as did the Molecular Psychobiology Laboratory, at York University—using labeled RNA to determine where in the recipient brain the injected RNA and RNA constituents were located (Shaeffer & Gaito, 1966).

Other researchers entering the field were Barondes, using RNA and protein synthesis inhibitors (e.g., Barondes & Jarvik, 1964); Agranoff, using mainly protein synthesis inhibitors (e.g., Agranoff & Klinger, 1964);

Glassman, concerned with the amount of labeled precursors of RNA entering brain tissue during shock avoidance conditioning (e.g., Zemp, Wilson, Schlesinger, Boggan, & Glassman, 1966); and a host of other individuals. At the present time there are many researchers, too numerous to mention, engaged in an attempt to uncover the relationship between gene and gene products (DNA, RNA, protein) and learning and memory events.

It is unfortunate, and shortsighted, that some of the reviews and papers by individuals entering the area during this period seem to show a superficial knowledge of the early phases of molecular psychobiology. For example, Cameron is seldom mentioned; yet he was one of the first individuals to conduct research in molecular psychobiology, and his yeast RNA experiments were a logical forerunner of the transfer experiment.

An interesting aspect of this history is the fact that during the early period many psychologists were involved (e.g., Corning, Halstead, Gaito, John, McConnell) whereas during the later development biochemists and geneticists tend to dominate the scene.

Important Questions

There are three important questions researchers have been trying to handle in this area. They are as follows:

1. Do quantitative changes in DNA, RNA, and/or proteins occur during learning and memory events?
2. Do qualitative changes in DNA, RNA, and/or proteins occur during learning and memory events?
3. Do these changes (quantitative and/or qualitative) lead directly to (i.e., cause) learning and memory events?

Methods Used

In attempting to answer these questions, a number of methods have been used. One can classify these methods in molecular psychobiology as either direct or indirect.

The *direct approach* uses behavior as the independent variable and neurochemical aspects as the dependent variable. For example, Hydén & Egyhazi (1962) trained rats to climb a wire to obtain food and analyzed the RNA base ratios to determine if these ratios differ in trained and untrained animals; the author contrasted the amounts, and specific activities, of RNA and protein in behaving and control rats (Gaito, 1967).

The *indirect approach* reverses the procedure: neurochemical variations are the independent variable whereas the dependent variable is a behavioral measure (e.g., Barondes & Cohen, 1968; Agranoff & Klinger, 1964; Zelman et al., 1963).

Summary of Research Results

It seems efficient to evaluate and summarize the research results relative to each of the three questions cited above.

Do quantitative changes in DNA, RNA, and/or proteins occur during learning and memory events?

Although some of the changes in amounts of DNA reported during learning events (e.g., Gaito et al., 1965) probably indicate a change in absolute amounts of DNA, by glial cell changes, for example, most of the reported changes are relative ones. With an increase or decrease in amounts of RNA and protein, or other cellular constituents, the amounts of DNA per gram of tissue will change also.

There have been many reports indicating RNA and protein changes during learning and memory (e.g., Hydén & Egyhazi, 1962; Gaito, 1967). However, such quantitative changes are not overly interesting, inasmuch as one would expect that during behavior many chemicals would change in quantity (e.g., oxygen consumption, ATP usage, etc.). Thus, although it is quite conclusive that quantitative changes in RNA and protein appear during learning and memory, such changes may be of trivial nature.

Do qualitative changes in DNA, RNA, and/or proteins occur during learning and memory events; for example, are new molecules formed?

The author's early theory in *Psychological Review* in 1961 suggested the possibility that qualitative changes resulted in DNA (with adenine changing to guanine, or vice versa, and guanine to cytosine, or vice versa) during experiental events. Thus the first research at Kansas State University evaluated DNA base amounts of dogs and rats subjected to varying degrees of experiences (Gaito, 1966). The results were negative. Unfortunately, even if qualitative changes had occurred in DNA, base analysis procedures are too gross to detect possible differences.

Hydén in his early work with RNA base ratios assumed that he was showing qualitative changes in RNA (Hydén & Egyhazi, 1962). Unfortunately, base ratio changes could indicate quantitative changes in RNA because this method is unable to differentiate qualitative and quantitative changes.

The procedures that appear to be the most appropriate for evaluating qualitative changes in RNA are the DNA–RNA hybridization methods. The only laboratory that has attempted to use these methods in a systematic program involving learning and memory is the Molecular Psychobiology Laboratory at York University. However, although the initial results appeared to be successful and suggested qualitative changes in RNA during learning, later experiments tended to question this result (Gaito, 1972). Unfortunately, the procedures are so complex and expensive in time, effort, and money that this approach had to be abandoned before conclusive results (positive or negative) were available.

There appear to be a few methods of value in determining if qualitative changes in protein occur during behavioral changes. One involves the use of chromatography or electrophoresis. For example, polyacrylamide gel electrophoresis has suggested that the profile of specific protein patterns may be different in learning and nonlearning animals (Yanagihara & Hydén, 1971). This procedure has the disadvantage that a protein band that appears to be lacking (e.g., in a nonlearning animal) may merely be available in such low quantities that it is undetectable by electrophoretic procedures. In spite of this aspect, the polyacrylamide gel electrophoresis appears to be a useful procedure and is being used presently by a number of researchers, including those in the Molecular Psychobiology Laboratory at York University (Hopkins, Gaito, & Howick, 1973), to evaluate protein patterns.

A very sensitive procedure is the immunological one, which involves the use of antibodies to detect the presence or absence of specific brain proteins (Jankovic, 1972). Yanagihara & Hydén (1971) have used this technique to advantage.

The most significant approach relative to the question may be provided by the *transfer paradigm*. This paradigm involves injecting brain material from trained animals into one group of naive recipients and material from untrained animals into a second group of naive recipients, then noting the behavior of both groups on the learning task. At first the results were positive, showing a superiority of the recipients with extracts from trained animals. Then a large number of individual researchers were unable to confirm this result. Recently, Ungar (1972a) has spelled out the conditions wherein an "interanimal transfer effect" will occur and many researchers have been successful with these conditions. Thus at this time the phenomenon seems to be genuine, although not always reproducible. The problem, however, seems to concern what is being transferred (memory or some type of cellular facilitation), what molecular species is responsible for the effect (protein or RNA), and whether the effect is task-specific (Gaito, 1971).

Recently, Ungar, Desiderio, & Parr (1972) have isolated from dark-avoidance-conditioned animals a polypeptide, a small protein called *scotophobin*, containing 15 amino acids, which is reported to induce dark-avoidance behavior when injected into naive recipients. This chemical in synthetic state is claimed to produce the same effect. A number of other researchers have obtained significant results (e.g., Bryant, Santos, & Byrne, 1972; Guttman, Mattwyshyn, & Warriner, 1972; Malin & Guttman, 1972; McConnell, personal communication). Other research, however, does not show this effect (e.g., Ali et al., 1971; Goldstein et al., 1971), and a detailed article by Stewart (1972) raises questions about the overall methodology and conclusions of the scotophobin advocates. Also there is some unofficial information that other researchers have not obtained significant results with scotophobin. Unfortunately some research with statistically nonsignificant results is never published, either because editors do not accept such papers or the authors do not desire to publish these results.

The positive scotophobin results would suggest a unique polypeptide or protein of 15 amino acids. The implication then would be that there is also a unique RNA of 45 nucleotides during dark-avoidance conditioning to code for this protein.

The overall conclusion relative to this question is that there is no consistent conclusive evidence to indicate that qualitative changes in either DNA, RNA, or proteins occur during learning and memory, although the transfer work may provide this conclusiveness within a few years. Unfortunately the answering of this question is difficult because of the methodologies required.

Do these changes (quantitative and/or qualitative) lead directly to learning and memory events?

Even if qualitative changes in DNA, RNA, and/or protein were shown conclusively, such results would not mean that these changes are the basis for the behavioral events. It is possible that the chemical and behavioral changes are correlative ones as a result of general cellular activity (Gaito, 1971). Although this is the most important of the three questions, most of the methods used have not been able to answer it. The only method pertinent to this question is the transfer paradigm. But the results are not clearcut at this time, as was indicated above.

Conclusions

It seems safe to conclude that quantitative changes in RNA and protein do occur. But such information is of trivial nature inasmuch as changes in many cellular constituents are also occurring during the behavior of concern. With regard to possible qualitative changes in DNA, RNA, and/or protein, the research has not been able to answer this question either affirmatively or negatively at this time. The most important point, that the changes lead to the behavior, can be evaluated at this time only by transfer experiments, and the results from these experiments, although suggestive in the hands of Ungar and McConnell and others, do not provide a clear-cut conclusion as yet.

Methodological Problems

There are a number of methodological problems faced by researchers in this area.

Stress

Most behavioral tasks assessing learning and memory include stress aspects. For example, the task of Shashoua (1968) in which fish attempt to swim with styrofoam attached to their ventral surfaces is an extreme example. Although Shashoua has a number of control groups to handle stress and other nonlearning variables, it is difficult to see how he would completely eliminate stress from his design. The shock-avoidance tasks are also replete with stress factors. Even the change-of-handedness design by Hydén probably includes some stress because of the forced changing of hand for retrieving food pellets.

Nonlearning

Many researchers contrast the brain chemistry and/or behavior of "learning" animals with groups of "nonlearning" ones so as to determine effects of learning. Unfortunately, it is difficult or impossible to obtain a completely nonlearning animal. Even though the nonlearning control may not be learning the task imposed by the experimenter, he may be learning many things about the situation, thus making difficult the attempt to determine the contributions of learning.

Motivation

In any design, the animals must be motivated to perform some task. The degree of motivation probably varies with each subject and this variability contaminates the results of the research.

Specificity of Chemicals Administered

The researchers using the indirect approach assume that the chemicals administered to the subjects have a specific effect and minimal, or no, side or general effects. Unfortunately, such an assumption appears to be completely unrealistic. Two or more drugs can have the same effect. And one drug can have multiple effects. Thus, it is quite difficult to attribute results specifically to one process with indirect procedures.

Memory vs Retrieval

A crucial problem faced by many researchers dealing with memory is that the results are assumed to be showing the presence or absence of memory factors when in reality retrieval events may be occurring. For example, a number of researchers inject chemicals such as puromycin or acetoxycycloheximide and note that these antibiotics result in a loss of memory at certain time periods and under certain specific conditions. However, if saline is administered during the period of loss of memory (Flexner & Flexner, 1968) or if the animal is stimulated (Barondes & Cohen, 1968), memory returns. Such results probably suggest that the researcher has been dealing with retrieval mechanisms rather than with memory.

In a series of important experiments, Myers (1972) has shown that researchers dealing with memory events might be advised to drop the use of terms such as "memory" and "loss of memory" and refer instead to "accessibility to memory" and "loss of accessibility to memory." He reported that rats who had been subjected to loss of memory by specific brain lesions were able to show the return of memory by later injections of amphetamine.

One Type of Learning?

The learning processes during behavior are quite variable because what has been labeled as learning may consist of a number of separate events rather than a single unitary process. There are two or more different types of learning recognized by psychologists. This aspect makes it quite difficult to determine the molecular correlates associated with learning.

A New Methodology

Because of the above problems there is the need to develop and utilize methods that minimize or eliminate some or all of the contaminating influences. One methodology that may offer promise is the "kindling effect." A group of researchers (Goddard, McIntyre, & Leech, 1969; McIntyre, 1970) have found that repeated low-level stimulation via unilaterally implanted electrodes in a number of subcortical sites lead eventually to bilateral clonic convulsions that are of relatively permanent nature. For example, daily administered electrical stimulation to the amygdala produces clonic convulsions, on the average, in about 10–15 days. The initial stimulations have little effect on the animal's behavior (stage 1—normal exploratory behavior); with several repetitions, overt indications of seizure activity can be observed, such as eyelid blinking, chewing, salivation (stage 2—behavioral automatisms). With further stimulations, these automatisms culminate in a complete convulsion (stage 3—clonic convulsions). The rat stands on its hindpaws, and bilateral clonic convulsions ensue; these continue after electrical stimulation is terminated. Attending these behavioral changes are modifications in the EEG. Such results may be indicating similarity to the memory aspect involved in learning. Thus, one might hypothesize that the kindling effect simulates the learning process in that behavior is being modified over time in response to an invariant stimulus.

Pressing levers, wandering into one chamber of two- or three-chambered apparatus, and the like, in usual learning paradigms are behavioral patterns that can be quite variable, and the subject may come upon these accidentally. However, clonic convulsions are automatic, involuntary, stereotyped responses that the subject never utilized previously, are clear-cut and easy to identify, and are responses he would not come upon accidentally. In addition, the kindling paradigm has the advantage of allowing for easy control of stress, motivation, and other aspects.

Two sets of experiments using the kindling procedures have been completed in the Molecular Psychobiology Laboratory at this time. Electrodes were implanted unilaterally in the amygdala in Wistar rats approximately 100 days of age (brain coordinates: 0.5 mm posterior to bregma, 4.5 mm from midline, 8.5 mm from skull). Six or more days later, experimental rats were subjected to 60 Hz sine waves of 100 μA intensity (peak to peak) for 60 sec at 12 hr intervals. Control animals were connected to the stimulator lead wires but were not stimulated.

In one set of three experiments, an evaluation of chemical events underlying the kindling process was attempted. The specific chemicals chosen were the prealbumin range (PAR) proteins of the soluble protein fraction, because some of these proteins have been reported to be brain specific (Yanagihara and Hydén, 1971; Kawakita, 1972). Electrophoretic patterns of the PAR proteins were the same for all rats utilized: nonstimulated, stimulated for several days (stage 1), stimulated until stage 2 was well underway, and stage 3 rats.

In a second series of four experiments, the transfer paradigm was incorporated with the kindling procedures. The results suggested that naive recipients that had received intraperitoneal injections of soluble proteins from kindled rats reached stage 2 and stage 3 at a slower rate than did recipients injected with soluble proteins from nonkindled rats, as long as the injection utilized two brain amounts. If the injection contained soluble protein from one brain, control and experimental recipients were not different in the rate of kindling. Table 1 shows the results of these four experiments. The retardation effect is of slight magnitude. For example, the mean number of trials to the first clonic convulsion for donors in the different experiments tended to be between 8 and 12, with a mean of about 10. The means for the control recipients with both one and two brain amounts were of this magnitude also. However, the experimental recipients with two brain amounts had a mean of 15.0, a 25% increase beyond the upper limit of the 8–12 range.

At present, experiments are underway using intracranial injections to determine if the retardation effect is a consistent phenomenon. If such consistency is indicated, later experiments will attempt to isolate and determine the properties of the chemical or chemicals responsible for this effect.

Acknowledgments

The intent of this article is not to review all the molecular psychobiological literature (which is becoming voluminous), but merely to discuss

Table 1   Mean Number of Trials to First Behavioral Automatism (Stage 2) and to First Clonic Convulsion (Stage 3)

	No. of Trials		
	To Stage 2	To Stage 3	No. of Rats
Two brain amounts			
E	9.1	15.0	28
C	5.2	8.3	13
One brain amount			
E	6.7	12.4	33
C	5.3	10.5	13

NOTE: E = naive recipients injected with soluble proteins from kindled rats.
          C = naive recipients injected with soluble proteins from nonkindled rats.

those contributions most significant to the goals of molecular psychobiology.

The author wishes to thank William Corning and James McConnell, two early contributors to the development of molecular psychobiology, for reading a preliminary draft of this paper and providing comments, especially on the History section.

References

Agranoff, B. W., & Klinger, P. D. (1964). Puromycin effect on memory fixation in the goldfish. *Science, 146*, 952–953.

Ali, A., Faesal, J. H. R., Sarantakis, D., Stevenson, D., & Weinstein, B. (1971). Synthesis of a structure proposed for scotophobin. *Experientia, 27*, 1138.

Babich, F. R., Jacobson, A. L., Bubash, S., & Jacobson, A. (1965). Transfer of a response to naive rats by injection of ribonucleic acid extracted from trained rats. *Science, 149*, 655–657.

Barondes, S. H., & Cohen, H. D. (1968). Arousal and conversion of "short term" to "long term" memory. *Proc. Nat. Acad. Sci., 61*, 923–929.

Barondes, S. H., & Jarvik, M. E. (1964). The influences of actinomycin-D on brain RNA synthesis and on memory. *J. Neurochem., 11*, 187–195.

Briggs, M. H., & Kitto, G. B. (1962). The molecular basis of memory and learning. *Psychol. Rev., 69*, 537–541.

Bryant, R. C., Santos, N. N., & Byrne, W. L. (1972). Synthetic scotophobin in goldfish: Specificity and effect on learning. *Science, 177*, 635–636.

Cameron, D. E. (1963). The process of remembering. *Brit. J. Psychiat., 109*, 325–333.

Cameron, D. E., & Solyom, L. (1961). Effects of ribonucleic acid on memory. *Geriatrics, 16*, 74–81.

Chamberlain, T. J., Rothschild, G. H., & Gerard, R. (1963). Drugs affecting RNA and learning. *Proc. Nat. Acad. Sci., 49*, 918–924.

Corning, W. C., & John, E. R. (1961). Effect of ribonuclease on retention of conditioned response in regenerated planarians. *Science, 134*, 1363–1365.

Crick, F. H. C. (1954). The structure of the hereditary material. *Sci. Amer., 191*, 54–61.

Crick, F. H. C. (1957). Nucleic acids. *Sci. Amer., 197*, 188–200.

Dingman, W., & Sporn, M. B. (1961). The incorporation of 8-azaguanine into rat brain RNA and its effect on maze-learning by the rat: An inquiry into the biochemical bases of memory. *J. Psychiat. Res., 1*, 1–11.

Dingman, W., & Sporn, M. B. (1964). Molecular theories of memory. *Science, 144*, 26–29.

Flexner, J. B., Flexner, L. B., & Stellar, E. (1963). Memory in mice as affected by intracerebral puromycin. *Science, 141*, 57–59.

Flexner, L. B., & Flexner, J. B. (1968). Intracerebral saline: Effect on memory of trained mice treated with puromycin. *Science, 159*, 330–331.

Gaito, J. (1961). A biochemical approach to learning and memory. *Psychol. Rev.,* **68,** 288–292.

Gaito, J. (1962). A biochemical conceptualization of learning and memory. *Papers Symp. Models in Psychol.* R. Forgus, chairman. *Midwestern Psychol. Assoc. Meet., Chicago, Ill., May 1962.*

Gaito, J. (1963). DNA and RNA as memory molecules. *Psychol. Rev.,* **70,** 471–480.

Gaito, J. (1966). *Molecular psychobiology: A chemical approach to learning and other behaviors.* Charles C Thomas, Springfield, Ill.

Gaito, J. (1967). Molecular psychobiology laboratory: Development and progress. Tech. Rep. MPL 11. York University, Toronto, Ontario.

Gaito, J. (1971). *DNA complex and adaptive behavior.* Prentice-Hall, Englewood Cliffs, N. J.

Gaito, J. (1972). Successive competition DNA–RNA hybridization procedures to detect the presence or absence of qualitative changes in RNA during behavioral events. *Int. J. Psychobiol.* **2,** 163–176.

Gaito, J., Koffer, K., & Mottin, J. (1965). The effects of auditory stimulation and motor activity on nucleic acids and proteins. Tech. Rep. MPL 1. York University, Toronto, Ontario.

Gaito, J., & Zavala, A. (1964). Neurochemistry and learning. *Psychol. Bull.,* **61,** 45–62.

Gerard, R. W. (1953). What is memory? *Sci. Amer.,* **189,** 118–126.

Goddard, G. V., McIntyre, D. C., & Leech, C. K. (1969). A permanent change in brain function resulting from daily electrical stimulation. *Exp. Neurol.* **25,** 295–330.

Goldstein, A., Sheehan, P., & Goldstein, J. (1971). Unsuccessful attempts to transfer morphine tolerance and passive avoidance by brain extracts. *Nature,* **233,** 126–129.

Guttman, H. N., Matwyshyn, G., & Warriner, G. H., III. (1972). Synthetic scotophobin mediated passive transfer of dark avoidance. *Nature,* **235,** 26–27.

Halstead, W. C. (1951). Brain and intelligence. In L. A. Jeffress (Ed.), *Cerebral mechanism in behavior.* Wiley, New York.

Hopkins, R. W., Gaito, J., & Howick, D. (1973). Electrophoretic histone patterns during shock avoidance conditioning and visual stimulation. *Int. J. Psychobiol.* **2,** 259–263.

Hydén, H. (1959). Biochemical changes in glial cells and nerve cells at varying activity. In *Proc. 4th Int. Congr. Biochem. Biochemistry of the central nervous system.* Vol. III. Pergamon Press, London.

Hydén, H., & Egyhazi, E. (1962). Nuclear RNA changes of nerve cells during a learning experiment in rats. *Proc. Nat. Acad. Sci.,* **48,** 1366–1373.

Jankovic, B. D. (1972). Biological activity of antibrain antibody—an introduction to immunoneurology. In J. Gaito (Ed.), *Macromolecules and behavior* (2nd ed.). Appleton-Century-Crofts, New York.

John, E. R. (1967). *Mechanisms of memory.* Academic Press, New York.

Katz, J. J., & Halstead, W. C. (1950). Protein organization and mental function. *Comp. Psychol. Monogr.,* **20** (103), 1–38.

Kawakita, H. (1972). Immunochemical studies on the brain specific protein. *J. Neurochem.,* **19,** 87–93.

McConnell, J. V. (1962). Memory transfer through cannibalism in planarians. *J. Neuropsychiat.* 3, 42–48.

McConnell, J. V. (1963). A tape recorder theory of RNA. *Papers Symp. Nucleic Acids and Behavior,* J. Gaito, chairman. *Midwestern Psychol. Assoc. Meet., Chicago, Ill., May 1963.*

McConnell, J. V., Jacobson, A. L., & Kimble, D. P. (1959). The effects of regeneration upon retention of a conditioned response in the planarian. *J. Comp. Physiol. Psychol.,* 52, 1–5.

McIntyre, D. A. (1970). Differential amnestic effect of cortical vs. amygdaloid elicited convulsions in rats. *Physiol. Behav.* 5, 747–753.

Malin, D. H., & Guttman, H. H. (1972). Synthetic rat scotophobin induces dark avoidance in mice. *Science,* 178, 1219–1220.

Myers, D. R. (1972). Access to engrams. *Amer. Psychol.,* 27, 124–133.

Schaeffer, E., & Gaito, J. (1966). The effect of RNA injections on shock avoidance conditioning and on brain chemistry. Tech. Rep. MPL 7. York University, Toronto, Ontario.

Schmitt, F. O. (1967). Molecular neurobiology in the context of the neurosciences. In G. C. Quarton, T. Melnechuk, & F. O. Schmitt (Eds.), *The neurosciences.* Rockefeller University Press, New York.

Shashoua, V. E. (1968). RNA changes in goldfish during learning. *Nature,* 217, 238–240.

Smith, C. E. (1962). Is memory a matter of enzyme induction? *Science,* 138, 889–890.

Stewart, W. W. (1972). Comments on the chemistry of scotophobin. *Nature,* 238, 202–209.

Ungar, G. (1970). Role of proteins and peptides in learning and memory. In G. Ungar (Ed.), *Molecular mechanisms in memory and learning.* Plenum Press, New York.

Ungar, G. (1972a). Biological assays for the molecular coding of acquired information. In J. Gaito (ed.), *Macromolecules and behavior* (2nd ed.). Appleton-Century-Crofts, New York.

Unger, G. (1972b). Molecular organization of neural information processing. In G. H. Bourne (Ed.), *Structure and function of the nervous system.* Vol. IV. Academic Press, New York.

Ungar, G., Desiderio, D. M., & Parr, W. (1972). Isolation, identification and synthesis of a specific-behavior-inducing brain peptide. *Nature,* 238, 198–202.

Ungar, G., & Oceguerra-Navarro, C. (1965). Transfer of habituation by material extracted from brain. *Nature,* 207, 301–302.

Yanagihara, T., & Hydén, H. (1971). Protein synthesis in various regions of rat hippocampus during learning. *Exp. Neurol.* 31, 151–164.

Zelman, A., Kabat, L., Jacobson, R., & McConnell, J. V. (1963). Transfer of training through injection of "conditioned" RNA into untrained planarians. *Worm Runner's Digest,* 5 (1), 14–21.

Zemp, J. W., Wilson, J. E., Schlesinger, K., Boggan, W. O., & Glassman, E. (1966). Brain function and macromolecules. I. Incorporation of uridine into RNA of mouse brain during short-term training experiences. *Proc. Nat. Acad. Sci.,* 55, 1423–1431.

Chapter 6

VISUAL RIGHT–LEFT CONFUSIONS
IN ANIMAL AND MAN

KAREN S. TEE† and AUSTIN H. RIESEN
University of California, Riverside

Many species learn to discriminate with greater difficulty a pair of lateral mirror-image stimuli than a pair of comparable stimuli in other orientations. For example, oppositely sloped diagonal lines are mirror-image stimuli, and for a number of species a discrimination between horizontal and vertical lines is easier to accomplish than a discrimination between the diagonals. This relative difficulty with the diagonals exists even though the diagonals are perpendicular to each other, just as horizontal and vertical lines are perpendicular to each other.

The confusion between two mirror-image stimuli, and the relative difficulty of learning a discrimination between them, poses a number of questions, some of which are discussed below. The mirror-image phenomenon is also of importance in a number of fields. It is relevant to psychologists and educators trying to determine how a normal child develops reading ability and why some children persist in confusing certain letters, such as b and d, or p and q, that are lateral mirror images of each other. (See Fellows, 1968, for a review and discussion of this literature.)

The mirror-image question is also of interest to investigators of the sensory capacities of various species. Even in the human adult, for example, it has been found that when reaction times are measured, lateral mirror-images (such as ⊏ and ⊐) take longer to discriminate than the comparable vertical mirror images (⊔ and ⊓)(Sekular & Houlihan, 1967). Further data on the abilities of different species to discriminate mirror-image stimuli are reviewed later in this section.

° Based on a doctoral dissertation submitted by the senior author in partial fulfillment of the requirements for the Ph.D. degree at the University of California, Riverside.
† Now at the Department of Psychology, Vanier College, Montreal, Canada.

The confusion of mirror-image stimuli must be taken into account by theorists who propose a particular information-processing system to explain how shapes are discriminated. Sutherland (1957a) proposed a theory of shape discrimination for the octopus (later extended to the goldfish and rat) that includes an explanation of why these animals could not discriminate the diagonals, or had great difficulty doing so. He proposed that the animals analyzed each shape in terms of its vertical and horizontal components. As mirror-image diagonal lines do not differ from each other on either of these variables, Sutherland's theory would explain why the discrimination between them could not be learned. Although the theory was modified and elaborated a number of times (e.g., 1960, 1961, 1963b, 1969), in each case Sutherland proposed that the confusion between mirror-image oblique lines (as well as some other kinds of confusions) occurs because of a neural coding mechanism that renders the diagonals identical.

Likewise, Deutsch (1955, 1958, 1962) and Dodwell (1957a, 1957b, 1958, 1961, 1970b) each proposed mechanisms of information processing that result in identical output for mirror-image diagonals. Although details were different, and the two theorists altered their proposals over the years, both suggested a scanning mechanism that sweeps across the visual field or a portion of it, much as an electron beam sweeps across a television screen. The scanning mechanism transforms the shape into a particular time-by-intensity function, resulting usually in a distinctive temporal signal for different shapes. In both theories the coding is done in such a way that mirror images are transformed to the same temporal pattern, making it impossible for the animal to learn such a discrimination.

Regardless of which of the above topics is under consideration, certain basic questions need to be answered. These questions are: when does the mirror-image confusion manifest itself (under what conditions), and why does it happen? This chapter is directed primarily to the former problem, of the conditions under which mirror images are confused; it discusses also a suggested basis for the confusion.

Studies of the Mirror-Image Phenomenon

If one reviews the experimental literature with a critical eye, it becomes harder to justify the assumption behind the theories of shape discrimination previously mentioned—that it is extremely difficult or impossible for the lower animals to discriminate mirror-image diagonals.

Octopus and Goldfish. The octopus seems incapable of performing at above-chance levels on a 45°–135° rectangles-discrimination when the stimuli are presented successively, although it learns the comparable horizontal-vertical discrimination (Sutherland, 1957a, 1957b, 1958). Goldfish learn to discriminate the oblique rectangles (mean = 125 trials to criterion) but the horizontal–vertical discrimination is easier (mean = 45 trials). The tasks were simultaneous discriminations, but in posttests, when the stimuli were presented successively, performance remained above chance levels (MacIntosh & Sutherland, 1963). These results applied when the rectangles were black against a light background. When the shapes were white, both problems became more difficult.

Pigeon. The pigeon seems capable of discriminating mirror-image oblique lines. Zeigler & Schmerler (1965) tested three pigeons on a horizontal–vertical discrimination, and three on a 60°–120° problem. Even though the angular difference between the two stimuli is smaller for the latter pair (only 60° difference), the pigeons appeared to learn the obliques discrimination as easily as they did the horizontal–vertical problem. The original task was with a simultaneous presentation, and when three of the pigeons were switched to a successive mode, there was only a slight deterioration in performance.

Over (1969) trained two pigeons on a simultaneous horizontal–vertical problem, and two on a 45°–135° task. The former two reached criterion after 5 and 12 days, respectively, whereas the latter two reached it in 9 and 13 days. After learning the first problem, each subject was taught the other discrimination, then finally was tested with the two discrimination tasks mixed. Reaction times were measured (*a*) when the subjects had learned the first problem, (*b*) when they had learned the second task, and (*c*) for both tasks when the two tasks were mixed in random order. Analysis revealed no difference in reaction times for the two types of discriminations.

Thus, it would appear that although the octopus cannot distinguish mirror-image diagonal lines, both the goldfish and the pigeon are capable of learning the diagonals discrimination. For the goldfish the diagonals discrimination is more difficult to learn than the horizontal–vertical task. For the pigeon, however, the two tasks appear to be of equal difficulty.

Rat. Lashley (1938) reported that distinguishing horizontal from vertical striations is one of the very easiest problems for rats to learn in the jumping-stand apparatus. Yet if the striped figures are rotated so that the lines are sloped 45° in opposite directions "the difficulty is increased" (p. 160). He noted that if the stimulus fields were circular, rather than square, "the contrast is still more pronounced." Lashley did not present data from the rats tested on the diagonals discrimination.

In discriminations with different mirror-image figures (Lashley, 1938), rats failed to perform above chance when the stimuli were, for example, N vs И or S vs Ƨ. Although the rats failed to learn, it would be unwarranted, on the basis of Lashley's work, to infer that they could not discriminate diagonals or that they had great difficulty doing so.

Koronakos & Arnold (1957) tested rats on a succession of eight different visual discriminations. (Each discrimination task had four identical negative stimuli instead of the usual one.) Because they were interested in whether rats could form learning sets, most of their data (for problems 2–7) are presented in terms of the percent correct on the first day's training for each of the several problems. The data for the first and eighth problems, however, are analyzed separately and presented in a different form. Half the rats ($N = 10$) were trained on problem 1 to discriminate horizontal and vertical striations. For these rats, problem 8 was to discriminate a 45° line from a 135° line. For the other 10 rats, the order of these two discriminations was reversed. Data were reported from each group only for rats that reached criterion on both problems. (The authors did not state how many rats this was, but elsewhere in the article they reported that only five of the 20 subjects could learn all eight problems.) The mean number of trials to criterion for the horizontal vs vertical stripes problem when presented first and last was 43.0 and 28.5 trials respectively. (Each trial represented two independent discriminations, since the apparatus contained two separate and independent choice points.) For the diagonal lines discrimination the respective means were 50.0 and 30.0 trials. The authors reported that "neither difference, however, was stable" (p. 13). If these respective differences are unreliable, it would seem unlikely that there is a significant difference between the horizontal–vertical discrimination and the diagonals discrimination. This evidence can not be considered conclusive because there is no information about how many rats failed to learn each of the problems. The Koronakos & Arnold study, then, does not contradict the possibility that rats find a diagonals discrimination harder to learn, but (contrary to the statement made in a review by Appelle, 1972, p. 270), neither does it support it. Koronakos & Arnold's study does indicate that at least some rats can learn the diagonals discrimination; five out of 20 were able to learn all eight problems.

Kinsbourne (1967) tested rats in a Y maze on both black–white and diagonals discriminations. For each type of discrimination, he had two separate groups run under different conditions. In the first condition the appropriate stimuli lined the far wall in each arm of the Y maze. For the oblique discrimination in the first condition, the stripes in both arms were oriented in the same direction. The rats were required to run in the direction of the upper or the lower ends of the stripes. Thus, it was a successive discrimination. In the second condition the stimuli lined *both* walls in each arm. For the oblique discrimination, the rats were required to choose either the arm lined with stripes in the two different directions or the one with stripes running in the same direction. In the first condition, eight of the nine subjects learned the diagonals discrimination (mean trials to criterion = 102.5). For the same–different diagonals task, nine out of 12 reached criterion (mean = 143 trials). These data indicate that under these experimental conditions, at least, it is possible for rats to discriminate between opposite diagonals. However, it is difficult to compare Kinsbourne's data on the mean number of trials to criterion with those from other studies. Kinsbourne allowed each rat a maximum of 300 trials to learn the task. It appears, although one cannot be certain, that the rats that never learned the problem were counted as having learned it in 300 trials. The present writers find it puzzling that only 62.5% (10 of 16) reached criterion on the black–white same–different discrimination when 75% (nine of 12) reached criterion on the diagonals same–different task. Perhaps strong pretraining preference behavior was involved.

Appelle (1972) reported that Dodwell (1970b) demonstrated the rat's difficulty with a diagonals discrimination that persisted regardless of the type of testing apparatus used. However, of the four experiments with rats that Dodwell reported, only the last two included a diagonally striped stimulus, and it was never paired with its opposite diagonal (only with horizontal or vertical stripes), thus shedding no light on the rat's ability to discriminate between the diagonals.

Ely (1970) tested rats extensively in a large number of simultaneous discrimination problems. He measured the ease of learning a discrimination between horizontal stripes and stripes of various orientations, between vertical stripes and stripes of various orientations, and between a number of different pairs of orientations. Each rat learned only one discrimination, and each was given 1056 trials on that problem. The mean number of correct trials for the horizontal–vertical discrimination ($N = 15$) was 859; the mean number correct for the 45°–135° discrimination ($N = 15$) was 723. The reliability of this particular difference was unfortunately not tested, although the difference would appear to be significant. These results show that rats could learn the 45°–135° discrimination, and suggest that the diagonals task was more difficult than the horizontal–vertical task.

In summary, it has been demonstrated that the rat can learn a lateral mirror-image diagonals discrimination (Ely, 1970; Kinsbourne, 1967) and that probably the diagonals discrimination is more difficult than the horizontal–vertical task (Lashley, 1938; Ely, 1970). Furthermore, it is possible but not certain, that the diagonals task and the horizontal–vertical task are of equal difficulty when there are multiple negative stimuli, allowing a type of "oddity" learning (Koronakos & Arnold, 1957).

Rabbit. The rabbit is capable of discriminating diagonal striations (van Hof, 1966, 1970a) or diagonal bars (van Hof, 1970b), in addition to horizontal vs vertical stimuli. The number of trials to criterion was not of primary importance to the author but it would appear that in the 1966 study, the rabbits ($N = 3$) learned the diagonals discrimination faster than the horizontal–vertical task. A simultaneous discrimination was used for training, but control testing on a successive task revealed only a slight drop in performance. In the two 1970 studies the horizontal–vertical discrimination was learned faster than the diagonals task. In these later studies, however, each subject was learning both problems at the same time.

Cat. Sutherland (1963a) trained eight cats on a simultaneous discrimination task. Half the cats learned a horizontal–vertical bar discrimination (mean trials to criterion = 220); the others learned a 45°–135° problem (mean = 215 trials). When the cats were switched to a successive discrimination, performance deteriorated somewhat, but was similar for the two problems and was consistently above chance.

Warren (1969) tested 35 cats on a series of four discrimination problems presented in a counterbalanced order. He found that all cats could learn a 45°–135° simultaneous problem and could learn it as quickly as a horizontal–vertical discrimination. A vertical mirror-image problem (⊔ vs ⊓) was not significantly harder than either of the rectangles discriminations, but the comparable lateral mirror images (⊏ vs ⊐) were harder to learn than any of the other three problems.

Parriss (1964), however, got different results from the four cats he tested on a successive discrimination. Regardless of which task was learned first, the discrimination between the 45° and 135° rectangles was much harder for each subject than was the horizontal–vertical discrimination; all subjects, however, learned both problems. There are obvious differences between a successive and a simultaneous discrimination, and Parriss suggested that Sutherland's cats (1963a) might have learned the simultaneous discrimination on the basis of the overall pattern formed by the two stimulus lines. Parriss also speculated that when Sutherland's cats were switched to a successive discrimination, they might have been responding to parts of a previously learned pattern. Parriss' cats never viewed the two stimuli at the same time, so it was not possible for them to use this cue. Thus, perhaps, the "true" difficulty of the obliques problem was revealed.

There is another factor that may be relevant in explaining the discrepancy between Sutherland's and Parriss' findings, and that is the difference in criteria that the two investigators used. Parriss required 90% correct responding over a period of 4 days (72 out of 80 trials). Sutherland's criterion for the simultaneous discrimination was 95% correct over 2 days (38 out of 40 trials). When Sutherland's cats were switched to the successive discrimination, performance fell below the 80% level on both the diagonals problem and the horizontal–vertical task. Training was continued for 4 days. The cats showed some slight improvement on the horizontal–vertical task, but none on the diagonals task. It is possible, therefore, that if Sutherland had retrained his cats until they met criterion, that Sutherland, also, would have found the diagonals task harder for the cats to learn.

Thus, although the cat can learn the diagonals discrimination (and the lateral mirror-images discrimination), there is some doubt about the true difficulty of the diagonals task, because the apparent difficulty has varied with different investigators and different procedures.

Chimpanzee. Nissen & McCulloch (1937) tested four chimpanzees in a variety of tasks. The results are somewhat hard to interpret because of the complex design of the experiment, but it would appear that the horizontal–vertical discrimination was easier to learn than was the diagonals discrimination, even though the former was always learned earlier in the series than the latter. The study was designed to compare a simultaneous, two-stimulus situation to one in which there were nine (identical) negative stimuli and one positive stimulus. In this latter situation (which occurred first for half the subjects), learning seemed faster, but the diagonals task was apparently still harder than the horizontal–vertical problem.

Human Child. Preschool children have great difficulty discriminating diagonal lines. Rudel & Teuber (1963) found that most preschoolers failed to learn the diagonals problem, although the same subjects could readily learn a horizontal–vertical discrimination. More of the older children (ages 6 1/2 to 8 1/2) learned the diagonals discrimination, but even then, approximately 30–50% failed to learn the problem. The same children were also tested on two other problems; the lateral mirror images (⊏ vs ⊐) proved harder to discriminate than did the vertical mirror images (⊔ vs ⊓). Both problems were harder for the younger children than for the older children, but especially the lateral mirror-image task, which most of the younger ones failed to learn.

Over & Over (1967) also found that young schoolchildren and preschoolers have great difficulty with the diagonals discrimination, although they could learn the horizontal–vertical discrimination. However, they found that when the children were required only to recognize whether the two diagonals were the same or were different, most subjects could easily learn the diagonals discrimination.

Over & Over's 1967 study was in some ways a landmark experiment. For essentially the first time, a distinction was made between the subject's ability to differentiate mirror-image diagonal lines and his ability to remember which stimulus was the positive one. As Over argued in a separate paper (1967) the traditional simultaneous or successive discrimination task cannot distinguish whether a failure to learn the discrimination indicates a failure in the perceptual analysis or in the memory traces. Over pointed out that problems of oddity, matching-to-sample, or same–difference judgments would not require the subject to remember which stimulus was the positive one, and in such situations we would be able to tell whether the subject actually can distinguish the two stimuli. Over & Over's study (1967) confirmed that young children *can* differentiate mirror-image diagonal lines as long as they are tested in a situation such as the matching-to-sample task that Over & Over used.

Bryant (1969) also used a matching-to-sample task for 5- and 7-year-old children. In one case the sample card was presented simultaneously with the two choice cards; in the other, the sample card was removed before the two choice cards were presented. When the sample was presented simultaneously with the choice cards, few errors were made in either age group on either the diagonals task or the horizontal–vertical problem. In the successive discriminations, however, the 5-year-olds performed at chance level on the diagonals task, although the 7-year-olds performed well on that problem and neither group had difficulty learning the horizontal–vertical task. Bryant's experiments also suggested that the younger children failed to learn the diagonals problem because the oblique lines were not parallel with any of the edges of the card. When a diamond-shaped border was superimposed on the stimulus card, performance was improved. He suggested that all the children used a match–mismatch code, but that only the older children recorded further information about the stimuli after a mismatch signal.

Human Adult. By the age of eight or so, most children can master the diagonals discrimination (Rudel & Teuber, 1963). The development of this skill is discussed at some length in Olson (1970). Because the human adult can obviously discriminate mirror-image stimuli, studies of adults are typically restricted to measuring reaction times to different pairs of stimuli. For example, Sekular & Houlihan (1967) determined that lateral mirror images ($\sqsubset$ and $\sqsupset$) take longer to discriminate than do vertical mirror images ($\sqcup$ and $\sqcap$). They also found that the relative difficulty with lateral mirror images persisted even when the stimuli were presented vertically, in a column, instead of in the more normal horizontal presentation. However, Wolff (1971) found contradictory results; his data indicated that when presented in a vertical array, vertical mirror images take longer to discriminate than do lateral mirror images. When the stimuli were presented in a horizontal array, the lateral mirror-image problem was harder than the vertical mirror-images task. Wolff's data agree with those previously found by Sekular & Rosenblith (1964) for first-grade children.

For a further review of such literature, see either Appelle (1972) or Wolff (1971). Wolff (1971) also discussed his data with reference to Deutsch's (1955) theory of shape recognition (discussed earlier in this paper), and he attempts to explain the difference between his data and those of Sekular & Houlihan (1967). Because the explanation of the relative difficulty of lateral vs vertical mirror images is not a central theme in this paper, it will not be discussed further here.

A Mirror Image Experiment—Memory vs Reception

The hypothesis for the present experiment was twofold: (1) that rats *can* tell the difference between mirror-image diagonal lines, and (2) that the difficulty rats have had in learning a diagonals discrimination is due to a difficulty in remembering which stimulus is the positive one, not a problem in perceiving the stimuli per se.

To test this hypothesis, it was necessary to have a task whose solution did not depend on the rat's ability to remember which stimulus was which. Four groups of rats were tested on a simultaneous discrimination task. The first two groups served as controls and were tested with a standard simultaneous discrimination procedure. That is, there were two test stimuli, and the rats were required to learn which was the positive one. One group was trained on a horizontal–vertical problem, the other on a diagonals task. The other two groups were tested on the same tasks in the same apparatus modified to present three stimuli simultaneously. Of the three test stimuli, two were alike, and the odd stimulus was the positive one. The extra stimulus (always a negative stimulus), however, did not represent a choice for the rat; it existed instead only as a cue, and the rat was required to choose either of the other two stimuli. This meant that the probability of a correct choice by chance was 50%, and that the data from these two groups could be compared with those from the first two groups, as well as with data from any other two-choice simultaneous discrimination task.

It was expected that if rats can perceive the difference between opposite diagonals, they should be able to learn the three-stimulus diagonals discrimination easily, inasmuch as that task required them only to perceive a difference (find the odd stimulus), rather than to remember which stimulus was the positive one. It was also assumed that with the traditional two-stimulus task, the rats would find the diagonals discrimination harder to learn than the horizontal–vertical task.

One final point about terminology should be discussed. Like Olson (1970), we feel that there should be a single term that refers to both horizontal and vertical stimuli, just as the term *diagonals* or *obliques* includes lines that slope either to the left or to the right. Like Olson, but independently, we concluded that the most suitable term would be the word "orthogonals" for lines that are either vertical or horizontal.

Inasmuch as mirror-image diagonals, like horizontal and vertical lines, are at right angles to each other, it might seem that "orthogonal" could apply to a pair of diagonals as well as to a horizontal–vertical pair. However, when we define 45° and 135° lines as diagonals or obliques, we don't mean that they are oblique to each other. We mean that they are oblique to our usual horizontal–vertical frame of reference. In a similar way, it is easy to see that horizontal and vertical lines are orthogonal to our usual horizontal–vertical frame of reference, hence justifying the use of the term *orthogonal* to refer to horizontal and vertical lines. In this study, the term *orthogonal* is used in this sense; to refer to horizontal and vertical lines, but not to diagonal lines.

Method

Subjects. The subjects were 48 male hooded rats, weighing 250–300 g at the start of the experiment. The rats were caged individually and were given free access to food and water at all times.

Apparatus. A Thompson–Bryant box (Thompson & Bryant, 1955) was modified so that it could be used in both a two-stimulus and a three-stimulus situation. The apparatus consisted of a 5 × 7 in. start

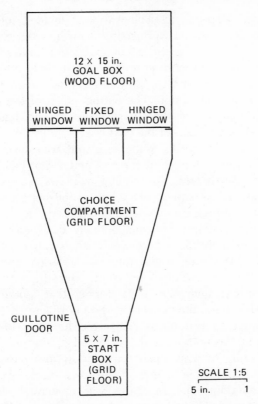

Fig. 1. A diagram of the apparatus as viewed from above.

box, a 20 in. long choice compartment that was roughly V-shaped, and a 15×12 in. goal box (see Fig. 1). The walls were 9 in. high.

The apparatus was constructed throughout of 1/4 in. plywood, painted medium-gray, and waterproofed with a coat of clear, semigloss Varathane. Each of the compartments (start, choice, and goal) was covered separately with a piece of 1/4 in. clear Plexiglas, fastened in place, but easily removable.

The floors of the start box and choice compartment were grids constructed of 1/8 in. brass rods placed every half-inch. A timed, constant-current, scrambled shock could be delivered to the grid floor from a Grason–Stadler shock generator. The floor of the goal box was wooden.

An opaque guillotine door separated the start box from the choice compartment. Raising the door triggered a timer that recorded the elapsed time for each trial.

The stimulus wall was a wall 15 in. wide separating the goal box from the choice compartment. The wall was divided into three equal sections by wooden partitions projecting 3 in. into the choice compartment. Each of the three sections contained a stimulus window. The windows were formed by cutting a 3.5 × 3.5 in. hole into the wall and mounting a larger piece of clear Plexiglas behind each hole. Each window was centered in its section. The bottom edges of the windows were level with the grid floor of the choice compartment, but were 1/4 in. above the slightly lower floor of the goal box.

The center window was fixed in place and was never opened. The two side windows were hinged at the top, and, if not locked shut, could be pushed open by the rat. The hinged windows were constructed of 1/8 in. Plexiglas, 4.5 in. square, with lips at the bottom and 1/2 in. in from the sides to hold the stimulus card in place.

These movable windows were not actually flush with the back side of the stimulus wall. Rather, there was a small gap (1/8 in.) between the window and the wall at the top, and a larger gap (1/4 in.) at the bottom. When the window fell shut after the rat's passage into the goal box, it fell against a small stopper that muted the noise of the window's slamming and prevented the loud bang that would otherwise occur. (Pilot trials indicated that the lightness of the window, the larger gap at the bottom, and the muted closing all facilitated the rat's initial learning to push open the window and pass through; this eased the task of the experimenter in the early stages of training.)

The room containing the apparatus was moderately bright and lit by standard fluorescent light fixtures. The start box and the choice compartment of the apparatus were situated directly beneath one of the light fixtures. Measurements taken from the grid floor of the choice compartment indicated a uniform illumination of approximately 32 ft-c with the Plexiglas cover in place. The goal box, less brightly illuminated, measured about 26 ft-c.

Stimuli. All stimuli were 3.5 in. square and were constructed of stiff cardboard. One set of cards was painted medium gray, matching the walls of the apparatus, and was used during preliminary training. Also, one of the gray cards was put in the center window whenever the box was to be used as a two-stimulus apparatus. A second set of cards was marked with 1/2 in. stripes of black and white, all parallel to one edge of the card. These cards formed the horizontal (0°) and vertical (90°) stimuli, depending on which way the card was oriented when placed behind the window. A third set of cards had the stripes extending diagonally and could form either a 45° or a 135° stimulus, depending on how they were placed.

Procedure. The rats were handled every day for 7 days before the experiment began. During the first 4 days groups of six subjects were allowed to explore a large cardboard box for 20 min per day. Each rat was picked up and handled at least four times during each session. The last 3 days were devoted to group exploration of the apparatus (20 min per day). For these sessions, the guillotine door was raised, all windows were transparent, and the two side windows were taped open to allow free passage to and from the goal box.

Preliminary Training. Each rat was given 4 days of preliminary training. On the first day of preliminary training each subject was individually trained to run down the apparatus and to go through either of the side windows in order to avoid shock. On the first four trials both side windows were taped open. On subsequent trials the windows were in place, but were unlocked. During this period all three windows were transparent; no cards were used. On any single trial the subject was placed in the start box facing away from the door, and the door was raised. If after 5 sec the rat had not left the start box, it was given a 1.5 sec, 1.3 mA shock. If after 30 sec the rat had not entered the goal box, it was given another shock. Further shocks were administered at 10–15 sec intervals until the rat entered the goal box. The rat was left in the goal box for at least 30 sec before the next trial was begun. A new trial was begun with the same rat approximately every 60 sec, until it made 10 consecutive runs without being shocked.

On the second day of preliminary training the rats were tested in squads of six. A squad was brought into the testing room in a carrier that provided individual holding cages for each animal. The rats were tested in rotation and were returned to the holding cages between trials. Each rat was given 10 trials; the intertrial interval (ITI) was 10 min. During these trials all the windows were transparent, the two side windows were unlocked, and the ·rat was shocked at the 5-sec and 30-sec mark if it failed to perform. Typically, a rat needed to be shocked only on the first few trials.

During the third and fourth days of preliminary training the subject was trained to run to the opposite side window if its initial choice was locked, because the correction method was to be used in subsequent testing. Each animal was given 10 trials per day with a 10 min ITI; shock was administered as before. On the first three trials both movable windows were unlocked; on the last seven trials one window was locked. The position of the unlocked window was varied according to a randomly selected Gellerman series (Gellerman, 1933). During these sessions the gray cards were put behind all windows.

Experimental Training.   Experimental training began immediately following the 4 days of preliminary training. There were four experimental conditions (four discrimination problems) as follows:

1. Zero degrees vs 90°, two stimuli (Orthogonals/2). This is an ordinary horizontal–vertical discrimination. Half the rats were trained with 0° positive and half with 90° positive.

2. Zero degrees vs 90°, three stimuli (Orthogonals/3). In this horizontal–vertical discrimination, there were always two negative stimuli, one of which was always on the (immovable) center window. Again, half the rats were trained to 0° positive and half to 90° positive.

3. Forty-five degrees vs 135°, two stimuli (Diagonals/2). This condition is identical to condition 1 except that the two stimuli were the mirror-image obliques.

4. Forty-five degrees vs 135°, three stimuli (Diagonals/3). This situation is identical to condition 2 with its two negative stimuli, except that the stimuli were the oblique stripes.

The subjects were run in the same squads of six as in the preliminary training. The composition of each squad was balanced so that a given squad had at least one member under each experimental condition, and no more than two members under the same condition.

Experimental training lasted for 13 days. Each rat received 10 trials per day under the correction procedure with an ITI of 10 min. The appropriate test stimuli were placed behind the windows. When three stimuli were used, the center window always bore one of the two negative stimuli. When two stimuli were used, the center window always held a gray card. In either case, the positive stimulus was always on one of the side windows, and only that window was unlocked. The position of the positive stimulus was varied according to a Gellerman series (Gellerman, 1933), randomly selected daily for each rat individually. The position of the positive stimulus was changed by rotating the cards 90° and replacing them in the same windows; the cards were not switched from one window to another.

If the rat failed to leave the start box within 5 sec of the start of a trial, a 0.6 mA shock (milder than that used during preliminary training) was administered for 0.5 sec. These shock values were used throughout the rest of the experiment. If the subject approached within 3 in. of the negative stimulus on the locked window (i.e., passed the beginning of the 3 in. partition), it was shocked and the trial was scored as an error. A rat was not shocked for approaching the center window, regardless of whether it held a gray card or a striped card. In fact, they rarely approached the center window. A correct trial was recorded when the rat pushed through the positive window into the goal box without having approached within 3 in. of the negative side window.

On the 14th day, each rat was tested with gray cards behind all three windows. In all other respects, the procedure was the same as for the previous 13 days. This control testing was to determine whether there were any incidental cues to indicate which window was the correct one. In all, each rat received 130 experimental trials. The total number of correct choices out of the 130 was used as the subject's score. Theoretically, an individual subject's score could range from 0 to 130 with a score of 65 indicating chance performance. Whether, and on which day, each rat reached a criterion of nine out of 10 responses correct was also recorded.

Results

The results of the experiment were analyzed in terms of the mean number of correct responses for each group. Fig. 2 shows the daily performance of each of the four groups in terms of the mean percent correct. The means of the total number correct for each group are presented in Table 1. Table 1 also includes the standard deviation and the range and median number of trials to criterion for each group

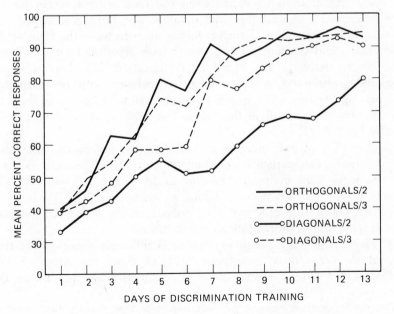

Fig. 2. Daily performance on four discrimination problems, in terms of mean percent of correct responses.

Table 1   Summary Data for Experimental Groups

			Trials Correct in 130		Trials to Criterion	
Group	Condition	N	Mean	SD	Median	Range
1	Orthog/2	12	100.75	11.97	50	30–120
2	Orthog/3	12	98.67	10.66	80	50–110
3	Diag/2	12	72.00	12.98	[a]	90–130+[a]
4	Diag/3	12	90.67	6.31	70	60–110

[a] Half the subjects in group 3 reached criterion in 130 trials (range = 90–120); the other half did not.

Within each group, a comparison was made between the subjects trained with one stimulus as positive and the subjects trained with the other. There was no significant difference in the total mean number correct for the two sets of subjects compared within each group ($p > .25$, all four t tests), suggesting no strong preference for one stimulus over the other.

Hartley's test for homogeneity of variance indicated that the four group variances were not significantly different ($F_{max} = 4.23$; df = 4,11; $p > .05$). An analysis of variance on the total correct scores for the groups yielded a significant overall F value ($p < .001$). A more detailed, two-factor analysis showed that both the main factors (the type of discrimination and the number of stimuli) were significant ($p < .001$ and $p < .05$, respectively) as was the interaction ($p < .01$). This two-factor analysis is presented, in spite of its redundancy with the individual comparisons below, for the benefit of the reader who would find the information more useful in this form. The analysis of variance is summarized in Table 2.

Because the overall analysis of variance was significant, individual (a posteriori) comparisons were carried out. The differences between various pairs were analyzed according to the Tukey (b) method[*]. The results of the individual comparisons are summarized in Table 3.

Inspection of the data and the analysis of the Tukey comparisons would seem to warrant the following conclusions:

1. The Diagonals/2 group performed significantly more poorly than any of the other three groups ($p < .01$, all three comparisons). This indicates that using the three-stimulus condition made the oblique dis-

[*] This method is more conservative with respect to type 1 error than either the Newman–Keuls method or the Duncan Multiple-Range Test, but is not as stringent, for example, as the very conservative Scheffé approach (Winer, 1962, pp. 85–89).

Table 2 Summary of Analysis of Variance

Source	SS	df	MS	F
Between groups	5421.90	3	1070.30	15.53***
A. Type discrimination	3657.69	1	3657.69	31.5***
B. Number stimuli	652.75	1	652.75	5.6*
A × B	1111.46	1	1111.46	9.6**
Within groups	5120.48	44	116.38	

* $p < .05$
** $p < .01$
*** $p < .001$

Table 3 Individual Comparisons Using the Tukey (b) Method

Condition No.	Condition	X	Difference from Condition No. 4	2	1	Critical Difference
3	Diag/2	884	204*	298*	325*	$D_{.01}(2) = 158.9$
4	Diag/3	1088		94	121	$D_{.01}(3) = 169.2$
2	Orthog/3	1182			27	$D_{.01}(4) = 175.3$
1	Orthog/2	1209				

* $p < .01$

crimination easier for the rats to perform. It also confirms, once again, that rats can perform an orthogonal discrimination better than they can a diagonal discrimination if the task is a traditional two-stimulus discrimination.

2. Performance on the Diagonals/3 problem, although it might appear from the data to be worse than either of the Orthogonals problems, was not significantly different from either of them ($p > .05$).

3. Performance on the two Orthogonals tasks was not significantly different ($p > .05$).

On day 14, when the subjects were tested with gray cards, no animal's score was above that expected by chance (binomial formula, $p > .05$), indicating that performance on the discrimination task was not learned on the basis of incidental cues such as might be communicated by the experimenter or by the locking of the windows.

Discussion

Using the Orthogonals/2 performance as a basis for comparison, we can see the procedure and apparatus of the present study allowed fairly efficient learning. For example, Boles & Sheridan (1969) used a Thompson–Bryant box after which the apparatus in our study was modeled. They found that rats learned the horizontal–vertical task to a criterion of nine out of 10 correct in a median of 65 trials. Thompson & Bryant (1955) reported that the range of trials to criterion for such a discrimination in the Thompson–Bryant box was 50–130 trials. As the rats in study under discussion learned the Orthogonals/2 task in a median of 50 trials and a range of 30–120 trials, it would seem that having the two stimulus windows farther apart, with a blank window between them (as was necessary in the present study) presented no particular problems. The slight superiority of the rats in the present study, if it is a real difference, is likely to be due to their having been given fewer trials per day (10 instead of 20) with a longer ITI (10 min instead of 25 sec).

The initial performance for all four groups in this study was in the 30–40% range (see Fig. 2). One would expect initial performance in a two-choice situation to be at the 50% level; however, the reason the initial performance was lower in this case probably is because of the criteria employed for classifying correct and incorrect responses. In order to make a correct response the rat not only had to approach the correct stimulus but had to push through the window into the goal box as well. An incorrect response was recorded if the rat merely approached the negative stimulus within 3 in. During preliminary training the rats were shocked for approaching within 3 in. of the locked window. They quickly learned to run to the opposite side window whenever they received the shock. During this stage of preliminary training and the early stages of discrimination training, rats were frequently observed to behave in the following manner: On a trial where the rat initially chose the negative stimulus, it would be shocked when it approached within 3 in. of the negative window and would immediately run to the other window. On other trials the rat would first approach the positive stimulus but would not always immediately push through the unlocked window. In such cases, it would often run instead to the other side window. On approaching the negative stimulus it would be shocked, causing it to run back to the initial (positive) window and, typically, it would then push through into the goal box. Because of the more stringent criterion for a correct response, the rat was thus often not credited with making a correct response, when, in fact, it had actually approached the positive stimulus. This below-chance performance usually disappeared within a day or two, but was sometimes noted to recur on day 14 when the stimuli were replaced by blank gray cards for control testing.

The rats were all tested on a simultaneous discrimination task and were not given any control testing on a successive task, so it is not possible to say definitely that the rats did not learn the task on the basis of the overall pattern, that is, on up–down cues. (When two mirror-image diagonal lines are placed side by side, they form a V that points either upward or downward. If the subject attends only to the bottom center of this V, it could learn the task by discriminating whether the tip of the V is pointing up or down, without learning which diagonal line is the positive stimulus.) However, it seems to the authors unlikely that the present rats did so, for several reasons. First, the stimuli were striped cards rather than single lines or rectangles; with single lines or rectangles the overall pattern (a V pointing down or pointing up) would seem a much more salient cue than in the present case with multiple strips on each card. Second, for the Diagonals/3 group to learn the task (as they all did) on the basis of the overall pattern would appear a rather difficult task, as the overall pattern would seem a very complex one, and not easy to solve on the basis of up–down cues. Finally, a number of rats that eventually learned the task started out position-responding, running head down, apparently ignoring the stimuli. Typically, when one of these rats began to learn the problem, it was often observed to run up close to the stimulus on the preferred side, and if the stimulus were not the positive one, it would come to a sudden halt just before passing into the zone where it would have been shocked. The rat would then run to the opposite side and push through the correct window without hesitation. Although these rats numbered in the minority, it would seem that these, at least, were viewing only one stimulus at a time.

In any case, if the rats could learn the diagonals task on the basis of an overall pattern, why did so many rats in the Diagonals/2 group fail to learn the task and why did the rats in the Diagonals/3 group perform so much better? Of course, none of these arguments can totally rule out the possibility that the rats learned the diagonals task on the basis of the overall pattern formed by the stimuli. Now that it has been demonstrated that rats can, indeed, learn a diagonals task—under certain conditions—it would be important to know whether the rats can maintain their performance if the task is changed to a successive discrimination.

The results of this study have implications concerning methodology when one is attempting to determine the sensory capacities of a given species. A failure to learn a two-stimulus discrimination task is not necessarily a failure to differentiate the stimuli. Such a point has been made before (Over, 1967), and several studies with children (e.g., Jeffrey, 1958; Over & Over, 1967; Bryant, 1969) indicated that although the children may not have been able to learn the required discrimination between two mirror-image stimuli, they could clearly perceive that the two stimuli were different.

Previous studies had, at the least, hinted at the rat's ability to differentiate diagonals although they may fail to learn certain diagonals tasks. Kinsbourne's study (1967) would seem to demonstrate that rats can differentiate mirror-image diagonals. Also, the data from the Koronakos & Arnold study (1957) demonstrate that at least some rats can learn a diagonals task when there are multiple negative stimuli. It was not possible, however, in Koronakos & Arnold's study, to compare a diagonals discrimination to the orthogonals discrimination for reasons previously discussed. Nor could there be any direct comparison between the five-choice oddity task and a traditional two-stimulus (two-choice) discrimination task. The present study makes it clear that a three-stimulus oddity situation greatly facilitates a rat's learning the diagonals task. This facilitation is not merely a general effect for all types of discrimination tasks, since the three-stimulus situation did not seem to facilitate learning the orthogonals task—performance on the Orthogonals/3 task was no better than that on the Orthogonals/2 task ($p > .05$).

The finding of the present study—that rats can distinguish between diagonals—also has implications for theorists, such as Sutherland, Deutsch, & Dodwell, who are attempting to explain a species' shape-discrimination abilities and confusions by postulating specific information-processing mechanisms. If rats, for example, do register that there is a difference between mirror-image diagonals, it is not necessary to presume a coding mechanism that transforms the two diagonals into identical stimuli, as all three above-mentioned theorists have done.

The question then remains why a diagonals discrimination is so hard to perform under certain conditions and why it is so much easier under other conditions. Also, what is special about diagonals and certain other mirror-image stimuli that makes a discrimination task between them so hard to learn under normal testing conditions? The suggestion that follows is one elaborated particularly by Noble (1966) and Corballis & Beale (1970a), but has roots back to before the turn of the century (Corballis & Beale, 1970a).

If there is a point-to-point connection between the two hemispheres of the brain, as has been indicated, for instance, by Sperry (1962) or Morrell (1963), then it may be that the cells stimulated on one side of the brain by a $+45°$ line would be directly connected to cells on the opposite side that normally would be stimulated by a $-45°$ line. If this is so, then in a mirror-image discrimination task, "both the positive and negative representations of a mirror-image pair will receive both positive and negative reinforcement," (Noble, 1966, p. 1265). Noble (1966) further proposed that for animals that can learn a mirror-image task, the learning that occurs from information crossing the midline must be "weaker" than that occurring from direct sensory input—otherwise the task would never be learned. Thus it may be supposed that the degree of symmetry in the interhemispheric connections would be correlated with the difficulty of learning a mirror-image task and that this would vary for different species. The greater the number of asymmetrical connections, the less will be the confusion between learning that crosses the midline (and gets reversed) and learning that does not cross the midline. Hence, the more "asymmetrical" the brain, the easier it should be for the subject to learn a mirror-image task.

One of the predictions of the above theory is that only lateral mirror-images would be confused in this fashion. Vertical mirror images (such as ⊔ and ⊓) would be unaffected by transfer across the midline. There is some support for this prediction in work with the octopus (Sutherland, 1957a, 1960a,b), the rat (Lashley, 1938), the cat (Warren, 1969), the rhesus monkey (Riopelle, Rahm, Itoigawa, & Draper, 1964), the human child Rudel & Teuber, 1963; Sekular & Rosenblith, 1964), and the human adult (Sekular & Houlihan, 1967; Wolff, 1971). There are, however, two factors that make it complicated to interpret studies such as the above. One is the possible tendency for the animal to attend to only a portion of the stimulus rather than the whole figure. For example, Lashley (1938) determined that his rats attended primarily to the bottom edges of the stimuli. This kind of attention bias would allow a subject to discriminate the vertical mirror images, such as ⊔ and ⊓ easily but would make it hard to learn a lateral mirror images task such as ⊐ and ⊏. A second confounding factor is that in most simultaneous discrimination problems the stimuli are presented in a horizontal array. Some of the studies with humans have found that the vertical mirror-images task is the harder one to learn when the stimuli are presented in a vertical array (Sekular & Rosenblith, 1964; Wolff, 1971). Wolff (1971) suggested that the data concerning the relative difficulty of lateral and vertical mirror-image tasks can be better explained in terms of the direction of scanning movements made by the subject. Most humans are taught to scan from left to right; this asymmetrical behavior may facilitate our discrimination of mirror images. It may be that preschool children and the lower animals have more trouble with mirror images because they scan outward from the center of the stimulus array. See Wolff (1971) for a further discussion of this point.

A second prediction of the symmetry theory is that interhemispheric transfer should be accompanied by a mirror-image reversal. Again, the relevant evidence is difficult to interpret. Ray & Emley (1964, 1965) found such an interhemispheric reversal in rats when one side of the cortex was depressed by KCl during training. The mirror-image reversal occurred on the first transfer trial, but it is not obvious how the transfer could have occurred, because the half of the cortex that was being tested had been depressed during training. Corballis & Beale (1970a) suggested that the cortical depression was not total, allowing the depressed hemisphere to function partially. Ettlinger & Elithorn (1962) found that when monkeys were trained to discriminate mirror images tactilely with one hand, it was easier to train the reverse discrimination with the other hand. Noble (1966, 1968) tested monkeys with split optic chiasmas. In these subjects an interocular transfer would then have to be an interhemispheric transfer. When the monkeys were tested with the untrained eye, they displayed a preference for the previously negative stimulus. Evidence for interocular reversal has also been noted in goldfish (Ingle, 1967) and pigeons (Mello, 1965, 1966a, 1966b). In both species each eye projects entirely to the opposite hemisphere so that an interocular transfer would be the same as an interhemispheric transfer. Beale & Corballis (1967, 1968) and Corballis & Beale (1970b) have argued that the apparent interocular reversal in the pigeon can be explained by *beak shift*—the tendency to view only one side of the stimulus key and then to discriminate on the basis of up–down cues. Mello (1965) anticipated such an argument but did not agree that the pigeons learned the task on the basis of up–down cues.

The strongest evidence, however, for the symmetry theory comes from studies like the present one that show that learning a discrimination task depends on more than just the ability to differentiate the stimuli. As shown here, the rat can learn the mirror-image diagonal task (as can children—e.g., Jeffrey, 1958; Over & Over, 1967) as long as it is not required to remember which stimulus is the positive one. Such studies support the idea that the difficulty with mirror-image tasks lies not in the perceptual analysis but in the memory-encoding process. It is important that investigators take this distinction into account before coming to conclusions about the nature of the perceptual analyzing mechanism or the sensory capacities of the subject.

Acknowledgments

This research was supported by Grant 2RO1-EY00573-09 from the National Institutes of Health, U.S. Public Health Service, to Austin H. Riesen.

References

Appelle, S. (1972). Perception and discrimination as a function of stimulus orientation. *Psychol. Bull.* **78**, 266–278.

Beale, I. L., & Corballis, M. C. (1967). Laterally displaced pecking in monocularly viewing pigeons: A possible factor in interocular mirror-image reversal. *Psychon. Sci.* **9**, 603–604.

Beale, I. L., & Corballis, M. C. (1968). Beak shift: An explanation for interocular mirror-image reversal in pigeons. *Nature,* **220**, 82–83.

Boles, T. J., & Sheridan, C. L. (1969). Enhanced pattern discrimination learning following unilateral damage to posterior cortex in rats. *Psychon. Sci.* **16**, 273–274.

Bryant, P. E. (1969). Perception and memory of the orientation of visually presented lines by children. *Nature* **224**, 1331–1332.

Corballis, M. C., & Beale, I. L. (1970a). Bilateral symmetry and behavior. *Psychol. Rev.* **77**, 451–464.

Corballis, M. C., & Beale I. L. (1970b). Monocular discrimination of mirror-image obliques by pigeons: Evidence for lateralized stimulus control. *Anim. Behav.* **18**, 563–566.

Deutsch, J. A. (1955). A theory of shape recognition. *Brit. J. Psychol.* **46**, 30–37.

Deutsch, J. A. (1958). Shape recognition: A reply to Dodwell. *Brit. J. Psychol.* **49**, 70–71.

Deutsch, J. A. (1962). A system for shape recognition. *Psychol. Rev.* **69**, 492–500.

Dodwell, P. C. (1957a). Shape recognition in the octopus and in the rat. *Nature* **179**, 1088.

Dodwell, P. C. (1957b). Shape recognition in rats. *Brit. J. Psychol.,* **48**, 221–229.

Dodwell, P. C. (1958). Shape recognition: A reply to Deutsch. *Brit. J. Psychol.,* **49**, 158.

Dodwell, P. C. (1961). Coding and learning in shape discrimination. *Psychol. Rev.,* **68**, 373–382.

Dodwell, P. C. (1970a). Anomalous transfer effects after pattern discrimination training in rats and squirrels. *J. Comp. Physiol. Psychol.,* **71**, 42–51.

Dodwell, P. C. (1970b). *Visual pattern recognition.* Holt, Rinehart & Winston, New York.

Ely, D. J. (1970). Discrimination of stripes at different angles by the rat. Unpublished doctoral dissertation. University of Nevada.

Ettlinger, G., & Elithorn, A. (1962). Transfer between the hands of a mirror-image tactile shape discrimination. *Nature,* **194**, 1101.

Fellows, B. J. (1968). *The discrimination process and development.* Pergamon Press, New York.

Gellerman, L. W. (1933). Chance orders of alternating stimuli in visual discrimination experiments. *J. Gen. Psychol.,* **42**, 206–208.

Ingle, D. (1967). Two visual mechanisms underlying the behavior of fish. *Psychol. Forsh.,* **31**, 44–51.

Jeffrey, W. E. (1958). Variables in early discrimination learning: I. Motor responses in the training of a left–right discrimination. *Child Develop.,* **29**, 269–275.

Kinsbourne, M. (1967). Sameness–difference judgements and the discrimination of obliques in the rat. *Psychon. Sci.*, 7, 183–184.

Koronakos, C., & Arnold, W. J. (1957). The formation of learning sets in rats. *J. Comp. Physiol. Psychol.*, 50, 11–14.

Lashley, K. S. (1938). The mechanism of vision: XV. Preliminary studies of the rat's capacity for detailed vision. *J. Gen. Psychol.*, 18, 123–193.

MacIntosh, J., & Sutherland, N. S. (1963). Visual discrimination by the goldfish: The orientation of rectangles. *Anim. Behav.*, 11, 135–141.

Mello, N. K. (1965). Interhemispheric reversal of mirror-image oblique lines after monocular training in pigeons. *Science*, 148, 252–254.

Mello, N. K. (1966a). Concerning the interhemispheric transfer of mirror-image oblique lines after monocular training in pigeons. *Physiol. Behav.*, 1, 293–300.

Mello, N. K. (1966b). Interocular generalization: A study of mirror-image reversal following monocular training in pigeons. *J. Exp. Anal. Behav.*, 9, 11–16.

Morrell, P. (1963). Information storage in nerve cells. In W. S. Fields & W. Abbott (Eds.), *Information storage and neural control.* Charles C Thomas, Springfield, Ill.

Nissen, H. W., & McCulloch, T. L. (1937). Equated and non-equated stimulus situations in discrimination learning by chimpanzees. I. Comparison with unlimited response. *J. Comp. Psychol.*, 23, 165–189.

Noble, J. (1966). Mirror-images and the forebrain commissures of the monkey. *Nature*, 211, 1263–1266.

Noble, J. (1968). Paradoxical interocular transfer of mirror-image discrimination in the optic chiasma sectioned monkey. *Brain Res.*, 10, 127–151.

Olson, D. R. (1970). *Cognitive development: The child's acquisition of diagonality.* Academic Press, New York.

Over, R. (1967). Detection and recognition measures of shape discrimination. *Nature*, 214, 1272–1273.

Over, R. (1969). Reaction time analysis of discrimination of direction of line by the pigeon. *Psychon. Sci.*, 17, 171–172.

Over, R., & Over, J. (1967). Detection and recognition of mirror-image obliques by young children. *J. Comp. Physiol. Psychol.*, 64, 467–470.

Parriss, J. R. (1964). A technique for testing cat's discrimination of differently oriented rectangles. *Nature*, 202, 771–773.

Ray, O. S., & Emley, G. (1964). Time factors in interhemispheric transfer of learning. *Science*, 144, 76–78.

Ray, O. S., & Emley, G. (1965). Interhemispheric transfer of learning. *Life Sciences*, 4, 823–826.

Riopelle, A. J., Rahm, V., Itoigawa, N., & Draper, W. A. (1964). Discrimination of mirror-image patterns by rhesus monkeys. *Percept. Motor Skills*, 19, 383–389.

Rudel, R. G., & Teuber, H. L. (1963). Discrimination of direction of line in children. *J. Comp. Physiol. Psychol.*, 56, 892–898.

Sekular, R. W., & Houlihan, K. (1967). Discrimination of mirror-images: Choice time analysis of human adult performance. *Quart. J. Exp. Psychol.*, 48, 204–207.

Sekular, R. W., & Rosenblith, J. F. (1964). Discrimination of direction of line and the effect of stimulus alignment. *Psychon. Sci.*, 1, 143–144.

Sperry, R. W. (1962). Some general aspects of interhemispheric integration. In V. B. Mountcastle (Ed.), *Interhemispheric relations and cerebral dominance.* Johns Hopkins Press, Baltimore.

Sutherland, N. S. (1957a). Visual discrimination of orientation and shape by octopus. *Nature,* **179,** 11–13.

Sutherland, N. S. (1957b). Visual discrimination of orientation by octopus. *Brit. J. Psychol.,* **48,** 55–71.

Sutherland, N. S. (1958). Visual discrimination of the orientation of rectangles by *Octopus vulgaris Lamarck. J. Comp. Physiol. Psychol.,* **51,** 452–458.

Sutherland, N. S. (1960a). The visual discrimination of shape of octopus: Squares and rectangles. *J. Comp. Physiol. Psychol.,* **53,** 95–103.

Sutherland, N. S. (1960b). Visual discrimination of shape by octopus: Mirror images. *Brit. J. Psychol.,* **51,** 9–18.

Sutherland, N. S. (1961). The methods and findings of experiments on the visual discrimination of shape by animals. *Quart. J. Exp. Psychol. Monogr.* (1) 1–68.

Sutherland, N. S. (1963a). Cat's ability to discriminate oblique rectangles. *Science,* **139,** 209–210.

Sutherland, N. S. (1963b). Shape discrimination and receptive fields. *Nature,* **197,** 118–122.

Sutherland, N. S. (1969). Outlines of a theory of pattern recognition in animals and man. In R. M. Gilbert & N. S. Sutherland (Eds.), *Animal discrimination learning.* Academic Press, New York.

Thompson, R., & Bryant, H. (1955). Memory as affected by activity of the relevant receptor. *Psychol. Rep.,* **1,** 393–400.

Van Hof, M. W. (1966). Discrimination between striated patterns of different orientation in the rabbit. *Vision Res.,* **6,** 89–94.

Van Hof, M. W. (1970a). Interocular transfer in the rabbit. *Exp. Neurol.,* **26,** 103–108.

Van Hof, M. W. (1970b). Mechanisms of orientation discrimination in the rabbit. *Exp. Neurol.,* **28,** 494–500.

Warren, I. M. (1969). Discrimination of mirror images by cats. *J. Comp. Physiol. Psychol.,* **69,** 9–11.

Winer, B. J. (1962). *Statistical principles in experimental design.* McGraw-Hill, New York.

Wolff, P. (1971). Mirror-image confusability in adults. *J. Exp. Psychol.,* **91,** 268–272.

Zeigler, P., & Schmerler, S. (1965). Visual discrimination of orientation by pigeons. *Anim. Behav.,* **13,** 475–477.

Chapter 7

THE VISUAL EVOKED RESPONSE AND PATTERNED STIMULI

CARROLL T. WHITE

Naval Electronics Laboratory Center, San Diego

The development of the first effective average-response computer shortly over a decade ago and the subsequent availability of several types of relatively inexpensive dedicated averaging devices have led to the rapid accumulation of findings regarding sensory evoked responses (Katzman, 1964; Bergamini & Bergamasco, 1967; Donchin & Lindsley, 1969; Perry & Childers, 1969; Regan, 1972).

Studies dealing with the visual evoked response (VER) have been especially numerous. The most complete review of this work to date is to be found in Regan's book (1972), which includes all relevant findings up to 1970–1971.

Of special interest have been those studies dealing with the VERs obtained with patterned stimuli. Our laboratory has been interested in this topic for over 6 years. During that period there have been a number of studies, and the nature of the studies changed as more information as to the nature of the VER was obtained.

This chapter will present some of the findings made during the past 6 years, in the form of representative records obtained in the various studies. This might be especially useful for those not personally experienced in this area of work, because the variety of ways in which VER records appear in the literature can be confusing.

Our intention is not to duplicate the other reviews, but to perhaps add to their usefulness regarding the earlier studies, and to discuss a number of important studies that have appeared since Regan's book was printed—in particular, those studies dealing with clinical application of the VER. Some previously unpublished work has been included, at times to corroborate earlier work and at other times to indicate the direction of some current undertakings.

Finally, a Reference section that should provide a rather thorough overview of this area has been included. No attempt has been made to reference all these works within the text, because this was not our goal. Earlier papers bearing a close relationship to our own projects have been referenced, as have major papers that have appeared subsequent to the Regan book.

Methodology of VER Studies

In our laboratory studies, the subjects (Ss) sat in an electrically-shielded, darkened room, viewing transparencies that were periodically rear-illuminated by a strobe lamp outside the room. The electrical activity elicited by the presentation of the stimuli was picked up by a single electrode placed on the midline of the scalp about 2.5 cm forward of the inion. Ear electrodes were used as references.

The electrical activity picked up at the scalp was amplified by a standard Beckman–Offner Type "R" Dynograph. After amplification and the desired filtering the output was fed into a TMC Computer of Average Transients (Model 400C). This device performed the necessary signal processing (averaging). The final results of this processing were then plotted on a Moseley X–Y Plotter. Such plots are our VER records.

The intensity of the flash illumination used to present the patterned stimuli is really not a very important piece of information in the present context. It is sufficient to say that it was a comfortable, low–medium level, white light source.

The number of individual responses summed to obtain VER records varied, the usual number being either 50 or 100, but this was quite arbitrary, and again not very important per se.

One last comment should be made regarding the records included in this paper. Surface negative is down, and positive is up in each case. This is apparently becoming the most frequent way of presenting such records, even though not the tradition in electroencephalography.

Physical Characteristics of Stimuli

The fact that the presence of pattern in the visual stimulus markedly affected the VER was discovered quite early (e.g., Spehlmann, 1965). Later work indicated that specific forms might elicit specific VER wave forms, regardless of such factors as size (John, Herrington, & Sutton, 1967). Certainly, some pattern characteristics gave rise to distinctive differences in the responses (Jeffreys, 1969; White, 1969a).

S = RE

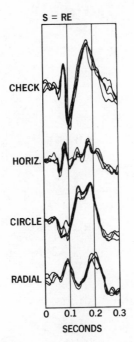

CHECK

HORIZ.

CIRCLE

RADIAL

0   0.1   0.2   0.3

SECONDS

Fig. 1. VERs obtained from a subject presented with four types of patterned
stimuli: row 1, checkerboard; row 2, horizontal grating; row 3, concentric
circles; row 4, radial lines. Each tracing represents the average of responses.
Negative downward. Total subtense of patterns about 2° visual angle.

Fig. 1 presents one subject's VERs produced by four different classes
of visual patterns: a checkerboard, a horizontal grating, a set of concentric circles, and a pattern consisting of straight lines radiating out
from a common point. Four replications of each condition were obtained,
each run consisting of 50 pattern presentations. The overall intensity
levels were the same in all four cases, so the differences appearing in
the wave forms must be brought about by other factors. Jeffreys (1969)
has shown that breaks in contours and the presence of corners seem
to be potent factors. This is probably related to the very marked responses
to the checkerboard.

The similarity of the four replications shows the consistency of the
responses. This is generally the case. Under well-controlled conditions
a given individual will produce essentially the same wave form in response to a given pattern. There are marked individual differences in
the VERs to a given pattern, however. This is shown in Fig. 2, which

PATTERN

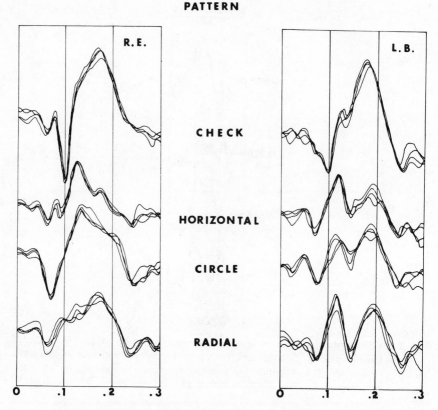

Fig. 2. VERs obtained with different patterned stimuli from two subjects. Same pattern types as for Fig. 1. Each tracing represents summation of 100 responses. Negative downward.

presents the responses of two subjects to the conditions described for Fig. 1. In spite of the individual differences both subjects gave the most marked responses to the checkerboard. This also is the general rule. For this reason we have devoted most of our attention to checkerboard-type patterns.

Having found that the checkerboard figure would be the most sensitive probe for our purposes, we had to know more about that class of pattern. What, for instance, would be the optimum check size to use? A study was carried out in which a number of adult subjects with normal vision were presented with a series of checkerboard patterns consisting of different sizes of check elements. An example of the results of this study is presented in Fig. 3. Three replications of each check-size condition were

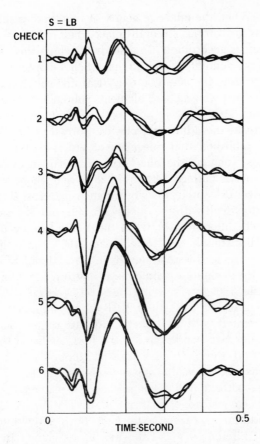

Fig. 3. VERs as a function of check-size (contour density). Large checks at
top, smaller checks at bottom of figure. Optimum response to checks subtending about 10 min of arc, visual angle. Negative downward.

made. Each tracing represents the averaged response to 50 stimuli. Starting from the top of the figure the wave forms represent responses to
checkerboards made up of check elements subtending 120, 60, 30, 20,
10, and 5 min of arc respectively.

The VERs shown are typical of the results obtained with all members
of our experimental group, and agree very well with the findings of others
who have studied this particular aspect of the problem (Rietveld, Tordoir,
Hagenouw, Lubbers, & Spoor, 1967; Lesevre & Remond, 1972). There has
been general agreement that the optimal check-size for producing the pattern VER is one that subtends around 10–15 min of arc. It must be noted
that the subjects used in these studies were adults having no marked visual

abnormalities. When the effective acuity of this type of subject is altered by having lenses of various strengths placed before his eyes, the optimum check-size changes accordingly. In a study in which this relationship was examined in some detail it was found that when 5 diopter lenses were used, effectively degrading the acuity a great deal, the subjects responded best to the checkerboard whose check elements subtended about 60 min of arc (Harter & White, 1970).

Let us return to the adult subject with normal vision, however. Once it had been established that one class of visual pattern (composed of closed elements, such as the checkerboard) was superior to others in its power to evoke pattern responses, and that there was apparently an optimum level of contour density for such patterns, the next question to be investigated dealt with the quality of such contour. Earlier work had revealed marked differences between the VERs produced by patterned stimuli and blank stimuli (e.g., Spehlmann, 1965; Spekreijse, 1966). We decided to investigate this relationship in some detail to determine just how sensitive the technique would be to pattern variations of this kind (Harter & White, 1968).

In the first phase of this study VERs were obtained from a group of subjects presented with a checkerboard pattern, of about the optimal dimensions, under two conditions. In the first condition the pattern was in sharp focus at the milk-glass screen. Under the second condition the pattern was clearly visible on the screen, but badly blurred. This blurring of the pattern was accomplished by placing the transparency behind the screen instead of in front of it. The VERs obtained under these two conditions were markedly and consistently different. Despite the individual differences in VER wave forms shown by the different subjects, there were consistent trends noted in all of them. Two components of all the subjects' VERs were especially noticeable in this regard, one occurring around 100 msec following the stimulus presentation and the other around 180 msec.

In every case (four subjects, three replications) the VER wave form was more negative at the 100 msec point when the pattern was sharply focused than it was when the pattern was blurred. Similarly, the wave forms were always more positive at the 180 msec point when the pattern was sharply focused than when it was blurred. On the basis of the demonstrated consistency of the evoked activity at these two points in time following stimulation it was decided to limit attention to these points in the remainder of the study.

In the next phase of the study the sharpness of focus of the patterned image on the subjects' retinae was varied over a wider range by placing a series of ophthalmic lenses in front of their eyes. The lenses used

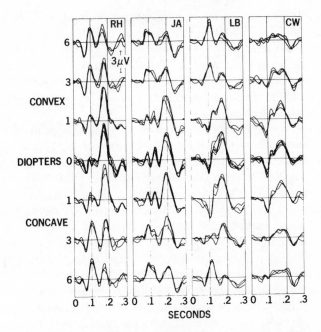

Fig. 4.   VERs obtained from four subjects as a function of sharpness of focus. Optimum checkerboard pattern. Each tracing represents summation of 100 responses. Diopter values represent strength of ophthalmic lenses used to control degree of contour degradation. Negative downward.

ranged from +6 diopters (convex) to −6 diopters (concave). The actual lens conditions were: +6, +3, +1, 0, −1, −3, and −6. Because our subjects all had normal vision, it was assumed that this series of lenses would result in badly blurred images at the two extremes and in clear vision around the 0 diopter, or plano, condition.

An example of the results obtained in this phase of the study is shown in Fig. 4. The VERs of the four subjects clearly show the transition from blur to sharp focus then back to blur. The two components described above are easily identified.

When we ran this study we had assumed that our subjects would exhibit the largest pattern responses when no lenses were being used, because one of the restrictions in choosing subjects was that they have 20/20 vision without correction. The expected pattern response was seen with subjects RH and JA but not with LB and CW. Subject LB definitely favored the concave lenses, whereas CW responded best to the convex lenses. These effects are most clearly seen if you compare the responses to the +3 and −3 lenses. Further investigation showed that LB was indeed slightly myopic and CW presbyopic. Subject CW had never worn glasses, and this was the first indication he had had that he was beginning to need reading glasses. Subject LB, on the other hand, did occasionally use glasses for reading. We therefore ran LB while he was wearing his reading glasses. This time he gave the largest pattern responses in the plano condition, and his responses to +3 and −3 diopter lenses were almost identical.

At this point we realized that the pattern VER was probably a very sensitive technique for determining the refractive error. This was proven to be true when we next studied subjects who required sizable corrections to achieve 20/20 vision. We found that we could determine their refractive errors quite readily by comparing the VERs obtained with a series of lenses. Later work showed that the sensitivity of the technique could be increased considerably by subtracting the VER to light alone from the VER to light-plus-pattern (White, 1969a; Jeffreys, 1968). By using this added step in the process we found that a small degree of astigmatism could be detected (White, 1969b). At this time details of the techniques were presented by the author to state and national optometric conferences. These presentations led directly to intensive evaluative studies by vision specialists at various centers and eventually to clinical application, as described in a later section.

Visual Field Effects

The nature of the pattern VER obtained is very much dependent upon the part of the visual field stimulated. The examples given thus far have all been with the subjects fixating the center of the patterned field. Jeffreys (1969) showed that the components related to the presence of pattern can apparently be of a completely different nature when the pattern falls in the lower visual field than when it falls in the upper field. In this study he found that the marked negativity noted around 100 msec after stimulation was apparently produced primarily by the reactions of the upper portion of the retina, corresponding to the lower visual field. Stimulation of only the upper visual field produced a marked positive component at this point in time following stimulation.

A replication of this study, done in our laboratory, illustrates the situation. Fig. 5 shows the VERs of one subject as he fixated successively the different rows of a checkerboard pattern. The topmost record shows the VER obtained when the pattern fell entirely within the lower visual field and the bottom record that obtained when the pattern was entirely in the upper field. The other records represent his responses to the various

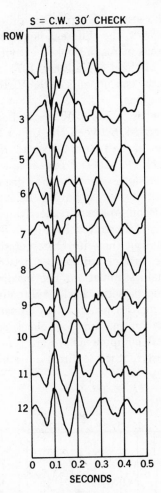

Fig. 5. VER for one subject as a function of focus of fixation on a checkerboard pattern. Top row represents fixation at top of pattern, bottom row at lower edge. Other rows show responses with intermediate fixations. Negative downward.

intervening conditions. It has been found that the reliability of these responses is such that an experienced subject can produce any one of a number of specified VER wave forms merely by fixating a given row of the pattern.

Further studies dealing with more restricted stimulus placements have provided additional data on this matter. Through the use of multiple electrode placement it has been found that the various positions of the stimulus patterns in the visual field produce different patterns of electrical activity over the cortex, the different field positions seeming to have corresponding focal areas of major evoked activity (Jeffreys, 1971; Halliday & Michael, 1970; Michael & Halliday, 1971). Moreover, Jeffreys' results indicate that specific components of the VER represent focal activity in different cortical locations.

A study carried out by Eason, White, & Bartlett (1970) indicated that there is an interaction between the upper and lower visual fields and the contour density in the pattern. A series of checkerboard patterns, each consisting of check elements of one of a wide range of sizes, was presented to the upper, lower, and central visual fields of a group of subjects. This was accomplished by having the subjects fixate the bottom, top, and center of the flashing pattern respectively.

The general results are illustrated by Fig. 6. These are the VERs for just one of the subjects but they are representative of the entire group. Here again we see the striking differences between the VER produced by lower and upper field stimulation. The maximum response from the lower field was produced with checks subtending around 20–30 min of arc, whereas the responses produced by upper field stimulation were still increasing even when the smallest check sizes were used.

Inasmuch as the VER components we are referring to as the *contour response* depend almost in their entirety on stimulation of the central

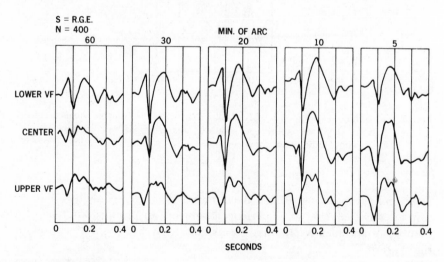

Fig. 6. VERs obtained from a subject for lower visual field, central visual field and upper visual field pattern stimulation, with check-size as a variable. Negative downward.

3° of the visual field (Spekreijse, 1966; Rietveld, et al., 1967), we are in reality dealing with the differential results obtained by stimulating the upper and lower 1.5° of the central retina. The possible functional significance of this difference, if any, is not as yet clear.

Again, the marked interindividual differences found in VER wave forms must be stressed. The same sort of individuality is shown in the relative wave forms produced by upper and lower visual field stimulation. As indicated earlier, the records of the one individual shown in Fig. 6 are presented as a means of describing the general trends observed in our group of subjects.

One thing has become apparent, however. The components of the VER that have been referred to as the contour response (negative component around 100 msec, marked positive around 180 msec) arise primarily from stimulation of the lower visual field. In some individuals, such as RGE (Fig. 6), the nature of the upper field response is such that it does not interfere much with the contour response from the lower field, therefore central fixation results in a potent response.

In the case of some individuals, however, the nature of the upper field response is such as to interfere with the lower field contour response, thereby causing that subject's VER to appear relatively unresponsive to pattern stimulation when the pattern occurs in the central field. This is clearly seen in Fig. 5. In this case the major components of the upper field response (row 12) are essentially out of phase with those of the lower field response (row 1). With central fixation this situation leads to a much reduced pattern VER.

Once again, there are no obvious functional correlates of these individual differences. One practical result of these findings, however, is that if we want to do studies dealing with changes in the contour response we often only deal with lower field stimulation.

Harter (1970) found that the relationship between contour density and the pattern VER was dependent on the eccentricity of the stimulation. When the central portion of the field was stimulated the maximum responses were obtained with relatively small-sized checks (subtending 7.5–30 min of arc, depending on the subject). When the stimulation occurred about 4.5–7.5° from the central fovea, however, the maximum response was to checks subtending 60 min of arc. These results appear to be analogous to the earlier findings of Harter & White (1970) relating to VER to effective visual acuity. This study also provided evidence for the probable functional differences of the processes indicated by the two major contour response components (surface negative around 100 msec and surface positive around 180 msec). The relationship noted between the VER and check-size with increasing eccentricity was almost entirely due to the negative (100 msec) component. The positive (180 msec) component remained most sensitive to the 30 min of arc checks for all stimulus locations except for central foveal stimulation. With central stimulation the positive component was most sensitive to the smallest checks used (7.5 min of arc subtended), whereas the negative component was most sensitive to check-sizes of about 30 min of arc subtended. The same differentiation between the two components was found in the earlier study by Harter & White (1968).

On–Off Effects

Harter (1971) obtained VERs to the onset and offset of patterned stimuli in order to determine whether the same relationships regarding contour sharpness and density would hold under the two conditions. Very similar results were obtained with regard to the degree of contour sharpness. Sharp focus maximized both the surface negative (SN) and the surface positive (SP) components, whereas a blurred image reduced them both markedly.

The amplitude of both the SN and SP components was much greater for onset than for offset. This fact is immediately apparent for SP, which is more than twice as large for the onset as for the offset. The SNs for onset and for offset appear very much the same in Harter's records, but this may be misleading. His records, obtained for essentially diffuse light, show a marked onset effect but very little offset effect. The major component of the onset effect is a positive wave peaking at 100 msec following stimulation. Therefore the onset SN of the contour response is opposed by the light onset response, resulting in an apparently small SN. If the subtraction technique had been used in this case (with light-produced VERs subtracted from pattern VERs) a truer picture of the situation would probably have resulted.

One very interesting finding was the fact that the most effective stimuli were smaller in angular subtense for offset than for onset. No immediate explanation is available as to why this should be.

Binocular Interaction

The studies described so far all used binocular stimulation. The impressive effects of changes in the refractive state, however, made it clear that the eyes must also be studied separately, inasmuch as it cannot be assumed that the two are perfectly matched in their physical characteristics.

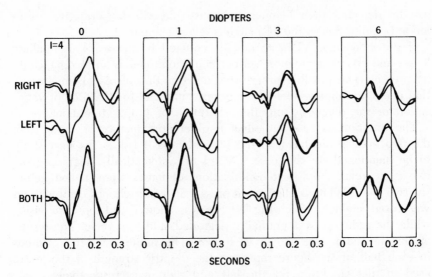

Fig. 7. Binocular summation in the VER as a function of image quality, both eyes having equal quality. The 0 diopter condition represents sharpest image focus, the 5 diopter condition the most degraded. Negative downward.

As a first step in determining the contributions of each of the eyes to the binocular VER a study was made in which the quality of the images presented to the eyes was systematically varied by the use of ophthalmic lenses of various dioptric powers (White & Bonelli, 1970). At each such lens setting VERs were obtained for each eye separately and for both together. A typical example of what was obtained is shown in Fig. 7. It can be seen that the degree of binocular summation shown by the VER is directly related to the quality of the image available to each eye. This effect is so striking that it suggests a possible clinical screening technique—to obtain VERs under monocular and binocular conditions and note how the addition of the second eye affects the response. A marked increase would indicate that both eyes are probably functioning well.

A mismatch in the physical conditions of the two eyes can usually be detected by comparing the VERs of each eye. Differences in amplitude or wave form would indicate that the two monocular systems are not reacting in the same way to the visual stimulation. This could, of course, be due to a number of causes, some benign but others serious. The benign causes would be such things as differences in refractive state or the presence of a minor astigmatic condition. Such conditions can be detected in a manner previously described. Corrective lenses might be prescribed if the mismatch is severe enough.

If the monocular VERs cannot be equated by means of ophthalmic lenses and prisms, some more serious condition, such as amblyopia, could be present. The possible progressive deterioration of visual functioning that could accompany such a condition would call for the prompt verification of the diagnosis and the institution of proper treatment.

The question as to what effect a differential quality of input from the two eyes would have on the binocular VER led to the next study to be mentioned. In this case, instead of systematically degrading the two eyes equally, different combinations of lenses were placed before the two eyes (White & Hansen, in press). Sixteen such lens combinations were used, eight in which the left eye was allowed to keep clear vision while the right eye was gradually degraded, and vice versa. The results of this procedure are shown in Fig. 8. The numbers in the columns in each half of the figure represent the dioptric strength of the lenses used in that condition for the left and right eyes respectively.

The top row of wave forms and the bottom row represent this subject's binocular responses to a sharply focused checkerboard pattern and to a completely blurred field respectively. The intervening conditions show the effects of gradual image degradation. It is seen that the response is not much depressed by a slight degree of blurring in one eye (the 0,1 and 1,0 conditions). A greater degree of blurring, however, sharply cuts the amplitude of the response. The first aspect of the VER to be greatly affected appears to be the positive component at around 180 msec. As lenses are now put before the previously unimpaired eye, the response is rapidly degraded.

The midpoint conditions are of special interest (0,6 and 6,0). A comparison of the two conditions would seem to indicate that when the right eye has clear vision the visual system can withstand somewhat better the blurred input from the other eye, than is the case when the left eye has the clear vision and the right is blurred. It might be that a technique such as this would provide information about visual dominance effects not available any other way.

When conditions are such that there is a marked degree of binocular summation such summation does not manifest itself as merely an expanded version of the monocular response wave form. Certain components of the complex VER are definitely more affected by binocular summation than are others. The most conspicuous such component is the positive peak occurring around 180 msec. By observing the changes that this component of the VER undergoes in the various studies it becomes clear that the component is quite sensitive to the binocular

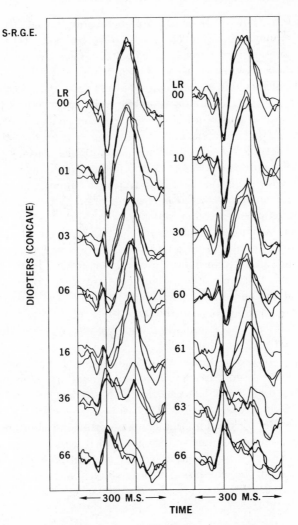

Fig. 8. Binocular summation in the VER as a function of image quality, the two eyes having images of varying quality. Negative downward.

summation of contour or pattern-related activity as well as being sensitive to the amount and quality of contour presented to one eye alone. Other components, although sensitive to pattern-related elements and contour quality, do not exhibit the same degree of sensitivity to binocular stimulation. Further discussion of the various components will appear in later sections as appropriate.

Harter has shown (personal communication) that the degree of binocular summation achieved is also directly related to the density of contour present in the monocular patterns. Thus the degree of binocular summation shown by the VER is determined by both the quantity and quality of the contour information available in the two inputs. Again, however, there is an optimum separation of pattern edges to be found, just as in the previously described studies when only binocular stimulation was used. If the pattern elements become smaller than that optimum level the relative degree of binocular summation decreases.

The studies discussed so far in this section on binocular summation have dealt with situations in which transient stimuli were used. In fact all have been concerned with the effects created by the onset of a lighted area that contained varying amounts and qualities of pattern. The phenomenon of binocular summation can also be demonstrated by means of *steady-state conditions,* wherein the intensity of each element of the pattern is modulated sinusoidally over a given range, the overall intensity of the stimulus display remaining at a constant level. Some earlier studies showed that the addition of the second eye in this situation would lead to practically a doubling of the amplitude of the ongoing electrical activity produced by stimulating one eye alone (van der Tweel & Spekreijse, 1968; Spekreijse, 1966).

No formal studies on that very special aspect of binocular interaction, stereopsis, have been carried out in our laboratory. The best work to date on this topic, as related to the VER, is the well-conceived study by Regan & Spekreijse (1970). This work is especially noteworthy for its demonstration of the importance of experimental controls in complex topics such as stereopsis, and indeed in all VER work.

Retinal rivalry, a situation in which the patterns presented to the two eyes cannot be combined into a single constant percept by the higher visual centers, has also been approached by some workers.

Temporal Summation

Preliminary studies done in our laboratory have shown that VERs produced by patterned stimuli exhibit marked temporal summation effects. This is in contrast to nonpatterned light stimulation, which produces such effects only around threshold. When using a checkerboard pattern a much larger contour response will be obtained if a train of flashes is used rather than just a single flash. This is shown by Fig. 9. The numbers to the left of the tracings indicate the number of flashes in the train.

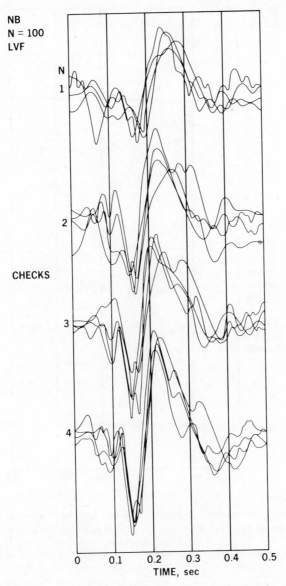

Fig. 9. VERs showing temporal summation of the pattern response. Responses to trains of 1, 2, 3, and 4 patterned flashes respectively. Negative downward.

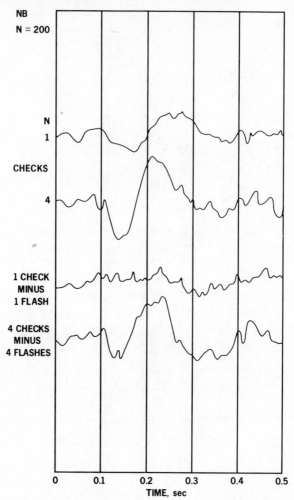

Fig. 10. Temporal summation of pattern VERs. Top two rows show responses to trains of one and four patterned flashes respectively. The two bottom rows show the result of subtracting the responses of trains of one and four light flashes from rows 1 and 2 respectively. Negative downward.

The flashes within the flash-trains were 10 msec apart, thus the total time represented varied from 10 μsec for $N = 1$ to about 30 msec for $N = 4$. At the flash separation used there was complete fusion, each train appearing as a single flash. The results of the temporal summation are clearly seen—an approximate doubling in amplitude and a decrease in the latency amounting to about 50 msec. Such changes would not have taken place in the VER if the pattern had not been present.

Evidence for this differential effect for patterned and nonpatterned stimulation is shown in Fig. 10. The two upper tracings represent VERs for trains of one and four flashes respectively—the two lower tracings show what remained of these responses after the responses to equivalent trains of nonpatterned flashes have been subtracted from them. The amplitude of the resultant four-flash train response shows that the subtraction of the nonpatterned flash responses had relatively little effect. This appears to be strong evidence for the idea that nonpatterned and patterned visual information are processed by different neural systems.

Movement (Pattern Displacement)

Most of the examples of the VER dealt with in this paper are concerned with the electrical events in the visual cortex associated with the sudden onset of a complex visual stimulus. The transient effects in the visual system are also complex—perhaps too complex for a straightforward analysis of what might be occurring. My own assessment of the situation is that it is important to study every type of visual stimulus condition in order to come to any sort of understanding of what might be involved.

One approach that has been tried is to record the reactions brought about by the sudden displacement of a pattern that has been stationary in the visual field. In this case we are not dealing with the onset of light per se, and thus we might be able to derive information concerning pattern processing in the purer sense.

Our group has not dealt with this particular aspect of the VER systematically, but we have done enough to be able to provide some corroboration to the reports of others and perhaps to suggest some direction for future work. Our work can be distilled into one figure (Fig. 11), which represents the findings we have made so far in this area.

The checkerboard patterns were reduced photographically to fit into an overhead projector, which presented the patterns on a screen. The small checkerboard transparencies were attached to a solenoid arrangement that, when activated, would move the transparency in any desired direction. A fixation point was provided so that the pattern would fall on any prescribed part of the retina. A system of rubber bands was attached to the patterned slide so that when the solenoid was deactivated the slide would return to its original position. With this admittedly crude arrangement we were able to present "fast" and "slow" pattern

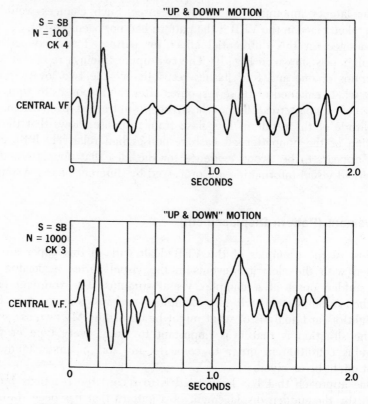

Fig. 11.   VERs obtained to the movement of patterned stimuli in the visual field.

movement. The solenoid gave "fast" and the rubber bands "slow" movements. No attempt was made to measure the velocity of this pattern shift—at this point it was sufficient to know that the velocities were perceptibly different. By arranging the slides it was possible to obtain left–right (fast–slow) sequences and up–down (fast–slow) sequences.

As is the case with others who have used comparable stimulus situations, we found this to be a very good way of obtaining VERs. Our results, admittedly very preliminary, show that velocity of pattern displacement is an important variable, the "fast" solenoid-induced movement producing larger responses than the slower return movement. Our results did not show any significant differences between up and down movements or between left and right movements, however. The differences apparent in the figure are related to the velocity of the pattern displacements.

The contour density within the patterns was an important factor. In Fig. 11 we see the different evoked wave forms produced by "check 3" (20' elements) and "check 4" (10' elements). The earlier parts of the wave forms are markedly different. This difference was noted on all the replications of these studies. The examples shown are typical.

In Fig. 11 one wave form represents the summation of 1000 responses, the other the summation of 100 responses. This is not an important factor. The difference between the wave forms evoked by the different patterns held for even smaller summation numbers. The example for a summation of 1000 responses is shown just because it was done, not because it was necessary.

Clinical Applications

As discussed in an earlier section, Harter & White (1968) demonstrated that the sensitivity of the VER to contour sharpness was such that an objective measure of the spherical refractive error of the eyes could be obtained with this technique, and it was later shown that the presence and degree of astigmatism could also be detected by this means (White, 1969b). During this same period it was found that the presence of amblyopia could be detected by comparing the monocular responses of the eyes evoked by checkerboard patterns (Lombroso, Duffy, & Robb, 1969). Earlier studies by a number of workers had shown that the evoked wave forms produced by patterned and blank visual stimuli were quite different, but the three studies just referred to were probably most responsible for alerting researchers in optometry and ophthalmology to the expanding clinical possibilities of the VER.

An extensive study of the possibilities of the VER as a visual diagnostic technique was undertaken by the U.S. Army (Duffy & Rengstorff, 1971). In the course of this work it was found that the VER could indeed be used for visual screening and for refraction. Tentative plans were also developed for automating most of the entire procedure. During this same period work was proceeding at the College of Optometry, State University of New York, to adapt the technique so it could be used with young children and other individuals who could not be adequately tested by regular optometric methods (Ludlam, Cohen, & Ludlam, 1970). A more recent report by this group presents the details of their findings and describes the techniques that have proven successful for dealing with very young patients (Ludlam & Meyers, 1972). Children 12 months old are now being tested on a routine basis by this group.

In both the major evaluative studies described above (Duffy &

Rengstorff, 1971; Ludlam & Meyers, 1972) the general technique developed by White (1969a, 1969b) was used. That is, VERs to flashed patterned stimuli were first obtained and then the VERs to blank field flashes of the same average intensity were subtracted from the pattern responses. Such a procedure has been found to greatly enhance the sensitivity of the VER technique (see White, 1969b).

Another technique, developed by Millodot & Riggs (1970), avoids some of the complexities inherent in the transient response approach. A modified checkerboard pattern was made up, with interlaced strips of polarizing material. This pattern was then illuminated from the back by a steady tungsten light source, which shone through a rotating polarizer. The result is a situation in which the average intensity level remains constant but where the intensity level of each square that does vary does so in a sinusoidal manner. The resultant condition is perceived as a pattern in motion. The VER produced is sinusoidal in nature, the amplitude of which is proportional to image quality. Using this type of stimulus these workers found that they could also refract the eye by noting the changes occurring in the averaged electoretinogram (ERG), but this response was much less sensitive to changes in contour quality than was the VER, undoubtedly because the VER is primarily related to foveal activity.

It has been found that in cases of optic neuritis the pattern VER is severely reduced in amplitude and has a markedly increased latency (Halliday, McDonald, & Mushin, 1972). Because the disease is often unilateral, rather dramatic differences can be seen by comparing the VERs obtained by stimulating the two eyes separately. There is no comparable increase in the latency of responses when light alone is used as the stimulus. This fact is interpreted as indicating that the pattern and light-alone responses are mediated by different fibers in the optic nerve.

Developmental Aspects of the Pattern VER

Age Factors

The interest of our group in the VERs produced by patterned stimuli was brought about by a question raised by Dr. Bernard Karmel, then of San Diego State College, as to whether such a technique could differentiate between stimulation by various check-sizes with any degree of accuracy. Karmel was interested in problems dealing with child development, and his question arose from his earlier studies dealing with the way in which infants' apparent preferences for patterns made up of various sizes of elements changed as a function of age.

The results of our work on this topic, along with the work of other laboratories, was summarized in an earlier section. For adult subjects with normal vision there was a range of check-size (spatial frequency) that produced the optimum pattern response. That the intersubject variability found as to which check-size was optimum was probably related to individual differences in visual efficiency was indicated by the results of the study in which the degree of retinal blur was systematically varied (Harter & White, 1970).

In this case the effective visual acuity of the subjects was varied by artificially introducing varying degrees of refractive error. It was assumed that variations in visual acuity, regardless of the cause, would bring about similar results as far as the VER was concerned. A visual system that had not fully matured would probably react quite differently from that of the normal adult to the series of checkerboard patterns, even if no refractive error were present—the relatively undeveloped system responding better to the larger checks. As the striate cortex matured, it was predicted, gradually smaller and smaller check sizes would produce the optimum pattern responses in the VER, approaching the situation found in the various studies dealing with normal adults.

At least three groups have started to study the developmental aspects of the pattern VER. Harter & Suitt (1970) carried out a longitudinal study with one subject. The study was begun when the child was 21 days of age, and continued until he was 155 days of age. VERs were obtained for a series of checkerboard patterns made up of pattern elements of varying size. Definite trends were noted in the VER wave forms that were obtained. Most important, there was a definite trend toward there being larger responses to gradually decreasing check-sizes as a function of age—as predicted. The data from this one subject cannot be used to describe general trends in the pattern VERs of maturing infants, but is more than adequate to show the value of obtaining normative data on this topic.

Karmel has continued his interest in this area, and now has a laboratory (at the University of Connecticut) at least partly devoted to this topic. A recent paper (Karmel, Hoffman, & Fegy, 1972) deals with the changes occurring in the pattern VERs obtained from a number of infants at two age levels.

Extensive work in this area is also being done by Marcus and associates at California's Sonoma State Hospital at Eldridge. In addition to being interested in the developmental aspects of pattern VERs in normal children, they are carrying out similar studies with children afflicted with

Down's Syndrome (mongoloidism) and other types of retardation. Work is also underway dealing with the effects of various drugs on the pattern VER, in this case drugs that are used in the treatment of some of those conditions (Marcus, 1970).

The fact that the number of published reports on this topic is not commensurate with the effort expended to date is tribute to the level and variety of difficulties encountered.

Sensory Deprivation Effects

When cats are deprived of patterned light stimulation during critical periods following birth very marked effects on visually guided behavior will occur. Although the cats are able to make light-intensity discriminations, pattern discrimination learning is lost and therefore also such things as the visual placing response and normal responses to impending collisions.

The findings relating to human pattern VERs described in earlier sections of this paper, especially those dealing with the quantity and quality of contour information contained in a pattern, suggested to Siegel, Coleman, & Riesen (1973) that the pattern VER might provide a physiological correlate of the degree of pattern degradation produced by being exposed only to diffused light. To test this possibility, two matched groups of cats were reared from birth on identical regimens except that during the 3 hr of exposure to light each day (following 10 days of complete darkness) one group's members had fine percale hoods placed over their heads. This diffused the light and effectively excluded those visual patterns that were available to the other group.

When the cats were 6 months of age, VERs were obtained from both groups. The stimuli consisted of blank flashes of light and also a series of patterns containing varying amounts of contour. The VERs of the two groups differed significantly not only at the primary visual area but also at the motor cortex.

The authors concluded that the "Contour Response appears to be a promising tool which might provide a quantifiable physiological correlate of both normal perceptual development and changes in perceptual abilities resulting from enriched or impoverished environments."

Discussion

It is hoped that the brief overview of the pattern VER given here will convey the richness of this field of research. A most fortunate brain topography has provided us with the means of studying the reactions of the visual system at its highest levels. The macular region of the retina is represented in magnified form on the occipital cortex, and we may find that even the various parts of the macula may have strikingly different functional characteristics.

Of great interest are the detailed studies of the various components of the pattern VER. It is quite clear that the major components of the contour response relate to different aspects of the processing of information contained in the complex visual stimuli. The various studies indicated that the surface negative response (SN) is most reactive to relatively low contour density stimulation. The general findings indicate that this component reaches its maximum when the contour elements are separated by around 30 min of arc.

The surface positive component (SP), on the other hand, is most responsive to much smaller contour elements. In some studies the smallest elements utilized (5–5.7 min of arc separation) apparently had not reached the point of greatest reactivity. It is also to be noted that this component of the contour response appears to be most sensitive to binocular interaction effects. In one study where a subject with a congenital strabismus was used, this component appeared to be lacking completely (subject JH, in White, 1969a).

Harter (1970, 1971) has discussed the possible implications of these findings in terms of receptive field centers. There seems to be agreement between these VER results in humans and earlier single-unit studies in animals having visual systems similar to that of man.

There also appears to be a relationship between the separation of contour elements and the part of the visual field that is stimulated. When the lower visual field was stimulated the larger contour element separations resulted in the greatest amplitudes of the VER (again around 30 min of arc separation appeared optimum). Upper visual field stimulation favored the much smaller separation.

The preliminary studies of temporal summation effects indicate a marked difference between the contour response and the light alone response. This same kind of differentiation is indicated by the studies of certain types of visual pathology that primarily affect the macular region. The evidence appears to be quite convincing as to the fact that there are some components of the VER that are related to pattern elements and some that are related to light alone. Probably the most direct evidence of that fact is afforded by the study dealing with the effects of visual deprivation on the pattern VER.

It is felt that one of the most interesting applications of the pattern VER will be in the study of the development of the visual capacities of human infants and young animals. The studies laying the groundwork for pediatric optometry and the ophthalmological applications have already proven the great value of this approach.

Acknowledgments

The preparation of this chapter and certain of the studies described in it were supported in part by a grant from the Office of Naval Research.

References

Armington, J. C., Corwin, T. R., & Marsetta, R. (1971). Simultaneously recorded retinal and cortical responses to patterned stimuli. *J. Opt. Soc. Amer.*, **61**, 1514–1521.

Bergamini, L., & Bergamasco, B. (1967). *Cortical evoked potentials in man.* Charles C Thomas, Springfield, Ill.

Buchsbaum, M., & Fedio, F. (1969). Visual information and evoked responses from the left and right hemispheres. *Electroenceph. clin. Neurophysiol.*, **26**, 266–272.

Chapman, R. M., & Bragdon, H. R. (1964). Evoked responses to numerical and non-numerical visual stimuli while problem solving. *Nature*, **203**, 1155–1157.

Childers, D. G., Perry, N. W., Halpeny, O. S., & Bourne, J. R. (1972). Spatio-temporal measures of cortical functioning in normal and abnormal vision. *Comput. Biomed. Res.*, **5**, 114–130.

Clarke, P. H. J. (1972). Visual evoked potentials to sudden reversal of the motion of a pattern. *Brain Res.*, **36**, 453–458.

Cobb, W. A., Morton, H. B., & Ettlinger, G. (1967). Cerebral potentials evoked by pattern reversal and their suppression in visual rivalry. *Nature*, **216**, 1123–1125.

Dawson, W. W., Perry, N. W., Jr., & Childers, D. G. (1968). Flash and scan stimulation of retinal fields and evoked response production. *Electroenceph. clin. Neurophysiol.*, **24**, 467–473.

Donchin, E., & Lindsley, D. B. (1965). Visually evoked response correlates of perceptual masking and enhancement. *Electroenceph. clin. Neurophysiol.*, **19**, 325–335.

Donchin, E., & Lindsley, D. B. (Eds.) (1969). *Average evoked potentials: Methods, results, and evaluations.* NASA AP-191, U.S. Government Printing Office, Washington, D. C.

Duffy, F. H., & Rengstorff, R. H. (1971). Ametropia measurements from the visual evoked respose. *Amer. J. Optom. Arch. Amer. Acad. Optom.*, **48**, 717–728.

Eason, R. G., White, C. T., & Bartlett, N. R. (1970). Effects of checkerboard pattern stimulation on evoked cortical responses in relation to check size and visual field. *Psychon. Sci.*, **21**(2), 113–115.

Gross, G. E., Vaughan, H. G., Jr., & Valenstein, E. (1967). Inhibition of visual evoked responses to patterned stimuli during voluntary eye movements. *Electroenceph. clin. Neurophysiol.*, **22**, 204–209.

Halliday, A. M., McDonald, W. I., & Mushin, J. (1972), Delayed visual evoked response in optic neuritis. *The Lancet,* Vol. 1, 7758, 982–985.

Halliday, A. M., & Michael, W. F. (1970). Changes in pattern evoked responses in man associated with the vertical and horizontal meridians of the visual field. *J. Physiol.,* 208, 499–513.

Harter, M. R. (1970). Evoked cortical responses to checkerboard patterns: Effect of check-size as a function of retinal eccentricity. *Vision Res.,* 10, 1365–1376.

Harter, M. R. (1971). Visually evoked cortical responses to the on- and off-set of patterned light in humans. *Vision Res.,* 11, 685–695.

Harter, M. R., & Salmon, L. E. (1971). Evoked cortical responses to patterned light flashes: Effects of ocular convergence and accommodation. *Electroenceph. clin. Neurophysiol.,* 30, 527–533.

Harter, M. R., & Salmon, L. E. (1972). Intra-modality selective attention and evoked cortical potentials to randomly presented patterns. *Electroenceph. clin. Neurophysiol.,* 32, 605–613.

Harter, M. R., & Suitt, C. D. (1970). Visually-evoked cortical responses and pattern vision in the infant. A longitudinal study. *Psychon. Sci.,* 18, 235–237.

Harter, M. R., & White, C. T. (1968). Effects of contour sharpness and checksize on visually evoked cortical potentials. *Vision Res.,* 8, 701–711.

Harter, M. R., & White, C. T. (1970). Evoked cortical responses to checkerboard patterns: Effect of check-size as a function of visual acuity. *Electroenceph. clin. Neurophysiol.,* 28, 48–54.

Jeffreys, D. A. (1968). Separable components of human evoked responses to spatially patterned visual fields. *Electroenceph. clin. Neurophysical.,* 24, 593–596.

Jeffreys, D. A. (1969). In D. MacKay (Ed.), Evoked potentials as indicators of sensory information processing. *Neurosci. Res. Progr. Bull.,* 7, 216–217.

Jeffreys, D. A. (1970). Polarity and distribution of human visual evoked potential (VEP) components as clues to cortical topography. *Electroenceph. clin. Neurophysiol.,* 29, 326.

Jeffreys, D. A. (1971). Cortical source locations of pattern-related visual evoked potentials recorded from the human scalp. *Nature,* 229, 502–504.

John, E. R., Herrington, R. N., & Sutton, S. (1967). Effects of visual form on the evoked response. *Science,* 155, 1439–1442.

Karmel, B. Z., Hoffman, R. R., & Fegy, M. J. (1972). Processing of contour information in human infants evidenced by pattern-dependent evoked potentials. *Papers Amer. Psychol. Assoc. September 1972.*

Katzman, R. (Ed.) (1964). Sensory evoked response in man. *Ann. N. Y. Acad. Sci.,* 112, 1–546.

Keesey, U. T. (1971). Comparison of human visual cortical potentials evoked by stabilized and unstabilized targets. *Vision Res.,* 11, 657–670.

Kopell, B. S., Wittner, W. K., & Warrick, G. L. (1968). The effects of stimulus differences, light intensity, and selective attention on the visual averaged evoked potential in man. *Electroenceph. clin. Neurophysiol.,* 26, 619–622.

Lawwill, T., & Biersdorf, W. R. (1968). Binocular rivalry and visual evoked responses. *Invest. Ophthalnol.,* 7, 378–385.

Lehmann, D., Beeler, G. W., Jr., & Fender, D. H. (1967). EEG responses to light flashes during the observation of stabilized and normal retinal images. *Electroenceph. clin. Neurophysiol.,* 22, 136–142.

Lehmann, D., & Fender, D. H. (1968). Component analysis of human averaged evoked potentials: Dichoptic stimuli using different target structure. *Electroenceph. clin. Neurophysiol.,* 24, 542–553.

Lesevre, N., & Remond, A. (1972). Potentiels evoques par l'apparition de patterns: Effects de la dimension du pattern et de la densite des contrastes. *Electroenceph. clin. Neurophysical.*, **32**, 593–604.

Lifshitz, K. (1966). The averaged evoked cortical response to complex visual stimuli. *Psychophysiol.* **3**, 55–68.

Lombroso, C. T., Duffy, F. H., & Robb, R. M. (1969). Selective suppression of cerebral evoked potentials to patterned light in amblyopia. *Electroenceph. clin. Neurophysiol.*, **27**, 238–247.

Ludlam, W. M., Cohen, S., & Ludlam, D. P. (1970). The visual evoked response: A new tool in vision research. *Amer. J. Optom. Arch. Amer. Acad. Optom.*, **47**, 505–519.

Ludlam, W. M., & Meyers, R. R. (1972). The use of visual evoked responses in objective refraction. *Trans. N. Y. Acad. Sci.*, **34**, 155–170.

MacKay, D. M., & Rietveld, W. J. (1968). Electroencephalogram potentials evoked by accelerated visual motion. *Nature*, **217**, 677–678.

Marcus, M. M. (1970). The evoked cortical response: A technique for assessing development. *Calif. Mental Health Res. Digest*, **8**, 59–72.

Martin, J. I. (1970). Effects of binocular fusion and binocular rivalry on cortically evoked potentials. *Electroenceph. clin. Neurophysiol.*, **28**, 190–201.

Michael, W. F., & Halliday, A. M. (1971). Differences between the occipital distribution of upper and lower field pattern-evoked responses in man. *Brain Res.*, **32**, 311–324.

Millodot, M., & Riggs, L. A. (1970). Refraction determined electrophysiologically. *Arch. Ophthalmol.*, **84**, 272–278.

Perry, N. W., Jr., & Childers, D. G. (1969). *The human visual evoked response: Methods and theory.* Charles C Thomas, Springfield, Ill.

Regan, D. (1972). *Evoked potentials in psychology, sensory physiology and clinical medicine.* Wiley, New York.

Regan, D., & Richards, W. (1971). Independence of evoked potentials and apparent size. *Vision Res.*, **11**, 679–684.

Regan, D., & Spekreijse, H. (1970). Electrophysiological correlate of binocular depth perception in man. *Nature*, **225**, 92–94.

Regan, D., & Sperling, H. G. (1970). A method of evoking contour-specific scalp potentials by chromatic checkerboard patterns. *Vision Res.*, **11**, 173–176.

Rietveld, W. J., Tordoir, W. E. M., Hagenouw, J. R. B., Lubbers, J. A., & Spoor, Th. A. C. (1967). Visual evoked responses to blank and to checkerboard flashes. *Acta Physiol. Pharmacol. Neerl.*, **14**, 259–285.

Riggs, L. A., & Whittle, P. (1967). Human occipital and retinal potentials evoked by subjectively faded visual stimuli. *Vision Res.*, **7**, 441–451.

Ristanovic, D. (1972) On the cortical responses to paired patterned flashes in man. *Acta Med. Iug.*, **26**, 207–216.

Sandler, L. S., & Schwartz, M. (1971). Evoked responses and perception: Stimulus content versus stimulus structure. *Psychophysiol.*, **8**, 727–737.

Siegel, J. M., Coleman, P. D., & Riesen, A. H. (1973). Pattern evoked response deficiency in pattern deprived cats. *Electroenceph. clin. Neurophysical.* **35**, 569–573.

Spehlmann, R. (1965). The averaged electrical responses to diffuse and to patterned light in the human. *Electroenceph. clin. Neurophysiol.*, **19**, 560–569.

Spekreijse, H. (1966). *Analysis of EEG responses in man.* W. Junk, The Hague, Netherlands.

Van der Tweel, L. H., & Spekreijse, H. (1968). Visual evoked responses. In *The clinical value of electroretinography, ISCERG Symp. Ghent 1966.* Karger, Basel New York. Pp. 83–94.

Van Hof, M. W. (1960). Open-eye and closed-eye occipitocortical response to photic stimulation of the retina. *Acta Physiol. Pharmacol. Neerl.,* 9, 443–51.

White, C. T. (1969a). Evoked cortical responses and patterned stimuli. *Amer. Psychol.,* 24, 211–214.

White, C. T. (1969b). In E. Donchin & D. B. Lindsley (Eds.), *Average evoked potentials: Methods, results and evaluations.* NASA SP-191. Washington, D. C. Pp. 118–124.

White, C. T., & Bonelli, L. (1970). Binocular summation in the evoked potential as a function of image quality. *Amer. J. Optom. Arch. Amer. Acad. Optom.,* 47, 304–309.

White, C. T., & Hansen, D. Complex binocular interaction and other effects in the visual evoked response. *Amer. J. Optom. Arch. Amer. Acad. Optom.* in press.

Chapter 8

THE EFFECTS OF SENSUAL DRUGS ON BEHAVIOR: CLUES TO THE FUNCTION OF THE BRAIN

HARDIN B. JONES

University of California, Berkeley

In 1954, Aldous Huxley published "The Doors of Perception," an account of his personal experiences with mescaline and other drugs (Huxley, 1954). The essay created a following. Huxley was not the first drug user to "confess" fascination, but his endorsement of mescaline and drugs in general had appeal: "Although obviously superior to cocaine, opium, alcohol, and tobacco, mescaline is not yet the ideal drug. . . ." The title was taken from a passage of "Prophesy" by William Blake, and the text provided an alien view of perception as opening the mind and freeing it through drugs to know reality. Huxley argued that the mind has a "reducing valve" that keeps it from full function and that drugs allow unreduced sensations: " 'This is how one ought to see' " wrote Huxley of his mescalinized gaze at his "jeweled books . . . 'how things really are.' " Huxley did say that ". . . the man who comes back through the door will never be the same as the man who went out." But he was referring to the educative aspects of the experiences rather than alteration of brain function by conditioning or by chemical trauma. Such romantic views of drug use have not shed light on how they affect the brain.

In early 1965, I became aware of the growing social movement advocating drug use. Most prominent then were cannabis, mescaline, and LSD, but the list now includes barbiturates, amphetamines, heroin, and many others. I immediately began to study the subject. My investigations included in-depth interviews with drug users from samplings throughout the United States and in Vietnam. My studies include my case history interviews of 200 users of tobacco who quit, 23 alcoholics, 1354 cannabis users, approximately one-third of whom used other, more powerful drugs as well, 352 heroin addicts, and users of a variety of other drugs. All these interviews were conducted when the subject was sober, for the purpose of gaining information about his subjective sensations and experiences. I observed as much as possible regarding the habits, attitudes, and character of each subject.

The sensual* drugs cause more than transient intoxications. They may involve persistent sensory changes and alteration of mental process. Drug users are often remarkable resources of comparative subjective sensory experiences, but a drug user has diminished criteria with which to judge the changes either in his health or personality before and after the commencement of drug use. Except for alcoholics, drug users of all other sensual kinds appear to lack an awareness of the change in themselves brought about by drug abuse, but may be aware of changes in their friends. However, each drug user, including users of alcohol, believes that he is a moderate user and that his use is tolerable or harmless. He is likely to rationalize that his situation (i.e., his health, personal relationships, his ability to function) is better than it actually is and that it will not degenerate. Most think of the brain as a nonphysiologic entity. The drug user may worry about his lungs, liver, or arm veins, but not about his brain. In the initial stages of drug use, a user almost always states that he will certainly not venture much beyond his present level of involvement.

Effects of Various Sensual Drugs

The ideas of safety and harmlessness in drugs are usually derived from the pleasure the drugs impart. All drug users report that they use drugs because they "like them." The sense of pleasure seems to diminish or eliminate any sense of present or future harm, even if the user notices the difficulties of other users. The effects of the sensual drugs are observed as follows:

Cannabis

In my interviews with young cannabis users, it soon became apparent that the appeal of this drug was the good feelings it induced. Relaxation

---

* Sensual drugs are those imparting, in certain forms of use, sensations of pleasure from effects on the brain. Ethyl alcohol, barbiturates, cannabis (marijuana and hashish), amphetamines, cocaine, LSD, psilocybin, mescaline, atropine, scopolamine, and opiates all have diverse effects on the brain, but they have in common the generation of sensations of pleasure and well-being, even though the sensations produced by the different drugs are discretely different. I use the term "sensual" to imply that there is an effect on the sensory mechanisms. Indeed, the sensual drugs probably act upon the higher centers that evaluate sensory information.

was often cited, as was the drug's ability to enhance sexual and other sensual pleasures, such as can be derived from music, color, and touch, for example. It remains to be shown whether such effects are indeed augmentations or deletions. I think the latter is more likely. It does appear that cannabinols concentrate in the limbic region of the midbrain, which shows atrophy on heavy chronic exposure to cannabis, according to the investigations of Campbell, Evans, Thomson, & Williams (1971). Although no brain function studies were done in cannabis users I have interviewed, I can tell roughly the extent of involvement with cannabis from differences in facial muscle movement. Facial muscles tend to reflect the nature of mental process. The bright, quick expressions of young faces are dulled when they have been using cannabis; the eye movements drift away and snap back with the lessened attention span. Some users are bleary in facial expression even though they are not actively intoxicated. Perhaps thoughts are less detailed, or perhaps the linkages between thought and facial muscles in the many associative centers of the midbrain are not working well. These structures are severely damaged in heavy use, as found by Campbell et al. (1971). It is therefore reasonable that there may be detectable functional impairment with less use.

The marijuana user often discusses the thought formation of intoxication as "stoned" thinking. I characterize this stoned thinking as free association and the use and acceptance of non sequiturs. Certainly something has gone astray in thought formation to permit this degree of uncritical thought. This tendency is still detectable, though in a lesser extent when the cannabis user is sober.

Generation of good feeling or enhancement of it is probably not different in kind from that induced by alcohol. It is my hypothesis that gratification mechanisms are stimulated and there is a strong association between feeling good and sexual inclination. In the use of alcohol, cannabis, and heroin, these sensual states are associated; these sensations fail or are enhanced in the same circumstance. Perhaps feeling good is a prerequisite step to sexual inclination. With cannabis the feeling is more powerfully generated than in the case of alcohol and this is in keeping with the fact that the frequency of use of cannabis progresses from occasional use to daily use in 3.5 years. The sexual and good feeling associated with heroin is more powerful yet, and when heroin is easily available, the average user progresses from trials to daily use and addiction in one month.

The occasional use of marijuana may enhance sexual sensation, but my interviews with those who use it several times a day suggest that the effects shift with heavy use from hypersensitivity to numbness and from sexual–sensual interest to disinterest. Such a user is comparable to the alcoholic, but he develops more pronounced and earlier sensory deprivation and motor impairment. He does not recognize the gradual reduction of sexual inclination or any of the other effects of his abuse of cannabis, though some users admit to the impairment of memory. It is reasonable to assume that the very elements of mental function that are missing are the ones that are necessary to initiate functions of that sort. Thus, the person with a hole in his memory is not aware of it from within. Likewise the person with diminished sexual function has correspondingly reduced inclination, and so he cannot be aware of the missing function until someone challenges him enough to have him remember the change in behavior.

This lack of awareness on the part of the cannabis user is an important symptom of its use. It makes the study of cannabis difficult because it limits the sources of information and the efficacy of interviews. Heroin and cannabis users have in common that they also cannot grasp the significance of their situation. Some mental linkages seem impaired.

In 1969, I began to test the mental status of cannabis users by challenging them to stop using the drug in order to observe the consequent changes. I reasoned that suppression of mental function is usually undetectable in going to sleep or suffering anoxia, but that in recovery from sleep, the suppression is easily noticed. This theory was supported by the first and subsequent users who agreed to abstain. The first abstainer had been using cannabis several times a week. The first 5 weeks of abstinence he noticed no changes, but with the sixth week, his sense of improvement in mental function was dramatic. I have suggested to more than a thousand college students: "If you use cannabis, you cannot know whether it has affected you unless you totally abstain for several months. Then you may notice a difference." Most of them are content to believe that cannabis is harmless. If they had any intention of abstaining, it was to prove that I was misinformed. To date, none have returned to make this claim, though 339 have reported marked improvement. Of these, 43 claimed some degree of mental clarity after 2 weeks, and 20 did not notice the marked change until the fifth week or so. The usual description of recovery included memory improvement and clearer thinking. Only six of the 339 have returned uncertain of any change, but the six were occasional users and presumably would have less recovery to notice. On the other hand, the number who were weekend users was 114; the noticeable recovery was not limited to daily users. These observations indicate the cumulative nature of the suppression of mental function by cannabis. Thirteen carefully studied cases of behavioral disorder causatively associated with cannabis were described by Kolansky & Moore (1972). All these cases were unable to comprehend personal difficulties, even though each became unemployed, deserted family responsibilities, and became indolent. Marked improvement occurred on full abstinence for several months, but only in those with less than 3 years of heavy use.

The novice cannabis users whom I interviewed usually stated they would not use more powerful drugs; yet marijuana smokers with over a year's experience had usually done so. All 210 LSD users interviewed as well as all* of the 352 heroin addicts said that they used marijuana before LSD or heroin. It became apparent to me that, in general, those who do not use cannabis will not use LSD or heroin. In my group interviews of U.S. soldiers in Vietnam who had not used cannabis but who did smoke tobacco, many of them said they had rejected cigarettes laced with heroin. Those who had smoked cannabis obviously accepted more readily the heroin cigarette, for only cannabis users became heroin users. It appears that the cannabis user has acquired deficient judgment, perhaps associated with his lack of awareness of the effects cannabis has had on him.

Alcohol

Alcohol users who begin with occasional use and who progress to daily use take about 15 years to reach this stage. It usually takes 20–30 years to become involved with the heavy daily use associated with a specific form of alcoholism. The alcoholic uses alcohol because it gives him pleasure and because he claims it is disagreeable to be sober. Many of them say "It's hell to be sober." This attitude is apparently the result of a functional brain change that is induced by the abuse of alcohol. The change can be viewed as functional failure of natural sources of sensory gratification, a form of sensory deprivation. Alcoholics also progressively develop motor tremor, impaired coordination, impaired sexual and sensual functions whether they are intoxicated or sober. Sensory correlative functions, motor coordinative functions, and autonomic control centers are weakened. Even with such degrees of brain damage, however, the alcoholic can comprehend his difficulty enough to know that he has a problem. Alcoholics frequently warn others; hence, alcohol apparently does not affect the same "comprehending" portion of the brain as do cannabis and heroin. Users of these drugs at the same level of dependency do not warn others. Perhaps they do not comprehend the problems because of chronic changes in brain function.

---

* Questionnaires to heroin users show a high percentage, usually about 90%, stating prior use of cannabis. The interview method is more likely to get correct information. The cases collected are from the drug movement, with high association with marijuana.

Those who use alcohol may have the sensation of clearheadedness, but the sensation develops, especially at a heavy dosage, out of mental confusion. The case of the loquacious drunk is well known. The conclusions can be drawn that alcohol induces only the sensation of clearheadedness, and that this is an effect of depletion of brain function during acute intoxication. There are severe symptoms, the delirium tremens, in withdrawal from addiction to alcohol, and these symptoms indicate that there is extensive involvement of the autonomic nervous system. The alcoholic does not continue to drink out of fear of withdrawal symptoms but from the pleasurable sensations it gives him and, in the usual example, natural good feelings fade. As in all heavy drug abuse, pleasure fades with illness; then the user seeks to become intoxicated to keep from feeling bad.

Barbiturates

Barbiturate users usually reach a state of addiction in a few weeks after beginning with a sensual abuse of sleeping tablets. In the drug culture, users are generally much younger than the adult alcoholic but they exhibit many of the same effects: sexual inactivity, intermittent use of alcohol or combinations of alcohol and barbiturates, and severe symptoms upon abstinence representing longstanding and long-persisting disturbances in the autonomic nervous system. The barbiturate addict also suffers from an inability to feel good when sober. He too feels that a sober state is painful. Intoxication from both barbiturates and alcohol is regarded as pleasurable, feeling good.

Stimulants

My subjects described the pleasures of amphetamines as a sense of well being but quite different from that of the depressant drugs or cannabis. The good feeling is associated with excitement. In further analysis of comments by stimulant users, I am led to postulate that these effects are, from the standpoint of the brain, like preorgasmic sensations as those derived from masturbation. More than a hundred amphetamine users state clearly that, whereas no sex is involved, the sensation is indeed quite similar to that of masturbation. I conclude that the amphetamines (and the similar drug, cocaine) simulate pleasurable mental excitement equivalent to the preorgasmic sexual sensations that are associated with sensory correlative functions and are linked to sympathetic nerve activity.

With amphetamine use, some interviewees report, if they attempt to perform the sexual act while under the influence of the drug, they cannot reach orgasm. It is only when the effects of the drug have subsided that the climax is possible. I postulate that the sex act is prolonged by a block of sexual climax. The orgasm depends on a natural burst of sympathetic activity and the abrupt transfer of dominance from the sympathetic to the parasympathetic control centers. This coordination of and transition between the sympathetic and parasympathetic control centers can be observed in the diameter of the pupil during the sex act. It widens slightly in the peorgasmic phase, dilates abruptly at the moment of impending orgasm and then narrows. The coordinated transition cannot take place when the brain's controls are overwhelmed by the amphetamine stimulation of the sympathetic nervous system. The prolongation of the sex act under the amphetamine, Preludin, was first reported by Louria (1968). This drug was thought to be aphrodisiac but it merely postponed the climax by interference with the sensual progression in the sex act.

Amphetamines or cocaine impart a sense of being awake, alert, and clearheaded. Judgment, however, is seriously impaired as evidenced from the acts ranging from harmless impetuosity to murder while "clear-headed" and stimulated. Paranoia is a common mental state associated with this clearheadedness and when it occurs there is reason to suspect that the brain is being deprived of the balancing forces of reason and sensory input. It is more likely then that the sense of hyperawareness is really a deception; the real state is still sensory deprivation. The "speed-freak" is about as clearheaded as the loquacious drunk but more dangerous because the speed-freak is hyperactive and does not have motor impairment to restrict the carrying out of his deluded inclinations. But he does have the sensation of clearheadedness, and he is capable of clear unslurred communication.

Cocaine sniffers describe their experience euphorically as a clear-headed high. Although amphetamines and cocaine have equivalent effects pharmacologically, the sensation reported by cocaine users experienced with amphetamines is that cocaine is more purely pleasurable—stimulation without the "muggy" feeling attributed to amphetamines. The person "high" on cocaine, although thinking of himself as clearheaded, responsible, and reasoning, is actually often rash and unreasoning.

Opiates and Heroin

Interviews of heroin addicts became easy to arrange because of the increase in heroin use in Berkeley from 1967 to 1968. Some of the addicts were students. All of the first 50 had been college students up to the beginning of their heavy drug use, and about half of them had come to Berkeley after drug use had become their life style. These first interviews provided some interesting facts. The frequency of dosage varied from one to 20 intravenous injections per day; the usual frequency was four times per day; there was a marked reduction in the pleasurable response unless the dosage was progressively increased; all subjects were multiple drug users and had been heavy cannabis users prior to using heroin; all had taken up the use of each drug in their experience through the advice of a friend; all described the effect of the intravenous "hit" as a rush, which, on detailed questioning, appeared to be like a sexual orgasmic sensation except that it lasted much longer and ejaculation did not take place. I was not, in these first interviews, aware of the sexual incapacitation of the young men. The needed insight was provided by a couple who stated that to have sex they had to reduce the dosage of heroin and after a small enough fix barely to abolish withdrawal symptoms, have sex within the hour. The same day, I interviewed a young man who, though a heroin addict, had not been in close touch with the drug culture. His difficulty in trying to eliminate drug use and his failure to do so was his sexual impotence, which would not disappear with simple abstinence. In his case, sexual activity had diminished rapidly as his use of heroin began, and sexual capacity was gone by the time he knew he was addicted. The young man clearly described the sensation of taking heroin intravenously as equivalent to sexual orgasm. He has linked his impotency, including his inability to have an erection, to heroin addiction. He had panicked when he made this deduction and began to inject himself about 10 times a day. Later, another case told me of now he panicked when he discovered he could not get an erection or have sexual sensations. He, too, then injected himself more and more frequently until he reached at least 20 injections a day. Both men were hospitalized for a cure, but when their sexual capacity did not return after several weeks of total abstinence, each returned to heroin.

Summary of Sensual Drugs and Sex

It became evident to me that the behavioral pattern of addiction could be traced to the close parallel between the sex-like sensations induced by drugs and natural sexual sensations. Other sensual and functional mechanisms were also affected by drugs, but sex was a function with important significance to everyone. Both addiction patterns and normal sexual habits are developed through conditioning to pleasure-giving stimuli. Each drug has its own way of affecting the sexual system, either by altering its function or mimicking sexual sensations. Each disrupted sexual functioning and eventually even the drug failed to produce the quasi-sexual sensations. The patterns of sexual substitution were as follows:

1. Cannabis as an aid to sex: In early use, it may lower the inhibitions and reportedly enhances sexual sensations. Sexual enhancement decreases, however, with prolonged use and increased doses. Daily use, for example, is frequently associated with depressed or absent sexual activity, including sexual dreaming.

2. Amphetamines and cocaine in high doses cause preorgasmic sexual sensations, with or without actual sexual activity, and they delay or inhibit sexual climax. There is sometimes ejaculation by the male promptly following injection of amphetamines but the preorgasmic phase of sexual sensations continues without transfer to the orgasmic phase. Thus, even though stimulants may temporarily prolong erection, they disrupt sexual function.

3. The use of amphetamines for prolonged sensations of hallucinations is followed by taking a "downer" to avoid the depression of withdrawal from amphetamines. The downers are either barbiturates or opiates. When high doses of amphetamines are injected, then followed by an injection of heroin, the sequence of sex-like events and sensations was ejaculation, preorgasmic sensations lasting several hours, then orgasm without ejaculation upon the injection of heroin. The sensations of this combination are wholly sex-like but occur entirely within the brain and without relationship to the sex organs themselves. Significantly, events related to these sexual sensations are out of sequence: ejaculation takes place before either preorgasmic excitement or climax.

4. Withdrawal from heroin itself causes malfunction of the sexual system, though the form it takes tends to be opposite to the malfunction during heroin use. The result is still confusion of the order of events in the full sexual experience. The person undergoing withdrawal is likely to have spontaneous ejaculation and either premature ejaculation or inability to reach climax if he masturbates. Sexual dreams return, but are often incomplete and become transitions to a vision of heroin injection instead of natural sexual climax. It appears that some sexual capacities return fleetingly during detoxification only to lapse again into post-withdrawal impotency, which may last for many months.

5. Heavy barbiturate or alcohol use coincides with sexual inactivity and there is usually sexual impotency even during periods between intoxication.

Heroin Smoking and Changes in Brain Function prior to Addiction

An opportunity to study drug-using soldiers in Vietnam in October 1971, and March 1972 served to extend my information about the effects of heroin (Jones, 1972). There are some significant differences between junkies who inject low-potency heroin and the soldiers in Vietnam. The soldiers who used heroin, with rare exception, smoked it. The effects of smoking were similar to injection in that both produced a prolonged sensual rush. Once addicted, a user often consumed several grams of heroin a day, whereas an addict in the United States injects from 4 to 100 mg daily, divided into about four doses. With allowance for a loss of heroin in the burning of the cigarette, it still appears that the addict who smoked heroin in Vietnam was exposed to considerably more heroin than a mainliner. A prevalent notion in Vietnam was that the heroin obtained there was nonaddictive because it was relatively pure. It *was* relatively pure, 90%, but there can be no question of its addictive properties, and its ability to give the same rush as injected heroin. Injection of heroin by soldiers, however, was a last resort when the heroin was in short supply.

There were consistent physical and behavioral changes among all the addicted soldiers (Jones, 1972). Regularly, they reported that they felt especially bad in the morning upon awakening; they had all stopped having sexual dreams and they no longer had morning erections. The men usually continued taking heroin to combat these symptoms and in doing so found an increasing sense of isolation, loneliness, and paranoia. All had stopped writing letters home shortly after the first use of heroin and explained that they no longer felt connected to their home, family, or friends. The failure to write letters is significant. These soldiers had, in most instances, been active in writing home. The writing filled the time and they could actively think of home. They were also anxious to receive letters in return. The cessation of writing was abrupt and dramatic. It was also recent enough so that each remembered the change in attitude. The few who were questioned about receipt of letters also make it clear that, after heroin useage began, they would allow letters to accumulate unopened, a clear indication that heroin results in a long-lasting mental change toward reduced interpersonal relationships. This effect is not due to the heroin high, for these soldiers, though uniformly affected, only occasionally smoked heroin during the month prior to addiction.

In the heroin user, the loss of sexual powers, good feelings, morning erection, and sexual dreams, all of which occur before true addiction, points to the significant changes caused by the drug in the brain's associative pathways. In addition, the disturbances of many psychic functions and of urinary and bowel functions indicate a profound degree of functional interplay in the normal brain between conscious process, the pleasure processes, and the regulative controls of the autonomic nervous system, which are located close to the pleasure centers of the limbic region. The extent of the changes in the function of the brain caused by heroin is indicated by the fact that functional disturbances not only precede true addiction but appear to continue long past withdrawal symptoms.

Effects of Cannabis and Heroin on Memory and Comprehension

Still other changes in behavior affect the drug user, as observed especially in heroin or heavy cannabis use. Immediate experiences are forgotten. The user cannot comprehend the significance of his situation. It is tempting to say that both of these characteristics may represent a difficulty of transfer from short- to long-term memory; this has been described for cannabis (Drachman & Hughes, 1971). A drug user can know about his difficulties but cannot comprehend them. The heroin addict knows he is sexually incapacitated but rarely seeks help or advice; the cannabis user does not really understand his altered mental functions, yet he may admit that he has changed in behavior and attitude.

Rehabilitation

Getting both cannabis and heroin users to understand their situation is possible and is an important step toward rehabilitation. To know that improvement follows abstinence from cannabis can be an effective step. When mental clearing develops, there is then a reason for continued abstinence. Leading the heroin addict to understand his sexual disorders and to recognize that there is a hope for recovery is a powerful incentive if the subject can remember his former function.

Sexual functioning and the ability to feel good return quickly if the addict in treatment is otherwise generally in good, robust health, if he exercises and trains physically, if he has only been addicted a short time and, most importantly, if he has a firm resolve to abstain. When the return of sexual powers is not prompt, however, the treated addict returns to heroin rather than working through his sexual incapacitation, the other forms of sensory deprivation, and the drug-conditioned reflexes that persist after detoxification. It takes from several months up to a few years for an addict to recover his ability to sleep soundly, to regain his appetite, and to recondition his capacities for interaction with his environment.

Hallucination

Though I will not attempt an analysis of the actual mechanism affected in hallucination, the reports of those who have experienced it imply that the effect involves interference with sensory correlative mechanisms. For example, the normal sensory correlative functions pertaining to vision are: (a) to stabilize the visual field by canceling out the effects of changes in position of the eye; (b) to detect real movement of objects; (c) to establish depth and perspective; (d) to perceive color veridically (different parts of the retina do not respond equally to a given wavelength; (e) to correct for minor mechanical defects such as astigmatism, focus, and the blind spot and small impairments of the retina; (f) to correlate sight with equilibrium, hearing, and memory; and (g) to pull together the responses of the three segments of the retina, which reach the visual centers by different nerve pathways. The normal brain sees "how things really are," even though the eyes do not. Huxley was wrong in thinking that mescaline improved the reality of vision (Huxley, 1954).

The hallucinatory aberrations of color, color distribution, motion in the field of vision, and indistinct separations of objects are all easily explained as failures of the visual correlative functions. The seeing of things that are not there, not seeing things that are there, and the fusing together of objects appear to be due to deletions in the field of vision, scotomata, which cannot be seen because the brain either picks up continuity from the other side of the gap or fills in from memory. Distortions in other sense modalities are analogous to visual hallucination, whereby the sensory correlative centers either fail to complete the correlative of a sensation or they fill in absent sensory data with incorrect information stored in the memory.

The Pleasure Mechanisms

The above data compiled from the responses of drug users have led me to postulate that drugs activate the pleasure mechanisms either through stimulaton or chemical mimicry. The brain then readjusts its pathways to function in the presence of the drug so that functions governed both through the autonomic nervous system and in conscious process are altered. In early use of heroin, before addiction, pleasure mechanisms are already dimmed. It is not that heroin is more pleasurable but that normal pleasures are persistently suppressed from the beginning of doping.

After a certain point of addiction, the pleasure mechanism fails to respond to nonchemical sources of pleasure and satisfaction. The user is said to be "burned out." By this time the only sensation of pleasure imparted by drugs is relief from utter misery. The pleasure mechanisms are responding only minimally, if at all, to either drugs or the normal pleasure stimulations.

The form of sensory deprivation induced by the sensual drugs is pesistent suppression of pleasurable awareness. Perhaps this is because the natural pleasure pathways are reconditioned to respond only to drugs. In heavy drug abuse they are traumatized, for they do not respond even to drugs, and they may not recover. Sensual drug action can interfere with sensory information and cause numbness; usually the effect is on the sensations derived from the primary senses. Sensory information can reach consciousness, but the drug user's sense of pleasure becomes dependent on alterations in sensory correlative functions and these form his understanding of pleasure. The drug user's responsiveness to external stimuli other than drugs is drastically reduced. Even the most powerful drives and their pleasure incentives are subordinated to the drug experience. Lost are interest in and capacity for sex, hunger and its satisfaction, the relieving of fatigue by sleep, bladder and bowel sensations and controls, and the need for positive response to and satisfaction from friends and family. These failures are evident to a dramatic degree in the heroin user, and are still apparent in the paranoid reactions and sensory deprivation associated with all sensual drug abuse. They also account for the "depersonalization" noted by Kolansky & Moore (1972) in persons who have been heavy users of cannabis.

Each of the various kinds of pleasure mechanisms has its characteristic sensation, and some of them, as described by Heath (1964), have been located anatomically by probing and stimulating parts of the midbrain. Many correspond to sensations at a visceral or sexual level; when we fill what's empty, empty what's full, and scratch what's itching, the brain receives appropriate rewards of pleasure. The mechanisms for feeling good, clearheaded, friendly, and the like are influenced by drugs, and the malfunction of them is a part of the pattern of sensory deprivation resulting from drug abuse.

Response systems of the brain appear to be arranged to provide standards against which consciousness searches for approval or disapproval. These pleasure standards, conditioned by experience and held beyond the range of the conscious process, constitute the only rewards we can know. They are easily disturbed by chemical stimulation. When De Quincey (1899) wrote, upon his initial discovery of the pleasures of opium eating, ". . . happiness might now be bought for a penny, and carried in the waistcoat pocket," he had no insight to the deprivation of happiness he would suffer through opium-eating. There can be no doubt that the brain's reward mechanisms can be weakened by the sensual drugs.

Intellectual pursuits can provide pleasurable and satisfying experiences, but similar illusory experiences are also induced by drugs. William James (1902) wrote of the semiconscious states produced by inhalation of ether or nitrous oxide (which in my opinion have their parallels to the current use of hallucinatory drugs): "Depth beyond depth of truth seems revealed to the inhaler. This truth fades out, however, or escapes, at the moment of coming to and if any words remain over . . . , they prove to be the veriest nonsense. Nevertheless, the sense of a profound meaning having been there persists. . . ."

Religion and Drugs

Large numbers of drug users have found that, in conversion to and exercise of religion, there are satisfactions greater than the drug experiences. My case histories of such persons indicate that drug use diminishes and finally stops as they respond to the new source of satisfaction and the new peer pressure against the use of drugs. The exception in this instance is in the Satanic forms of religion; they are not healing and they do not free the person from drug dependency.

I have collected 27 cases of persons who have had a spectacular spiritual experience involving Christian religious conversion and simultaneous relief from involvement with drugs. They all had in common a craving for sensual experience, drug addiction of a severe form, severe sensory deprivation, and illness giving a premonition of death. They then resorted to prayer and at that moment had a sensation of light from within the head. Afterward, they all had full, rapid recovery of sensory functions, including sexual functions, without withdrawal symptoms. I believe that the interesting phenomenon of light arises within the visual correlative centers and is a sign that the paranoia and severe sensory deprivation are suddenly lifted. These cases and the more commonly encountered person who has found comfort in religion are an indication that, whatever the nature of the sensations of joy or pleasure that are associated with religion, they are not damaged by drug abuse as are the sensory mechanism; and, more importantly, this form of joy is able to reactivate the sensory functions. Several abstaining heroin addicts, still affected by sensory deprivation, have reported that they were tempted to try religion because religious music caused them to have "a stir of feeling inside." The long association of religion with rehabilitation of addicts is well known in the work of the Salvation Army, Alcoholics Anonymous, and other organizations. It is also evident as a help in drug rescue efforts involving rehabilitation from any kind of sensual drug dependency.

Conclusions

1. In spite of the notions that the sensual drugs enable a person to reach higher, altered states of consciousness, evidence indicates that the brain under the influence of these drugs is in fact denied the full use of mental powers.

2. Sensual drugs commonly induce various pleasurable sensations and especially the sense of well-being. These effects seem to be due to chemical titillation of the pleasure mechanisms. In each case, the capacity of the sensory mechanism to respond to stimulation through normal pathways is impaired in proportion to the prior use of the chemical agent. This leads to a form of sensory deprivation in the capacity to feel good, in the function of the sexual system, and in the domain of interpersonal responses. The brain essentially tricks the individual into believing all is well when actually, for his own health and safety, he should perhaps be responding otherwise.

3. The experiences that result from stimulant drugs and from some forms of alcoholic intoxication do not lead to a genuine increase of mental abilities but rather to the illusory sensation that the brain is clearheaded.

4. The similarities of the effects of sensual drugs to sexual sensations stem from the fact that cocaine and amphetamine stimulants mimic the preorgasmic phase of sex, whereas the opiate depressant drugs mimic the orgasmic phase. No stimulant or depressant drug, or combination thereof, can enhance the full sex act itself or duplicate the normal sequence of sensations of the sex act, for that depends on an intricate balance between the sympathetic and parasympathetic control centers.

5. Brain changes induced by drugs lead to the lack of ability to comprehend the degree of change. It appears that the very parts of the

brain that are perturbed are the very ones needed to comprehend the degree of loss.

6. Sensual drugs excite or inhibit pathways through the brain, creating functional disturbances throughout the brain, from the controls of the autonomic nervous system to the higher levels of memory, association, and reason. These disturbances appear to begin before true addiction is established and persist in varying degrees even after withdrawal and detoxification.

7. The pleasure from drugs is relatively magnified by comparison with the feeble or absent natural function of those gratification mechanisms that are injured through drug abuse.

References

Campbell, A. M. G., Evans, M., Thomson, J. L. G., & Williams, M. J. (1971). *Cerebral atrophy in young cannabis smokers. Lancet,* 2, 1219–1224.

De Quincey, Thomas (1899). *Confessions of an English opium eater.* F. M. Lupton, New York.

Drachman, D. A., & Hughes, J. R. (1971). *Memory and the hippocampal complexes. Neurology,* 21(1), 1–14.

Heath, R. G. (1964). Pleasure response of human subjects to direct stimulation of the brain: Physiologic and psychodynamic considerations. In R. G. Heath (Ed.), *The role of pleasure in behavior.* (Hoeber) Harper & Row, New York.

Huxley, Aldous (1954). *The doors of perception.* Harper Colophon, New York.

James, William (1902). *The varieties of religious experience.* Longmans, Green, New York.

Jones, H. B. (1972). *A report on drug abuse in the Armed Forces in Vietnam. Medical Service Digest,* 23, 8.

Kolansky, H., & Moore, W. T. (1972). *Toxic effects of chronic marihuana use. JAMA,* 222(1), 35–41.

Louria, D. (1968). *The drug scene.* McGraw-Hill, New York.

AUTHOR INDEX

SUBJECT INDEX

social behavior in, 138

Ribonuclease, intraventricular injection of, 226

Right-left differences, in visual cortical cells, 100, 110

RNA, and dark rearing, 60
modification of, 226–228

Sacrifice, procedure for, 89

Scanning mechanism, in visual discrimination, 242

Scopolamine, and pleasure sensation, 298

Scotophobin, and dark-avoidance, 228ff

Selective Model, of RNA modification, 227

Sensory deprivation, and drug use, 303
effect on visual evoked response, 290

Sensual drugs, 298
and sex, 304, 305

Septal lesions, and male sexual behavior, 16

Serotonin, and male-male behavior, 18

Sex act, and Preludin, 303

Sexual behavior, adaptation in, 5
and castration, 4
cerebral cortex in, 25
and cortical depression, 25
and early experience, 4
heterotypical, 11–13
and hippocampal lesions, 16
hormonal control of, 7ff
in male, 44ff
measurement of, 1–3
and medial forebrain bundle, 16
and menstrual cycle, 13
neural control of, 14ff
and neuroendocrinology, 1ff
nonhormonal factors in, 4
and ovariectomy, 8
quantification of, 1–3
in rat, 1ff
and receptivity, 4
restoration of, 8
and septal lesions, 16

Sexual climax, and drug use, 303

Sexual differentiation, in the brain, 35ff

Sexual receptivity, in cat, 27
and endogenous progesterone, 10, 11

Sexual satiation, and monamines, 19

Sexual sensation, in cannabis use, 299

Social behavior, in malnutrition, 135, 166
recording of, 174

in rhesus monkey, 139ff

Social hierarchy, and diet, 167

Social isolation, and aggression, 167

Social rearing conditions, monkey, 139

Soldiers, drug use in, 306

Solicitory behavior, in rat, 2

Spherical refractive error, measurement of, 287

Starvation, and motivation, 135

Steady-state conditions, in binocular summation, 282

Stereotypy, and noxious stimulation, 182

Steroid hormones, radiolabeled in brain, 14

Stimulants, subjective response to, 302, 303

Stimulation, in caudate, 211
of frontal cortex, 202
in hippocampus, 212

Stimuli, mirror-image, 241

Stimulus, in visual evoked response, 268–274

Stress, and learning, 233

Superior colliculus, and visual deprivation, 99

Symmetry, in mirror-image discrimination, 261

Synapses, density in visual cortex, 102

Synaptic ribbon, 66

Tactile contact, and protein diet, 177

Temporal summation, in visual evoked response, 282–285

Testosterone propionate, autoradiographic localization of, 14
conversion to estrogen, 12
hypothalamic implant, 47
and lordosis quotient, 5
mammillary region implant, 17
and mating behavior, 18
receptor neurons, 35

Tetrabenazine, and serotonin synthesis, 33

Thompson-Bryant box, 250, 258

Threshold, for electric shock, 155
for retrograde amnesia, 200

TMC computer, 268

Tobacco, and perception, 297

Tonic-clonic convulsion, 197, 198

Training-treatment interval, in ECS, 195

Transcorneal *versus* transpinnate ECS, 194

Transfer research, with planarians, 226–228

Transpinnate ECS, 194

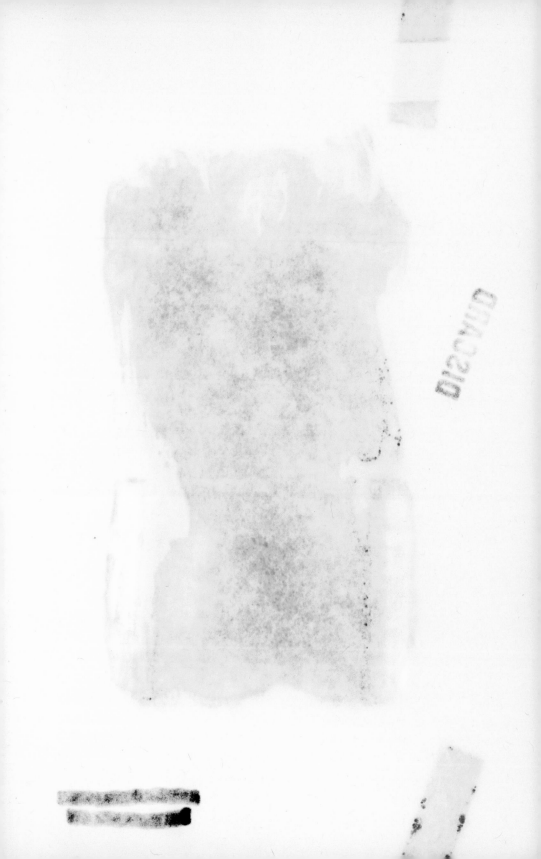

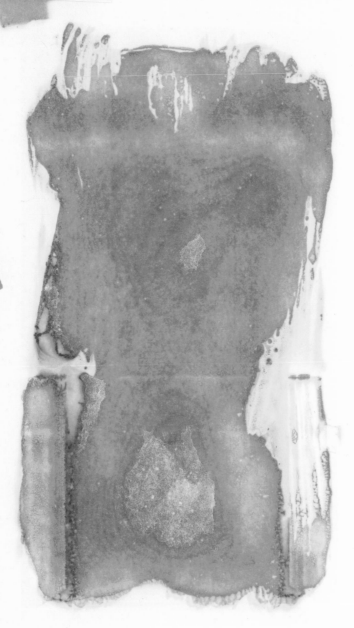